SHOOTING STRAIGHT

Praise for *Shooting Straight*

'Among the few biographies of an outstanding modern military leader, *Shooting Straight* is a beautifully written book on military leadership, filled with lessons that are relevant across domains and disciplines.'

—**Indra Nooyi**, global corporate icon; Class of 1951 chair for the Study of Leadership at US Military Academy, West Point; and author

'*Shooting Straight* is an extraordinarily researched, lucid, authoritative and objective biography of a senior Indian military leader who "led from the front" and demonstrated high levels of truthfulness, integrity and professional excellence. Rostum was an uninhibited challenger and never a "yes man"—he stood firm on what he believed to be right. Arjun Subramaniam offers deep insights into life and growth in the Indian Army and the security environment through the lens of Lt Gen. Rostum Nanavatty's military career.'

—**General V.P. Malik**, former Chief of Army Staff

'This deeply researched and beautifully written book by an accomplished military historian explores the life and times of Lt Gen. Rostum K. Nanavatty. A physically tough soldier with towering leadership qualities, unflinching moral courage and a sharp mind, he demonstrated an uncompromising concern for the complete battle-readiness of the men he commanded. Besides tracing the memorable career of an accomplished soldier, this volume provides a rare and honest insight into the internal functioning of the Indian Army and the country's higher defence management machinery. This book should be essential reading for all military officers, politicians and bureaucrats involved in the functioning of the national security apparatus.'

—**N.N. Vohra**, former Governor of J&K; Union Home and Defence Secretary

'An engrossing biography of a complete soldier—physically fit, professionally competent and with immense courage of conviction. He is a soldier's general worth emulating.'

—**General N.C. Vij**, former Chief of Army Staff

'This carefully researched and perceptive biography of Lieutenant General Nanavatty is at once an account of the making of a distinguished military commander and a window to the transformation of the Indian Army over the past six decades. Everyone interested in the Indian military should read this book.'

—**Srinath Raghavan**, professor of International Relations and History, Ashoka University

'Arjun Subramaniam has done some remarkable research and utilized his historical lens to produce a laudable biography of an outstanding soldier. To those who have had the honour of serving under him, the portrayal is indeed authentic and accurate. The dovetailing of his family life into the narrative adds to its flavour.'

—**Lt Gen. (Dr) Prakash Menon**, former Military Advisor to NSA; and director of the Strategic Studies Programme, Takshashila Institution

'Arjun Subramaniam combines his passion for writing and contemporary military history most admirably as he offers a sharp look at the personal and professional journey of one of India's finest military leaders, Rostum Nanavatty. A fine read.'

—**Nitin A. Gokhale**, author; and National Security Analyst

'General Nanavatty's life provides a prism to view the Indian Army's role in "less-than-war" contingencies, its counterinsurgency roles in the Indian northeast and Kashmir, and its operations in Siachen and Sri Lanka. In intertwining Nanavatty's journey as a soldier with this big picture, the author ably makes use of Nanavatty's own notes and papers, interviews with those who worked with him, as well as conversations with the man himself. The emergent portrait of the general is even-handed: obviously intelligent, dutiful and frank—but also sometimes stubborn and too tough. An accomplished military historian, the author also asks the big questions on India's endgame in these less-than-wars and lessons for soldiering and strategy. A unique book on a unique life that deserves broader reading.'

—**Vinay Sitapati,** professor; and author of *Half-Lion: How P.V. Narasimha Rao Transformed India* and *Jugalbandi: The BJP before Modi*

'In *Shooting Straight,* Arjun Subramaniam has given us more than a biography. This is the story of the evolution of the contemporary Indian Army, told through the lens of one soldier and many conflicts. Writing with compelling flair, Subramaniam draws a portrait of a four-decade-long military career at a cracking pace. Lt Gen. Rostum Nanavatty strides through these pages with integrity, professionalism and courage.'

—**Narayani Basu**, historian; biographer; and author of *V.P. Menon: The Unsung Architect of Modern India*

'*Shooting Straight* is a compelling read on the complex challenges of soldiering and leadership in an era of grey zone warfare.'

—**Syed Akbaruddin**, dean, Kautilya School of Public Policy; and former Permanent Representative of India to the United Nations

'Military historian Arjun Subramaniam's meticulously researched book, *Shooting Straight*, is a gripping biography of Lt General Rostum K. Nanavatty (Retd) ... General Nanavatty's long service in the Indian army, his intellectual explorations and bold assertions about defence and security issues continue to have a contemporary relevance in an era of major power contestation, protracted wars, evolving threats and challenges faced by India, and, the rapidly changing character of warfare.'

—***Hindustan Times***

'Subramaniam's writing, lucid and accessible, aided by the protagonist's (Lt Gen Nanavatty) painstaking notes, brings out the clarity in Nanavatty's thinking, which underpinned his career philosophy.'

—***The Hindu***

'The life and times of soldiers like General Nanavatty become all the more relevant because they have truly been there and done that—from the icy heights of Siachen, the Kashmir terror theatre, and the Sri Lankan civil war, to the insurgency-plagued swathes of Nagaland, Manipur and Tripura.'

—***The Week***

'A gritty, no-nonsense Indian military history through the lens of a relentless commander.'

—***Swarajya***

'This biography will give readers a well-rounded picture of the life and mindset of an exemplary soldier and of the way soldiering has evolved in the face of the security challenges India faces.'

—***Business Standard***

'*Shooting Straight* by AVM Arjun Subramaniam (retd) is an excellent account of this dyed-in-olive-green Gurkha officer. Lt Gen. Nanavatty's military accomplishments—despite his no-nonsense personality—speak volumes about his professional excellence.'

—**The Print**

'Meticulously researched and written, the book offers a close look at soldiering, command and leadership in turbulent times. It offers a glimpse into counterinsurgency and counterterrorism operations, operations by Special Forces, high-altitude operations and "No War No Peace" contingencies.'

—***The Statesman***

SHOOTING STRAIGHT

A MILITARY BIOGRAPHY OF LT GEN. ROSTUM K. NANAVATTY

ARJUN SUBRAMANIAM

HarperCollins *Publishers* India

First published in hardback by HarperCollins *Publishers* 2025
4th Floor, Tower A, Building No. 10, DLF Cyber City,
DLF Phase II, Gurugram, Haryana – 122002
www.harpercollins.co.in

This edition published by HarperCollins *Publishers* 2026

2 4 6 8 10 9 7 5 3 1

P-ISBN: 978-93-7307-338-5
E-ISBN: 978-93-6569-508-3

All photographs used in this book are from the Nanavatty family albums.

Typeset in 10.5/13.5 Adobe Caslon Pro
by HarperCollins *Publishers* India

Printed and bound at
Saurabh Printers Pvt. Ltd.

This book is produced from independently certified FSC® paper to ensure responsible forest management.

HarperCollins *Publishers*, Macken House, 39/40 Mayor Street Upper, Dublin 1, D01 C9W8, Ireland

To
My family

CONTENTS

	List of Maps & Sketches	xi
	Introduction	1
1.	Early Days	9
2.	Into the Deep End with the Gorkhas	25
3.	Peacetime Soldiering	50
4.	First Command	76
5.	Learning from the Americans and the British	97
6.	Into Sri Lanka with the PARA Commandos	117
7.	On the Saltoro Range	138
8.	Interlude between Operations	177
9.	Covert War in Baramulla	184
10.	Return to the Eastern Cauldron	217
11.	A Minefield Called Northern Command	247

12. Almost War and Adios 266

13. Soldiering, Leadership and Strategy 289

Acknowledgements 310

Appendices 313

List of Interviewees 337

Notes 340

Index 366

LIST OF MAPS & SKETCHES

1. 2/8 GR at Along
2. 2/8 GR in Nagaland
3. 2/8 GR in Tawang
4. PARA Commando Task Force
5. Field Sketch: Siachen Region
6. Field Sketch: Operation Ibex
7. 19 Infantry Division Area of Responsibility (AOR): 1993–94
8. 3 Corps AOR
9. Northern Command AOR
10. J&K: Deployment and Hot Spots

INTRODUCTION

'Military strategy is the art of distributing and applying military means to fulfil the ends of policy.'[1]

—LIDDELL HART

I first met Lieutenant General Rostum Kaikhushru Nanavatty in Pune in early 2015 where he was visiting his sister. I was mid-way through the narrative for my first book—*India's Wars I: A Military History 1947–1971*. The meeting was instructive and interesting. Nanavatty quizzed me on my project and seemed sceptical of the vast landscape I was attempting to cover, but he gave me a patient hearing. After retirement from active service, he had written a robustly researched book on counterinsurgency and internal security—*Internal Armed Conflict in India: Forging a Joint Civil-Military Approach*,[2] and it was clear that he was sizing me up before consenting to speak to a stranger about his operational experiences. As we parted, he wished me 'the very best' and suggested we might 'continue our conversation in Dehradun'.

I had by then already commenced research for the sequel to my first book that would take the narrative as far forward as possible into the present. Lieutenant General Shamsher Mehta, a former Western Army Commander and veteran of the 1971 War in East Pakistan and a key protagonist in my chapter on the war, together with being a generous mentor for almost a decade, had suggested that I meet Nanavatty, a course-mate of his. 'He has a sharp mind and is a thinking soldier who's had a ringside view of several key military events and operations during the post-1971 period.'

Since then, my exploratory journey into the deep recesses of contemporary Indian military history has been akin to a rollercoaster ride. Nanavatty has been partly instrumental in intellectualizing and putting that journey into a proper framework. The quartet—Nanavatty, Shamsher Mehta, Air Marshal Vinod Patney and Admiral Arun Prakash—offered me much content, impeccable in its honesty and depth. More importantly, they gave me the inspiration and momentum to take contemporary Indian military history to a diverse readership that extended beyond the armed forces.

I visited Dehradun in March 2017 to attend the annual Old Boys Reunion at the Rashtriya Indian Military College (RIMC), of which I am an alumnus. Taking time off from the revelry at the RIMC, I coaxed Nanavatty to speak to me about his early soldiering experiences in counterinsurgency operations against 'Naga hostiles', as they were then called, his involvement with the para commandos in Sri Lanka and his brigade commander's tenure in Operation MEGHDOOT across the icy battleground of the Siachen Glacier. Our first long conversation took place in 'Saltoro', a stone bungalow in Dehradun, named after the Saltoro Range that lies west of and dominates the Siachen Glacier where Nanavatty commanded his brigade. He followed up by helping me understand Pakistan's covert war in Jammu and Kashmir (J&K), which unfolded in the first half of the 1990s, with him in command of a division in the Kashmir Valley. When I pushed for more, he reluctantly spoke to me about two assignments that offered microscopic insights into the transition of Indian military commanders from the operational to the strategic domain. The first was his tenure in command of 3 Corps in the insurgency-ridden North-east. The second was his stint as the Northern Army Commander dealing with multi-dimensional operations along the Line of Control (LoC) with Pakistan and the Line of Actual Control (LAC) with China in Eastern Ladakh. The covert war in J&K peaked during this tenure and resulted in Operation PARAKRAM the ensuing short-of-war face-off between India and Pakistan in 2001–2002.

By then, I had interviewed scores of veterans, thoroughly mined the limited primary sources available, extensively researched secondary sources for my two books, and developed a hybrid research pedagogy of my own. The approach I adopted involved recording events and personal perspectives of combat veterans and triangulating their views with those of others from the same era. By so doing, I could accurately ascertain events, consequences and outcomes and overcome the near-total absence of declassified material from the service headquarters and Ministry of Defence in the post-1972 period.

No one I had interviewed thus far had referred to their old papers, diaries or notes beyond the odd logbook until Nanavatty pulled out several olive-green satchels during my first interview with him. Each satchel comprised his jottings and notes for each of his tenures as a formation commander. Neatly handwritten with a calligraphic touch, his papers emerge chronologically. They have yellowed with age but constitute a treasure trove of information and are worth their weight in gold. I asked him whether he planned to hand over his papers to an archive at any war college in India or to his regiment. He had no such plans! As the writing of my second book, *India's Wars II: A Military History 1972–2020,* progressed, propelled in no small measure by the contents of Nanavatty's satchels, I wondered about their future, because in them lay much of the history of the Indian Army from the early 1960s to the 2000s.

With *India's Wars II* done, dusted and successfully published during the COVID-19 pandemic, the logical question for me was, 'What next?' From this proposition emerged the idea of writing a military biography based on what I started calling 'The Nanavatty Papers'. Good military biographies are not only life and career stories of the central protagonist; they must also serve as a lens through which the reader can glimpse soldiering during the period. Embedded vignettes of communities, societies, attitudes and culture as perceived by the central character and interpreted by the biographer add value to such narratives. What was compelling in Nanavatty's case was the sheer depth and breadth of his chronologically arranged writings on diverse issues of leadership, training, operations and policy matters. They would permit a closer look at the evolution of the Indian Army through four decades of war and conflict.

Nanavatty brushed away my initial approaches, arguing that if I wanted to write a biography, others would fit the bill better than him. The unconvincing argument that he offered rests in the belief of an era gone by that soldiers, sailors and airmen had a worthwhile story to narrate if they had fought in the 1962, 1965 or 1971 wars against China and Pakistan. Nanavatty had missed out on them for reasons beyond his control. Not having participated in them rankles with the proud infantryman that he is. All I had was a hunch that Nanavatty had much to offer future generations of military officers and general readers than what had emerged during my episodic interviews with him while writing *India's Wars II*.

Every time I met him, I prepared lawyer-like arguments that failed to breach the 'Nanavatty Fortress' even though I received some initial support from his gracious wife, Suniti Nanavatty, who gently chided him for shying away from sharing his rich repository of operational experience. During a visit to the US in 2021, I broached the idea to the Nanavattys' elder son, Rushad, who thought it was excellent and promised to try to convince his father to consent to my request. Recounting my final pitch to Nanavatty in early April 2022, I argued and pushed him hard. I said, 'Sir, there is a misplaced conception in India that only those soldiers, sailors and airmen who have fought and engaged in combat at the tactical and operational level, particularly in the 1965 and 1971 wars and in various other conflicts such as Kargil, and have then risen to senior ranks, are worthy of being written about, or have a story to tell. Military legacies are also about leadership in various genres of conflict, prolonged less-than-war situations and during peace; they are also about the art of soldiering and leading armies with vision and integrity; they are also about strategy, planning and delivering outcomes and, in recent times, about providing the intellectual edge to warfighting and understanding the political outcomes of war. Please consider my request.' I continued without giving him a chance to interject, 'I have a detailed plan ready, including the schedule of interviews, proposed chapters and much more that will fit into your way of doing things with discipline, method and integrity. I can assure you that this book will be more than "subaltern history"[3] considering that your repository of written work indicates that you have been a prescient observer of military affairs and politics.' I got a cryptic answer: 'Arjun, I will seriously consider your request and get back to you.' All I could do was wait!

Despite the stellar contribution of independent India's Armed Forces in the evolution of its fledgling democracy, military autobiographies, memoirs and biographies have not been a part of the literary landscape. On the other hand, biographies and memoirs of political leaders, diplomats, scientists, business and industry pioneers, social activists, film stars, and even 'cricketing stars' seem to emerge with regularity from leading publishing houses. Few books of quality and scholarship have profiled and recorded the lives and accomplishments of outstanding soldiers, sailors and airmen after Independence. Among them are the memoirs of Air Chief Marshal P.C. Lal (*My Years with the IAF*), Lieutenant General S.P.P. Thorat (*From Reveille to Retreat*), Lieutenant General Harbaksh Singh (*War Despatches*), Lieutenant General S.K. Sinha (*A Soldier Recalls*), Lieutenant General J.F.R. Jacob (*An Odyssey in War and Peace*) and Admiral S.M. Nanda (*The Man Who Bombed Karachi*). Notable biographies are fewer: General K.S. Thimayya by Humphrey Evans (*Thimayya of India*), Field Marshal Sam Manekshaw by Behram and Zenobia Panthaki (*The Man and His Times*), Depinder Singh's (*Soldiering with Dignity*) and S.D. (Shubhi) Sood (*Field Marshal Manekshaw*), Marshal of the Indian Air Force Arjan Singh by Air Commodore Jasjit Singh (*The Icon*), and Lieutenant General Sagat Singh by Major General Randhir Singh (*A Talent for War*). Interestingly, all these soldiers, sailors and airmen were commissioned before Independence. On the other hand, the shelf of comprehensive and objective military biographies about military leaders who achieved the pinnacle of their careers in the 1980s, 1990s and later is rather bare.

Effusive biographies that portray the central protagonist as a 'Superman' have not been uncommon throughout history. Writing in his masterly biography of three US military generals and icons, Eisenhower, MacArthur and Marshall, titled *15 Stars,* Stanley Weintraub caustically writes: 'MacArthur arranged for both generals (Willoughby and Whitney), neither of whom had commanded anyone in combat, but whom MacArthur lavishly be-medalled, to write and publish hagiographic post-war biographies of him which he freely and imaginatively dictated.'[4]

The ever-probing Nanavatty sent me an excerpt from a book review he had recently read as if to ask, 'Arjun, where do you stand?' In that review of a biography on the former Indian Prime Minister V.P. Singh, titled *The Disruptor: How Vishvanath Pratap Singh Shook India*, Prem Shankar Jha, a veteran journalist, political commentator and bibliophile, wrote: 'As the pre-eminent psycho-sociologist of our times, Erich Fromm, pointed out, biographies are the most difficult things to write. Biographers usually choose their subjects because something in their subjects' lives has resonated with something in their own lives. Those connections affect the biographers' perceptions of their subject, often in ways they are unaware of. Therefore, the challenge that writing a biography poses is identifying those perceptions.'[5] I wrote back immediately: 'Interesting, Sir! In your case, the two things that resonate with me have been your consistent ability to speak truth to power throughout your career and to contextualize and simplify the intellectual dimension of warfighting. Besides, hidden in your diaries and papers is a fantastic story worth telling.'

On the issue of objectivity, biographies written by aides, staff officers, regimental officers, friends, protégées and commissioned authors tend to suffer from a familiarity bias. With very few professional historians taking on the task of writing military biographies because of the lack of institutional and archival resources that could help investigate an accomplished military career, this genre of writing in India is as unattractive as plain vanilla military history. I am not an army officer nor have I ever been associated with Nanavatty during our respective military careers. In short, I ticked most of the boxes needed to write an objective biography.

Nanavatty has his share of critics, which makes for an essential ingredient in an exciting biography. Finally, as a military historian, I reckoned that I had an opportunity to write a memoir that stays true to history because of the vast repository of 'the Nanavatty Papers' made available to me rather than bank on oral recollections. As Robert S. McNamara wrote in his eloquent memoir on Vietnam, *In Retrospect: The Tragedy and Lessons of Vietnam:* 'Too often, I believe, memoirists rely on their recollections. This reliance on memory leads them, however honest in their intent, to remember what they wish to remember—what they wish had happened—rather than what happened.'[6] Like McNamara, I have tried to minimize this real and human danger and organize the material in a way aligned with history.

I was thrilled when Nanavatty suggested in mid-April 2022 that I make my final pitch to the entire Nanavatty family, including his elder sister, Erna. I outlined the way ahead and answered questions from the family, even a few pointed ones from his ten-year-old grandson. The family vote was unanimous and I was ready to undertake a challenging journey across India's diverse battlegrounds with a soldier who 'shoots straight', epitomizes the ethos of the Indian Army and has led his officers and men with integrity and courage.

Nanavatty's 'lived experience' comprises a complex and varied journey through multiple genres of modern conflict that constitute what is now commonly termed 'Grey Zone' conflict. Apart from a brief glimpse into his Parsi legacy and his introduction to soldiering at the Indian Military Academy, Nanavatty's career highlights include an early introduction to fighting against skilled Naga guerrillas in the 1960s followed by a long period of peacetime soldiering culminating in the command of his battalion—2nd Battalion 8th Gorkha Rifles (2/8 GR). Experiential learning abroad in the US and the UK were interesting and invaluable interludes before he was briefly pitch-forked into operations in Sri Lanka with the para commandos in 1987. Thereafter, Nanavatty's successive command assignments of a brigade, division, corps and army command were all in active operations in Siachen, North Kashmir, the North-east and, finally, the entire Northern Command that stretches from Eastern Ladakh to the plains of North Punjab during some of the most turbulent times in India's recent history (1987–2003).

His last tenure as Northern Army Commander, with its broad canvas of events, calls for an entire book, an endeavour that Nanavatty, with his memory and meticulously kept papers could well have undertaken on his own but chose not to for reasons best known to him. Consequently, I have cherry-picked events from this tenure and squeezed them into two chapters that offer readers a glimpse into the complexities of apex military leadership in turbulent times. Vignettes of his leadership style, operational acumen and strategic foresight will befittingly conclude the book.

Lieutenant General Rostum Kaikhushru Nanavatty represents the best in soldiering and leadership the Indian Army has produced since Independence. For that reason and more, his life offers much to absorb, not only for those who wish to dedicate themselves to the vocation of arms but to leaders across domains and disciplines.

In much of the book, he is referred to as 'Nanavatty', but the narrative alternates between the latter and his first name, 'Rostum'. To many of his mates in the army, he was 'Nana', and in school, he was 'Rusty'—a name coined by his Housemaster, Mr Peter Rogerson.

1

EARLY DAYS

'Parsis have contributed to the Armed Forces far out of proportion to their dwindling numerical strength, a fact not generally appreciated.'[1]

—Lieutenant General A.M. Sethna, a former Vice Chief of Army Staff

Rostum was born on 18 May 1943 into a service-oriented middle-class Parsi family at Karwar in the North Kanara District of the erstwhile Bombay Presidency. The younger of the two siblings, Rostum's sister, Erna, was four years and eight months older. Their father, Kaikhushru (Keki) Jehangir Nanavatty, was then the District Superintendent of Police, Karwar. Kaikhushru, born in 1907 in Bombay, was the second child of his parents and one of four siblings—three brothers and the youngest a sister. Rostum's mother, Dhan, was born in 1913 into the Kothavala family, which had roots in Rajpipla in Gujarat. Her illustrious grandfather, Dhanjishah Kothavala, after whom she was named, was the Divan of the princely state of Rajpipla. An exceptionally able administrator he was revered by the people of the state.

Scholarly works suggest that large numbers of Zoroastrians fled[2] Persia because of religious persecution during and after the Arab-Muslim conquest between the seventh and the eleventh century. They followed the sea route across the Arabian Sea from the island of Hormuz at the head of the Persian Gulf to India. Powered by the westerly winds, some made landfall on the island of Diu and the Junagadh Peninsula to the north. Others sailed further south and east, landing along the Bharuch–Surat–Navsari coastline that was later part of the erstwhile Bombay State in British India and now lies in the Indian state of Gujarat. They were deemed Parsis—people from Pars (Persia). Sanjan, a few miles inland, was the first known settlement of the Parsis. Initially acquiring land along the fertile stretch of coastline, including the riverine deltas of the Narmada and Tapi Rivers, early generations of Parsis developed good farmlands and orchards. Several built good businesses and were important merchants in places like Bharuch, Khambhat, Surat and Navsari. Drifting inland over centuries, several families settled in various parts of modern Gujarat, while others made their way down India's west coast to Bombay's emerging trading hub.

Kaikhushru's father passed away when he was seventeen. At the time, his elder brother, Jal, was pursuing higher studies and his younger brother, Dadi, was still in school. Acutely aware of his responsibilities, Kaikhushru saw himself as the breadwinner in the family and aspired to a career in the British Indian Army. In 1927, he applied for a King's Commission in the British Indian Army from Sandhurst and reached the stage in the selection process where he was interviewed in Shimla by the Commander-in-Chief (C-in-C) of India, Field Marshal William Riddell Birdwood. Unlike most candidates, Kaikhushru did not come from a privileged background. Considering the modest financial resources at the family's disposal, the C-in-C gently pointed out that he would not be able to sustain himself through the years at Sandhurst and later as an officer in the Indian Army. Deeply disappointed, he briefly contemplated a career in the Indian Forest Service but eventually joined the Bombay Presidency Police as a directly recruited Deputy Superintendent instead. Ten years later, he was absorbed into the Indian Police (I.P.) cadre. At the beginning of World War II, Kaikhushru once again attempted to join the army. He sought to be released from the police so that he might apply for a wartime commission, only to receive a terse reply from his superior officer that there was a continuing need for 'good officers in the police force' and that he should 'get on' with his job. Ironically, his brothers would join the Indian Army as war-time emergency commissioned officers. While Jal joined the Education Corps, Dadi, a happy-go-lucky soldier, chose the infantry and the Punjab Regiment. 'A bachelor who liked his rum, played his bridge and made good use of the club, Dadi Kaka (uncle) retired as a Major, married after he left the army and, sadly, passed away early,' said Nanavatty.[3]

Dhan's parents, who had lost their two sons in childhood, were persuaded to send their only daughter to Bombay in the care of her fuiji (aunt) Shirin and uncle Hector to ensure a proper education. Unfortunately, as things turned out, adverse circumstances resulted in Dhan having to abandon her schooling in her teens and devote time to nursing and caregiving in her aunt's household. Hector Ratanji Kothavala, OBE, MVO, KPM, was a remarkable man. He joined the Bombay Police as a constable and retired as a much-decorated Inspector General of Police of the princely state of Sirohi, Rajasthan, with a formidable reputation for police intelligence, investigation and detective work. During the First World War, he was a Special Service Officer attached to the Army General Staff of the 'War Council' in the Straits Settlement (Singapore). Instrumental in establishing an intelligence and counter-intelligence centre in Singapore, which eventually evolved as the Special Branch of the Singapore Police, he was presented with a Sword of Honour for his counter-espionage work in parts of Southeast Asia by the Government of the Straits Settlement, mentioned in the London Gazette for his extraordinary service, and was awarded the Order of the British Empire.[4] While Hector remained a mentor to Kaikhushru throughout his life, it was a Parsi merchant in Rajpipla, Nadirshah Seth, who first suggested to Dhan's parents that she meet Kaikhushru, a promising young police officer who was then a Deputy Superintendent of Police in Rajkot. Dhan and Kaikhushru were married in Rajpipla on 6 December 1937.

Kaikhushru had a notable career in the police. Apart from serving with distinction in several districts of Bombay State, he raised, trained and nurtured the Bombay State Reserve Police (SRP). He was specially selected and twice sent on deputations, first to Rewa in Vindhya Pradesh to help tackle the unremitting dacoit menace in that state and then to raise the Railway Protection Force. His reputation for effectively dealing with mob violence and riots preceded him. In the late 1950s, as the Deputy Inspector General (DIG) Northern Range (Ahmedabad), he was falsely framed for the use of excessive force in suppressing vicious Hindu–Muslim riots in Ahmedabad city. It resulted in a lengthy, drawn-out Judicial Inquiry. 'It was a harrowing time for our parents, but eventually, all the charges against the police were proved false and were rejected,' said Nanavatty. Kaikhushru had the privilege of serving as the Inspector General of Police (IGP) of three states: Bombay, Maharashtra after the 'bifurcation' and, finally, post-retirement, the newly formed state of Nagaland.[5]

It was during the turbulent and acrimonious stage preceding the bifurcation of the erstwhile state of Bombay that Kaikhushru was the Deputy Inspector General (Criminal Investigation Department) for much of the time. For his services rendered, the Chief Minister, Y.B. Chavan, while addressing a volatile state Legislative Assembly, in an unusual gesture, is on record to have stated that Kaikhushru Jehangir Nanavatty was 'the best police officer the state ever had'. At 'bifurcation', the Y.B. Chavan government insisted that he continue as the IGP Maharashtra and subsequently granted him a three-year extension of service on his superannuation at the age of fifty-five years. After that, in 1964, the Central government sought his assistance to organize the police in the newly formed state of Nagaland and assume responsibility for 'restoring and maintaining public order' therein, a task he accepted with alacrity. Unfortunately, intractable professional differences with the army persisted despite his excellent relations with the senior military leadership in Kohima and Eastern Command in Calcutta. Seeing that the Indian Army was adamant in its view that the 'task was beyond the capabilities of the state police', Kaikhushru saw no valuable role for an officer of the rank of an IGP and decided to finally hang up his boots.[6]

Several facets of his father's personal life and professional career influenced Rostum's personality. 'He was of medium height, powerfully built, very strong and possessed tremendous powers of endurance,' recalls Rostum. 'He "could walk the hind legs off a donkey". As the IGP of the state, he would often, after a full day's work, walk home all by himself from his office near the Oval to our flat on Nepean Sea Road!' Incorruptible and forthright Kaikhushru possessed great physical and moral courage. As the DIG Northern Range (Ahmedabad) responsible for dealing with the dacoit menace in the area astride the Gujarat–Rajasthan border, he walked alone, unarmed and 'escorted' by two dacoits across the border into West Pakistan to successfully negotiate the surrender of a notorious dacoit leader, Balwant Singh, and his gang. A strict disciplinarian, Kaikhushru brooked no nonsense and was quick to anger but was kind and understanding towards his subordinates. 'Shikar was his passion,' Rostum remembers with awe and admiration. 'According to the rules, he shot by the book—on foot, no vehicles, no lights, no machans and no bandobast. One subordinate called him the "Indian Jim Corbett"! Calm and cool in dangerous situations, he was the finest shot with a rifle I have ever seen. Gunsmithing and car mechanics were his hobbies. Many would request him to "zero" their newly acquired weapons.'[7]

Rostum recalls his mother as a self-made woman. More spiritual than religious, she was mentally strong, highly disciplined, blessed with good common sense, and a positive outlook. Despite missing out on formal learning, she educated herself in the true sense of the word. She was fluent in several languages, had acquired through practical application the skills of nursing and caring for the young, sick and elderly, and quickly adapted to the role of a police officer's wife. Apart from taking complete charge of the children, house and home, she was deeply involved with the well-being of policemen's families and, later, with the work of the Indian Cancer Society in Bombay. She was a pillar of strength to Kaikhushru. 'For Ma, her home and family mattered most; a good listener and grounded, she was the "rock" that family and extended family members turned to in their hour of need,' recalls Nanavatty.[8]

Realizing that his career as a police officer would keep them on the move across the undivided Bombay State and deprive the children of a stable education, Kaikhushru and Dhan decided to send their kids to boarding school. Erna was the first to go to the Kimmins High School in Panchgani, a hill town in Bombay State. Rostum followed soon after. And so! Off he went at the age of five to an independent 'holding house' facility for young children attached to his sister's school. Nanavatty recalls a story his mother would often tell of his first day in school. She had said her goodbyes and left him in a music class with the others. However, yearning to see her boy once more before heading back to Satara, where Kaikhushru was the Superintendent of Police, Dhan returned to the classroom and, failing to see any sign of her son, said to an equally perplexed teacher, 'But I just left him here a few minutes ago.' A frantic search ensued, and a short while later, they found him hiding behind a piano. Embarrassed by his mother's return and desperately trying to control his tears, he fiercely and repeatedly said to her, 'Go away, go away, why have you come back?'[9]

Soon after, Rostum transferred to St Peter's, the boys' school literally 'across the road'. He would spend five years in Panchgani. His report card from St Peter's was glowing except for a modest performance in mathematics, which was his weakest subject.[10] St Peter's was also Rostum's first time in a boxing ring. Soundly thrashed by an older lad named Ansari, an outstanding student and sportsman, the only saving grace was that Rostum lasted the three rounds and was declared the 'best loser'. About the time Rostum was ten, circumstances compelled a change of schools.

Kaikhushru and Dhan looked at several schools, but Kaikhushru's posting to Ahmedabad clinched the issue in favour of the Rajkumar College (RKC) at Rajkot. Set up by the British in 1870 to provide wholesome education to the young princes from the Kathiawar region of Gujarat, the school opened its doors to deserving students after Independence. With the Jam Saheb of Nawanagar as its patron, the school boasted several illustrious alums. Among them were General Rajendrasinghji, the Indian Army's second chief; Ranjitsinghji, the legendary Indian cricketer who played for England in the early 1900s and even toured Australia; and his nephew, the talented batsman Duleepsinhji, who played for England in the 1930s. A keen and accomplished sportsman in school, Rostum recalls that Duleepsinhji, then in his early fifties, occasionally came and watched over the First XI practising in the nets. In the school team, primarily for his fielding prowess, Rostum would often find himself sent in as a night-watchman during a two or three-day game. Cricket, though, was not Rostum's main game at school. He preferred football and hockey, playing as a forward in both sports for the school team alongside his good friend and classmate, Owen D'Sena, who later joined the India Air Force (IAF) as a fighter pilot and was tragically killed in an accident on takeoff during a training sortie at Air Force Station Jamnagar.

Academically proficient at RKC, Rostum consistently stood second to Abdul Razak Kiddie, who took 'pole position' in every class. He secured good grades in all subjects except mathematics, which continued to be his bugbear.[11] He also developed an early interest in military history thanks to Peter Rogerson, his housemaster in the Senior Wing, who was to become the Principal later. Rogerson, who joined the Indian Army just after the Second World War, was commissioned into the Sikh Regiment and was actively involved in the work of the Punjab Boundary Force, struggling to safeguard the refugees crossing over in both directions during the Partition of India in 1947.

One of the last British officers of the Regiment to leave India after the horrors of Partition, Rogerson went back to Cambridge for further studies but returned to India in 1949, responding to an advertisement in the *Times Educational Supplement* for an English teacher's position at the RKC.[12] Later, Peter Rogerson was to become the longest-ever serving Principal of the school—twenty-eight years! He was to 'die in harness' literally while standing and bidding farewell to the Class of 1991. He was awarded the Order of the British Empire (OBE) by Her Majesty Queen Elizabeth II of England for his contribution to education in India.

'Roggy', as the boys called him in school, was, according to Nanavatty, a wonderful human being, an excellent teacher, an outstanding sportsman and a talented pianist. He was a great motivator, large-hearted, had a fine sense of humour, and excelled at anything and everything he put his hand to. 'He loved India as much as he did his own country,' said Nanavatty.[13] Rogerson also raised and nurtured the National Cadet Corps (NCC) at the school, helping the college compete against contingents from other military schools in multiple competitions and parades. Like many young boys his age, Rostum devoured books about the Second World War, notably the Battle of Britain and the air war elsewhere.

Being a Prefect as a senior did not keep Rostum away from pranks and other signature traits of the quintessential teenager. Always on the lookout for challenges, Rostum 'walked' the precariously narrow ledges all around his first-floor dormitory, crawled over the roof past his housemaster's windows in search of the delicious 'ber' fruit or jujuba, the sour 'imli' or tamarind pods, and much more. Appreciating Rogerson's approach, Rostum acknowledges, 'Roggy knew all the tricks we had up our sleeves, but let boys be boys. He rarely asked us what we had been up to—consequently, one never had to lie. He hugely influenced us and taught us several life lessons that stood us in good stead in later years.'

At the RKC, students had two long-term breaks, one in the summer and a shorter break in the winter. Rostum went home for the holidays first to Ahmedabad, a relatively short train ride away, and then in the last couple of years at school to Bombay. In Ahmedabad, the DIG Northern Range's bungalow was in a large sprawling compound on the banks of the Sabarmati River and nudging the cantonment. Apart from the small garden that Dhan nurtured, the rest was wild and covered with scrub that harboured partridge, quail and hare. Pigeons and doves, of course, were aplenty. Rostum had just graduated from using a .177 to a .22 airgun and couldn't have asked for more. With two sets of cousins and one lot of friends from school within the range of a cycle ride, the boys were in and out of each other's homes all the time. On Sundays and public holidays, it was more serious stuff. The areas around Ahmedabad abounded in small game, and in the shooting season, Kaikhushru was out at every opportunity. 'I would tag along and slowly pick up the nuances of "beating", "marking", "fetching" game, using a shotgun, and shooting on the wing. It was great learning and fun, too. Life was idyllic.'

Life for a teenager was uncomplicated in the Nanavatty household, with enough room for escapades. 'Father set the example but rarely "lectured us". Our mother confided in us, explained things, corrected, encouraged and disciplined us. I cannot remember a single instance when my father admonished me except when I was dangerously naughty as a teenager on holiday in Ahmedabad.'[14] He went on, 'One day, a cousin older than me who lived on this large ancestral property and seemingly had a running feud with his neighbour, a crusty old relative, suggested we teach the latter a lesson. He suggested I shoot out the windowpanes of his bathroom, which was nearest to the common boundary wall with my airgun. Accordingly, we hatched a plan, carefully selected a "firing position", and at last light, three windowpanes were knocked out with three successive shots. Pleased with what we thought was a well-planned and executed "covert" operation we quietly withdrew, pretending we knew nothing. The following day, I was mortified when Father summoned me and, with Mother present, asked me if I had done what I did. I pled guilty. He then spoke to me quietly, but very firmly. He said that I had violated the basic rule of handling firearms that he had drummed into me, that I could have, even with an airgun, caused serious injury to a person and that he expected me never to act so stupidly and irresponsibly again. And, that was the end of the matter.'

Rostum finished school by mid-1959, and excerpts from his school report indicate that he was an all-rounder of exceptional ability. The Principal, Mark Alexander Wynter-Blythe, endorsed his progress and conduct as 'Excellent'.[15] Mr Ayaaz Khan, his close friend from school, two years his senior and a future Principal of Rajkumar College, has fond memories of his association with Rostum. Responding to the author's request to share some of his recollections of the carefree times they spent together at boarding school, Ayaaz wrote back: 'Rusty, as we called him, was a diminutive young lad, but in his stature, he turned out to be a colossus. It was in his DNA, as it were, to give his hundred per cent in whatever he took up, whether it was academics, co-curricular activities, games and sports, NCC, or leadership. Rusty was an extremely competitive mate—but the rivalry was always healthy and fair. He was an outstanding student, a much-admired member of the cricket, hockey and football teams, an outstanding performer at debates, recitation and English-speaking competitions, and an exemplary Prefect. Finally, let me say, Sir, what makes you want to write a biography of this officer and gentleman is the knowledge and admiration of his qualities of head and heart. I say that he displayed all those as a school lad.'[16] 'Rusty' was a name that stuck for a lifetime.

Having decided in senior school that he would join the Indian Army, Rostum acquiesced to his mother's suggestion that he should give himself a few years to explore the freedom of college before committing to a lifetime of service. Joining St Xavier's College in Bombay, Rostum felt like a fish out of water among the young and upwardly mobile Bombayites and sorely missed the organization, regimentation and discipline of life in school. However, he enjoyed spending time with his family and never regretted not joining the National Defence Academy (NDA). Impatient and wanting to get on with life, the moment he completed his Intermediate Exam at St Xavier's College in Bombay, Rostum applied and was selected to join the Indian Military Academy (IMA), Dehradun, in March 1961. While Rostum had set his heart on the Indian Army, his sister Erna sought and excelled in a career in the manufacture of high-end garments for export using hand-woven Indian fabric. She joined Paville Fashions in Bombay as a Production Manager and served some thirty-two years with the company, of which twenty years were spent as one of its Directors.

The Indian Military Academy is a revered military institution. It first commenced training officer candidates, traditionally referred to as Gentlemen Cadets, for the Indian Army in 1932. The 1st Course (the Pioneers) that included Field Marshal Sam Manekshaw passed out in 1934. After that, for a few years post-Independence, it took on the additional responsibility of serving as a joint services institution providing initial military training to officer candidates of all three services until the National Defence Academy, Khadakvasla, came into being in 1954. Whereas in 1932, the strength of the 'Passing Out' Course was forty Gentlemen Cadets, by 1960, the average strength of a Passing Out Course had grown to around 150 and currently stands at about 350–400 Gentlemen Cadets, including a complement of Technical Course cadets.

IMA in the early 1960s comprised three battalions with three companies in each battalion. A Lieutenant Colonel commanded the battalion, with a Major as the company commander and Captains commanding platoons. The latter constituted the first link in the chain of command: they acted as mentors, trainers and assessing officers of the Gentlemen Cadets. In their first two terms, the Direct Entry cadets comprising Y Cadets: selected soldiers deemed fit for a commission as officers; OTU and NCC Cadets; and students fresh from two years of college concentrated on acquiring the requisite basic military knowledge and leadership skills. Additional course-mates joined them in their third term from the NDA. It was only in the second term that deserving Gentlemen Cadets began to tenant appointments—Lance Corporal in the second term, Corporal in the third, and Sergeant and above in the fourth and final term.

Joining the IMA in July 1961 and assigned to Panipat Company in Charlie Battalion, Rostum embarked on a forty-two-year career as a soldier that would take him from the jungles and mountains of the North-east to strife-torn Sri Lanka, the icy heights of the Siachen Glacier, and deep into the fight against insurgents and terrorists in the North-east and J&K.

The 31st Regular Course was scheduled to 'pass out' of the portals of the IMA in December 1963. When the Indian Army's frontline in Ladakh and the North-East Frontier Agency (NEFA), or what is today the Indian state of Arunachal Pradesh, wilted in the face of the Chinese onslaught in late October 1962, Army HQ decided to fast-track the commissioning of the 31st Course in December 1962 itself together with the 30th Regular Course. Nanavatty recalls that the month that followed was a blur. The emphasis shifted to practical training in military subjects to the exclusion of all else, with activity stretching well into the nights. Despite the woeful lack of authentic information about the two-front war with China, cadets, especially from the passing out courses, were keyed up at the thought of going straight into battle.

Brigadier (later Lieutenant General) P.S. Bhagat, an Engineer Officer and the first Indian to be awarded the Victoria Cross during the Second World War, was the commandant of the IMA. He was an impactful and inspirational commandant whom the cadets worshipped in those troubled times.[17] Nanavatty, at the time, was a hard-driving third-term corporal in the Panipat Company of Charlie Battalion. An excellent sportsman in school, his single-minded focus at the IMA was on the core military disciplines—endurance and physical fitness, drill, weapon training, marksmanship, small unit tactics and leadership. Among several friends that Nanavatty made at the IMA, most, for obvious reasons, were his mates in his company.

Perhaps his closest friend was J.K. 'Jojo' Sengupta of the 22nd Course NDA, whom he got to know only in the third term. Jojo was a gold medallist 'twice over', first at the RIMC and then at the NDA. He was exceptionally talented—a fine mind and brilliant in the academic field, he was a swimming and boxing blue. He was held in high esteem by his NDA coursemates. In what must surely be a record of some kind, Jojo passed out first in the order of merit in the 31st Course, winning a third successive gold medal. A mere two and a half years later, in the India–Pakistan War, 1965, Jojo, then with 16 Cavalry, was severely wounded in a tank battle in the Sialkot Sector. He went through months of painful surgery, treatment and rehabilitation in India and abroad to recover, but was visually impaired for life and was 'boarded out' of the army on medical grounds. Unfazed by this setback, Jojo married after he left the army. Together with his wife, Rita, a remarkable person in her own right, he set up 'Prerana', a school for disabled and underprivileged children in Salugara (Siliguri), North Bengal, which brings much relief to those less fortunate. Rostum and Jojo were to remain lifelong friends till the latter's passing in 2013.

Brigadier Shamsher Singh from the Corps of Signals, like Nanavatty, joined the IMA in June 1961 as part of the Direct Entry Course 31. Housed in a twin-sharing room in Collins Block next to the one occupied by Nanavatty, the two became lifelong friends. Of the several recollections Shamsher has of their time together as buddies at IMA, the two that stand out reflect the traits of professional excellence and humility that Nanavatty demonstrated throughout his career. 'Rostum at the firing ranges fired every shot with total deliberation, whereas we would poop off the ammunition in haste. He was the archetype marksman who made every shot count. On sentry duty in a trench with me one day, I asked him what he would do if the enemy attacked at that moment. In his typical Parsi accent, he said, "*Saale ko pass aane do aur phir fire kholo* (Let the enemy close in before opening fire)." One day, we were to fill the forms with personal information. In the column relating to the "profession of father", Rostum wrote, "Police Officer" and immediately filled in a relatively high salary that I found hard to understand. On goading Rostum, he revealed that his father was the Inspector General of Police of the undivided Bombay State. Till then, we were unaware that Rostum was the son of a renowned police officer.'[18]

Professor Gautam Sen, a Direct Entry who joined the Panipat Company at IMA with Rostum in June 1961, is a family friend and has intellectually jousted with the latter for over five decades. Serving in the Indian Army for thirteen years before embarking on a fulfilling and noteworthy academic and writing career, Sen's strongest memory of Rostum in the IMA is that apart from his performance in the field, 'Rostum was always immersed in reading and understanding the careers of accomplished field commanders from the Second World War, people like Rommel and Slim. He was always talking about the Chindits, small-team operations behind enemy lines and Major General Orde Wingate, their talismanic commander.'[19] His introduction to Wingate sparked Nanavatty's deep and continued interest in Special Forces and 'small team operations' throughout his career.

Nanavatty stood third in the Order of Merit of the 31st Course. He bagged the Sword of Honour as the Best All-round Cadet of his course and received the Drill, Marksmanship, Tactics and Leadership and Infantry Prizes. Despite being in the same company in their third and what became their final term, Nanavatty says that he never felt he was in competition with Jojo or, for that matter, anyone else. 'I thoroughly enjoyed the IMA and endeavoured to do my best, and that was about it. I hadn't a clue that I was in the running for the Sword of Honour. It was at the Passing Out Course regimental dinner night before the Passing Out Parade, where several prizes were distributed, that the commandant, Brigadier Bhagat, put his arm around my shoulder after I had collected the Infantry Prize and said, with a twinkle in his eye, "Do you know that you are getting the Sword?"—it was a bolt from the blue. I did not know what to say!'

Dr Sarvepalli Radhakrishnan, the erudite and learned President of India and the Commander-in-Chief of India's Armed Forces, reviewed the Passing Out Parade at the IMA on 10 December 1962. It was a very long parade, considering that the President was presenting Colours to the Academy for the first time after Independence, and two courses were 'passing out' simultaneously[20] and, Rostum's proud parents and sister were there to see him receive the coveted 'Sword'.

In the 1960s, the Indian Army broadly comprised Arms, Supporting Arms and Services. The Arms comprised the Armour and the Infantry; the Supporting Arms included the Artillery, Engineers and Signals; and the Services comprised the Army Ordnance Corps (AOC), the Army Service Corps (ASC), the Electrical and Mechanical Engineers (EME), the Army Medical Corps (AMC) and the Remount Veterinary Corps (RVC). Allotting Arms and Services to the passing out cadets was and remains a complex exercise for the Military Secretary's Branch (MS Branch) at Army Headquarters. Several factors—the number of vacancies in the various arms and services, the recommendations of the IMA, the personal choice of each Gentleman Cadet to include 'parental' claims, the class composition of regiments, and the need to balance out the quality of individuals in units—are all carefully considered. Adding to the woes of the MS Branch is the manoeuvring—albeit unofficial—by the Directing Staff at the IMA, keen on getting the best young men into their regiments! In those days, cadets strived to join the Arms and Supporting Arms with the Armoured Corps, invariably attracting the best.

Nanavatty's heart was set on joining the infantry from the day he joined the IMA. To begin with, he had three regiments in mind: the Maratha Light Infantry, the Sikh Regiment and the Gorkha Rifles. Once in the Academy, in the snatches of time available, he would leaf through various regimental histories in the library. As time went on, Nanavatty 'firmed in' on the Gorkha Rifles and his final three choices were the 5th, 8th and 3rd Gorkha Rifles, in that order.

Nanavatty's decision to join the 5th Gorkha Rifles (Frontier Force) was heavily influenced by the regiment's exploits in the Second Burma Campaign in 1943–44, wherein the Second Battalion won three Victoria Crosses. It was Captain H.C. Attri, his impressive young platoon commander in Panipat Company from the 8th Gorkha Rifles (8 GR), who persuaded the young Nanavatty to switch his allegiance to 8 GR. Attri assured Nanavatty of there being a vacancy in the First Battalion. Nanavatty was unimpressed. 1/8 GR had been in the news. They had already been involved in severe fighting in November 1962 in the Sirijap, Pangong Tso and Kailash Range Areas in the Chushul Sector, where they had taken heavy casualties, and Major Dhan Singh Thapa had won a Param Vir Chakra. In his young mind, Nanavatty knew that the unit would be pulled out of the line for rest and refit sooner rather than later. He wanted to go to a battalion that would likely go into action if the fighting restarted. Attri backtracked and quickly contrived to see that the subaltern was allotted to 2/8 GR, his battalion. Neither he nor Nanavatty knew that the 2/8th had received a severe mauling in the Eastern Sector, something that the latter was to realize only when he reported for duty on 29 December 1962.

Though Nanavatty never wore his Parsi legacy on his sleeve, he maintains that it is indeed a matter of pride that Parsis have contributed four Service Chiefs since Independence: Field Marshal Sam Manekshaw, Admiral Jal Cursetji, Air Marshal Aspy Engineer and Air Chief Marshal Fali Major. As an aside, Nanavatty proudly recalls that he had the privilege of serving alongside three other Parsi C-in-Cs in 2002. Nanavatty was the sole army officer in the quartet as a Lieutenant General and General Officer Commanding-in-Chief (GOC-in-C) of the Indian Army's Northern Command. The others were all Air Marshals from the Indian Air Force: T.J. Master, Adi R. Ghandhi and Manek Madon, the Air Officer Commanding-in-Chiefs (AOC-in-Cs) of Training Command, Western Air Command and Eastern Air Command respectively—four out of a total of seventeen such posts in the three services then. 'Today, the scene is bleak; hardly any Parsi youth join the Armed Forces,' laments Nanavatty. Among the several Parsi recipients of gallantry awards, two stand out according to him: Lieutenant Colonel Adi Tarapore, 17 (Poona) Horse, and Second Lieutenant (later Major General) Cyrus Pithawala, JAK RIF. Tarapore was awarded the Param Vir Chakra (Posthumous) in the India–Pakistan War in 1965 and Pithawala the Ashok Chakra fighting insurgents in Manipur in 1980.

These vignettes of Parsis in uniform are by no means complete. They offer a lens into the exploits of a small community that has punched well above its weight in the service of the nation in multiple arenas. Delivering a lecture on 'Parsis in the Armed Forces' at a Bombay University Seminar in March 2000 to honour the memory of Sir Pherozeshah Mehta, one of the founding members of the Indian National Congress and the 'uncrowned' king of Bombay, Lieutenant General A.M. Sethna, a former Vice Chief of Army Staff and veteran of WWII and the 1971 Bangladesh campaign, argued that it was worth noting that the contribution of Parsis in matters related to national security was wide-ranging and went beyond the famous few such as Manekshaw.[21]

Like most Parsi families at the time, the Nanavattys were a nuclear family. They maintained a low social profile in Bombay. Though his relatives and friends knew about his being commissioned and assigned to the Chinese front, there were no celebrations or family gatherings, considering the sombre mood prevailing across the nation. Nanavatty spent his two weeks' leave at home and used the Willingdon Club's sports facilities to keep fit. His mother thoughtfully presented him with a transistor radio to stay abreast of the world around him. 'It only seemed to come alive when the antenna touched the CGI sheet of my bunker, and I would get a crackling signal,' said Nanavatty with a wry smile. A firm handshake from his father and hugs from his mother and sister on the railway platform at Bombay's V.T. Station were the only goodbyes he got. Still, it was the whisper in the ear from his mother that he remembers with great fondness every time: '*Fateh kar je*' she would say in Gujarati, which translated in English meant 'may victory be yours'.

On the train from Bombay to the farthest corner of the North-east in late December 1962, 'Mr' Nanavatty—as subalterns were more properly addressed then—had embarked on the journey of his life in the service of his country. At his detraining station, Tinsukia in Upper Assam, he was met by a Gorkha Non-Commissioned Officer (NCO) and driver and bundled with his 'tin trunk and bedding roll' into a one-ton truck bound for Dinjan (Chabua), a WWII Allied airfield reactivated during the operations in 1962. Dinjan would much later become the headquarters of 2 Mountain Division. After spending a night in a tent at the airfield, he flew into the airhead at Along the following day in an IAF Dakota from Chabua. This IAF base was the air operations hub for the Along and Walong sectors. Arriving in a unit in utter disarray and reeling from the effects of a disastrous withdrawal from Mechuka, Nanavatty's career began with a very sobering lesson on the harsh realities of war.

2

INTO THE DEEP END WITH THE GORKHAS

'Had definite orders to hold out been given, the Gorkha soldier would have obeyed them to the letter. He has done it before and would do it again.'

—Second Lieutenant R.K. Nanavatty, 29 June 1963

When the young lads of the 30th and 31st Regular Courses from the IMA first reported for duty to their respective units, the humiliating India–China War of 1962 had just given over, and the future, to say the least, was uncertain. A brief review of the role played by the 2nd Battalion 8th Gorkha Rifles (2/8 GR) in the war provides an exciting backdrop to the start of Nanavatty's career as a professional soldier.

Ever since the Chinese occupation of Tibet and the escape of the 14th Dalai Lama to India via Tawang in March 1959, relations between the two countries had deteriorated rapidly. The gloves finally came off on 20 October 1962 when the Chinese People's Liberation Army (PLA) launched an offensive against India on a broad front stretching from Ladakh in the west to the North-East Frontier Agency (NEFA) (now Arunachal Pradesh) in the east. The attacks in NEFA were on several widely separated axes—Tawang, Mechuka and Walong.[1] The offensive caught the Indian Army ill-prepared and unbalanced, resulting in an overwhelming defeat. The Chinese quickly signalled victory in what they deemed a punitive operation, and on 21 November 1962, they declared a unilateral ceasefire. They withdrew to positions they held before the commencement of the conflict, allowing a distraught Indian Army to limp back gradually into the territories it had lost. Why the Chinese should have withdrawn from an area that they now claim to be theirs is a question they ought to be made to answer.

In 1962, 2/8 GR under command Lieutenant Colonel Derek Taylor, an officer commissioned into 1/8 GR, had just completed a tenure in counterinsurgency (CI) operations in Nagaland and was based at Ramgarh, Bihar, as part of 62 Infantry Brigade. The unit had barely settled down in its 'peace station' when the fighting erupted, and the brigade was leapfrogged, first to Jorhat and then to Dinjan in Assam.[2] From Dinjan, two of the brigade's integral units (battalions) were sent in quick succession to two different formations in two divergent directions. 4 SIKH went to 11 Infantry Brigade in Walong and 4 GARH RIF to 4 Infantry Division in the Tawang Sector: the latter were destined to garner just glory and acclaim for their gallant action as divisional covering troops in the battle for Jaswantgarh on the Tawang–Sela–Darang–Bomdila Axis.[3] That left the brigade headquarters and 2/8 GR in Dinjan—but not for long, as Chinese troop concentrations were reported opposite Lo La to the northwest of Mechuka. A subsidiary thrust by the enemy along the Nissangong–Mechuka–Tato–Along axis was a distinct possibility. Accordingly, Alpha Company 2/8 GR under Major S.N. Dar was airlifted from Along to Mechuka using the Otter aircraft of 59 Squadron IAF. With a platoon of Assam Rifles in location and under command, the company was ordered to occupy a screen position at Nissangong astride the Lo La–Mechuka track approximately ten kilometres ahead of Mechuka.[4]

Over 400 kilometres to the east, an ominous situation was developing in the Walong Sector following the fall of Kibithu. Accordingly, on 25 October, two rifle companies of 2/8 GR, Bravo under Second Lieutenant J.S. Sesodia and Delta under Major G.D. Pun, were mobilized and dispatched posthaste as reinforcements, first using Dakota aircraft of the Kalinga Airways from Chabua to Tezu, and thereon by IAF Otter aircraft of 59 Squadron to Walong. Sesodia, a plucky youngster and the reigning 9 mm Sten Machine Carbine shooting champion of the Indian Army, was itching to get into the fight. On the other hand, calm and composed G.D. Pun was a grizzled veteran commissioned through the ranks. Both companies were placed under command 6 KUMAON and 4 SIKH respectively, which were deployed astride the fast-flowing and dangerous Lohit River. The river was only crossable using a precarious steel wire rope, pulley and harness contraption, one individual at a time. With Chinese patrols probing forward aggressively along the limited tracks in the area, the two companies were soon in contact. They acquitted themselves well, inflicting several casualties on the enemy in the ensuing skirmishes, even recovering the first few Chinese weapons. In the process, they imposed caution and delay on the PLA and prevented a headlong dash by them to Walong.[5]

On 4 November 1962, 2/8 GR at Along was placed under the command of 192 Infantry Brigade and commenced the move of its headquarters, Charlie Company and elements of Support Company from Along to Mechuka, once again via an air bridge established by the ubiquitous Otters. On 6 November, Charlie Company had barely concentrated at Mechuka when they were ordered by the brigade to revert and occupy a layback (reserve) position with a Company less a platoon in the general area of Rego–Tato, where the tracks from Mechuka and Tuting converged. At this stage, 2/8 GR in the Mechuka–Nissangong Area had, in addition to its Alpha Company and a platoon of Charlie Company, a company of 2 MADRAS and two platoons of the Assam Rifles under command.

On the Walong front, on 12 November, Bravo & Delta Companies were relieved by integral units of 11 Infantry Brigade and re-joined the battalion in Along. They had done well there and had earned a commendation from the brigade commander, Brigadier N.C. Rawley, MC, conveyed to the commanding officer (CO) by a signal on 10 November. On 13 November, the corps commander, Lieutenant General B.M. Kaul, visited the battalion in Along and gave them a 'shabash'.[6]

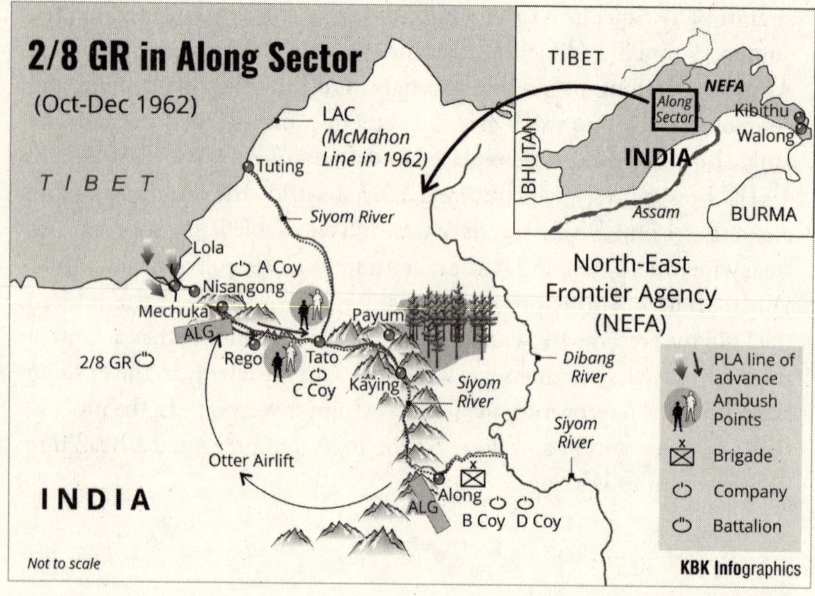

On 17 November, the advancing Chinese PLA columns contacted the screen and launched a quick attack on Alpha Company. The attack was repulsed and the enemy forced to retreat. Even as the screen from Alpha Company fought on, Bravo Company less a platoon was ferried by air from Along to beef-up the defences at Mechuka. Amidst this chaos, the brigade commander of 192 Infantry Brigade arrived on the scene with a new set of orders for the CO. He informed the CO that the troops from Mechuka and Tuting were to withdraw to Along via the layback position in the Rego–Tato Area on the night of 18/19 November to occupy a brigade-defended sector in the Along area.

18 November was particularly eventful. The brigade commander, arrived in Mechuka with a fleet of empty Otter aircraft, and ordered the evacuation of all the non-essentials and sick personnel, heavy baggage and stores. Despite the CO remonstrating in the strongest terms possible, the brigade commander was adamant and, to make matters worse, insisted that the battalion's 3-inch mortars be loaded onto the returning Otters. At that time, the battalion lay spread-eagled—Alpha Company at Nissangong in contact with the enemy; battalion headquarters with

Bravo Company less a platoon and a platoon of Charlie Company at Mechuka; Charlie Company less a platoon in the Rego–Tato Area; and a platoon of Bravo Company with Delta Company at Along—over some 150 kilometres of the most challenging, trackless mountainous and jungle terrain imaginable.[7] At 1600 hours that day the PLA mounted a deliberate attack on the screen. The attack was repulsed once again after which the screen withdrew in good order and reached the battalion-defended area at Mechuka around midnight. Simultaneously, the battalion received executive orders from the brigade headquarters to commence its withdrawal from Mechuka.[8]

Not a single individual of the battalion had walked the distance between Mechuka and the designated layback position at Tato to the rear. The few maps they held were utterly inadequate, and locals who could have served as guides were not forthcoming for fear of reprisals by the Chinese. Even the minimal logistical arrangements for a rearward move on foot were non-existent. Chinese patrols, on the other hand, bypassed Indian troops and isolated them by making extensive use of locals as guides. The fear of being cut off was omnipresent indeed. Faced with a difficult decision, Colonel Taylor ordered his sub-unit commanders to withdraw and stay clear of trails and tracks at all costs to avoid ambushes.

The withdrawal, predictably, was a disaster and degenerated into a desperate escape and evasion operation. The battalion lost a total of thirty-eight personnel of all ranks, who perished owing to a combination of enemy action, hunger, thirst and the ill effects of weather. Some of the wounded were captured and taken prisoner of war. Of the eight officers in Mechuka at the time, the CO, Adjutant and regimental medical officer (RMO) were killed; three officers, including one who was severely wounded, were taken prisoner. One officer, Lieutenant Anand Gore evaded the enemy. He hid amongst tribals who were suspicious and unfriendly at first but later were helpful till he was eventually recovered by helicopter after the cessation of hostilities.[9]

Only one young officer, Second Lieutenant B.K. (Manju) Barooah, came through unscathed. And yet, there were stirring examples of good leadership at the lowest levels. Almost all the sub-units that withdrew in good order were led by platoon and section commanders who ordered their men 'follow me', and force-marched down the only track to Tato despite the orders to do otherwise. For several days after that, bewildered, bruised, bleeding, and emaciated men with their clothing and equipment in tatters, desperately clinging to their weapons, kept trickling into Tato and Taliha.

Over the preceding four weeks, the unit had experienced a bewildering set of changes in command and control, locations and tasks, with scant attention being paid to unit and sub-unit cohesion and preparation for tasks—difficult even to comprehend on paper; it must have been a nightmare for commanders and troops on the ground. [10]

When the two newly commissioned subalterns, B.C. (Roni) Sarma and Nanavatty, joined the battalion at Along at the end of December, the unit was bivouacked around the Along airfield licking its wounds. The mood in the makeshift tented Officers' Mess was sombre. Its members comprised three officers left out of battle (LOB) for no fault of their own, Barooah, the Senior Subaltern who had miraculously come through the ordeal without a scratch, and the two 'pip-squeak' subalterns. The unit looked like a sad, rag-tag bunch. It was not a pretty sight. The men were despondent and bitter; their frequent refrain, 'We should have stayed and fought'—*Kafir hunu bhanda marnu niko* (It is better to die than be a coward) is what they always say in Gorkhali.

Brooding over the events of the recent past was not an option. The unit commenced regrouping despite having no CO, a shortage of officers, and glaring material deficiencies. It moved to prepare and occupy fresh defences to secure the Along airfield—virtually its lifeline.

Consequently, routine operational, training and administrative activities followed. Nanavatty was assigned to Charlie Company and appointed commander of 8 Platoon. His company commander, Major R.K. Majumdar, was typically 'old school'—intelligent, erudite, soft-spoken, well-mannered and reserved. He had served on the personal staff of the Colonel of the Regiment before reverting to the unit. Assigned to organize the layback position around Tato to cover the withdrawal from Mechuka, he was devastated by the loss of the CO and the Adjutant, his close friends. He left his subaltern alone to settle down and find his feet.

Nanavatty recollects 'that it was a while before Majumdar acknowledged his presence, even though their command posts were only a few hundred yards apart'. The ice finally broke when he was invited to share 'dal-roti' with his company commander in his bunker. 'Come and have supper with me,' he said.

The preparation of defences provided Nanavatty an ideal opportunity to 'mix it' with the men of his platoon. Living, eating, sleeping and constructing defences, he was fortunate to have an outstanding Platoon Havildar in '31' Dil Bahadur Gurung. In a Gorkha battalion wherein you have several soldiers with similar sounding first names and castes, tradition has it that you know a person by the last two digits of his Service No. too! Mature beyond his years, he was constantly by his platoon commander's side. Nanavatty immersed himself in the innumerable activities involved in the defence—analysing the attack approaches, locating early warning elements, spit-locking weapons, and carrying out endless rehearsals of the various procedures, drills and contingencies integral to any defensive battle. It was also a god-sent opportunity to talk to the men individually and get a feel of the ordeal they had just been through.

As he talked to his Junior Commissioned Officers (JCOs), Non-Commissioned Officers (NCOs) and men in a mix of Hindi and broken Gorkhali, he began jotting down his thoughts, not something that a Second Lieutenant would typically do. In an email to the author, Nanavatty wrote, 'Here is possibly the first "professional"—actually, quite un-professional—paper I wrote after commissioning. It is dated 29 June 1963 and was lying with an Emergency Commissioned officer friend who left the army in 1967–68 and chose to preserve it. I wrote the paper in response to orders from our brigade commander, Brigadier Gurbux Singh Gill, Commander, 192 Infantry Brigade. He required all of us officers serving in the brigade to write and share our thoughts on the just concluded India–China War of 1962. It is an awful piece of military writing and just shows how little I knew. I am sending it to you because it will give you an idea of how I and others like me felt at the time.'[11]

Little did Nanavatty realize that, for a researcher and historian, a sixty-year-old paper of this kind was worth its weight in gold. It is an emotional piece written in anger that portrays a sense of disappointment, betrayal, and hope. With the corrections and comments scribbled alongside, it offers insights into Nanavatty's intellectual and analytical potential still in his teens. Brigadier Gill's prompt for the officers of his brigade to reflect on was simple enough: 'During the fighting along our northern borders in October and November '62, we suffered serious reverses at the hands of the Chinese. Why did the enemy beat us? What steps do you suggest we take to overcome our shortcomings?'

In response, Nanavatty wrote about the abject lack of preparedness of the Indian Army: 'It was neither the "antiquated" arms nor the insufficiency of ammunition that everybody seems to point out and say, "That's the reason." I agree there probably was not enough at the right place and time. But what is this, if not fumbling and disorder at the top, a complete lack of foresight and planning? There is no doubt our Army was a mere "peacetime machine". Physically unfit, ill-equipped and ill-trained, with little or no effort to increase its fighting efficiency, we got what we deserved. Brilliant politicians wanted to do away with the Defence Services completely. It might have spared us the shame!' Responding to these opening paras, the Brigade Major (BM), Major V.K. Sood, later the Vice Chief of Army Staff in the late 1980s, remarked, 'I do not think things were so bad; don't be so emotional in your writing.'

Focusing on border defence, which is still a vexing issue, particularly along the LAC, Nanavatty highlights in his article the scattered defensive dispositions. These comprised posts manned by the police and the Assam Rifles, a paramilitary force raised by the British specifically for India's eastern frontiers in 1835. Complemented by a few regular Indian Army battalions split into small sub-units, the force paid little attention to training or getting to know their areas of responsibility and the people therein. Exploiting these vulnerabilities at an opportune moment, Nanavatty suggests that after a few years of probing, the Chinese finally struck where it hurt, eliciting angry cries from India's political leaders for the Indian Army to 'throw them out'.[12] Assessing the Chinese modus operandi, Nanavatty wrote: 'Chinese intelligence had already subverted and brainwashed the tribals of our border areas. Taking advantage of our unpreparedness, the Chinese pushed strong columns guided by locals along the innumerable shortcuts and mountain passes leading straight to the few and far between posts. They enveloped our defences from all sides and cut them off from any reinforcements. Despite gallant efforts to stave off the onslaught, without a shadow of a doubt, it was too late. Units were unable to call in adequate or any fire support at all. Commanding officers found themselves holding positions with poorly acclimatised troops from other fronts with little familiarization with the area.'

Influenced by the recent events in 2/8 GR, he was unsparing in his indictment of the senior leadership; Nanavatty argues that they should have been familiar with the tactics employed by the Chinese, given their experience with the Japanese in the Burma Campaign of the Second World War and the feedback from the Indian Army contingent that oversaw the repatriation of prisoners after the Korean War.[13] Nanavatty also questions the decision and timing of the withdrawal orders given to his battalion despite the spirited action of the screen. He voices the feelings of his Gorkha troops, who told him that they should have fought on at Mechuka rather than withdraw: 'Surely the best way would have been to fight back. Had firm orders to hold out been given, the Gorkha soldier would have obeyed them to the letter. He has done it before and would have done it again. He suspected that the abrupt and sudden decision to withdraw would have given rise to fear amounting to hysteria. Withdrawal, just in name, started as a retreat and was very soon a rout. For days on end, they marched back, heading in the direction they hoped was home, many of them frostbitten and wounded, struggling along as best as they could. The fit and the lucky made it back. There were the unfortunate ones who died of starvation and exhaustion, while others were mowed down in ambushes.'[14]

After the farcical resignation episode of India's Chief of Army Staff General Thimayya in March 1960, following a bitter feud with the Defence Minister and his subsequent retirement,[15] Lieutenant General B.M. Kaul was appointed the Chief of General Staff (CGS). The Forward Policy then gained momentum through the summer of 1961 and spring of 1962. This translated into over sixty posts being established in Ladakh and NEFA, many of them being within territory claimed by China and 'behind enemy lines' in Ladakh. From a military and operational perspective, the Forward Policy was a poorly conceived politically driven military posture with almost no coercive potential against a much stronger adversary. Ruminating on the ill-fated policy albeit through a tactical lens, Nanavatty's paper questions why pockets of troops were 'shoved out so far forward and away from any help'. Instead, he reckons 'the Chinese should have been forced to come forward and extend their communication lines, containing them in an area where it was much more feasible to supply and administer their own forces before striking back when the snows clamped down on the passes'.

Addressing his brigade commander's second question seeking remedial measures to overcome the army's shortcomings, Nanavatty's early obsession with preparation and training rings loud and clear, a trait he would demonstrate throughout his career. He wrote: 'We must build our defences in an area where we can provide easy logistics support. Ahead of our main defences, we should have specially trained formations gathering information, doing intensive patrolling and, in the case of an attack, harassing the enemy, cutting off his communications, and destroying his dumps. We should train extremely hard, aiming at top physical condition, especially the officers, and sack anyone not meeting the required standards. We must train junior commanders to take the initiative and deal with sudden situations. There is too much going by the book at lower levels. Emphasis on endurance training should be laid on long marches off tracks and cross-country, with adequate opportunities provided to units for battle inoculation under live firing conditions. Above all, we must create an offensive spirit to beat the enemy at his own game. No enemy is invincible!'

Concluding his paper with a flourish that would do a seasoned military historian proud, Nanavatty wrote: 'To obliterate this, one of the blackest moments in our country's fighting history, will mean sweat and blood, and when the opportunity arises again, we must show the world that what happened was an aberration.'

While the BM was tough on Nanavatty, remarking that the latter had not tackled the problem logically and that there was too much emotion in his considerations, he marked it a 'fair' effort. Brigadier Gurbux, though, was more appreciative of the youngster's candid writing and offered some encouraging comments: 'You are full of ideas and keen to see things improve at a fast rate, as they should. I would describe your writing style as "journalese", which will do if you write for the *Blitz* or *Current* [two popular Bombay-based tabloid newspapers!]. But as an officer, you must deal with the subject objectively without allowing your emotions to override logic. You can express yourself well. What you must do is to alter your style to military writing.'[16] This early habit of speaking truth to power without worrying about his brigade commander's response and any ensuing consequences would strongly influence Nanavatty for the rest of his career. Excerpts from the original paper are placed at Appendix A.

But we are getting ahead of ourselves here. Just as the preparation of the defences at Along was progressing nicely, the battalion was ordered to stop work, disable the earthworks, abandon the area and concentrate again at the airfield to await further orders. The grapevine suggested that the situation in the Naga Hills was hotting up!

The Naga insurgency was a secessionist movement that gained momentum in the northeastern portion of India bordering Burma (Myanmar) in the early years after India gained independence from colonial rule. Spearheaded by the Naga National Council (NNC) with the charismatic A.Z. Phizo as its leader, it soon morphed into a violent armed struggle between the secessionists and the Indian state. The insurgency has waxed and waned for some seventy-three years and has emerged as the longest-surviving insurgency since the Second World War. Though the state of Nagaland is now integrated with the Union of India and the secessionist flavour no longer exists, a final political solution and complete peace still eludes the region and its people.[17]

The Indian Army was first deployed in the Naga Hills & Tuensang Area (NHTA) to quell the Naga Rebellion in April 1955. Coming to grips with counterinsurgency operations against Naga Hostiles (the term 'insurgent' was not in vogue at the time), a genre of warfare that was new to the Indian Army, was challenging. The evacuation of the Indian Army formations and units from the Naga Hills in 1962, because of the India–China War, further compounded the problem. The vacuum introduced a new dimension to the secessionist movement: covert support to insurgents by nation-states inimical to India, such as Pakistan and China. For the first time in the conflict, Naga Hostiles, taking advantage of the void in the NHTA and with the full connivance and support of Pakistan, exfiltrated into East Pakistan for training, equipping and financial support. Subsequently, this strategy was to be replicated by the Chinese, too, and in early 1963 intelligence reports suggested that Naga gangs were beginning to return from East Pakistan. It was now a race against time. 192 Infantry Brigade, with its three battalions, 2 MADRAS, 1 JAK RIF and 2/8 GR, was rushed into Nagaland to try and intercept the returning gangs and re-establish a measure of control over critical areas in the NHTA. Part of 23 Infantry Division during its earlier stint in Nagaland, the brigade was now part of the newly raised 8 Mountain Division, which had its headquarters at Zakhama. While at Along, Nanavatty read his first book on counterinsurgency operations in Malaya, *Shoot to Kill* by Colonel Richard Miers, who commanded his unit in those operations.[18]

Waiting for executive orders—and given that their experience of operations in the Naga Hills was relatively recent—2/8 GR tried to use the time they had gainfully. They organized and conducted a very satisfactory battle inoculation exercise (preparing troops in realistic conditions prior to induction into active operations), held a few discussions at the NCO level on counterinsurgency procedures, tactics and techniques, and even carried out a few situation-based small unit exercises. And, there was time for some fun, too. The unit organized an inter-company Khud race (a cross-country run in the mountains) over a challenging course calling for participation by a large contingent from each company. The three subalterns had to participate, too. And, though none of them was near a 'podium finish', cheered on by the lads, they finished in creditable times. The author asked, 'How did you win the respect of your Gorkha troops during your early days in the battalion?' Nanavatty replied, 'By partaking in all their activities, and I mean everything; by sharing in their privations, demonstrating genuine concern, earnestly giving your best always and, above all, being your true self. It took me almost a year to realize that the soldiers had accepted me both in letter and in spirit.'[19]

Airlifted to Chabua, the unit moved by troop train from Dinjan to Dimapur, arriving at its destination late at night on 10 February 1963. On the station platform awaiting the arrival of the troops were company distribution points where items of clothing and equipment were issued to needy troops courtesy the new CO, Lieutenant Colonel Shamsher Singh, who had arrived only a few hours earlier. Nanavatty recalls being introduced to his first CO by the newly appointed Adjutant, Captain Anand Gore. It was past midnight; the CO lay stretched out on a camp cot tucked under a mosquito net in the compound of the Dimapur Dak Bungalow, and the Adjutant had only just reverted to the battalion after sick leave following his escape and evasion ordeal during the withdrawal.

According to Nanavatty, 'Colonel Shamsher Singh, originally of the 6th Battalion, came to us from a staff appointment. He was the Assistant Quarter Master General (AQMG) in Headquarters 4 Infantry Division during the rout on the Tawang–Sela–Bomdila axis in the India–China War. His recent personal experience and the unit's disaster at Mechuka had left him bitter. As our CO, he was a man on a mission from the word go, determined to see that misfortune did not strike the battalion twice. The tough, no-nonsense Jat adopted a singularly simple approach: "If the Army Battle Physical Efficiency Test (BPET) standard is 2 miles in 18 minutes, then *'Sikand Aite'* (2/8 GR) will do 4 miles in 36 minutes," he said! And that was the criteria he applied to all things military: we had to strive to be twice as good as the rest! He may not have been popular with some, but to him must go the credit for licking the battalion into shape, and quickly, too.'

The very next morning the 2/8 GR convoy snaked its way from Dimapur to Kangpokpi, a village on the Kohima–Imphal Road short of Imphal. Halted at the Assam Rifles post at Kangpokpi the battalion had a few days to shake itself out—reorganize and attend to critical administrative issues before assuming operational responsibilities. Much to the annoyance of the new CO, it was from here that the battalion had to dispatch a large draft of personnel of all ranks below officer level to assist in the re-raising of the 3rd Battalion of the regiment (3/8 GR) in Dehradun. Under the circumstances the 'Shamsher Solution' was to send the entire battalion on a ten-mile battle physical efficiency run and drop the bar at the finish line to exclude the last 100, and you had your draft!

From Kangpokpi, the battalion marched to Tamenglong. It deployed with its headquarters and three under-strength companies in the general area of the small township, with Charlie Company occupying a separate patrol base on an adjacent ridgeline in Saramba, a small Rongmei Naga village a few hours' march away. The Rongmei are a relatively poor Manipuri Naga tribe. They were peaceful and had little to do with the insurgency. They earned a living doing their 'Jhum' (slash and burn) cultivation in the summers and manual labour in the Imphal Valley in the winters. Their misfortune was that their villages lay astride some of the traditional routes of exfiltration and infiltration used by the Naga Hostiles to and from East Pakistan (now Bangladesh) and they were often coerced and compelled to provide information and logistical support to the latter.

Describing the terrain in Nagaland as mesmerizing, beautiful to look at but a nightmare to negotiate, Nanavatty wrote about it and his first encounter and firefight with the Nagas on 7 March 1963, in an article that appeared in the *Infantry Journal*, Autumn 1963: 'A mass of tumbling, twisting, climbing jungle green, here and there a speck of earthy red to mark a track, cascading mountain streams, a steep dominating feature, bare and brown in marked contrast to the surrounding green, a few hazy bamboo huts and a wisp of blue smoke gently curling into the dusky March skies, a Rongmei Naga village. Deep down in the valley almost four thousand feet below, a lazy jungle stream winds along the narrow valley floor. Over on the other side, the valley floor rises again steeply, very steeply, to another razorback ridge, like our own and running parallel. If viewed from the air, the whole area consists of a succession of ridges and narrow valleys with almost monotonous persistence. It is the season of the "Jhum", the Naga is labouring away at clearing patches of the jungle and burning the cut and dried underbrush for his fields of "kodo" (a form of millet) and maize this year. The air is thick with smoke; the roar and crackle of big forest fires, and the gunshot-like crack of splitting bamboo is wafted across by the March winds. Some of the most difficult terrain as described by men who had fought through it during World War II, and one dare not disagree.'[20]

It was early March 1963. Nanavatty and his under-strength platoon had already done three patrols, familiarizing themselves with the terrain, the tracks, the villages and the Gaon Buras (village headmen) astride the

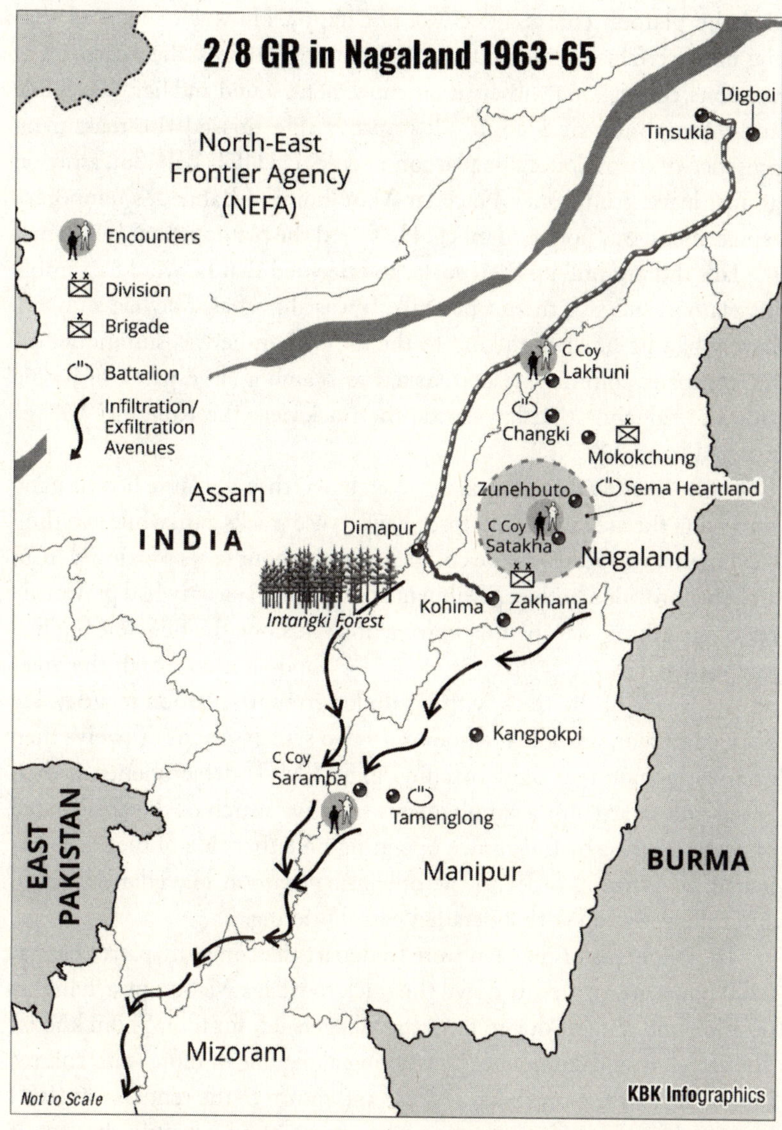

2/8 GR in Nagaland 1963-65
North-East Frontier Agency (NEFA)
Encounters
Division
Brigade
Battalion
Infiltration/ Exfiltration Avenues
Digboi
Tinsukia
C Coy
Lakhuni
Changki
Mokokchung
Zunehbuto
Sema Heartland
C Coy
Satakha
Nagaland
Assam
INDIA
Dimapur
Intangki Forest
Kohima
Zakhama
Kangpokpi
C Coy
Saramba
Tamenglong
EAST PAKISTAN
Manipur
BURMA
Mizoram
Not to Scale
KBK Infographics

ridgeline on which the company patrol base was established. So far, it was all 'nothing to report' (NTR). The older hands were not at all surprised. But the platoon commander was not happy. He was concerned that the men were losing their edge and becoming careless: their carriage of weapons, concealment, observation, movement, sound and light discipline and general alertness could all improve. He missed the reassuring presence of the redoubtable platoon Havildar '31' Dil Bahadur, away on annual leave. And Lance Havildar Mandhoj, Dil Bahadur's temporary replacement, was not up to much. He feared the platoon would slacken if the lads did not pull up their socks and decided that he would assemble his platoon and give them a pep talk. It was almost as if he had a hunch. Barely had he finished talking to the men when he was summoned by his company commander and tasked to search a large patch of jungle atop the ridgeline that lay astride the track near the Rongmei Village referred to as 'M'.

In the last few days, Nanavatty concluded that any large hostile gang traversing the area would perforce have to use tracks and, while avoiding staying in a village, would be compelled to harbour in its proximity in an area that provided both concealment and water. Nanavatty had previously negotiated the area using the prominent track along the ridgeline but had not searched it. He realized it would be impossible to search the areas on either side of the track with his under-strength platoon in a day. He decided to reorganize his platoon into two search groups of twelve men each to include two light machine gun (LMG) detachments in each group and to attempt a simultaneous selective search of the areas based on water sources by the groups operating on either side of the track. He issued his warning order to the officiating platoon Havildar Mandhoj and followed it up with a detailed patrol briefing.

The essentials of his plan were to depart the company patrol base at 0200 hours, move rapidly down the track to village M, occupy a 'lying up position' and remain 'doggo' until the villagers left for their 'Jhum khetis'. The search would commence by working along one or more watercourses in their area of responsibility (AOR) and return to the rendezvous (RV) by 1600 hours. If either of the groups encountered a hostile element, it would take immediate offensive action. The irony of what he said did not escape him. According to what he had garnered thus far it was rare indeed for a patrol to locate a 'live' Hostile camp without reliable guides and even more difficult to extricate one self from an ambush.

Things went as planned the following morning, and Nanavatty led his search patrol out of the harbour. On the edge of the village was a maze of tracks, and he decided to follow one that seemingly led to the 'Jhum khetis' in the direction of the area they were to search. His scouts working ahead of him saw a solitary figure wearing black trousers and a white vest with a 'dao' (a traditional multipurpose Naga machete) strapped to his waist, and 'went to ground'. The Naga was seemingly at work on a small bamboo shelter in a burnt and semi-cleared patch of jungle. Covered by his scouts, Nanavatty approached the individual and attempted to question him in sign language and the few words of Nagamese—a combination of Assamese and the tribal Naga tongue that he knew. All he got in reply was a mumble and a continuous shaking of the head. The patrol filed past quietly as the 'villager' looked on intently.

The patrol leader was pleased with how his men were moving that morning—slowly, cautiously, and spaced out, each member alert scanning the jungle with his weapon at the ready. Suddenly, the scouts went to ground again and signalled him to come forward. They pointed to two sets of banana leaves on the ground behind a pile of stones. The thought that it was a lookout post crossed his mind, but he waved it aside, thinking it was the handiwork of villagers in the Jhum. A few hundred metres further down the slope, the leading elements came to a small amphitheatre-like area with dense cover and a gentle stream crossing their path. The patrol went to ground again, and the patrol leader and his buddy Lance Naik Kumraj Gurung went forward. Almost immediately, they noticed the remnants of a still-warm cooking fire. In that very instance, Kumraj happened on an ordnance pattern khukri, which he picked up to show his patrol leader softly saying, 'A Naga would never leave a khukri behind!' Something was undoubtedly amiss, and yet the patrol leader still thought it was the villagers.

Events thereafter unfolded like an edge-of-the-seat narrative. Nanavatty signalled one of his two LMG groups to cross the stream and occupy the far bank, and the rest of the patrol went to ground in a tight semicircle, peering into the amphitheatre. Nanavatty's pulse quickened and a strange, dry feeling gripped his throat. Somewhere to his front, he heard a loud whisper, hesitant and somewhat fearful, 'Hostile!' He recognized Amardhoj's voice; a single shot rang out; a split second later he shouted, '*Nazdik dushman*—fire! (Enemy close—fire!)' and all hell broke loose. Nanavatty went to ground, and Kumraj dived for cover to his right. The jungle, a green wall and the echo and re-echo of sound in the confined rock-lined place made it impossible to 'find' the enemy. He knew the enemy was close, in fact only a few paces away. Then he heard the deep-throated and comforting thudding as his LMG across the stream went into action. Nanavatty was relieved that his men were in the fight with spirit.[21]

Suddenly, hostile fire from his front ceased. For a split second, all was quiet, and then he heard the distinct sound of movement over dried leaves. Steeling himself for the rush of a Naga 'dao party', Nanavatty shouted, '*Grenade nikaal* (Take out your grenades).' A smiling Mandal Gurung by his side remarked, '*Grenade prime chhaina* (Our grenades are not primed).' Rendered speechless, he hurled his own grenade, got to his feet as it exploded and moved forward with Kumraj and two others, only to realize that all was quiet and still. The hostiles had disengaged in a well-executed rearguard action. As Nanavatty checked on his men, Mandal reported that Indra Bahadur was hit and lying in the stream bed. He was dead—shot in the head. From the time the first shot rang out, the encounter had barely lasted five minutes.[22] Realizing that pursuit was not an option, a weary and watchful Nanavatty led his group back to the RV. He had been squarely bested by his enemy but felt no hatred.

Much later, as Nanavatty analysed the encounter, he appreciated the elaborate early warning system of the hostiles, their battlefield discipline that required every individual to pack his 'kit' every morning and be ready to move out in a flash, the main body abandoning camp at the earliest leaving behind a rearguard to execute an opportunity ambush and attempt to steal a weapon or two if possible. He pondered over his errors. Firstly, the splitting of his under-strength platoon. Secondly, ignoring the evidence—the lone individual working on the kheti hut, a possible lookout, and the banana leaves on the ground—and continuing to attribute every sign to villagers. Thirdly, on discovering irrefutable evidence—the warm ashes of a cooking fire and a khukri—failing to pull back, readjust and probe the area cautiously. Fourthly, Amardhoj's inappropriate reaction on seeing a hostile at close quarters—failing to open fire and initiate a '*turant hamla*' (an immediate action drill).

After the above encounter and a futile effort to follow the group over the next few days, the search was abandoned, and the battalion was de-inducted from the Tamenglong area and concentrated in Kohima. From here, it marched to Satakha, some 120 kilometres away, where Major Ranjit Majumdar was posted out; and young Nanavatty, all of twenty years old, assumed command of Charlie Company. The Satakha—Zunheboto—Atoizu area is the heartland of the Sema Naga. The Sema are the ultimate Naga warriors and the dominant component in the self-styled Naga Army.

During its relatively short stay in Satakha the battalion carried out several large-scale 'cordon and search' and 'search and destroy' operations. They were operations essentially to show the flag, to send the message that the army had returned to the Naga Hills and with purpose. Nanavatty recalls that in one such battalion-size operation in the deep recesses of the remote Satoi region, Indian Air Force Vampire jets, in a two-aircraft mission, strafed a suspected hostile camp location. He reckons that in his entire service, this was the only occasion when he witnessed the use of offensive airpower in a counterinsurgency operation! However, it is another matter that the Indian Air Force was extensively used during the early years of counterinsurgency operations in Nagaland in 1961 and 1962 in search-and-strike missions against Naga camps; particularly along the India–Burma border where there was little or no collateral damage. Coordinated at the division headquarters, it is not surprising that the young Nanavatty did not get to know about the early airstrikes. The author has had access to several logbook entries that corroborate these operations and has covered offensive air operations in Nagaland and Mizoram in his book *India's Wars II*.[23]

Demanding great endurance, these operations, by way of results, had little to show. Major Arjun Singh, who then was in command of Bravo Company, went on several long patrols with Nanavatty and found him to be 'tough as nails with phenomenal endurance and always leading from the front—intelligently never recklessly'. In lighter vein, he recalls, 'When we returned from patrols that lasted a week and more on backpack rations, we would be ravenous and have to send the Mess Cook to the Quartermaster store looking for more "atta" (wheat flour).'[24]

Satakha had been a double company location of the Assam Rifles with a vast AOR. The perimeter of the post demanded that more than half the strength of the company carry out protective duties every night. Men for missions the following day had frequently to be 'milked' from the posts after midnight. The Sema Naga hostiles were constantly probing, looking for any opportunity to steal a weapon or ambush a patrol. As always, patrols and escorts carrying out routine inescapable tasks—water collection, road-opening, convoy protection—were particularly vulnerable. It put a tremendous strain on the troops.

Nanavatty pondered his tasks and consulted his 'Orders' (O) Group, comprised of his JCO platoon commanders. He decided on two fundamental principles. First, the company would concentrate its efforts on dominating the area and villages in its AOR within a turnaround distance of twelve hours from the post and no more. Anything further away would call for extra strength and support from the battalion. Second, offensive counterinsurgency operations would be based on specific intelligence. This strategy required the company to develop its intelligence sources in Satakha itself. This simple approach helped in several ways. It helped reduce the company's vulnerabilities and consequently enhanced its security. It compelled the company to concentrate on the conduct of small-team operations and avoid unduly taxing the already over-extended manpower. Consequently, there was not a single adverse incident against Charlie Company during their nine-month stint in Satakha, and it resulted in several successful small unit operations boosting both the skills and the self-confidence of the men.

Nanavatty cites a typical operation, which was a partial success. Late one afternoon, a reliable source in Satakha sought a clandestine meeting with him. They met in the small medical inspection (MI) room of the local Government Dispensary. The source informed Nanavatty that

'Brigadier' Tukhovi, the self-styled commander of the 1st Naga Brigade, together with some other 'officers', was slated to meet with the Gaon Bura (headman) of Village Vishepu the next morning. The information was considered reliable. Vishepu was barely three kilometres from the company base. It was a large village spread along the spine of a curving ridge with rocky jungle-covered slopes on either flank. Nanavatty assessed that it would require a battalion to cordon, and even then, there would be gaping holes. Nevertheless, Nanavatty decided that they would chance it and focus on the Gaon Bura's hut in a 'snatch' operation.[25]

At 0100 hours, the small patrol led by the company commander comprising one JCO and nine other ranks divided into three subgroups of three men each, slipped out of the company base. They were familiar with the tracks and the terrain in the area. Moving quietly and carefully, they approached the village and halted. Just as dawn broke and the village showed the first signs of stirring, they moved silently into a lying-up position at the jungle's edge from where the Gaon Bura's hut was visible. It was less than sixty yards away. The patrol members bided their time and concealed themselves in a hollow, cramped and uncomfortable space. Silent and motionless, they prayed that a curious village dog or pig would not chance upon them and give them away. They waited until the mass of villagers left for their 'Jhum khetis'. The village was relatively silent and still again. The lookout signalled suspicious activity around the Gaon Bura's hut, and the patrol leader and two sub-groups moved silently and rapidly towards it, leaving the JCO and the third sub-group to cover their move.

Glancing through the hut's open door, Nanavatty saw a group of men seated around the cooking fire, and as he went past, he saw them rise and split, making for an exit on the other side. Luckily, Tike Pun, a big, strong lad from Baglung, and his sub-group were already there. Tike struck the first man, who emerged from the hut, a hard blow at the nape of his neck and the Naga went down like he had been pole-axed. Seeing this, the two men behind him sat down on their haunches, their hands in the air. The Gaon Bura then emerged, bowing and scraping, making apologetic noises expressing helplessness. He was followed by a fourth person—an elderly Naga, his upper body bare, dressed traditionally and with a typical Naga haircut. He was the splitting image of the Gaon Bura. His manner was humble and one of utter helplessness, bowing with his hands folded and apologizing. He walked past unhurriedly just as another person burst out of the hut and made a break for it. Nanavatty was distracted and shouted a warning, darting after the man and stopping every few yards to take a pot shot at him with his pistol, to no effect whatsoever. Just then, Subedar Kaman Singh Gurung drew abreast, huffing and puffing and shouting at his Company Commander, '*Chhordnus Sahib*, *ma haan chhu* (Leave him to me, I'll get him)', fired a long burst of his Sten Machine Carbine and bowled the fugitive over. Gurung stopped briefly to change his magazine, and the downed Naga was immediately up and away. Disgusted, the company commander returned to the hut where an agitated Gaon Bura was still trying to explain things, muttering 'Tukhovi, Tukhovi' and pointing in the direction where the old Naga, who emerged from the hut after him, had unhurriedly walked away. That is when it dawned on the company commander that an incognito S.S. Brigadier Tukhovi had got away scot-free in all the commotion. Nanavatty swore under his breath and, from that day onwards, decided to carry a rifle as his personal weapon—an oath he kept until the day he departed the battalion for good. The tally of persons apprehended during that operation was three out of a possible five, with the prized Tukhovi getting away. The only solace was that among the three persons apprehended, one was a notorious and vicious self-styled captain.

The exploits of Charlie Company at Satakha earned their young company commander the award for being the 'Best Junior Leader' in the battalion in 1963. It was an award instituted by Colonel Shamsher Singh, and Nanavatty cherishes it but adds, 'If memory serves me right, that was the first and last time the award was presented in the unit!' In the early '60s, Nagaland was a good learning ground for counterinsurgency operations, and the Naga hostiles were worthy adversaries. According to Nanavatty, the Naga hostile of the 1960s was a genuine guerrilla—he would enter a fight only when sure of success. If cornered, he would make a break and be gone in a flash—there was no question of standing and fighting to the last man. Not given to dramatics, Nanavatty added, 'If the Nagas took you on in a fight, it was extremely well planned. In an ambush, he would open fire only when he could see the whites of the eyes—literally at handshaking distance.'[26]

After a stressful deployment in the Satakha–Zunehboto–Atoizu area, the battalion was relieved by 56 Mountain Brigade and redeployed with its headquarters and Delta Company at Changki with Alpha Company at Warmong, Bravo Company at Mokokchung alongside the brigade headquarters and Charlie Company with Nanavatty still in command at Lakhuni. Later, consequent to a ceasefire in Nagaland, all offensive operations ceased, and on 1 December 1963, the NHTA was granted statehood, and Nagaland became the sixteenth state of the Indian Union. Early in 1964 Nanavatty was ordered to report to the battalion headquarters at Changki to eventually take over the duties of the Adjutant from Captain Anand Gore.

It was during the handing/taking-over period, that he received orders posting him as Aide-de-Camp (ADC) to Lieutenant General S.H.F.J (Sam) Manekshaw, GOC-in-C Western Command and Colonel 8th Gorkha Rifles. Taken aback, he asked Anand Gore what this was about. The latter said he knew nothing and suggested he speak to the CO. Colonel Shamsher Singh was understanding: he said that he had forwarded Nanavatty's name in the best interest of the unit and the individual and that there was little he could do about the matter now. In the Adjutant's office, which he shared with Anand Gore, Nanavatty ruminated over the events. He then picked up a standard pink 'Forces (free issue) Letter' and wrote to Manekshaw that he was not a volunteer to be an ADC, that he had less than two years of service, that the unit was in operations and that he would like to continue with it. Lo and behold! A few days later, Nanavatty received a reply from the GOC-in-C himself that read, 'I am in receipt of your letter for which I thank you. I have deemed your posting be cancelled.' And, that was the end of the matter.

In 1964, the Indian Army introduced a Commando Course at the Infantry School, Mhow. 2/8 GR was allotted its first vacancy on Commando Course Serial 7 in December 1964. Nanavatty was the first individual from the battalion to do the course. It was his first exposure to post-commission formal learning in the Indian Army. Lieutenant Colonel (later Lieutenant General) Tirath Singh Oberoi, a paratrooper and a graduate of the United States Army Ranger School at the Infantry School, Fort Benning, and the Special Forces Centre and School, Fort Bragg, was the first commander of the Commando Wing. He was assisted by an outstanding bunch of officers and Junior and Non-Commissioned Officer (JCO and NCO) instructors who constituted his formidable team.

In the early years, each course comprised a cross-section of officers, JCOs and NCOs. Nanavatty found the composite—officer, JCO, NCO—composition of the course particularly enriching. Paired with an NCO from the Dogra Regiment, a unit wrestler, as his buddy, the two shared the same bivouac, cooked their meals together, performed varied tasks, including unarmed combat, and supported each other during speed marches and exercises. Nanavatty recalls his experience on the course with a sparkle in his eyes: 'I enjoyed the course very much, with its emphasis on the physical aspects of soldiering—unarmed combat, speed marches, confidence tests, cliff assaults; small unit tactics, patrolling, ambush, immediate action drills, and raids; and the use of explosives. It was a wonderful first course to do after the IMA.'[27]

Leafing through his Infantry School Commando Course Précis, with all his neat annotations, which he preserves to date, underlines his continuing interest in infantry individual and small unit skills, techniques and tactics. His course report by his Senior Instructor and Commander was glowing: 'A very fine specimen of a young officer with plenty of determination, stamina, and initiative. He is cooperative and tactful in his dealings with others and inspires confidence with his calm and reassuring demeanour. He is physically and mentally robust and capable of fast cross-country movements over difficult terrain. He possesses effective leadership qualities and should make a good commando leader. Recommended to be a commando instructor upon completing four years of regimental service.'[28]

The outbreak of hostilities between India and Pakistan in Kutch in April 1965 lent urgency to the training of the battalion's support weapons platoons, which had been neglected during the previous two years of counterinsurgency operations. It was also a period of change, as Colonel Shamsher Singh's tenure ended in May 1965, and the reins of the battalion were handed over to Lieutenant Colonel R.S. Pathania. Major Anand Sarup assumed the appointment of the second-in-command (2IC).

In July 1965, the battalion handed over its operational responsibility in Nagaland to 4/1 GR. After seeing off the last convoy, Nanavatty and his old buddy Kumraj Gurung of Charlie Company, now a full-fledged NCO, said goodbye to Changki in style. They speed-marched approximately forty kilometres from Changki to Mariani via the shortcut through the vast Disai Forest hoping to shoot something for the pot. And sure enough, towards dusk, they encountered a couple of wild boars crossing the track at close quarters, but much to Nanavatty's chagrin and Kumraj's amusement, the former's faithful old shotgun with hammers misfired, and the pigs got away scot free. Perhaps it was just as well, for Kumraj, a staunch Gurung from Lamjung, would have had nothing to do with a dead pig, and as far as Nanavatty was concerned, there was only so much that he could have carried! Tired and hungry, the pair reached the Battalion 'Rear' at Mariani well after eleven that night.

Nanavatty had completed his first operational tour of duty with the battalion, and it was a happy and well-knit team of officers and men that arrived in Calcutta for their next tour of duty on 27 July 1965.

3

PEACETIME SOLDIERING

'Wear the Green Beret, whether dark or light, with pride and remember despite every technological advancement, you will still close in with the enemy to destroy him.'[1]

—Major General O.S. Kalkat's closing address to the young officers of the First YO Course at the Infantry School, Mhow, 1969

Lieutenant General S.H.F.J. (Sam) Manekshaw was the General Officer Commanding-in-Chief Eastern Command when the troop train carrying 2/8 GR from Mariani rolled into Calcutta (now Kolkata). As Colonel 8 GR, he would have had a hand in getting the battalion to Calcutta for its tenure in a 'peace station'.[2] Firmly entrenched in Shimla as the GOC-in-C of the prestigious Western Command before his move to Fort William in January 1965, India's proactive defence minister, Y.B. Chavan, moved him east in the backdrop of the renewed violence in Nagaland and growing Chinese and Pakistani support for what had by then clearly emerged as a secessionist Naga insurgency. Manekshaw's earlier experience in the North-east in 1963–64 as the Corps commander of the Tezpur-based 4 Corps influenced that decision significantly. Some also saw the move as an attempt by the Government of India to create leadership space for another outstanding general, Lieutenant General

Harbaksh Singh, who had considerable operational experience in the Western Sector. Harbaksh and Manekshaw would emerge as serious contenders to succeed General P.P. Kumaramangalam to the post of army chief in 1969.[3]

Fort William, built by the East India Company in 1781, is a remarkable architectural monument and a township. It houses the Headquarters Eastern Command, Bengal Area, Calcutta Sub Area, an infantry battalion, and several other ancillary military units and sub-units and is off-limits to civilians.[4] As the 'Fort William Battalion', 2/8 GR was responsible for ceremonial and internal security-related duties in Calcutta. This called for a rapid makeover in the battalion after the previous three years of 'jungle bashing'.

Senior Subalterns Sarma and Nanavatty and a boisterous brood of half a dozen or so Emergency Commissioned officers were residing in the Officers' Mess without knowing what peacetime soldiering was about. Major Anand Sarup, the Second-in-Command (2IC) of the unit, soon had the officers grappling with unfamiliar yet essential peacetime activities—officers' classes, boards of officers, Courts of Inquiry and other sundry duties. He even had Messrs Edde & Co., the regimental tailors in Delhi, send out a couple of darzis (tailors) to 'measure' the young officers for their ceremonial uniforms. But first things first; the CO, assisted by the 2IC after due notice, put Sarma and Nanavatty through the Retention Exam, a formal test, now defunct, to see how much they knew of the Unit Standing Orders & Procedures, administration, interior economy and customs of Service & the Officers Mess, e.g.: Which knife do you use and how do you butter your toast? It was good fun, and both young officers, after a 'gruelling' two days, were pronounced fit for retention, which was duly entered under the heading 'Particulars of Examinations' in their respective Records of Service. It was the last Retention Exam held in the unit, with the army scrapping the test all together.[5]

Following the Retention Exam, there was a scramble to pass the Lower Standard Nepali Exam, with only the very brave and literate attempting the higher standard. While in Calcutta, Nanavatty travelled to Sikkim to appear for his Part A, a practical Promotion Exam, which he passed with a 'Distinction'. Later, he was to appear for and pass the written Part B Promotion Exam in Calcutta.

Nanavatty was now the Adjutant, having been an acting major as a company commander with Charlie Company in Satakha and Lakhuni and then the Intelligence Officer and Assistant Adjutant as a Captain. In 1965, together with several other units, particularly from the 9 Infantry Division, 2/8 GR had the misfortune of 'sitting out' the India–Pakistan War. The closest it came to doing something useful was when Charlie Company patrolled the deltaic region of the Sunderbans to counter any infiltration. Once again, 2/8 GR sent a large draft of reinforcements to 3/8 GR, which was involved in a series of tough battles in the Tangdhar region in J&K, and had suffered heavy casualties in the process. Nanavatty requested the CO that he accompany the draft and deliver them to their destination but was curtly told that there was no need. 3/8 GR deservedly earned the Battle Honour *Sanjoi* for their fine effort during the war.

Lieutenant Behram Panthaki, a fellow Parsi who had joined the battalion in 1964, had by then been appointed ADC to Sam Manekshaw. One morning Nanavatty dropped in to share a cup of 'chai' with 'my good friend Behram', and was taken by surprise when the latter ushered him into Sam's office to meet the Colonel of the Regiment for the first time. 'Hello boy, what are you doing?' asked Sam, and when Nanavatty mumbled something about being the Battalion Adjutant, Sam retorted, saying 'Good for you,' and signalled the meeting over picking up a file. More was to follow: as Nanavatty and Panthaki returned to the latter's office, waiting there was Maja (later Maja Daruwalla), Sam's younger daughter, who when introduced to Nanavatty stumped him good and proper saying, 'Isn't it an honour for a young officer to serve as the ADC to the Colonel of his regiment,' and walked off leaving him at a complete loss for words!

In November 1965, Nanavatty attended the Platoon Weapons (Officers) Course at the Infantry School, Mhow. He excelled on the course, returning with a Course Grading D (Outstanding). He was the runner-up in the bayonet fighting competition, losing out to a fellow Gorkha officer and, a marksman with both the 7.62 mm Light Machine Gun and 7.62 mm S.L. Rifle and in doing so established a new Infantry School record in the Rifle Classification Practices. He was awarded the silver spoon for being the best shot on the course and his report adjudged him 'fit to be an instructor at this School on (the) Platoon Weapons Course'.[6]

It was around this time that Nanavatty spoke to his CO about volunteering for the PARA Cdo units that were being raised. Lieutenant Colonel Pathania said he could apply but added, 'I will not recommend you!' A man of few words, Pathania's refusal put an end to the matter.

Having done both the Commando and Platoon Weapons Courses at the Infantry School, Nanavatty felt equipped and confident to do the job of the Adjutant and set to his task with gusto. Apart from drill, discipline and ceremonial events, he was responsible in good measure for physical training and oversaw various central promotion and pre-course training cadres. The 'one-hour P.T.' schedule five days a week, introduced by Colonel Shamsher Singh, involved endurance training, strengthening exercises and physical proficiency and battle physical efficiency tests (B.P.E.T.) at regular intervals and has remained an article of faith with the unit.

On 13 April 1966, the first Raising Day of the Battalion after it arrived in Calcutta, Sam Manekshaw, the Colonel of the Regiment, was the reviewing officer at a special ceremonial parade. Desmond Doig, the editor of the *Statesman*, wrote of the 'battalion's scintillating performance' that morning. On another occasion, Nanavatty recalls General J.N. Chaudhuri, the Chief of Army Staff, after inspecting the residential guard provided by the battalion at the Inspection Bungalow where he was staying, turning around and complimenting the Subedar Major, saying that 'it was the smartest guard he had ever seen'. Then there was the Colonel of the Regiment's Stick Orderly: always the smartest soldier selected at the mounting of the Quarter Guard each day by the duty officer—standing rock-like outside his office and making a great impression with the staff. On one occasion during the annual Republic Day Parade in Calcutta, the entire unit contingent comprising a draft exclusively of young soldiers was adjudged the best marching contingent.[7]

Given the environs of the Fort and the various commitments of the unit—ceremonial and otherwise—training remained focused on young soldiers joining the unit from the training centre—the draft cadre, promotion cadres, and pre-course training for personnel proceeding on army courses of instruction. Good use was made of the short-range in the moat of the Fort, and the classification ranges at Barrackpore by camping at the ranges. Once a year, the battalion moved out to Ranchi and Panagarh for six weeks to do its collective training and field firing. It was by no means enough, but better than nothing.

Calcutta also offered Nanavatty the opportunity to participate in sports at the competitive level for the first and last time. He coached and played as a right half and captained the battalion football team, which in 1966 came very close to winning the Gorkha Brigade Trophy, losing by a whisker in a replayed final to an extremely skilful 5/5 GR team. In 1967, he was captain of the Eastern Command team for the Inter-Services Football Championships in Bangalore. During a practice match against East Bengal, he sustained a severe injury to his right knee, resulting in a 'completely disrupted Anterior Cruciate Ligament'. That and a recurring dislocation of the left shoulder first sustained while boxing in his third and final term at the IMA were injuries that plagued him throughout his service but failed to deter him from physical activity of any form.

Writing in the Regimental Newsletter as the unit's scribe, Nanavatty put the battalion's sojourn in Fort William in the proper perspective: 'We wouldn't want you to get away with the idea that all we did in Calcutta was "night clubbing" and, as the Americans call it, "R&R" (an acronym for Rest and Recuperation). It has been a singular honour for the battalion to have served in the same station as the Colonel of the Regiment, Lieutenant General Sam Manekshaw. Despite the tremendous administrative commitments, the battalion did all it could to remain in fighting trim. The roads around the Strand and the Maidan rang to the thump of hobnailed boots working at double time. Elderly Bengali gentlemen and "rotund yoga enthusiasts" were often jerked out of their early morning reverie by the sudden appearance of the battalion in full battle order, speed marching by in column. The short ranges resounded to the crackle of musketry, and the GOC Bengal Area's vegetable garden was invariably the RV for all commando raids. The polo grounds reverberated with the crash of demolitions, and the rifle companies were pushed out to the long ranges whenever the time and space permitted. As was inevitable in West Bengal, we had more than our share of Internal Security Duties. The mere sight of Johnny Gorkha, that grim combination of man and equipment, his "tin hat" at a jaunty angle, the magnificent Khukri which speaks volumes for itself, and his "no nonsense" approach was enough to give any would-be rioter the fright of his life.'[8]

Soon after the Indo-Pakistan War, in 1965, Major Anand Sarup was selected by the Colonel of the Regiment to assume command of the 1st Battalion (1/8 GR) for a few months to resolve a few command-related issues that had arisen in the unit. Anand Sarup then attended the Command and General Staff Course at Fort Leavenworth in the United States and on his return in 1967 the Colonel of the Regiment saw to it that he assumed command of the 2/8th.

According to Nanavatty, 'Anand (Nani) Sarup embodied the ideal commanding officer, physically tough and mentally very robust. He had nearly twelve years of service when he did the Ranger's Course in the US, completing it with distinction even though his fellow US students had less than half his service. A voracious reader, he was a repository of knowledge not restricted to military matters alone. He had a fine mind, great clarity of thought, excellent communication skills and a sense of the practical. He had an enviable record on courses of instruction at the Infantry School, the Jungle Warfare School and later at the Staff College. A CO with strong convictions, he was firm, resolute and forceful. He possessed this extraordinary ability to speak his mind and differ with others without causing offence. It was little wonder that his counsel on professional matters was much sought-after and explained his frequent periods of absence from the unit. Kind and caring, I never recall seeing him flustered or losing his temper. He would quietly convey his disappointment if you failed to meet his expectations, which usually sufficed.'

As a soldier, Anand Sarup's finest hour, undoubtedly, came during the Indo-Pakistan War of 1971 in East Pakistan, now Bangladesh. He had just assumed command of the Counterinsurgency and Jungle Warfare School (CIJWS) on promotion. A mere two weeks before the war commenced, he was given command of a hybrid formation called 'KILO Force'. It comprised two infantry battalions (with no support weapons and minus a rifle company each), a BSF battalion, a CRPF battalion and two Bangladesh Rifles (BDR) battalions. The force had no artillery resources worth the name. Their task was to capture Feni, an essential communication centre, and assist in capturing Chittagong. Where others may have hesitated, Nani grabbed the opportunity with both hands. Positioning himself well forward, he led his formation to capture Feni and Chittagong. A well-deserved Maha Vir Chakra for gallantry and distinguished service in war was a fitting reward for his leadership of KILO Force.[9]

Anand Sarup first met Nanavatty in December 1962 when he, as the Adjutant 58 Gorkha Training Centre, Dehradun, used to make it a point to meet Gentlemen Cadets of the Passing Out Course commissioned into the regiment. His first impression of Nanavatty was that he was a calm, collected young man of few words, who always made sense. 'That he had won the Sword of Honour made it easy for me to acknowledge his potential.' Later, he was to identify Nanavatty as a 'soldier with immense integrity and leadership potential'.[10] The two developed a close bond over the years as Anand Sarup became an influencer and mentor for much of Nanavatty's formative years as a military leader. Nanavatty never had the opportunity to work directly with him again. Nevertheless, Anand Sarup kept a benevolent eye on him, as he indeed did with the others. Nanavatty recalled at least two instances in later years where he intervened on his behalf. The first was when Lieutenant General K. Sundarji, Colonel of the Mechanized Infantry and later the army chief, was considering him for a transfer to the regiment on its raising, and later, when there was a move afoot to introduce a serving officer in the Institute of Defence Studies and Analyses (IDSA) to work with Dr K. Subrahmanyam. Both assignments would have taken the die-hard infantryman away from the regiment and the challenging operational environment that was emerging in the 1980s.

When Anand Sarup assumed command of the battalion, Nanavatty had done a good two years as the Adjutant. He requested a change, was relieved by Captain K.M. (Ben) Mandanna, and took over command, this time of Bravo Company. Later, Nanavatty was to recall, 'with Nani at the helm, K.M. (Ben) Mandanna his Adjutant and Bajar Bahadur

Gurung the Subedar Major, I believe the 2/8th possibly had one of its best "command teams" in place'.

In December 1967, Anand Sarup led the battalion back into NEFA, this time to 5 Mountain Division. The division was commanded by Major General Onkar Singh (*Dhante Pun*) Kalkat, a fiery salt-of-the-earth, much loved and respected officer of the regiment. Kalkat had a distinguished war record. Originally from the Punjab Regiment, he had fought in the bloody battles of the tunnels in the Buthidaung–Maungdaw region in 1943.[11] In 1947, as a Major, Kalkat had uncovered Pakistan's plans to invade Kashmir in his brigade commander's office at Bannu in the North-West Frontier Province. He made a daring run across the border to apprise the Indian military leadership of the impending Operation GULMARG, a covert operation in J&K planned by Colonel Akbar Khan. He was ridiculed by both the British and Indian military brass. When the raiders struck a few weeks later, a livid Prime Minister Jawaharlal Nehru admonished his military commanders for not paying heed to the early warning from Kalkat.[12]

Moving by train from Calcutta, the Gorkhas detrained at Misamari in Upper Assam on the North Bank of the Brahmaputra and, as was the custom then, picked up their battle loads and marched to Tenga via Chaku—170 kilometres in five days. They trucked over Bomdila to Sapper Camp, a short distance from Darrang. Initially designated the Division Defence Battalion, 2/8 GR was the GOC's 'go-to' unit. Subsequently, in an operational rearrangement, the unit was re-allotted to 190 Mountain Brigade in Nuranang.

Within a week of their arrival in the Darrang Valley, the battalion was involved in a divisional exercise with troops. Two days into the training, Bravo Company was pulled out with orders to immediately relieve a 14 RAJPUT company deployed in the 'early warning' (EW) role at Penga Teng Tso north of Tawang on the Bumla–Tawang Axis. The company was deployed with a platoon at Bumla and company less a platoon at Penga Teng Tso astride the Class V track the Chinese had constructed in 1962—an excellent bit of improvisation and engineering using local resources, which was then perhaps deliberately allowed to lapse into disuse.

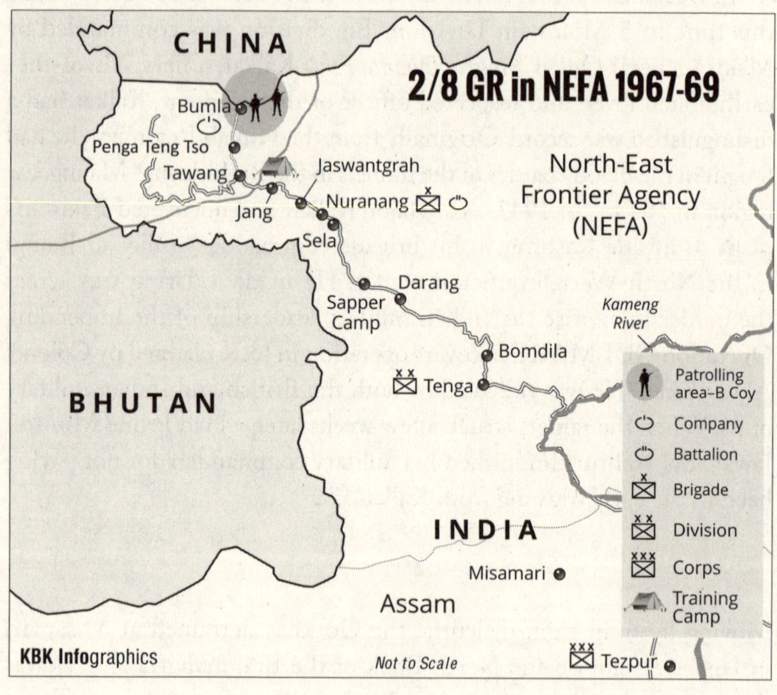

Nanavatty was lucky; he had two fine youngsters—Raghunath Thorat and Dileep Parab, one after the other—as the Early Warning (EW) platoon commanders at Bumla. And, one of the finest JCOs he ever had the privilege of serving with was his senior JCO. Subedar Bajar Bahadur Gurung was later to become the Subedar Major of the battalion during Anand Sarup's tenure itself. It is interesting to note that while Bajar Bahadur's father was with the battalion in France and Flanders during the First World War, his son, Chitra Bahadur Gurung, was commissioned from the IMA and retired as a Lieutenant General in the Nepal Army in 2005 after a distinguished career. Many of the officers in the battalion believed that Bajar Bahadur himself would have made an excellent battalion commander!

Bravo Company spent almost a whole year as the EW Company—patrolling extensively, familiarizing with the terrain, selecting observation posts, observing and reporting Chinese activities, deciding on ambush sites, routes of withdrawal and identifying 'hides'. Nanavatty recalls that the GOC visited him, insisted on spending the night with the platoon at Bumla at 14,000 feet and rode out the next morning with a foot patrol to the centre of the pass—a striking figure on a riding mule—cocking a snook, as it were, at the Chinese. Bumla in the 1960s was a broad and relatively flat piece of ground devoid of structures for Border Meetings. No man's land here was vast, with the Indian Army Early Warning Platoon locality at Bum La some 1000 metres short of the Pass, and the closest Chinese positions opposite a good three kilometres and more to the north on a feature named Snout.

Second Lieutenant Dileep Parab, fresh out of the IMA, was perhaps the first officer in the regiment to consider Nanavatty his mentor. Dileep's father, Colonel H.S. Parab, the first Indian CO of 2/8 GR, is best known as the General K.S. Thimayya–appointed governor of Leh and its saviour in 1948. A former commandant of the Rashtriya Indian Military College, India's premier military school that has among its alums several chiefs from the armed forces of India and Pakistan, Colonel Dileep Parab remembers his first winter patrol with his company commander in deep snow: 'This was a difficult winter reconnaissance patrol which involved movement out of the EW locality at night and establishing an observation post (OP) covered by a firebase on a feature we had named Lion's Tooth well before first light. Nanavatty invariably led these difficult patrols, requiring the person in front to beat a path through the snow for the others to follow. After a few hours of leading on one such patrol, I was surprised when he asked me to take over the lead. When I got tired after a while and asked Johnny Gorkha behind me to take over, Nanavatty stepped in and remarked with no fuss, "No problem, I will take over." That was a huge leadership lesson for me.'[13]

Parab continued, 'We patrolled practically every inch of the border—the term Line of Actual Control (LAC) was not part of our vocabulary then. Among our tasks within our area of operational responsibility was identifying and naming several landmarks and selecting suitable observation posts that allowed us to view the Chinese dispositions from different angles. In our area, the Chinese dispositions were comparatively some distance away. The closest we came to the PLA was on one of our patrols led by Nanavatty, wherein our OP to the rear in the Bumla EW locality warned us of a PLA patrol headed in our direction, which, owing to the lie of the land, we could not see. Though their patrol came close, they remained unaware of our presence, and there was no incident.'

As Parab matured under Nanavatty's tutelage, the latter assigned him a tough night patrol mission. Parab briefed the men in what Nanavatty assessed to be a 'good briefing', and the patrol turned in for some rest before the mission. But that was not to be, as Nanavatty asked Parab, 'Are you not supposed to fire your automatics before the patrol?' Parab retorted, 'But we cannot do it along the border.' At once came the reply from Nanavatty, 'Then you have to go down to Me La (a post about an hour's march away) and fire your weapons there.' The patrol did just that, and to Parab's surprise, Nanavatty accompanied them down to Me La and back.

Parab concluded his recollections of those times with a narration of Nanavatty and Bravo Company de-inducting from Penga Teng Tso in the autumn of 1968: 'When Bravo Company was ready to leave Penga Teng Tso, everyone except Nanavatty headed back to the battalion location at Sapper Camp by motor transport from the nearest roadhead at Bomdir (Tawang). Nanavatty and his "Runner" Sri Prasad, self-contained, walked cross-country from Tawang to Sapper Camp in eighteen hours flat via the Divisional Headquarters below Sela, where, stopping briefly, he met the GOC, who was trying to understand how the Chinese had moved so quickly in 1962!'[14]

In those days, the *Padyatra*—a ten-day self-contained man-pack exercise with battle loads held just before the onset of winter with the entire division participating—was an annual feature. Instituted by Major General Sartaj Singh, Kalkat's predecessor, the gruelling exercise remained a significant event on the 5 Mountain Division training calendar for several years. The aim was to shake units and formations out of their billets, familiarize all ranks with their areas of operation, test their endurance and give them the confidence to operate in the harsh environs.

The winter of 1968 saw 2/8 GR in snowbound Nuranang as part of the 190 Mountain Brigade. The unit had two options: sit around their smelly kerosene bukharis (local heaters) biding their time, or move ahead of Jaswantgarh—where the Garhwalis had fought so gallantly in 1962—and train just below the snow line. Anand Sarup persuaded the Brigade Headquarters to permit the battalion to move out and train for the winter. A tented camp was established just below the snow line near the village of Jang. The village elders were liaised with and a training area with specified 'no-go areas' for the locals was identified and 'acquired' temporarily. Its unique feature was an ad hoc field firing area. Included in the works was an improvised classification range, a jungle lane, a grenade 'golf course', an ambush range, a space for individual and section fire and move exercises, 'Immediate Action' drills and Battle Inoculation.[15] Training was restricted to section and platoon level to improve individual and sub-unit fighting skills. Nanavatty led a central training team responsible for the planning, programming and coordination of training and the conduct of all the lectures, demonstrations and 'live fire' exercises. The battle inoculation area comprised four large and stout bunkers with overhead protection, each capable of accommodating a rifle section at a time. All the personnel in the battalion were 'inoculated' in platoon lots, bringing down 3-inch (81 mm) mortar and MMG fire directly on the bunkers.

For those three months, the valley reverberated with the pitter-patter of small arms, blasts of grenades and explosives, and the 'crump' of mortars throughout the day, and often at night. When it looked like the battalion would run out of training ammunition, they 'borrowed' from their sister battalions, who were only too happy to part with their share. And, as Nanavatty terms it, 'we had a marvellous time'. But, there was a stark reminder that, when training with live ammunition, one cannot be too careful. On one occasion, during a rehearsal for a lecture demonstration on the ambush, a battalion runner came down from the Adjutant to Nanavatty at the demonstration site with the message that he should report to the CO immediately. A calm and composed Anand Sarup pointed to three holes in the outer fly of his 180 lb office tent where a burst from an LMG had gone through and said in an even and matter-of-fact tone, 'Rostum, be careful and re-site the LMG.' Nanavatty reckons it was one of the best spells of training the battalion underwent during the seventeen-odd years he spent in the 2/8th in various ranks.[16]

In April 1969, done with leading a rifle company in high-altitude terrain and supervising an extraordinarily satisfying and extended sub-unit level training programme, Nanavatty headed for another round of professional military training, the Junior Commander's (JC) Course at the JC Wing in the Infantry School at Mhow. Considering his experience in jungle and mountainous terrain and his exposure to training under his COs Shamsher, Pathania and Anand Sarup, he was well equipped to do the course. Excerpts from his end-of-course report said that he 'should make an above average infantry officer' and recommended him 'to be an instructor in the Tactical Wing of the Infantry School'.[17]

In September 1969, Nanavatty, with approximately seven years of unbroken service in the battalion, was posted out of the unit as an Instructor Class C (Captain) in the Platoon Commander's (PC) Wing of the Infantry School. Barely had he settled down when he was ordered to join the first ever Infantry School Shooting Team, the brainchild of the commandant, none other than General Kalkat of 5 Mountain Division fame, for the annual Army Rifle Association (ARA) competition. Notwithstanding his fondness for shooting and marksmanship, Nanavatty knew that he was at the school for a purpose and that his instructional assignment should be his priority. He sought an interview with the commandant and requested him to allow him to revert to his role as an instructor in the PC Wing. In the context of this incident, when asked whether senior officers in the early years were better listeners and tolerant of dissenting professional opinions, Nanavatty replied, 'Absolutely! Young officers were unafraid, and senior officers listened.'[18]

Nanavatty reverted to instructing the JCOs and NCOs on the PC Course and was just about beginning to enjoy himself when he received fresh orders. The infantry had decided to introduce an Infantry Young Officers' (YO) Course, combining instruction on platoon weapons, platoon tactics and the commando course. Nanavatty was deputed to assist Lieutenant Colonel (later Lieutenant General) Mathew Thomas, PARA, an Instructor Class A in the Senior Officers' Wing and the commander designate of the YO Wing in organizing and designing the YO Course. Working with Mathew Thomas was an education and resulted in a professional association to last a lifetime. Unfortunately, with the stage set to commence the first Infantry Young Officers' Course in 1970, Mathew Thomas was pulled out and dispatched on a studytour to the US before establishing the Counterinsurgency and Jungle Warfare School in Vairengte, Mizoram.

During the Tactical Leg of the course, student syndicates were organized based on their regiments and allotted Syndicate Directing Staff (DS) from the same regiment as far as possible. Nanavatty was responsible for the Young Officers commissioned into the seven Gorkha Rifle Regiments. Sifting through his notes in a blue cloth-bound exercise book, I found handwritten briefing points that read like a list of leadership imperatives for young officers particularly relevant to officers serving in the Gorkha Rifles. More of that will emerge when Nanavatty's perspectives on leadership are discussed in the final chapter. By mid-1971, the first two YO courses were concluded and done, with young officers of the Rajput Regiment walking away with the Best Young Officer trophy. Among them was Second Lieutenant V.K. Singh, a future Chief of Army Staff. He was to go into battle in East Pakistan soon after the course as part of an infiltrating force.

In 1970, a College of Combat was carved from the existing Infantry School, Mhow, with the responsibility to conduct three all-arms command courses: the current Junior and Senior Command Courses for sub-unit and unit commanders, respectively and an entirely new course designated the Higher Command Course (HC) for formation commanders. Major General Onkar Singh Kalkat was the first commandant of the College of Combat. In January 1971, Nanavatty was posted from the Infantry Young Officers' Wing as a staff officer in the General Staff Branch of the Headquarters College of Combat. Following the military crackdown in March 1971 in East Pakistan, now Bangladesh, Kalkat moved quickly to Eastern Command to organize and train the Mukti Bahini: Major General Eric Vas, 9 GR, replaced him as the head of the college. Eric Vas was an ideal choice: an astute military thinker with great clarity of mind, a man of solid convictions and wide experience. To him the credit must go for organizing and designing the Higher Command Course. In 2003, the College of Combat was renamed the Army War College (AWC).

The Infantry School and College of Combat were the wellsprings for Nanavatty's writing on professional matters. His initial interest was in individual and group infantry fighting skills, techniques, and small unit tactics at the section and platoon levels. Driving home an argument in a paper written when he was at the Infantry School titled 'Training the Infantry Company Commander', Nanavatty insisted that the Indian Army would remain an infantry-oriented army for a considerable period in the foreseeable future owing to its commitments in the poorly developed northern and eastern border areas and the ever-present threat of irregular warfare (Sub-Conventional Operations). While mechanization and other technological advancements would help take much load off the infantryman's back, the prime role of the foot soldier would remain unaltered. Highlighting the need for better-trained and empowered company commanders with superior leadership skills to cope with the multiple threats, Nanavatty suggested the creation of elite and self-contained infantry units that could operate independently from widely dispersed company locations to disrupt and confuse the enemy.[19]

From Nanavatty's notes, it is apparent that Field Marshal Rommel and the Israeli Army influenced him greatly and helped shape his intellectual moorings as a 'thinking soldier'. A mention of the contents of two books frequently featured in his writings: *The Rommel Papers* edited by the eminent British strategist and military historian Liddell Hart, and *The Making of the Israeli Army* by Yigal Allon, one of the founders of the young state's armed forces. Occupying pride of place in these notes is a paragraph from *The Rommel Papers* that reads: 'Exasperating to staff officers, he was worshipped by his fighting troops, and what he got out of them in performance was far beyond any rational calculation.'[20]

From Yigal Allon's book, the most strikingly relevant observation that Nanavatty absorbed relates to the factor of surprise in battle. Allon writes, 'Of all the major principles of war, surprise is the most important;

all other principles are either secondary or are a means to achieve it. The three important principles that facilitate surprise are fighting spirit, concentration and mobility. When these three means are achieved, surprise is achieved. When surprise is achieved, the battle is won.'[21]

In the 1970s, notwithstanding the ups and downs in India–US relations, the Indian Armed Forces, notably the Indian Army, continued to take advantage of the US military aid programmes that allowed subscription to a limited selection of courses of instruction for junior and mid-level officers at their various training establishments. One such course was the Infantry Officers' Advance Course (IOAC)—a career course for US Army Infantry Officers of the rank of Captain—at the Infantry School, Fort Benning, Georgia. Major (later Major General) Ashok Verma, a relatively senior staff course-qualified officer of outstanding merit of the Rajput Regiment, was the first officer detailed for the course. On his return, he was emphatic that the army select relatively junior officers for the course, considering the service bracket of the average US Army officer. Nanavatty was not on the panel of officers for the following course, but when the list was put up to General Sam Manekshaw, the army chief, Captain Behram Panthaki, the chief's ADC, glanced at the names on the panel and as a matter of interest pointed out to the chief that, given the criteria for selection, Rostum Nanavatty's name should have been on the panel for selection, too. The panel of officers for the course vacancy was drawn up again, and Nanavatty's name topped the list, and that is how he found himself on the nine-month-long IOAC 1-72 at the US Army Infantry School in August 1971. More on that course in Chapter 5 along with salient aspects of his tour of duty as the Indian Army Liaison Officer (IALO) at the British Army's School of Infantry, Warminster, in the mid-1980s.[22]

As the war clouds gathered again over the subcontinent, Nanavatty was mortified at the thought of being left out of battle (LOB) once more. Following Onkar Singh Kalkat's departure from the College of Combat, Nanavatty wrote to him volunteering his services to train the Mukti Bahini. In a prompt reply, Colonel Yadav, an officer on the General's staff, acknowledged receipt of the letter and conveyed the General's thanks and advice that he should proceed on the course to the US as ordered, as there was no certainty about the future. After the commencement of the course in Fort Benning and as the outbreak of hostilities became imminent, Nanavatty spoke to the Military Attaché in the Indian Embassy in Washington to ask whether officers on training abroad were to 'return to their units' (RTU) given the situation in the subcontinent. He was told that there were no such orders. He then wrote a letter to the army chief and Colonel 8 GR, General Sam Manekshaw, requesting he be withdrawn from the course, to which he received a prompt reply from the staff stating that officers on duty abroad were not being recalled. As a last resort, he appealed to his father, who had more than just a nodding acquaintance with the chief, to do the same. The chief's reply to Kaikhushru was polite but firm. He wrote: 'I am in receipt of your letter dated 10 December '71, for which I thank you. I quite understand Rostum's anxiety to get back and be where the fighting is—indeed, I would expect nothing less from him. He, too, has a job to do there, which is to imbibe higher education for the higher ranks that await him in the future. He must, therefore, complete his course, and I would not like to recall him prematurely from the course that he is now undergoing.'[23]

When the author asked Nanavatty about his propensity to shoot off letters to senior officers and whether it constituted overreach, arrogance or a tendency to leverage connections, Nanavatty replied: 'I never thought about it that way. As an officer, I was well within my rights to write to the Colonel of my Regiment. I did not "shoot off" letters to curry favours or further my career. I did so when I felt strongly about something and was willing to bypass the chain of command.'

In June 1972, on his return from Fort Benning, Nanavatty was posted back to his battalion and assumed the appointment of officer commanding Support Company responsible for providing specialist weapons and communications support to the rifle companies. The unit, now commanded by Lieutenant Colonel S.N. Dar, was doing the duties of the Rashtrapati Bhavan Battalion and was split between the Red Fort and the President's Estate. Preoccupied with ceremonial duties, the unit struggled to stay in trim. In January 1973, Nanavatty had the singular honour of commanding the Guard of Honour to Field Marshal S.H.F.J.

Manekshaw on his demitting the office of the Chief of Army Staff. Soon, it was time for the 2/8th, now under the command of Lieutenant Colonel H.C. (Joe) Joshi, to head north into the field again, this time into J&K. The unit's role demanded it familiarize itself with a vast area in the Kashmir Valley and its surroundings.

For Nanavatty, it was his first time in J&K as a soldier. Even then there was palpable, simmering resentment against all things Indian. On one occasion, returning from the Field Firing Ranges driving a jeep through Khrew village, south of Srinagar in the Pulwama District, with his CO beside him, he accidentally ran over a rooster that darted across the road. Pulling up immediately, he got down from the vehicle, apologized and offered to pay for the fowl. By then, a small crowd had gathered, and a sullen young man in a loud voice summed up the mood, '*Kal aap isi tarah aadmi maar doge aur maafi mangoge* (Tomorrow you will kill a human and say sorry).'[24] 'I put the money down and drove off, realizing that we were not welcome in that part of the world.'[25]

Nanavatty was back commanding Charlie Company and Khrew and its surroundings with a classification firing range beside the Officers' Mess was well suited for individual and small unit training. A notified Field Firing Range around the corner where mortars and other battalion support weapons could be fired offered excellent areas was an added advantage. By now, it was de rigeur in the battalion to select and isolate a sub-unit, ensuring the presence of its full complement and setting it apart under its OC in a suitable training area for a fixed period, free of all routine encumbrances. Nanavatty's early combat reflections in the unit continued as he broke down the critical and final portion of a platoon attack on a well-defended and fortified enemy position, in a detailed paper titled 'Training in Covering the Last 200 Yards and Fighting on the Objective'. In the paper, he wrote, 'It is over the last 200 yards to an objective, a combination of individual fighting skill, good small unit battle drills, courage and leadership will inevitably decide the issue.'[26]

In 1974, one year from becoming a substantive major, Nanavatty decided to take the Staff College entrance exam. Attempting the exam in Mhow, he passed the entrance test, earning a competitive vacancy on the 31st Staff Course at the Defence Services Staff College (DSSC), Wellington.[27] The year 1975 was spent in the sylvan surroundings of the

DSSC. It was hard work and a lot of fun, too. There was time for sport, for making friends and socializing. Shooting and fishing for sport was permissible in the Nilgiris then, and Nanavatty spent many a happy holiday scouring the 'sholas' and grasslands of the Nilgiris with Susai, his local shikari, looking for kakkar (barking deer), pig and jungle fowl. On one occasion in the upper reaches of the Nilgiris, after two days of tracking in poor weather, he was lucky to bag a fine specimen of a Nilgiri Tahr (a Saddleback) that might have found mention in Roland Ward's *Records of Big Game*.

As the Course ended, Nanavatty was appointed leader of one of the two Syndicates selected to write the *Nav Kalpana* (New Ideas) paper—in some respects, the culmination of thought and written work on the Course. With Major Jaswant Mann, an accomplished 'Gunner' (an Artillery officer) to assist him as the deputy leader of the syndicate, they attempted to break the shackles of existing thinking in the Indian Army. They recommended reorganizing offensive formations in the Western theatre based on brigade-size composite Battle Groups of all arms capable of functioning independently or being grouped as necessary based on the mission under lean floating Divisional Headquarters. The staff rubbished their paper, and the honour of presenting the *Nav Kalpana* recommendations to the Course went to the other syndicate. Unfortunately, the author was unable to retrieve the *Nav Kalpana* paper written by Nanavatty's syndicate as it was not archived at the DSSC.

At the Staff College, Nanavatty got to know and struck a lasting friendship with Major (later Lieutenant General) T.S. (Maun) Shergill, 9 (Deccan) Horse, a soldier and friend he admires greatly. Opting at the end of the course either to return to regimental duty or a staff assignment in a formation headquarters in a counterinsurgency environment, Nanavatty was surprised when he was posted as the BM of HQ 1 Armoured Brigade, a part of 1 Armoured Division. Maun Shergill suggested to his hardnosed infantryman friend that a short attachment with the Armoured Corps Centre and School, Ahmednagar, by way of introduction to and familiarization with Armour before reporting for duty, would be of immense value. Even though his attachment was cut short by a few days owing to his father suffering the first of a series of debilitating strokes, Nanavatty felt the attachment was useful and a gesture that conveyed the right message. On the termination of his leave, he drove from Bombay to Patiala to begin an exciting phase in his career. It was to be the beginning of a distant but meaningful and mutually respectful professional relationship with Major General (later General and army chief) Krishnaswamy Sundarji.

1 Armoured Brigade, located in Patiala, was commanded by Brigadier Gurdev Singh Kler, a cavalryman and a veteran of the 1965 War, who had commanded an infantry brigade in counterinsurgency operations in Nagaland. The mercurial and brilliant Major General Krishnaswamy Sundarji, an infantryman from the Mahar Regiment, was the General Officer Commanding (GOC) 1 Armoured Division.[28] A good mix indeed! Viewed at first with scepticism by the COs of the T-55 regiments that made up the brigade, they relented somewhat when they realized that Nanavatty had a reasonably sound—theoretically, at least—understanding of mechanized warfare thanks to his stint at Fort Benning and that he was more than willing to watch, listen and learn its practical application in the existing operational environment. As Nanavatty made the transition from being a die-hard footslogger (infantryman) to an exponent of manoeuvre warfare, he turned to Rommel's propositions that 'the fundamentals of mobile warfare are speed of judgment and action, which allow us to create changing situations for the enemy faster than he can react'.[29]

The winter of 1976 saw the Brigade concentrate in the desert around Suratgarh in North Rajasthan for its collective training. Towards the end of the training, the entire Western Command hierarchy comprising the GOC-in-C (Army Commander), Lieutenant General I.S. (Inder) Gill, the GOC 2 Corps Lieutenant General Z.C. (Zoru) Bakshi and the GOC 1 Armoured Division Major General K. Sundarji—interestingly, all infantrymen and outstanding soldiers to boot—were to descend on the hapless brigade to witness the final stages of an exercise wherein a Combat Group would 'bounce' (cross) a canal obstacle and secure a quick crossing from the line of march.

The previous evening, all three visitors had arrived and were ensconced in caravans in the brigade HQ location. Nanavatty was deputed Liaison Officer (LO) to the Army Commander and was responsible for escorting him to the mobile view point—a Topaz Armoured Personnel Carrier (APC)—on the canal bank to view the event. Nanavatty recalls: 'I knocked on the general's caravan door at 4.30 a.m.; sat him in the jeep and subjected him to a rather bumpy, uncomfortable ride through the badly rutted tracks in the wake of the tanks. Driving on dimmed lights in the pitch black that precedes the dawn, the drive to him must have seemed interminable. After several minutes, he asked, "Do you know where you are going?" I said a confident "yes sir" but was getting a trifle concerned myself when, suddenly, we were at the "mobile vantage point" and well in time.'

The Army Commander 'boarded' the APC to join the corps, division and brigade commanders already present, and after a cheerful round of greetings, everyone settled down to a patient wait. As dawn broke, they heard the T-55 tanks of 73 Armoured Regiment Combat Group before they were seen—engines straining and tank tracks clanking. Then, slowly over the dunes, one could discern silhouettes against the sky as tanks jockeyed to occupy hull-downpositions about 1000 metres from the canal. Controlled explosions, Light Machine Guns (LMG) firing into pits and weapons using blank ammunition on the home bank simulated enemy fire. Suddenly, three Topaz APCs of the mechanized company of 1 Sikh that was part of the Combat Group appeared line abreast, raced through the gullies and came to an abrupt halt about a hundred metres away. There was a moment's pause, and then from behind each APC appeared an 'apparition'—a burly Sikh soldier—bare-bodied except for his 'kachha', 'patka' and 'kirpan'—with a large tyre tube around his waist carrying a coil of rope in one hand and charging up to the canal as best he could, diving in, swimming across the water obstacle and securing the rope. Soon after came the infantry, which manfully struggled across the obstacle using the ropes. In the Topaz APC, there was a stunned silence. Even the simulated fire of the enemy had come to a stop. Suddenly, Inder Gill chuckled, and everyone burst out laughing and just could not stop—it was 'humour in uniform' at its best.

It was different though during the exercise summing up by the Corps Commander. Zoru Bakshi was scathing in his criticism and implored all to return, think hard, dig deep and find practical solutions to tactical problems. Sundarji was perturbed, and rightly so. He aimed to set things right and quickly at that. He 'called on' Brigadier Hanut Singh, of 17 (Poona) Horse fame widely acknowledged as the Army's expert on mechanized operations, then commanding an Independent Armoured Brigade in Ambala, and his GSO 1, Lieutenant Colonel Ajai Singh, of the same regiment, and a veteran of the tank battles in both India–Pakistan wars to assist him. Mechanized operations of the division were broken down into parts and the responsibity of writing detailed operational notes assigned to formations and units in the division to be finalized after demonstrations and detailed discussions. Nanavatty recalls that 1 Armoured Brigade was assigned the responsibility of writing an Operational Note on combat engineer support to an armour heavy combat group.

Nanavatty observed that Sundarji lived and breathed military operations and was forever asking questions. In discussions with his brigade commanders, rank and appointments mattered little. He was just as happy discussing a matter at the operational level with a brigade commander as he was talking to a young officer about tank troop tactics. He often insisted that the BM sit directly behind his respective brigade commander saying, 'I know you gentlemen are going to say "yes" to everything I suggest, and so I would like to hear what your BM has to say!' In many ways, Nanavatty believed Sundarji was the best thing that happened to 1 Armoured Division. However, in his later years, Nanavatty felt that Sundarji's intellect, command over the language, use of military terminologies and comprehension of operational concepts so outstripped that of many of his immediate subordinates that he became impatient, intolerant and over-bearing.[30]

In 1976–77, drawing heavily from Chaim Herzog's book on the 1973 Arab Israeli conflict titled *War of Atonement*, Nanavatty wrote a paper on the 'Training of Armoured and Mechanised Forces' and argued, 'The lessons of the war dictate the conversion of ground forces into one large inter-arm battle team controlled by one HQ. There should be two types of teams, armour being dominant in one and infantry in the other and resorting to groupings that would include air defence weapons, artillery and combat engineers.'[31]

Another idea that Nanavatty floated during his tenure as BM was based on the knowledge that the British Army periodically transported entire mechanized battle groups by air, less their heavy weapons and equipment, from Germany to the British Army Training Unit Suffield (BATUS), a training area in Canada for their live fire training under realistic conditions. The Armoured Fighting Vehicles (AFV), guns and heavy equipment required prepositioning and being made available in the location. Similarly, Nanavatty felt that the Indian Army should acquire large tracts of land in uninhabited and remote areas, including Ladakh, and convert them into Field Firing ranges. This thought may have helped in developing the Mahajan Field Firing Ranges in Rajasthan in 1982 when Sundarji was the Deputy Chief of Army Staff, a feather in his cap considering how valuable the range has been since.[32] Summing up his equation with Sundarji, Nanavatty reckoned, 'I think he liked me. He would invariably chat with me, and it always was "shop"—about tactics and operational art, irrespective of where we were. I never found him to be intimidating or difficult.'

Wedded to the Indian Army, friends and family had been unable to convince him to embrace the softer side of life and share his space with someone other than Johnny Gorkha. Rostum was not averse to matrimony; he had just not found the time to look for a life partner. Until now, he had also assumed that he would not contemplate wedlock until his sister, Erna—almost five years his senior—tied the knot. However, as time passed, it became apparent that Erna, now thirty-six, could choose to remain single. He began to have a rethink, and fate chose to intervene. His former local guardian from his school days, Som Maira, decided to play Cupid. One weekend in February, he invited Rostum to spend a day at his farm in Panipat. Little did Rostum know that by accepting the invitation he would meet his fate in the pretty form of Som's niece, Suniti Khanna. Her uncle's favourite, quiet and serious, Suniti, appeared to Som to be the perfect match for Rostum. A Gold Medallist from The Lawrence School at Sanawar, Suniti's experience at boarding school had taught her to be a team player, feel comfortable in the company of boys, have josh or spirit, and never give up, no matter the odds.[33] She graduated with an Honours Degree in English from Lady Shri Ram College, Delhi, and among other activities in college, dabbled in debating, acting, modelling and going 'Dutch' to the discotheque. Finishing at the top of her class in the Teachers' Training course at St Bede's College in Shimla, she realized that teaching was her calling.

'I won't marry an army officer,' Suniti used to tell her father, Lieutenant Colonel K.K. Khanna 2nd Lancers (Gardner's Horse), every time he half-jokingly offered to introduce her to eligible young 'faujis'. Although her father, an alumnus of the RIMC and a Services Squash player, had taken premature retirement after commanding his regiment and had set up a successful business in Delhi, his heart had stayed with the army.

Som's machinations worked. They met in February, and Rostum proposed to Suniti late one night in June by the sea in Bombay. Independent and strong-willed, Suniti had to eat her words when she accepted Nanavatty's proposal. The wedding on 9 October 1976 was a simple affair attended by only close family and friends. It started with a civil ceremony presided over by the Magistrate, who had acceded to Mrs Khanna's and Suniti's request to come home. Vedic rituals and a *Tandorosti Ashirvaad* Zoroastrian prayer by Rostum's father followed. Later that day, Suniti's parents hosted a large reception at the India International Centre.[34]

Rostum was thirty-three, and Suniti was twenty-six. Two seemingly mature adults, seldom prone to impetuous or impulsive behaviour, took their families and themselves by surprise when they announced their engagement. According to Suniti, 'Rostum's friends had assumed he was a confirmed old bachelor, and Rostum reckoned that I was on the shelf when he met me. The cheek of the man!' From the start, Rostum laid all his cards on the table well. He told her that life was tough for an infantry officer and his family and that he would be away from home 50 per cent of the time. She would have to cope with his frequent absences, and start speaking Gorkhali within three months of joining the battalion.

Subsequently, she received another warning from him. All Parsis were eccentric. Did that include him, she asked. His prompt response was in the affirmative! 'Now, he was covered on all fronts,' she said with mock indignance.

Suniti rode her bicycle around the military station in Patiala, her first station as a military wife, and soon made friends. One day, she asked her loving husband about the movies the other wives watched and talked about. Where did they view them, and how did they know which movie was showing? His reply was priceless! The movie programme came every month, and he tore it up and threw it into the wastepaper bin! The possibility that she could be interested had not even occurred to him!

During the final stages of a very satisfying tenure as the BM of an Armoured Brigade, it was back to Mhow for the umpteenth time, this time to the College of Combat, to undergo the Senior Command course. It was a three-month preparatory period for senior majors or just-promoted lieutenant colonels who were likely to get command of units soon. It was also a platform for mentoring and sharing command experiences by Directing Staff and faculty members. Little did Rostum know it would be the last time he would be formally associated with every Indian infantryman's alma mater.

Married by then for under a year, Suniti was in the first trimester of her pregnancy. She insisted that she accompany Rostum as he drove from Patiala to Mhow with a stop in Delhi. Despite opposition from her doctor in Delhi, who advised that she travel by train to Mhow, the family budget did not permit such extravagance. Her doctor reluctantly acquiesced, insisting that they travel in easy stages. Rostum, of course, felt that the doctor was making a big fuss about nothing and declared rather disdainfully, 'Women have babies all the time.' And so, they set off! The roads were terrible, but Suniti suffered no discomfort as Nanavatty carefully circumnavigated each pothole and slowed to a crawl when the road was bumpy. His love and consideration touched her despite him being unconvinced by what the doctor had said. So, they made their leisurely way to Mhow, making three halts enroute when they could have made the trip with a one-night break! Suniti suffered no ill effects from the journey and soon put it out of her mind.

Years later, when they were dining with friends, the talk turned to driving. Their hostess regaled them with amusing stories of her husband's reckless driving. There wasn't a soul who had ever sat in a vehicle driven by him and had not been amazed that they were still alive to tell the tale! All this talk of driving brought back memories of Suniti's journey from Delhi to Mhow. When she reached the part about Rostum avoiding every pothole, he cut her short, saying, 'Naturally, after the monsoon, the roads were in bad condition, and if I had gone any faster, I would have damaged the car.' And, after saying that, he studiously avoided looking her in the eye. Suniti recalls, 'That was when I discovered that, though some may try their best to deny it, all good soldiers have soft centres.'[35]

After completing the Senior Command Course, Rostum was posted back to 2/8 GR at Ferozepur. Suniti stopped in Delhi to spend the final few days of her pregnancy in her parents' home. Before becoming parents, Rostum and Suniti had to think seriously about their children's upbringing. They were in total agreement that the children would be enriched by learning about both the Zoroastrian and the Hindu faiths.

On 14 February 1978, Rostum and Suniti welcomed Rushad, born in the Moolchand Hospital in South Delhi. Six weeks later, the family gathered in Delhi for the Vedic Naamkaran ceremony for baby Rushad. On that note, it is time to move to the tenure closest to every infantry officer's heart: command of a battalion.

4

FIRST COMMAND

'The commander must also have the courage of his convictions, defying when necessary entrenched conventional ideas.'[1]

—YIGAL ALLON IN *THE MAKING OF ISRAEL'S ARMY*

In the infantry, the command of a battalion, especially the unit one is commissioned into, is special. Indeed, in the past, all that some officers aspired to was the command of a unit, and having done so, they would leave the service voluntarily, their desires fulfilled. In the early 1970s, among the transformative initiatives sweeping through the Indian Army was the contentious issue of selecting infantry battalions for conversion into mechanized infantry battalions, which, together with armoured regiments, comprise composite armoured brigades. As a mark of honour, the first battalions of some of the oldest regiments in the Indian Army were chosen for conversion. Amongst the Gorkha Rifle Regiments, the 1st Battalion 8th Gorkha Rifles (1/8 GR), with Lieutenant Colonel Anand Gore in command, was chosen to be one of the select few. Lieutenant General Sundarji, the first Colonel of the new Mechanized Infantry Regiment, not only championed its raising and expansion but went further, looking for suitable officers to transfer to the Mechanized Infantry. He knew Nanavatty when he was the Brigade Major 1 Armoured Brigade and asked Anand Sarup whether Nanavatty would be keen on converting to the Mechanized Infantry. 'No, Sir,' was Nanavatty's reply.[2]

In December 1977, after completing the Senior Command Course, Nanavatty was posted back to the 2/8th, then part of 48 Infantry Brigade in 7 Infantry Division in Ferozepur, a bustling town in the Punjab. Lieutenant Colonel Prakash Chauhan, who had recovered from his grievous wounds during the 1962 conflict, was the CO, Janak Sesodia the 2IC and Nanavatty, a senior Major, once again with Charlie Company. Ferozepur was a typical peace station with a crowded annual calendar comprising training, sports, visits and social events. In the case of 2/8 GR, rifle companies rotated through a two-month operational tour of duty in the Hussainiwala Enclave. A dreary, waterlogged, snake and insect-infested area on the banks of River Sutlej, the only compensation it offered was some excellent partridge, duck and geese shooting in the season. In November '78, Janak Sesodia, the ebullient 2IC, was posted out on promotion to command 17 Assam Rifles in Sikkim; and three months later, on 28 February, Prakash Chauhan handed over command of 2/8 GR to Nanavatty.

At that time, Nanavatty had an aggregate of approximately twelve years of regimental service, all with the battalion. He'd had the good fortune of commanding two of the four rifle companies in the field; he was familiar with the specialist platoons while in command of the Support Company; functioned as the Adjutant in a peace station; acted as the OC of an Advance Party during the relief of units in Khrew; and, on several occasions, oversaw the training of sub-units, promotion and pre-course training cadres. The men knew him, and he understood them. His stint as an instructor in the PC & YO Wings of the Infantry School and his tenure as the BM of an armoured brigade had added to his knowledge, experience and confidence, and so had the stint at the US Army Infantry School, Fort Benning.

In his brief opening address to the battalion on the day he assumed command, he said: 'We are all members of one family—the battalion. Our glorious history is written in the blood of our forefathers. But, we cannot afford to rest on our laurels. It is not what we "were" but what we "are" that counts. We cannot be satisfied merely by maintaining high professional standards in the unit: standards do not remain the same; either they improve or they decline. We must make every effort to enhance our standards continually. And remember, everything we do in the unit—training, administration, sport, even celebrations—must be with one aim: to be prepared to fight. You must live for the unit and, should the occasion demand, be prepared to die for it.'[3]

A grizzled old JCO sipping his raksi (Nepali for alcohol in general; in the army essentially it means rum during a barakhana—community meal) once said to Nanavatty, '*Sahib, Paltan ma quaida, dastoor ra tarkib hunu parchha* (Sir, in the battalion we must respect custom and tradition, adhere to rules and regulations and do things methodically).' While that stuck in his mind, he was reminded of what Rommel had to say about tradition: 'However praiseworthy it may be to uphold tradition in the field of soldierly ethics, it is to be resisted in the field of military command.'[4]

Lieutenant Colonel Rostum Nanavatty knew what he wanted to accomplish during his tenure as the CO. His primary concern was training with emphasis on the 'how to fight' aspects—individual and sub-unit fighting skills, techniques and small unit tactics. With training, he was determined to refine and update policies and procedures in the unit. He believed that policies, procedures, rules and regulations were not sacrosanct. He felt that changes could and should be made wherever necessary but only after due deliberation and that such change should be introduced formally. He was convinced that policies and procedures would only endure if there was widespread participation in their formulation and would insist that JCOs and NCOs, where required, were a part of the process.

His first step was to reorganize the Pioneer Platoon in the Support Company as a Commando Platoon—the forerunner of today's Ghatak Platoon in infantry battalions. This was to entrust promising young officers with a sense of responsibility, ownership and purpose on their return from the YO Course. The platoon commander would select the members of his platoon, train them to carry out tasks that demanded higher levels of skill, and administer and manage this small group of soldiers—his very own command.

During his command tenure, Nanavatty systematically revised training syllabi of young soldiers' draft cadres, promotion cadres, specialist platoon new entrant and refresher cadres and pre-course training cadres. Similarly, he would formulate guidelines and lesson plans for all the important lectures and lecture-cum-demonstrations in the unit. In the administrative arena, he would review and revise policies and Standing Orders for War and Peace and introduce the concept of Standard Operating Procedures (SOPs).

Nanavatty's command tenure started inauspiciously, though. Cycling to the sports ground to attend the routine afternoon games and PT session on his first day in command, he observed a commotion outside the Station Swimming Pool. On reaching the pool, he realized that one of his lads had just been fished out of the water and was being administered first aid—not very efficiently—by the side of the pool. It did not take him long to realize that his soldier was dead. He learned that the fixed rope used as an aid to get across the water obstacle had snapped, and the soldier, a non-swimmer, weighed down by his equipment, had gone under.

While the medical report opined that the soldier had died of shock, the formation headquarters understandably ordered a Court of Inquiry. The Court blamed personnel in the chain of command and recommended disciplinary action against those responsible. Nanavatty wrote back, disagreeing with the proceedings and accepting full responsibility for the incident. His brigade commander was livid and had him marched up to the GOC, Major General J.S. Gharaya, a highly decorated soldier and the only one to have been awarded both the Kirti Chakra and the Maha Vir Chakra, the second highest peacetime and wartime gallantry awards. Gharaya rebuked and dismissed him, saying, 'I thought you were a good officer.' Nanavatty, standing stiffly to attention and looking at the wall above the seated GOC, said not a word, and that was the end of the matter.

Since their arrival in Ferozepur in 1976, the battalion had suffered a couple of drowning deaths and, with Johnny Gorkha never quite in his element in water more than knee-deep, a pall of gloom seemed to have descended on the unit. Then, in 7 Infantry Division, infantry assaults across water obstacles using improvised aids was the flavour of the day, and Nanavatty was determined to rid the battalion of its fears. He issued instructions to make full use of the Station Swimming Pool and for practices to be carried out progressively, eventually culminating in crossings in complete battle order. Since most of the improvised aids for water crossings were, to put it mildly, ludicrous, the unit experimented with and finally improvised a square 'three-man bamboo raft' with outriggers on either side using inflatable tyre tubes that were hauled across the obstacle with a tow rope. It proved 'unsinkable' even in a fast current, and instructions to Johnny Gorkha were simple: 'No matter what: hang on to the raft.'

A few weeks after the unfortunate incident in the swimming pool, the battalion was out on the banks of a large canal conducting watermanship training in preparation for the collective training to come when the brigade commander decided to pay them a surprise visit. Seeing everyone from the CO downwards—officers, JCOs and men—'mucking in' and criss-crossing the canal with gay abandon on their rafts, he was rendered speechless.[5]

The summer of 1979 proved a testing time for the 2/8th in Punjab. The harvested wheat fields lay fallow. It was time for collective training, and the battalion enthusiastically approached its task. In 7 Infantry Division under Gharaya, the collective training was well structured: sub-unit training was followed by an exercise or two at the battalion level, and then came the brigade exercise.

In a staff paper Nanavatty wrote on 'Leadership Training in the Army' while doing the staff course at the DSSC in Wellington, he argued: 'Many of today's senior officers belong to the pre-independence era. Unfortunately, some of them continue to reflect past attitudes and are governed by the values of yore. Blind to today's requirements, they refuse to face reality and changed circumstances and shelter behind traditional systems that may have outlived their utility in their present form and require scrutiny and examination. The great danger lies in just such an uncompromising attitude.'[6]

Taking his cue from what he believed in, Nanavatty spoke to his officers and decided it was time to do away with the archaic legacy of the Officer Mess functioning—crockery, cutlery, glass and even silverware—in operations and exercises as the hallmark of a 'fine old battalion'. It was decided that officers would depend on their sub-unit '*langar*' (cookhouse), and the Officers' Mess staff would augment the cookhouse staff as necessary.

As luck would have it, Nanavatty's brigade commander announced that he would like to visit the battalion in the exercise area and have breakfast with them the following morning. After a short briefing on the conduct of the exercise, it was breakfast time. Expecting a regulation breakfast of 'fried eggs and bacon, hot buttered toast, cheese or jam washed down with a cup of coffee', he was taken aback when Dhan Bahadur—a Mess Waiter who invariably finished in the first ten places in every khud race—handed him a steel plate with 'puri-aloo ki sabzi' and soldier's tea in an enamel mug. Seeing the quizzical look on his commander's face, Nanavatty was at pains to explain that 'he was doing away with officer mess functions in operations and exercises as it was a waste of time, manpower and effort'. He may have been out of sync with his brigade commander but stood by his conviction that the battalion must train as it hoped to fight.

A brigade exercise followed the battalion exercise. This time it was going to be an attack across a wet 'ditch cum bund' or DCB, and the whispers doing the rounds were that the brass—the Western Army Commander, corps commander and division commander—would be present. In the work-up training before the exercise, besides ensuring the serviceability of their bamboo rafts to get them and their reorganization stores across the ditch, Nanavatty and his officers were busy refining their night attack drills and techniques. The battalion was experimenting and decided to do away with some existing tactics and take some cues from what the Israelis and British were doing in night operations. All this experimentation made the brigade commander a trifle nervous and compelled him to come around more than once to find out if the 2/8th knew what they were doing!

Once again, Nanavatty was to encounter Inder Gill, the formidable GOC-in-C Western Command, in an exercise area in the dark. As the unit approached the Battalion Release Point, a point where companies are released from centralized control, the Army Commander, with the brigade commander hanging on his every word, stepped out of the shadows and quizzed the CO: 'Tell me what's happening,' he said. The CO explained how the battalion was working the release point method of attack, and after a few questions, he sent the battalion on its way with a 'shabash'. Subsequently, the crossing of the wet ditch with rafts being niftily hauled from one side to the other, the securing of the Bund, and the arrival of the reorganization stores worked satisfactorily, and the exercise, no doubt to the relief of their brigade commander, was called off the following morning.

In Ferozepur, as elsewhere, inhabitants of villages within and on the fringes of field firing areas made a living out of collecting and selling metal scrap resulting from exploding munitions. Watching scrap collectors dart in and out between explosions with their scrap collection cloth bags in their hands, the Gorkhas could not help but marvel at their daring and finesse. The joke going around was that they were better inoculated than battle-hardened soldiers. Their handiwork was particularly 'impressive' when units carried out their shoots in a standard pattern that the scrap collector 'knew by heart'. Unfortunately, the 2/8th were doing things differently and the range safety officer, seeing a scrap collector collapse in the dust and smoke of a 3-inch mortar bomb burst, immediately ordered all firing to cease. When he walked up to the site and questioned the small group of people huddled behind cover, they shook their heads and behaved as if nothing untoward had happened. Later, when the bugle sounded the ceasefire for the day, a sentry on the perimeter observed a small group of people quietly carrying a body away. Accepting the odd casualty was a price they were willing to pay for their lucrative trade—a professional hazard as far as they were concerned. Despite the army regularly promulgating their firing schedules and sensitizing the villagers around of the dangers of venturing close to firing ranges, this exploitative and dangerous practice continues, and there is little that state governments or the army can do to stop it other than declaring it illegal.[7]

At the end of the collective training period in 1979, the 2/8th was ordered to move to 202 Mountain Brigade in Hasimara in West Bengal.

In his first command report, Nanavatty was rated relatively poorly by his brigade commander: 7 out of a possible 9. That was not surprising, considering the several run-ins between the two. Despite that, Nanavatty did not hold a grudge against him. He described him as 'keen, fond of sport with a special interest in officers' games and fitness, sociable, and someone who liked the good things in life. It was just that our approach to soldiering differed.'[8]

By the time the battalion moved, it was the month of July, and the heat and humidity in Ferozepur was wicked. The Military Special was loaded and standing by for departure. The Mess Secretary had very carefully planned for a 1-ton vehicle of a local unit to dash into the Ferozepur bazaar and pick up a basket of live chicken for the Officers' Mess kitchen. The 'Chicken Truck' arrived and pulled up alongside the train, and the basket was rushed to the waiting train with blocks of ice awaiting its arrival, and that is when the Mess Secretary almost burst into tears. Every poor chicken in the basket was dead, presumably from suffocation and heat, and all his meticulous planning had gone for a toss. Anyway, the whistle had gone, the green flag was up, and so, chicken or no chicken, the battalion was on its way.

In the late 1970s, Hasimara was a small town in the picturesque tea-growing district of Alipurduar in North Bengal, with Phuntsholing, the gateway to Bhutan, a hop and a skip away. While a fully-fledged peace station for the air force, for the army, literally 'across the road', it was a field area with very limited self-help bamboo 'Basha' type of family accommodation. Similarly, 202 Mountain Brigade was a part of 20 Mountain Division in Binaguri Cantonment, a peace station only a short distance away. 20 Mountain Division, in turn, was a part of 33 Corps. The latter, with its headquarters in Sukhna, close to the town of Siliguri, was responsible for the defence of an area that encompassed Sikkim, Bhutan and North Bengal to include the Siliguri Corridor, a thin sliver of land that connects peninsular India with its North-eastern states famously referred to as another 'Chicken's Neck',[9] the first one being a narrow strip of Pakistani territory also called the Akhnoor Dagger, which extends into J&K.

As soon as the battalion arrived in Hasimara, it was ordered to despatch a large draft to the 58 Gorkha Training Centre at Shillong, where the 7th Battalion of the regiment was being raised. Lieutenant Colonel Gurpreet Singh of the 6th Battalion, a coursemate of Nanavatty and an outstanding officer of the regiment, who was to retire years later as the Chief of Staff, Northern Command, was deputed as its first CO. This time, great care was given to the selection of personnel for the draft. The four officers of the 2/8th who went to the 'new raising' were selected by the MS Branch and were amongst the best they had. Nanavatty mildly protested to the Colonel of the Regiment but had no answer when he turned around and said, 'Surely our new raising, the 7/8th, must have their share of good officers, too!' While the youngest of the four voluntarily left the army early, the three others, Ashok (Tally) Dewan, Chandrakant (Chandre) Tembe and S.K. Singh, all commanded battalions of the regiment. Interestingly, Chandre returned to command the 2/8th, and S.K. became the Vice Chief of Army Staff and the Colonel of the Regiment!

Because of the mixed peace/field configuration of the formations and units in 20 Mountain Division, 202 Mountain Brigade and its units were sucked into a web of peacetime routines and activities in the division, much to Nanavatty's dislike. Despite excellent areas for training in jungle and 'riverine' terrain, there was little time, thought or opportunity for planned training at the unit level. It did not take long for Nanavatty to get into trouble again. At a meeting in the brigade headquarters, the visiting GOC of the division towards the end rather expansively asked the assembled COs 'if they had any problems'. Nanavatty was quick to respond. He said there was very little time for planned training at the unit level owing to administrative and ad hoc commitments being thrust on units by higher headquarters. 'We need to be left alone to train; as of now, I cannot even lay out a training programme at the section and platoon level in my unit.' The silence was deafening; the GOC turned to the brigade commander, arched his eyebrows and signalled the end of the meeting.[10]

When Lieutenant General Sundarji, then the GOC 33 Corps, visited the formation, Nanavatty was tasked by the brigade commander to 'stage' a specific training event for the visit. The CO informed the BM that the training in the unit would continue as per the existing programme and no changes would be made to the training schedules because of the corps commander's visit. General Sundarji came and did a walkabout in the unit, complimenting it on the layout of its 'F' (fighting) and 'B' (administrative) echelon stores. He then witnessed a small demonstration of battle loads for troops operating self-contained for five days in the mountains, a hot topic at the time; he also witnessed a demonstration of the intelligence section establishing a makeshift battalion command post with stores carried on a man-pack basis. In the CO's office, he commented, good-humouredly, on its austere appearance minus all the usual displays, and had a lively discussion with Nanavatty on compiling data for a unit-ready reckoner. Sundarji departed after a working lunch with the officers in the battalion's field area mess. He seemed pleased with what he had seen.

Notwithstanding the above incidents, the battalion managed two opportunities to train purposefully in the winter of 1979–80. In the first instance, the unit established a Watermanship Training Camp in bivouacs on the River Sankosh, approximately sixty kilometres east of Hasimara, which marked the inter-state border between Bengal and Assam. It was a picturesque spot, and the river was fast-flowing and treacherous. This time, it was to practise opposed river crossing techniques and drills using the standard engineer equipment called assault boats, and there was to be no fiddling around with improvised aids. Given his recent experiences in Ferozepur, Johnny Gorkha was confident and quickly settled down to the task at hand. Upon its conclusion, the battalion 'speed marched' fifty-five kilometres through the night to their lines in Hasimara, getting there for an early lunch the following day!

The second training event of significance was a field firing camp with the battalion again in bivouacs in the Raimatang Field Firing Ranges. Raimatang was a beautiful range in a thickly forested area and was underutilized. Here, the battalion had the honour of hosting Eric Vas, then the GOC-in-C Eastern Command. He spent the better part of the day with the unit, sportingly donned a helmet and walked along, witnessing small sub-units go through various situational training exercises with live fire; he would now and then make the comment 'interesting' in his monosyllabic manner! A short while later, the brigade commander was posted out on completing his tenure and Nanavatty, not surprisingly, 'bagged' yet another 7-point report; that made it two in a row! Nanavatty, however, was unfazed; he had a job that he loved and would do it his way. And the best was yet to come.

Every summer, an infantry battalion from 202 Mountain Brigade would proceed to Bhutan for joint training with a contingent of the Royal Bhutan Army for three months. A liaison officer from the Indian Military Training Team (IMTRAT) would remain attached to the battalion throughout the training period. The training was usually conducted in Dukhye Dzong near Paro in Western Bhutan. Fortuitously, in an answer to Nanavatty's prayers, in the summer of 1980, it was the 2/8th that was deputed for the task. Nanavatty recalls the weeks up in the mountains training with the Royal Bhutan Army as the best during his command: 'The news took me back to Jang in NEFA in 1968. It was a god-sent opportunity to do some meaningful training. Despite raising the 7/8th, I still had a good team of officers with me. In Behram Panthaki, my 2IC, I had a close friend and an officer of impeccable integrity whom I could trust with my eyes shut: he would ensure I did not stray from the straight and narrow. Raghunath Thorat was down to earth, a pugnacious Maratha devoted to the battalion and his Alpha Company; L.T. Singh, a Meiti from Manipur, an outstanding sportsman, calm and quietly efficient, was my Adjutant. Murlidhar, a young officer with great promise, would be my OIC Training Team. And Bidhi Chand, our Quartermaster, could "get the job done" come what may.'[11]

The camp and training areas were in a bowl-shaped re-entrant on the west bank of the Paro Chu (rivulet) with dense mixed vegetation of pine and rhododendron. The surrounding high ground on three sides provided an excellent backstop to the live ammunition in continuous use in the valley. The small Dukhye Dzong Fort, relatively well preserved, lay to the north of the camp and astride the track leading to Guni Chava. Later, it would serve as the ideal location for the conduct of a realistic Prisoner of War exercise for the ummedwars (riflemen who had the potential to become NCOs).

The first task for the battalion, as always, was to map out the area and create the necessary training infrastructure to include a site for the conduct of central lectures and demonstrations, a 200-metre improvised classification range, an ambush range, a jungle lane, a 'grenade golf course' and an area where immediate action drills and sub-unit battle drills could be practised realistically. Not being a designated field firing range, the only self-imposed limitation was that all live fire exercises were restricted to small arms. The area had pheasant and deer, but according to Bhutanese rules, customs and traditions, 'shikar' was taboo. The aim of training, once again, was to refine and practise individual, group and small unit fighting techniques, battle drills and tactics.

Since it was not possible to do a battle inoculation exercise this time around, the training culminated in a company night attack in the mountains using the release point method wherein enemy fire was simulated amongst other devices by LMGs on the objective carefully sighted and firing on interlocking fixed lines with tracer cum ball over the heads of the attackers as they passed through company and platoon release points and finally skirmished forward onto the objective.

In addition to routine training, officers and JCOs were required to familiarize themselves with the terrain and that entailed several long-range reconnaissance patrols. Lieutenant General K. Balaram, the corps commander, visited the 2/8th in Bhutan. When the CO briefed him on the battalion's training, his intuitive reaction was unfavourable. He asked the CO why they were not using the opportunity to do exercises on the various operations of war at the battalion level. Nanavatty was at pains to explain that he was fully aware of the training needs of the unit and the men. He also requested the GOC to walk up to the training area to get a feel for what they were doing that day—a live fire exercise where individuals were skirmishing forward in pairs using the ground and cover. The General looked at his watch and said, 'Another time, perhaps,' and went into the mess tent for a working lunch before departing.

Towards the end of the stint in Bhutan, the battalion received orders to relocate to Cooch Behar on the completion of its joint training and relieve the artillery regiment there. The move necessitated the early dispatch of an Advance Party under Raghu Thorat from Bhutan. It involved the arduous and thankless task of moving personnel and families in the 'Rear', vehicles, weapons and equipment, stores and baggage—from Hasimara to Cooch Behar and assuming responsibility for the essential station duties even before the main body arrived.

Suniti and three-month-old Rushad, accompanied by Suniti's mother, travelled by overnight train to join Rostum in Ferozepur. Briefed by her husband, Suniti lost no time settling into life with the paltan (a colloquial term in Hindi for a military unit). Not for her, the carefree years of a young officer's wife. She was plunged straight into the responsible position of a 2IC's wife and, within a few short months, the wife of a CO.

As the wife of the 2IC, she closely observed the conduct of the CO's wife and came to admire her greatly. So, when her turn came, she knew what to do. She had acquired a rudimentary knowledge of Gorkhali, enough to make herself understood. Recollecting her experience of learning Gorkhali and getting to know Johnny Gorkha, she recounted, 'Gorkhas are cheerful and helpful and never judgemental. They never laughed at me when I made mistakes but made sure they corrected me on an equal footing; I soon realized that subservience is alien to a Gorkha.'[12]

Her work experience as a teacher helped her to organize her time so that baby Rushad was not neglected. Her priorities were clear—family welfare in the real sense. She organized comprehensive immunization of all the children in the paltan and facilitated medical intervention for those who were having difficulty conceiving, a common problem in those days primarily due to the long, forced separations. The acute shortage of family accommodation resulted in Johnny Gorkha bringing his family to a peace station only once every seven years. Fortunately for her, the other officers' wives were most supportive. The majority had been with the paltan longer than Suniti and helped her as best they could.

When the battalion moved from Ferozepur to Hashimara by troop train, Suniti looked forward to travelling on it, having heard stories about such journeys since she was a little girl. But 'CO Sahib' had other plans: the men would travel by troop train, and the families would follow in relative comfort, giving the men sufficient time to make adequate living arrangements for the women and children. However, he did ensure that their twenty-year-old Fiat was loaded onto the train, the intention being that when Suniti and Rushad joined him in Hashimara, she would be mobile. No 'sarkari gaadi' (official vehicle) for the CO's wife! Like it had been in Ferozepur, Suniti, with eight-month-old Rushad in tow, arrived in Hashimara to find the larder stocked with essentials, the camp-style kitchen set up and the beds made. Living on the edge of a wildlife sanctuary was one big adventure—with no electricity and running water, no neighbourhood grocery store and no cooking gas, but with the odd rampaging elephant and friendly snake likely to pay them a call at short notice. The lantern was turned down in the Nanavatty household at nine at night, and reveille was sounded at five in the morning. 'CO Sahib' had no intention of going soft just because his family was with him! On one of her early visits to the family lines, she became aware of the need to run adult literacy classes in Nepali. Fortunately, Suniti found a trained teacher amongst the families, who readily agreed to run the classes.

Rushad soon grew accustomed to wandering around the hut in the dark. And when the water bowser came, he, too, grabbed his little beach bucket and ran to get it filled! It was a short six-month stay for the family. Suniti was expecting their second child and was keen to have the baby at the Air Force Hospital in Hashimara. But Rostum was adamant that she should return to the safety and comfort of her parents' home. Their younger son, Veer, was born on 3 October 1980 at the Moolchand Hospital, delivered by the same doctor. Rostum was out on exercise with the paltan in Sikkim. He received the news via a signal from the Rear HQ that read, 'For Tiger, cub born!' A week later, Suniti received an acknowledgement in a 'pink' forces letter from the cub's father.

On the battalion's return from Bhutan, 20 Mountain Division had a new GOC, Major General S. Mazumdar of the Engineers and 202 Mountain Brigade, a new commander, the legendary Brigadier V.P. (Ved) Airy of the GRENADIERS and of the Battle of Basantar fame.[13]

The impact on their respective commands was immediate. Mazumdar, a Sapper, was an intellectual—meticulous, deliberate and scholarly in his approach. He would later rise to be the Adjutant General of the Army. On the other hand, Airy was the salt of the earth, bold, practical and all fire and brimstone with a wicked sense of humour. He would retire as the Director General of Infantry. Though poles apart in many ways, they were professionals to the core, non-interfering and encouraging of their subordinates.

Of his brigade commander Nanavatty had this to say: 'The gods had smiled on me. My next brigade commander was Brigadier V.P. Airy, an outstanding soldier who, as CO 3 GRENADIERS, was awarded the Maha Vir Chakra for gallantry in the Battle of Basantar on the Western Front in the India–Pakistan War in 1971. He would visit the battalion several times when we were out on training, often turning up in the most unlikely places and at the shortest possible notice. Once, during a battalion attack by infiltration exercise wherein the unit infiltrated by night along multiple routes through dense jungle, he met the CO's Party at the Battalion RV, a six-figure grid reference, at 0400 hours, to witness an attack by the battalion that morning. On another occasion, he was with the battalion through the better part of a cold and wet night in an opposed river crossing on the Sankosh River, complimenting it on its various drills and procedures.'

Nanavatty continued effusively, among the few times the author noticed during his many interviews, 'It was always a pleasure having him around. I was flattered when, in one of my reports, he wrote, "This commanding officer has his battalion by the nose." It was my solemn belief that it was his report on my performance as a CO that kept me afloat.'[14] Airy, on his part, told his staff at the brigade headquarters that he looked forward to visiting 2/8 GR because he always learnt something new during these visits.

In October 1980, the battalion was involved in an important exercise in North Sikkim. After that, it was a rerun of what they had done the previous year—watermanship training, attacks by infiltration, and field firing in Raimatang. The only addition was an exercise in defence in the mountains wherein the GOC had expressed a specific desire to witness offensive actions in defence at the battalion level. He would spend the whole day with the unit, and his only request was for a good riding mule to get around the defences. He will have gone to bed very sore that night!

Nanavatty received his posting orders to the Defence Services Staff College in Wellington (Nilgiris) as a Directing Staff (DS) in the New Year, and on 25 February 1981, it was a happy and contented soldier who handed over command of the 2/8th to his 2IC Behram Panthaki in Cooch Behar. They had their fingers crossed because previously, as the story goes, apparently the only other time two Parsi officers had handed and taken over a unit in the Indian Army—and that too a Gorkha Battalion—the unit had been disbanded!

Several months earlier, a friend posted in the section in Army HQ that looked after the postings of officers, officially called the Military Secretary's (MS) Branch, sounded Nanavatty on his relatively weak reports, one after the other, as a CO. He said they could come in the way of his selection for promotion to the rank of Colonel and had suggested that he 'represent' against them. Nanavatty thanked him for his concern and thoughtfulness but said, 'I will be damned if I am ever going to represent against a report on me by a senior officer.'

Dilip Parab, who was also later in the MS Branch at some point, had a different take on the matter. He told the author that General Sundarji had overruled the report of the Commander 202 Mountain Brigade. Blissfully unaware of these happenings, when asked whether he lost any sleep over the issue, he said, 'None whatsoever: I would have left the army if I was unhappy.' Recounting these incidents without malice, Nanavatty attributed his recovery during his command to providence. Later, he would re-encounter similar hurdles in his career.

Professional papers would flow from Nanavatty's pen before, during and after his command tenure but began to taper off as he rose to the level of a formation commander. Nanavatty grappled with several issues that he felt were pertinent at the time and where he genuinely believed that change was needed in organizational interest. They would deal with aspects of leadership, training and tactics. His writings reflected a deep concern and commitment to the institution and were written without fear or favour, reflecting an ability and willingness to speak truth to power.[15]

Passionate about shooting as a teenager, and an accomplished marksman himself during his career, weapon training became almost an obsession with Nanavatty during all his command assignments. Recognizing that the Indian Army had inherited the belief in 'controlled accuracy of its small arms fire' from the British Army, he pointed out in a paper written during his command tenure that there was a 'staleness and aimlessness' creeping into weapons training. He also pointed at the urgent need for a 'reappraisal of the aim, organization and conduct of Weapon Training (WT)'. Highlighting that accurately delivered small arms fire was no longer the most critical battle-winning factor, Nanavatty drew on General Patton's early recognition in the Second World War that 'marching fire', with its emphasis on volume of fire rather than accuracy, had to complement well-directed small arms fire to 'suppress and shock the enemy'. Instead of 'To kill with speed and accuracy', he suggested reorienting to a more nuanced aim: 'To deliver controlled, accurate and sustained fire to destroy/neutralize a given target.' He argued that infantry battalions must move from an unrealistic parade ground atmosphere to a more regular small arms training in a Field Firing Range, the only way to recreate an operational environment.[16]

Intimately associated with the discipline of medium and high-altitude warfare by the end of his career, Nanavatty's early experiences with operations in the mountains were influenced by the professionally stimulating tenure under the command of Anand Sarup in NEFA in the Tawang Sector. With an eye on China, the deployment in Bhutan allowed Nanavatty to cement his ideas into suggested infantry tactics for what he termed 'Offensive Defence in the Mountains' from the battalion to the division level. About defensive operations at the philosophical level, he argues, 'Defence, the word itself, serves to conjure in the mind of the defender, an act of waiting and watching and reacting.' Suggesting that the only way to 'ensure the successful outcome of the defensive battle is to attempt to wrest and retain the initiative', Nanavatty argues that defensive operations must be aggressive in design and offensive in conduct.

Assessing the likely trajectory of Chinese operations in the early 1980s based on what he learnt during the aftermath of the 1962 debacle and reinforced by his experiences at Bumla, Nanavatty listed some of the most likely tactical actions by the Chinese People's Liberation Army (PLA) in offensive operations in mountainous terrain. Combining extensive reconnaissance and probes with harassment to induce fatigue and fear in the defender, the PLA was likely to concentrate forces to create overwhelming superiority against weak points. Nanavatty suggests that the Indian Army must be prepared to cope with a tri-pronged aim of infiltration, envelopment and encirclement as among the likely courses of action that the PLA would employ in the mountains.

Nanavatty realized that the retention of crucial terrain was an inescapable reality in the Indian context, given the political rhetoric that 'every inch of Indian soil must be defended' that emerged from New Delhi whenever there was tension along the Line of Actual Control (LAC). The only way out, he argued, was to observe the principles of depth, reserves, mutual support and compactness in planning defences. Further, the paper emphasized the value of 'early warning screens with fighting potential to commence the destruction of the enemy as far out as possible and then have the option of withdrawing to multiple defensive locations in depth'.

Nanavatty highlighted the importance of 'Special and Stay Behind Missions' in creating a sterile buffer zone between the attacker and the defender. According to him, the other essentials were effective ambushes and sniper deployments, close coordination of fire, including Close Air Support, and the ability to launch 'Spoiling Attacks' by earmarked troops. Differentiating between 'Spoiling Attacks' and local counterattacks, Nanavatty argues that while the former is deliberate, the latter will invariably be a result of quick decision-making by a local tactical commander down to the company or even platoon level when a vulnerability is spotted/sensed in the enemy during an ongoing attack.

The paper wisely limits the overarching objective of 'Limited Offensive Operations in Defence' to 'offensive operations undertaken by the defender to improve his overall defensive posture'. To achieve this, Nanavatty writes: 'The defender must overcome the static Maginot Line complex. He must be prepared to move out of his field fortifications to find the enemy and destroy him. In the final analysis, the spirit of the offensive will ensure the success of defensive operations in the mountains.'[17]

Convinced early in his career that leadership insight did not come instinctively to everyone and that it could be taught and ingrained in military professionals, Nanavatty's writings on leadership during and after his first command tenure indicate the close linkages that he established between leadership and performance. He highlighted several issues in another paper titled 'Improving Performance Levels in the Army'.[18] Among these was the need to abandon 'ceremonial customs and traditions, much of it foreign and little understood' and concentrate on functional efficiency. 'Ceremonial trappings should be trimmed ruthlessly and field forces backed by good administration and service conditions should remain "stripped for action".' Strengthening his argument for operational efficiency over everything else, he invoked Field Marshal Rommel's cautionary advice to the Wehrmacht against unquestioningly embracing Nazification or following dated Prussian models during the early years of the Second World War.

That Nanavatty was an idealist, a perfectionist, and an outlier was increasingly evident by the end of his command tenure. That he backed his ideas with solid leadership and continuous monitoring of the operational environment meant that he developed a high order of situational awareness (SA). Lastly, the translation of ideas into detailed writings that would have taken hours to execute in the backdrop of a command assignment indicated mental stamina and the ability to intellectualize the profession of warfighting. However, as Shergill, his close friend, very aptly pointed out, quoting the French revolutionary and philosopher Voltaire, 'Perfection is often the enemy of the good.' Nanavatty may have missed a trick or two in enabling the performance of his subordinates with the consistently high standards that he expected of himself and those around him. Dileep Parab, one of his company commanders, added, 'I have since told officers that it is impossible to emulate Nanavatty, and the secret was to learn from him and do what you could within the limits of your own capabilities.'[19]

Hasimara and Cooch Behar in North Bengal and Wellington in the Nilgiris are almost 3000 kilometres apart but share one thing: both are home to miles and miles of lush tea plantations. A posting to the Defence Services Staff College (DSSC) in Wellington as a Directing Staff (DS) was a welcome break for Nanavatty and the beginning of a long and uninterrupted spell of quality family time for the Nanavattys. Upon relinquishing command, Rostum came to Delhi to collect the family. A three-day journey by train, with three-year-old Rushad and five-month-old Veer, took the Nanavattys from Delhi toWellington. 'For Rostum, it was a time well spent with old friends, peers, and bright young student officers,' said Suniti. 'It allowed me to forge new friendships, some of which have lasted a lifetime. Those were good times.'

Lieutenant General S.R.R. Aiyengar, a faculty colleague of Nanavatty at Wellington from the Corps of Signals, a future commandant at DSSC, and a highly respected soldier was only an acquaintance but remembered Nanavatty as a 'true professional who many thought one day would become our chief. He was a man of few words who always called a spade a spade. He is a fine example of an officer and a gentleman.'[20] However, the good times in Wellington did not last. Before they knew it, distant shores beckoned, not once but twice. Nanavatty was asked if he was willing to go as a Military Attaché, and he expressed his unwillingness without batting an eyelid. Unsurprisingly, Suniti only learned of it through the grapevine. She recalls, 'As far as postings went, a pattern was also beginning to form. First, everyone knew where the Nanavattys were going. Then, some kind soul informed me. Then I told Rostum! He was always the last to know!'

Despite his earlier refusal, Nanavatty was selected a few months later to proceed as the Indian Army Liaison Officer (IALO) to the British Army's Infantry School at Warminster in the picturesque county of Wiltshire. Surprised at being selected for an interesting overseas assignment in mid-1982, despite a turbulent command tenure, it was clear that the Indian Army was keeping track of the 'thinking' commander that Nanavatty was emerging to be. Combining a razor-sharp intellect with a sprinter's impatience and a marathon runner's mental stamina to convert ideas into action and test them on the ground, he was an ideal candidate to fill the slot at Warminster.

Describing his professional experience at the DSSC as 'only modestly satisfying', excerpts from his farewell talk during his 'Coffeeing Out' in the presence of the commandant, Lieutenant General Balaram, who had earlier been his corps commander, were instructive. Following the traditional thanks to colleagues, the Army Wing, and others who made his stay comfortable, he got to the point, echoing the views of many who have served in that great institution as faculty members, including the author: 'Quite frankly, professionally I did not find the job as challenging and satisfying as a command. For your sake, I sincerely hope the commandant succeeds in his endeavour to restructure the syllabus and make the DS workload more interesting. That will allow more reflection, interaction and contribution, making the whole intellectual experience as a faculty member worthwhile.'[21]

Now, it is time to head overseas, first to Fort Benning, Georgia, US, and then to Warminster in the UK, and assess whether Nanavatty went there to 'have a jolly good time' or bring back significant takeaways for the Indian Army.

5

LEARNING FROM THE AMERICANS AND THE BRITISH

'The "Honour Code" at USAIS was unique, and plagiarism was unacceptable.'

—LIEUTENANT COLONEL R.K. NANAVATTY, MHOW, NOVEMBER 1977

Rewinding to August 1971 and heading overseas, Major Nanavatty flew into Washington, D.C. and then onwards to Columbus in southern Georgia, where he was picked up and driven to the US Army Infantry School (USAIS) Fort Benning. Before the US Congress mandated the 'Base Realignment and Closure' (BRAC) reorganization of the Department of Defence in 2005, Fort Benning had been the home of the infantry in the US Army since 1919. All basic and advanced training of infantrymen—officers, Non-Commissioned Officers and soldiers, airborne forces and Ranger training in the US Army—was conducted here.

Having done the Junior Command Course in 1969 and fresh from being an instructor in the YO Wing at the Infantry School in Mhow, it did not take Nanavatty long to settle down on his Infantry Officers' Advance Course (IOAC 1-72). The IOAC, together with the erstwhile

Armor Officers' Advance Course at Fort Knox, both career courses, were the forerunners of the current 'Manoeuvre Captain's Career Course' (MCCC) for officers of the Infantry and Armoured Corps at the Manoeuvre Centre of Excellence, Fort Moore (earlier name Fort Benning), Georgia, since 2011. The IOAC aimed to prepare students for the command of a company and for executing the tactical planning responsibilities of a S3 (GS Branch) staff officer at the battalion level.

The course comprised around 190 student officers, all captains with one lone major, the class senior student from the US Army, a trio from the US Marine Corps, and twenty foreign student officers referred to politely as 'Allied Student' officers. The latter were all assigned volunteer sponsor officers from within the class. The course was for nine months and included classified sections restricted to host country officers only, during which the Allied Students proceeded on well organized tours to places of interest, including Disney Land in Florida, if you please! At Benning, the Allied Student Training Division went the extra mile to administer and assist the Foreign Student Officers. In Nanavatty's opinion, they tended to 'pamper and spoil us', something he disapproved of thoroughly and felt it was 'best to treat foreign students correctly as one would one's own'.[1]

The Infantry School was organized along specialized faculties called Departments, i.e., Stability Operations, Airmobile Operations and Leadership, among others. A senior civilian educationist advised the Commandant on methods of instruction, and each department had a mix of military and civilian faculty members. Nanavatty observed that the 'faculty were of high quality; they had an open-door policy that encouraged and facilitated research and serious study. All the various departments maintained a close liaison with field formations, conducted frequent field studies and collaborated with other schools of instruction to ensure a uniform teaching model.'

Highlighting a facet of training that remains a 'grey area' in institutions of military learning in India, he said that military and civilian faculty members were required to undergo a two-week intensive course on

Methods of Instruction that the Department of Instruction conducted. They were only assigned to their respective academic departments if they passed a test that involved making presentations on their allocated subject to the Department of Instruction. Should they not succeed, they were assigned to perform administrative tasks. Instructors were also continuously rated and evaluated by their peers and their students. Lack-lustre feedback once too often meant relegation. This academic rigour ensured that the standards of delivery were consistently high.[2]

Conversely, Nanavatty assessed that instructors ran the risk of boredom since they were required to deliver the same module repeatedly. The only method of instruction employed was the lecture presentation to the entire course in a large classroom that was centrally air-conditioned with excellent acoustics and lighting, CCTV, film projection facilities, slide projectors, and glass and magnetic boards. A short Q&A Session would invariably follow a talk. Lecture presentations were thoroughly rehearsed and 'choreographed'. Lecturers did not refer to notes, used throat microphones, and spared no effort to make their presentations enjoyable. The use of dual lecturers was sometimes resorted to during long presentations and lectures on controversial subjects. Lecture presentations demanded that the students concentrate, listen carefully and assimilate what was said without being distracted.

By comparison, Nanavatty felt that the Indian Army model, a combination of lecture-cum-presentations, and tutorial discussions, followed by Sand Model (table) discussions and Tactical Exercises without Troops (TEWT), was more interesting. Convinced that a good professional soldier applies his theoretical knowledge to situations as they obtain on the ground at the time, he felt the Indian system, theoretically at least, encouraged students to think on their feet and apply their knowledge accordingly.

Apart from two very engaging, comprehensive and well-conducted Lecture cum Demonstrations in the outdoors, one on the Rangers and the other on Airborne Forces, there was, surprisingly, no outdoor work at all. The only outdoor exercise during the course was a simple yet wonderfully challenging orienteering-type individual map reading exercise in a dense patch of forest on the Post. Every officer was provided a unique plan that required the individual to go from one numbered stake in the ground to another and complete the course within the time stipulated. While the total distance covered during the exercise may have been modest, it demanded unerring compass work, accurate assessment of distances covered and an 'eye on the clock'. Nanavatty recalls that nearly two hundred students were in the exercise area, and he barely encountered a couple. Completely engrossed in the navigation, he suddenly realized he was 'running late' and had to make a desperate run to the finish, where he was received with a rousing welcome from the whole course that had fallen in and was about to be dismissed for the day—a welcome icebreaker for all![3]

What Nanavatty found interesting was that even on a career course of this nature, there were elective opportunities, both academic and non-academic, on offer. US officers were compulsorily required to choose any two subjects. These included topics such as speed reading and effective speaking and writing, all conducted by civilian academics. The elective programme was demanding and offered individuals an opportunity to pursue civilian educational programmes to further their academic qualifications through affiliations with nearby universities. It enhanced rehabilitation and second career prospects.[4]

Reflecting on the assessment methods, Nanavatty highlights the variety. There were testable and non-testable blocks of instruction, diagnostic tests to assess proficiency, innumerable spot quizzes, and subject-wise tests primarily of the 'multiple choice' type on the completion of each module. There were forums where students could discuss controversial issues and present contrarian views, all in an uninhibited environment. On class behavioural issues, despite the uninhibited academic atmosphere, there weren't many 'Spring Bucks' who needed to make their presence felt and be noticed. What was startling to Nanavatty, at least to begin with, were instances of clapping to commend and, equally, rude noises and booing to express disapproval—all good-natured.

In one instance, after the India–Pakistan War of 1971 had ended, the lecturer, probably seeking to provoke a complex and long-winded politico-military reply, asked, 'I believe we have an Indian Army officer in the class and would like to know what his views are on the subject of US military aid to Pakistan?'

Nanavatty stood up and said, 'Sir, as long as you pass on your old tanks, weapons and equipment, we have no problems,' drawing a raucous round of applause that brought the house down.[5] In another incident, in an exclusive closed-door address to the US Officers at Benning on the refashioning of the army after its withdrawal from Vietnam, General W. Westmoreland, the Chief of Staff of the US Army (CSA), was reported to have said that 'the Army would retain the best and get rid of the crud'. The unfortunate use of the word 'crud' so incensed the officers that the student leadership confronted the General and sought an apology before he departed the station!

Nanavatty's short verdict on the course was, 'Apart from the latest teaching methodologies and the academic concentration, the biggest takeaway was that it helped me understand the organization, concepts, doctrines and conduct of operations by mechanized forces. This stood me in good stead when I was thrown into the deep end a few years later as the Brigade Major of an Armoured Brigade.'[6]

It was not all-work-and-no-play for Nanavatty. The even pace of the course and the excellent facilities on Post allowed him to indulge in sport and regular exercise. He voluntarily participated in the standard US Army Physical Tests, like those conducted in the Indian Army and administered by a team of P.T. ustaads (Instructors), except that the tests were carried out in combat boots rather than P.T. shoes. Finishing first in the one-mile run, he received a joyous ovation from his coursemates. Interestingly, all the upper body strength-related tests were time-related, e.g., the number of push-ups and sit-ups in sixty seconds, and the only test he found difficult was the horizontal ladder, which required a specific technique. He made several friends on the Course: Wayne Porter, his student sponsor, David Newman, Peter Dalton, Bob Amiot, Lee Purdy and John Alexander.

Among the Allied Students, Captain Dorcha Lee, Irish Army, and Lieutenant Abdul Rahim Wardak, Afghan Army, his neighbours in the Bachelor Officers' Quarters (BOQ) were particularly close. Colonel Dorcha Lee would later serve as the Irish Military Advisor to the

European Union and is now a prolific commentator on strategic affairs. Wardak, on the other hand, was doing practically every course that the USAIS had to offer, one after the other! A big, burly Pushtoon (Pathan) and a baby at heart, he would seek Nanavatty's moral support at every trying juncture. He was promoted to 'four-star' rank in the Afghan Army and served two terms as the Afghan Defence Minister in the Hamid Karzai Government.

Nanavatty did well on IOAC 1-72 and was adjudged the Distinguished Allied Graduate of the Course. His friend Dorcha, however, had a different take on the matter. 'Rusty came first on the Course.' Reportedly, a foreign officer topped the class for the first time in the fifty-odd years of the Infantry Officers' Advanced Course.[7] Where did Dorcha get this nugget of information from? Nanavatty does not know!

Colonel Dorcha Lee shared his recollections of 'Rusty' in a long email to the author. The only occasion on the Course when Dorcha saw Rusty upset was when war broke out between India and Pakistan in December 1971: 'I found him in his room drafting a letter to the Indian Chief of the Army, requesting to be recalled for combat duty. His chief turned down his request gently, highlighting Rusty's duty—to stay, study and learn from the Americans.' Some weeks after the war ended, a Pakistani Major arrived at Fort Benning, and Lee was impressed with the kindness and courtesy that Rusty extended to him as he helped the Pakistani settle in.

According to Colonel Lee, Rusty was socially at ease in the US and had a wicked sense of humour. At one of the many receptions Lee and Rusty attended, they met several well-heeled ladies, perhaps older, too. Lee recollects one such occasion: 'When two of these ladies spotted us two unaccompanied foreign males, they came across and introduced themselves, American style, first names only. Rusty introduced himself as me, taking off my Irish accent to perfection, expounding on Ireland and how great it was for him, as an Irishman, to be in America! Of course, I had to pretend I was him and that I had served in the 8th Gorkha Rifles. Somehow, we got away with it.'[8]

When Lee's wife Eileen arrived in Fort Benning, they rented a house in nearby Columbus, Georgia and Rusty was a regular visitor. Eileen was interested in Indian cooking, and Rusty offered to cook dinner for them and two other guests one evening. He made up a long list of ingredients for Eileen to get from a specialized international shop with everything on its shelves. The meal took many hours to prepare and was truly memorable, not too hot, but with an excellent taste and lots of pots and pans to wash up! Lee reckons Rusty would have made more money running the best Indian restaurant in Dublin than in the Indian Army![9]

Underlining Rusty's professionalism during a critical operational discussion regarding the inadequacy of the existing US defensive doctrine, the Commandant of the Infantry School and his team developed a new concept called Force Oriented Doctrine (FOD). Tested for two days at the Corps level, most US participants favoured the FOD concept, which involved conducting operations behind enemy lines with small teams to cause disproportionate attrition. When Allied officers offered their comments, Lee expressed his reservations about the methodology used to arrive at the deemed success of the concept, suggesting that the computerized model favoured the defending force and that it may be unsafe to conclude on FOD based on this exercise alone. There was pin-drop silence; this was not what the Commandant wanted to hear.

Up went Rusty's hand as he agreed with Lee's assessment and presented his arguments with clarity and coherence, with more examples to back Lee's arguments. The exercise was deemed a success, and the Commandant thanked the two Allied officers for their contribution. Two months later, the Commandant got his third star and was sent to Germany to implement the FOD into US doctrine! Nanavatty capped an eventful year in the US with a stopover in Ireland on his way back to India, where he spent a few days with the Lee family.[10]

In early 1982, over ten years since his course in the US and a year into his assignment as a faculty member at the Defence Services Staff College, Nanavatty was asked by the MS Branch to furnish his 'willingness' or otherwise to proceed on a posting abroad. He promptly replied that he was unprepared to provide his 'willingness' to an overseas posting unless he knew where he was headed. He was not in the least bit interested in a Defence Attaché's job unless it happened to be in Nepal, and at no stage did the appointment of the Indian Army Liaison Officer (IALO)

at the British Army School of Infantry, Warminster, cross his mind. Several colleagues at the Staff College suggested he was being 'stupid' turning down an assignment abroad, that the MS Branch had a long memory, and that 'refusing a foreign posting' could reflect adversely on his career profile.

A few weeks later, the army chief, General K.V. Krishna Rao, visited the Staff College. During the customary introduction of the faculty members to the visiting dignitary, he paused as he shook hands with Nanavatty and said, 'So you are going to the UK as the IALO.' Nanavatty replied, 'I am sorry, sir, I know nothing about it.' The chief glanced at his accompanying staff officer and moved on.

Soon after the chief's visit, Nanavatty received his orders, attaching him to Army Headquarters for his pre-foreign posting preparations, which included staff briefings at Army Headquarters and visits to a few select training establishments. Nanavatty hoped to understand the army's requirements clearly, thus making his work more organized and purposeful. Unfortunately, his interactions were disappointing. People did not seem to have the time or the inclination, and the common refrain was 'Congratulations, all the best, have a good time.' Fortunately, that was not so in the Military Training Directorate, his sponsor directorate. There, he was painstakingly briefed and greatly encouraged by Colonel (later Major General) Vinod Sehgal, the Colonel GS, MT 3. Nanavatty soon realized that he would have to chart his own course, and the assignment would turn out how he wanted it to—either a fun trip or a learning experience of a lifetime.[11] He chose the latter.

Rostum, Suniti, Rushad (4), and Veer (2), flew into London late evening on 6 September 1982. Barely had they moved into their hotel room when he got a call from Brigadier Vijay Madan, the Indian Military Attaché in London, from the hotel foyer inviting him to a drink in the bar followed by dinner with Lieutenant General Sundarji, then the Deputy Chief of Army Staff who was on an official visit to the UK. Nanavatty politely declined the invitation saying that they were settling in and his wife needed help with the children after the long non-stop flight. A while later, there was a knock on the door, and you had Sundarji with Madan in tow, facing Nanavatty in his pyjamas and dressing gown! General Sundarji, who knew the family from his 1 Armoured Division days, had insisted on seeing what the 'stubborn chap was up to'. Nanavatty apologized for not being able to invite them inside the room or join them for dinner. Sundarji and Nanavatty exchanged pleasantries while Madan looked on incredulously as if to say, 'Look at the gall of this fellow talking to the future Chief in his pyjamas.'[12]

Colonel O.P. Kaushik, the incumbent IALO, and his wife, took the Nanavattys under their wing at Warminster. After making them comfortable in temporary accommodation, 'O.P.' did a painstakingly thorough job in the handover of responsibilities. He introduced Nanavatty to the staff, familiarized him with the School of Infantry and briefed him on the nature of work and the various procedures in place. It would be a few weeks of routine maintenance before Mr Havelock-Allan, the Estate Officer, a descendant of Lieutenant General Henry Havelock-Allan, VC of the British Indian Army, handed over '134 Elm Hill', the house within the School campus traditionally allotted to the IALO, to the Nanavattys!

The first thing that struck Nanavatty was that the Infantry Directorate and the School of Infantry were co-located at Warminster. To Nanavatty, that made perfect sense. At the time, he thought the Indian Army could emulate this arrangement to good advantage and reduce the congestion in Army Headquarters. The school's Commandant was Brigadier Ian Mackay, an officer highly regarded by the officers and staff. The school also hosted Exchange and Liaison Officers from the Australian, French, German and US Armies.

The British Army had a familiar ring to it. Individuals with strong family connections with India and the old Indian Army, the regimental system, military etiquette and customs of service, the language and military lexicon, and even sports—squash, cricket, hockey and football—all made for a comfortable and 'easy to slip into' professional and social environment as far as the IALO was concerned. The appointment of the IALO itself was a legacy of the British Indian Army, which boasted liaison officers in several British Army institutions. Perhaps the best known was Lieutenant Colonel (later Field Marshal) W.J. (Bill) Slim, the

IALO at the Staff College, Camberley. The IALO was not a diplomatic assignment, nor did the appointment carry any special perks or privileges. Suniti, on one of her brief visits to the NAAFI (the equivalent of the Indian Army's Canteen Stores Department or CSD), talking to a soldier's wife, was amused to learn that a private soldier's pay was on par with that of the IALO! And yet the Nanavattys did not do too badly: they bought a car, travelled extensively, entertained appropriately and lived comfortably![13]

Professionally, what the job offered was immense. The rules were simple: the IALO had access to information classified as Confidential and below in the British Army without reference to any higher authority. He was free to interact with the staff in the School of Infantry and military establishments and units throughout the army and plan his visits accordingly. This opportunity allowed the IALO to view the working of one of the finest armies—albeit a small one—of NATO and, indeed, the world at close quarters. Equally, British military papers and literature invariably provided a distilled explanation of US and NATO military weapons, equipment, concepts and doctrine as seen through the eyes of an experienced and critical ally.

Apart from housing, the Infantry School provided the IALO with office accommodation, limited clerical support and motor transport support for official purposes whenever necessary. Since this was before the advent of the computer, Nanavatty chose to submit handwritten reports for various reasons, the security of information being one of them. Every month, he would make the round trip to London to meet with the Military Attaché at the High Commission and deliver his bag of accumulated outgoing mail for dispatch to Army Headquarters in India, where the Colonel GS (MT 3) would do the sorting and further distribution as deemed fit.

Nanavatty was quick to realize that the appointment of the IALO at the School of Infantry, Warminster, did not, in any way, restrict him, and that he could, if he so wished, assume the role of an ex-officio IALO to the British Army! This opened the door to enormous possibilities. While his primary concern would remain the infantry, he would address many other issues of interest as they cropped up in his three years there. Existing procedures required Nanavatty to seek the Military Attaché's permission for visits outside Warminster. Nanavatty took up the issue with Brigadier Vijay Madan, stating that it was needlessly cumbersome and time-consuming and invariably led to missed opportunities. The Military Attaché agreed unhesitatingly and permitted him to plan and execute his visits as required, keeping him informed and claiming his travel expenses accordingly.

In the British Army, units and establishments were generally aware of the existence of the IALO. Service customs and etiquette required that you identify the person you wished to interact with, pick up the telephone, speak directly to the individual and fix whatever you wanted to see, discuss or do. While walking into an office unannounced and sitting down for a chat invariably drew a frosty response, doing it 'properly' could fetch you a pleasant surprise: your host might even offer you a glass of fine sherry before getting down to business! Greeted with courtesy on his visits, patience, camaraderie and frankness characterized Nanavatty's interactions notwithstanding the occasional mischievous chant of 'Here comes the Indian spy!' And, it was not uncommon for a commanding officer to invite him to revisit his unit or establishment.

Early during his posting, Nanavatty had set up a meeting with the Commander of the Small Arms Wing in his office without mentioning its exact purpose. After exchanging pleasantries, he broached the subject of training snipers, which had been discontinued at the Infantry School in Mhow for some reason. Embarrassed by the flood of questions, the Colonel responded, 'Ah! If it is all about sniping, Staff Sergeant Harverson in the Sniper Division is the man for you.' Similarly, Nanavatty recalled visiting the Guards Depot (Training Centre), where he watched young soldiers carry out a live fire exercise—skirmishing forward in pairs using cover—being supervised by an NCO with no officer in sight. Considering it was an exercise with live ammunition, out of curiosity, he asked, 'Staff, why isn't there an officer on parade?' to which the NCO, in the blink of an eye, replied, 'Colonel, in the Guards, the officers play polo.' Three things immediately stood out: first, rank did not matter, subject knowledge and expertise did; two, the professionalism and confidence of the Non-Commissioned Officer cadre was remarkable; and lastly, their worth and the trust they enjoyed was commendable.[14]

In September 1982, the after-action reports of Operation CORPORATE, the complex joint operation in the Falklands involving the Royal Navy, British Army and Royal Air Force, were of immediate interest to Nanavatty. Fought some 7000 nautical miles away from home in challenging sea, terrain and climatic conditions, the conduct of operations by the Land Forces offered several lessons. Declassified after-action reports were available for perusal, and a composite travelling team of officers and Non-Commissioned Officers was making presentations in all the military stations. Interestingly, one of the individuals on the team was the NCO, who was CO 2 PARA's bodyguard. He spoke briefly of the incident where the CO, Lieutenant Colonel H. Jones, was killed in action, leading his unit in the battle of Goose Green, for which he was awarded the Victoria Cross (VC) posthumously.[15] Another aspect that intrigued Nanavatty was typically British—the convention of appointing an official 'Military Artist' for every campaign. The artist would be responsible for ensuring a realistic pictorial record of the campaign through drawings and sketches, and often involved a revisit to the site of an incident together with eyewitnesses! Nanavatty found the after-action report and analysis to be frank and forthright, with no attempt to conceal failures.

In April 1984, the Indian Army occupied several heights on the Saltoro Ridge that ran along the western flank of the Siachen Glacier. Called Operation MEGHDOOT, the pre-emptive and audacious operation was a signature moment in High-Altitude Warfare. MEGHDOOT triggered Nanavatty's interest in NATO force operations in extreme cold weather conditions. A Royal Marine Commando officer friend on the staff at the School of Infantry suggested he interact with the Royal Marine Commando Mountain and Arctic Warfare Cadre at Lympstone in the UK. Later in the winter of 1984; he would travel to Norway to spend a few days with the Royal Marines on their annual winter training in arctic conditions along the northern flank of NATO. Interestingly, his visit would coincide with that of a group of members of the House of Lords. Nanavatty says 'it was amusing to see a Royal Marine Sergeant Tent Commander painstakingly issue precise instructions to a Baroness member of the group on how to prepare for a night in the tent in minus-fifty degree celsius!'

Highlighting the niche and elite nature of the force, Nanavatty observed that motivational levels in the force transcended normal levels. While intelligence, general education and awareness of even the junior-most trooper were remarkable, self-discipline, self-reliance, comfort with specialist weapons and equipment, versatility and complexity of skills were omnipresent.

Less than two years into his assignment as IALO, the Indian Army was involved in Operation BLUE STAR in June 1984, its first major operation in an urban environment against Sikh separatists and terrorists holed up in the Golden Temple in Amritsar. The heavy casualties suffered by the Indian Army during the operation prompted Nanavatty to seek exposure to the techniques and tactics of Urban Counterterrorist (CT) operations in Northern Ireland, where the British Army was battling the Irish Republican Army (IRA). He would spend a week with an infantry battalion undergoing work-up (pre-induction) training at a special purpose-built facility in England before deployment in Northern Ireland. Surprisingly, the CO extended him a standing invitation to visit the unit after it was deployed. However, much to Suniti's relief, this was one occasion where permission was denied and understandably so.

During his tenure, Nanavatty had planned to write a report on the Special Air Service (SAS), the British Army's famed Special Forces (SF). Try as he might, he could not gain access to the organization. As his term entered its last lap, he approached the HQ Director SAS (D SAS) in London directly. He was delighted when he received an invitation to visit the headquarters, where he was given a briefing of a general nature on the force. An interesting feature that caught his attention during the briefing was the complementary support provided to the SAS by specialist crews and aircraft of the RAF. It was a beginning. Subsequently, based on the briefing and information from open sources, he painstakingly compiled a comprehensive report highlighting the role, organization, selection of personnel, career management, training and concepts of employment of the force. Nanavatty signed off his report by recommending that 'much benefit will accrue from effective liaison between the SAS and the Indian Army's PARA Commando (PARA Cdo) units'. He suggested that initially, it could be in the form of joint training. He felt, 'if nothing else, it would allow us to gauge our standards vis-à-vis a force acknowledged to be among the best SF in the world'.[16] He would like to believe that a positive spin-off of his initial meeting and the report that he submitted to Delhi of his visit to the HQ D SAS opened a channel of communications between the two and facilitated a first-time visit to HQ D SAS by Colonel S.S. (Sukhi) Mann, Director Commando Cell in the Indian Army's Directorate of Military Operations.[17]

In between, Nanavatty recalls, he found the time to investigate and report on several other interesting features of the British Army. The role of Schools Liaison Officers who were retired officers with official 'self drive' cars who helped to identify, keep tabs on, and encourage young school-going lads who possessed the aptitude and showed an interest in the army as a career. The efficient management of field firing areas within the country despite the limited space; how British Army Training Units operated abroad in Canada and Kenya creating the required infrastructure with pre-positioned vehicles, weapons and equipment, e.g., British Army Training Unit Suffolk (BATUS) in Canada, were novel ideas.

One of the most enjoyable tasks he undertook was to do a short course for officers who would serve in appointments associated with adventure training in the army. By definition, adventure training in the British Army is categorized as a 'recreational activities that pose a threat to life and limb': Motor car rallies, cycling expeditions and treks did not qualify! Before doing the course, Nanavatty completed the Basic Free Fall course at Netherhaven, and during the course, he was introduced to canoeing, caving and rock climbing. He did not particularly enjoy caving, finding it claustrophobic. A couple of days before the course ended, while negotiating a rockface in the Brecon Beacons with a SAS Sergeant as his lead climber he dislocated his shoulder. Failing to set it right on a narrow ledge halfway up the rockface, his rescuers expertly lowered him and walked him to a small medical facility where a prim and proper nurse asked, 'What's wrong with you?' He replied, 'I have a dislocated shoulder,' to which she took offence. 'How do you know: are you a doctor?' she asked. When Nanavatty replied that it was a recurring problem, her manner quietened. After fixing the shoulder, he rested in the hospital for a few hours before returning to his bivouac. The interlude was delightful as he watched India beat the West Indies in the 1983 One Day Cricket World Cup Final.

The three-year stay started with great sadness for Suniti. In England for barely three weeks, news came that her father had passed away in Delhi of a cardiac arrest. Suniti returned to India with baby Veer, leaving five-year-old Rushad in his father's care. Fortunately, Rushad was already at a full-day school, and kind neighbours helped fill in the gaps. Upon her return from India, Suniti plunged into an exhausting routine of housework and childcare. Fortunately, Nanavatty's working hours were regulated and allowed him to help with housework. They were happy family times. For the first time, the family enjoyed the most extraordinary privacy imaginable. Nanavatty could clown to his heart's content, leaving the boys in splits, often threatening to kiss their mother, making them shriek and cover their eyes in horror. The boys, Veer especially, learned to do their share of household chores. Once, after a late night, entertaining dinner guests, Nanavatty and Suniti were awakened by Rushad and Veer serving them morning tea in bed. 'No comments, though, on the quality of the beverage!' remarked Suniti.

Every weekend brought travel opportunities, and thanks to their parents' British Indian Police and Indian Army expat friends, doors opened in homes across England, Scotland, Wales and Ireland. The weekend trips prepared them for a four-week camping holiday in Europe. They learned how to say 'ice cream' in French before they crossed the Channel and in Italian before they crossed the border into Italy, and so it went! Despite her busy schedule, Suniti found time to help at Rushad's school, which welcomed help from willing parents. Helping there was a tremendous learning experience for her as a teacher, adding value to the Open University correspondence course, 'Childhood, 5 to 10', in which she enrolled.

In September 1985, Nanavatty's term as the IALO ended after three years. It was to be his longest and, for the family, the most enjoyable posting ever. Lieutenant General Satish Nambiar, a Vir Chakra from the India–Pakistan War, 1971, and later a UN Force Commander in the Balkans was then the Military Attaché in London as a brigadier. He recollects receiving 'meticulously written reports in Rostum's calligraphic writing' and adds, 'Rostum was a professionally outstanding officer with great integrity; he is only one of the four officers I have graded as "Outstanding" in my entire career.'[18]

The legacy of the IALO was to continue for several years after Nanavatty's return. He would receive a letter every few years, presumably when a changeover was in the offing from Army Headquarters, asking for his views on whether the Indian Army should persist with the appointment. His reply was prompt and consistent. He firmly believed the appointment was worth continuing for its professional opportunities, even if it meant a compensatory reduction in the military staff at the Indian High Commission in London. Sadly, in 2012, in a casual conversation with his predecessor, O.P. Kaushik, in Dehradun, he was to learn that Army HQ had scrapped the appointment.

Back in India, Nanavatty acknowledged the value of his experience in the UK and its positive impact on his attempt to negotiate his next assignment in the just-established Directorate of Perspective Planning (PP) under the Additional Director General of Perspective Planning (ADG PP) in Army HQ. By then, Sundarji had become the army chief, and Army Headquarters was buzzing. The chief enquired, once again of Anand Sarup, then the Deputy Chief, whether an 'educated' Nanavatty would be happy to join Dr K. Subrahmanyam and his band of strategic thinkers at the Institute of Defence Studies and Analyses (IDSA). Like earlier, Nanavatty, not surprisingly wanting to remain in the mainstream, deflected the question.

The PP Directorate and other similar changes in the Indian Army's higher defence organization, e.g., Army Training Command (ARTRAC), were more akin to the organizational structures obtained in the US, and it took a while for them to settle down and find their feet. The crucial, established and all-powerful directorates, military operations and military training, felt 'threatened', and it took much time and effort to define the roles for the new verticals. The changes at the top of the PP Directorate—the rotation of three Additional Director Generals PP—in the two years he was with the directorate did not help. Nanavatty felt and still feels it was wrong to wring such farfetched organizational changes piecemeal.

The first task Nanavatty was assigned in the ADG PP was to write the draft 'Battlefield Milieu 2015', which would, once approved at the highest level, seemingly set the scene for perspective planning in the army. Next, he would spend a fair amount of his time as a member of different 'study groups', the first of which was a study on the 'Conduct of Officers' spurred by General Sundarji's famous letter addressed individually to every single officer serving in the army on the day he assumed the appointment of chief.[19] Sadly, the study would never see the light of day due to inherent contradictions within the system that baulked at introspection and tinkering with the legacy value systems that Sundarji sought to challenge.

Seeing Punjab's deteriorating internal security situation, Nanavatty wrote to Julio Ribeiro, his father's one-time Assistant IG and now the no-nonsense Director General of Police in Punjab. He offered to share all the material he had painstakingly collected and collated on counterterrorism operations in Northern Ireland. Ribeiro's response was electric. He had a senior intelligence officer of the Punjab Police report to Nanavatty in Delhi to collect the material. Several weeks later, Ribeiro returned the notes with a letter saying, 'You have gone to great lengths to retrieve the notes you made during your stay in London and pass them on to me. I am touched by your gesture and the interest you have shown in my fight against the terrorists in Punjab. I have gone through the material very carefully, and I intend to make use of the knowledge in our planning. I have made notes and copied out the relevant material (almost the entire material is relevant). I am also writing to my friend Sunith Rodrigues (Lieutenant General Rodrigues, the Vice Chief of Army Staff) about your effort.'[20]

On another occasion, the then ADG PP Major General (later General and army chief) B.C. (Bipin) Joshi walked into the office that Nanavatty shared with two of his colleagues and their clerk five minutes before closing time on a Friday evening. Slapping a file on his desk, he said, 'I want your comments on the financial aspects of this proposal when you come into work on Monday morning.' Nanavatty's mild protestations that his colleague, Colonel Vijay Jetley, the Director (Financial Planning), was the man for the job, were ignored. At home, over the weekend, Nanavatty went through the file. He was surprised by its contents and could not restrain himself. He was severely critical of the proposal and was compelled to offer his detailed comments on the entire proposal. Come Monday morning, he handed over the file to General Joshi.

A couple of hours later, he was sent for. The General was livid and said, 'Why have you commented on the entire paper when all I asked you to do was to give me your views on the financial aspects of the proposal?' Before Nanavatty could explain that he felt it necessary to offer his opinion because he felt that the Indian Army's conventional fighting potential would be degraded if the proposal went through, Joshi brusquely dismissed Nanavatty's critique and suggested that the latter stay away from this initiative and ended the discussion. He continued, 'You will have nothing to do with the file and its contents from now on—now get out of my office.'

Suniti recalls, 'That evening when Rostum came home he said in all seriousness, "We better start packing our bags."' Nanavatty believes that file was the first draft of the proposal to raise a counterinsurgency force called the 'Rashtriya Rifles'. Ironically, he would have the entire force under his command in the final stages of his career.[21] Joshi, however, was not someone to brood over professional dissent from his juniors. Nanavatty faced no blowback for his considered professional opinion and he enjoyed an excellent professional and personal relationship with Joshi till the latter's untimely demise in December 1994 while still the army chief.

Soon after the 'file incident' Joshi's interest was sparked when Nanavatty spoke of the need for a detailed study of Special Forces in the Indian context. His report as the IALO on the British Special Air Service (SAS) came up for discussion and was duly dissected. General Joshi was enthused and wasted no time in pursuing the matter. He proposed a study on reorganizing the existing PARA Cdo units into Special Forces. Sundarji, committed to the transformation of the Indian Army in more ways than one, approved Joshi's formal proposal and an Army Headquarters study on Special Forces was ordered. The Study Group comprised Brigadier N. (Nico) Bahri, GUARDS, Nanavatty and Colonel Sukhi Mann, the Director PARA Cdo Cell in the MO

Directorate. It had the authority to co-opt individuals as necessary and accordingly Colonels Dalvir Singh, 10 PARA Cdo, K.D. Pathak, 9 PARA Cdo, and H.S. Lidder also of 9 PARA Cdo, all three outstanding officers, were to be closely associated with the deliberations of the Study Group.

The study was completed in February 1987 and the first presentation was made to the COAS on 26 May 1987. In July, Sundarji gave the go-ahead to restructure the Indian Army's PARA Cdo units into Special Forces (SF). The two main features of the restructuring involved the establishment of a composite Headquarters SF to perform the dual role of a directorate and an operational HQ; and the conversion of the existing three PARA Cdo units into versatile SF units capable of a wide range of Special Ops.[22]

By June 1987, however, the balloon had gone up in Sri Lanka with fierce fighting raging in the Jaffna Peninsula between the Liberation Tigers of Tamil Eelam (LTTE) and the Sri Lanka Army (SLA). The LTTE sounded a call for the secession of the northern and eastern parts of Sri Lanka and the creation of an independent state of Tamil Eelam, for the region's Tamil majority population. Stepping in to play peacemaker and prevent a massacre of the Tamils by a rampaging SLA, the Indian PM Rajiv Gandhi persuaded President Jayewardene of Sri Lanka to sign the India–Sri Lanka Accord (ISLA) on 29 July 1987. The primary objective of the Accord was to enforce a ceasefire between the warring protagonists and ensure a withdrawal of Sri Lankan forces and the LTTE to pre-1987 positions. India's actions were also prompted by the need to safeguard its strategic interests in Sri Lanka,[23] and exclude any external meddling in its backwaters.

On the night of 29 July, Operation PAWAN commenced as India dispatched an Indian Peacekeeping Force (IPKF) comprising the Secunderabad-based 54 Infantry Division (54 Inf Div) to Sri Lanka to enforce the mandate of the Accord and disarm the LTTE. Unfortunately, a lack of trust, grave misunderstandings, and a series of untoward events rapidly turned peacekeeping into peace-enforcement operations, which, in the blink of an eye, led to open hostilities and fierce fighting between the LTTE and the IPKF. A complex politico-military campaign would keep the Indian Army at bay for nearly three years.[24]

By now, Nanavatty had already done close to two years 'flying a desk' in the ADG PP, and had put in a formal request to General Joshi to be assigned to a post in Operation PAWAN in Sri Lanka. Soon thereafter General Joshi himself was promoted and took over the key appointment of the Director General of Military Operations in Army HQ.

At that time 10 PARA Cdo, on the order of battle of Southern Command, was well and truly involved in the operations and had suffered casualties in the Jaffna University operation. The situation presented a unique opportunity for the PARA Cdo units to gain valuable experience in operations. Joshi decided that the other two, 1 and 9 PARA Cdo, should also join the fray.

The timing proved providential: all three PARA Cdo units were to to be committed to operations in Sri Lanka; there was a felt need for a HQ to oversee—coordinate, control and direct—the conduct of special operations; and, Nanavatty, a member of the Study Group on SF had volunteered for an assignment in Op PAWAN.

Joshi promptly had him posted to Sri Lanka as the Commander HQ PARA Cdo Task Force (Adhoc). Nanavatty packed his bags and, in less than twenty-four hours, was 'winging' his way to Jaffna as the commander designate with all three PARA Cdo battalions under his operational control.[25] The stage was set for a few eventful months in the 'Tiger's Lair'.

6

INTO SRI LANKA WITH THE PARA COMMANDOS

'Our Special Forces are arguably the best infantry units in the Indian Army. However, they lack government authorization and do not yet possess the covert and clandestine skills necessary for conducting Special Operations.'[1]

—NANAVATTY, AT A SEMINAR ON SPECIAL FORCES: NOVEMBER 2004

Megh Force, an ad hoc group of volunteers from various units of the Indian Army, was proposed and raised by Colonel Megh Singh, a maverick from the Brigade of the Guards, during the 1965 India–Pakistan War. Megh Singh was then serving on staff in Headquarters Western Command and was itching to inject some offensive content into the grim defensive battle that 10 Infantry Division was fighting in Chhamb. His proposal received the approval and full support of Lieutenant General Harbaksh Singh, GOC-in-C Western Command. Megh Force executed several small-scale operations behind enemy lines during the war with a measure of success. The exploits of the force gave birth to the idea of introducing commando-type units in the Indian Army.[2] The members of Megh Force provided the nucleus for the raising of the Indian Army's first two Parachute (Commando) (PARA Cdo) battalions in 1966–67: the 9th Battalion Parachute Regiment (Commando) (9 PARA Cdo) and the 10th Battalion Parachute Regiment (Commando) (10 PARA Cdo). These raisings were followed by converting the 1st Battalion Parachute Regiment, a traditional airborne unit, to the commando role as 1 PARA Cdo in 1978.

1 PARA Cdo, together with 10 GUARDS, led the storming of the Golden Temple in Operation BLUE STAR on 1 June 1984 in Amritsar to flush out Sikh extremists and terrorists led by the radical preacher Sant Jarnail Singh Bhindranwale.[3] The army suffered severe casualties during Operation BLUE STAR, during which the PARA Cdo were employed like regular infantry and had little impact. The PARA Cdo units were incorrectly used despite there being a cell in the military operations directorate expressly to advise and assist the Director General of Military Operations (DGMO). Following Operation BLUE STAR, the Government of India formed the National Security Guard (NSG), a force dedicated to counterterrorism and anti-hijack operations. It comprised the Special Action Group, which includes officers and men from the Indian Army, and the Special Protection Group, which comprises men from the Central Armed Police Forces.[4] The Ministry of Home Affairs has overall command and control over the NSG.

The narrative in this chapter primarily deals with the employment of the Indian Army's PARA Cdo units during the five months following the disastrous heliborne operation launched by the IPKF at Jaffna University on the night of 11 October 1987. The operation was based on intelligence reports and aimed at neutralizing the LTTE leadership. It was a bold attempt that involved Mi-8 helicopters landing PARA Cdos of 10 PARA Cdo and troops of the 13th Battalion Sikh Light Infantry (13 SIKH LI) in the heart of Jaffna University. The operation was doomed from the start due to several reasons ranging from hasty planning, lack of synergy between stakeholders and the LTTE being partially prepared for the assault after they intercepted the IPKF's radio transmissions.[5]

Arriving in Jaffna in October 1987 with 'Sukhi' Mann from the Military Operations (MO) Directorate as a Liaison Officer, Nanavatty was struck by the peacetime environment prevailing in HQ 54 Inf Div. He was appalled at the manpower, weapons and equipment-related deficiencies in the units, their lack of preparedness and training, as well as the surreal preoccupation with peacetime procedures in the divisional headquarters such as sit-down lunches and concern over matters frivolous. Mellowing his criticism, Nanavatty adds, 'To be fair, all this underwent a rapid change after Major General (later Lieutenant General) S.C. Sardeshpande took over the reins of the division in January 1988. I am convinced the story would have been different if he had initially led the division into Sri Lanka. The importance of selecting the right man for the job rang true during the initial days of Operation PAWAN, and I learned much by observing what was happening around me in the politico-military domain.'[6]

The print and electronic media gave the unrest in Sri Lanka and the subsequent induction of the IPKF comprehensive coverage. But it all seemed relatively remote for Suniti until the day that Rostum came home to say that he was leaving, very shortly, for that distant shore. Despite being aware of the dangers, Suniti had no choice but to take the news calmly; she did not want to alarm Rushad and Veer. Before they knew it, Rostum was gone. She went about her work as an English teacher at the Junior Modern School in Delhi, with both boys studying in the same school. Seated in the school van, Suniti prayed daily for her husband's safety to and from work. The only time she became tearful was in the principal's office when she first informed her of Rostum's overseas assignment.

A few weeks later, the family had a visit from Colonel Sukhi Mann, who had just returned from Sri Lanka. He came to bring them news of Rostum. However, he gave them a highly sanitized account and ended by telling them that, as far as he was concerned he had never met anyone who was so 'Olive Green', or OG, as they term it in the army for someone who is a stickler. He was convinced that if Rostum had removed his socks, his toenails would also be OG!

When Nanavatty arrived in Palaly, the airfield-cum-divisional HQ of 54 Inf Div, 1 and 10 PARA Cdo and a team of 9 PARA Cdo were located within the airfield's perimeter. A few days later, the rest of 9 PARA Cdo had also arrived. Subsequently, with the arrival of 36 Inf Div at Trincomalee on the east coast of Sri Lanka in November 1987, HQ IPKF decided to detach 1 PARA Cdo and place it under the command of the newly inducted division. Nanavatty was thus left with 9 and 10 PARA Cdo as part of his Task Force (TF). Nanavatty lived with the officers of 10 PARA Cdo as a member of their Officers Mess. He recollects that the conversation in the Mess seldom strayed from the ongoing operations, questioning India's decision to intervene in Sri Lanka and criticizing the conduct of operations. Nanavatty sought to set this right immediately. With the permission of the commanding officers, he spoke to the officers of all three units, essentially making three points. He emphasized, 'First, it was not for us to question the decision to intervene in Sri Lanka. Second, we were there to do a job; and third, being the best infantry combat units in the army, it was up to us to show the way in planning, preparing for and conducting our operations.'[7]

Nanavatty spent his first few days in the theatre, familiarizing himself with the area and the conduct of conventional operations by the formations and units of the division thus far. The two things that struck him were the woeful lack of intelligence about the adversary and the haphazard use of commando sub-units to 'pull the fat from the fire' in nasty situations. He concluded that the commandos were being asked for and used because 'they were there'. This was understandable considering the infantry were stretched, and reserves were non-existent, but it had to stop. He realized that his task would be to provide direction and infuse professionalism in the conduct of operations by the PARA Cdo units. To do so, he needed to address the fundamental issues of command and control, tasking, planning and remedial training 'on the job'.

With support from his two units, Nanavatty set up a skeleton HQ PARA Cdo Task Force (TF) with two staff officers, one from each battalion, a clerk and a signals detachment, all lodged in a small shelter within shouting distance of HQ 54 Inf Div. Nanavatty's HQ in Palaly was 'lean'. Colonel Awadhesh Kumar from 9 PARA Cdo, then a Captain, has fond memories of his stint as Staff Officer to Nanavatty. Awadhesh recollects that Nanavatty often introduced him to senior commanders who visited the TF as 'my Chief of Staff'. One of Awadhesh's principal responsibilities was to liaise with the hierarchy and protocol-conscious HQ 54 Inf Div staff, who understood little about SF operations and were 'nonplussed', even suspicious, of Nanavatty's presence in their midst!

In the operations room, paperwork was minimal. Information and intelligence were collated meticulously, directly transferred onto maps and duly annotated. Orders and instructions were handwritten in the Commander's notebook—no files, reports or returns! Awadhesh recalls that eighteen-hour days were standard, and it was not uncommon for Nanavatty to share the 'Duty Officer' roster with his staff officers. After an early supper, he would often walk into the operations room, dismiss the signal operator and the officer on duty, roll out his groundsheet and settle down for the night with the radio set for company. Awadhesh soon had an excellent working relationship with Nanavatty and won his implicit trust,[8] often acting as his sounding board.

Sceptical of Nanavatty's role initially, the commando units soon realized the value he added to their operations with his meticulous process and systems-driven approach. He accompanied them on a few missions to see for himself their tactics, techniques and procedures (TTP) and re-familiarized himself with all the weapons used by the commandos on a makeshift firing range with the help of the unit NCOs. This conveyed to all that he was serious about his role and fully invested in their operations. Superbly fit and demonstrating enviable marksmanship skills, it did not take long for Nanavatty to gain their acceptance. Indeed, there was a sense of déjà vu in the whole situation, considering that Nanavatty had wanted to volunteer for the PARA Cdo early in his career.

He discussed the employment and tasking of the PARA Cdo units with Headquarters IPKF in Chennai and 54 Inf Div and insisted that all demands for the support of PARA Cdo sub-units should be for specific tasks and be routed through the TF. He quickly realized that classical Special Operations tasks in a counterinsurgency situation—covert operations, pseudo gang operations, and rival gang operations—were beyond their current capabilities. Therefore, there was an obvious need to cut one's coat according to the cloth available.

To begin with, he assigned clearly defined areas of operation to 9 and 10 PARA Cdo. He tasked the units with intense reconnaissance, surveillance and intelligence collection as a precursor to carrying out small-scale offensive operations. In addition, in conjunction with the Indian Marine Special Forces (IMSF)—now called MARCOS—the para commandos were employed to dominate the inland waterways and off-shore islands.[9] Soon, small successes started coming their way. In one 'search and find' operation, a patrol recovered eleven weapons, and in a series of 'snatch operations', several important operatives, including the LTTE's financial brain, were captured. There were disappointments, too. An elaborate dragnet to snare the new LTTE commander of the Jaffna Region amounted to nothing owing to an accidental leak about the ongoing operations during a press briefing in HQ 54 Inf Div.

Colonel (later Major General) Dalvir Singh, who had taken command of 10 PARA Cdo just before the IPKF deployed in Sri Lanka, had just completed a tour of duty with the Special Action Group (SAG) of the National Security Guard (NSG). He says he was not surprised when Nanavatty followed him to Jaffna. Now in his late seventies and still actively involved with training policemen of the Rajasthan Police, Dalvir acknowledges the role that Nanavatty played in transforming them from a 'group of daredevils into professional commandos'. In an email exchange with the author, he wrote that he soon realized that Nanavatty 'wanted us to plan and execute our missions professionally. He felt a little method combined with our "bring it on" approach would benefit us. For example, he insisted that all planning, even for the smallest of operations, commenced with a review of the available intelligence. Detailed mission briefings and rehearsals followed intelligence briefings. Every mission was followed up with a "debrief" to identify shortcomings and ensure corrective action. His insistence on training during operations did not go well with some of my officers, who were confident of their skill sets. I was, however, convinced his advice had the wisdom of an experienced soldier, and irrespective of the reaction of my officers, I insisted on following through with all the procedures throughout my command of the unit in Sri Lanka.'[10]

Colonel (later Lieutenant General) Tej Pathak, the Commanding Officer of 9 PARA Cdo, known affectionately as the Phantom, was a taciturn soldier who sized up Nanavatty carefully before they became friends. He, too, acknowledges that Nanavatty's 'insistence on adopting the right processes and procedures was a game-changer in the highly complex and uncertain operational environment that prevailed in Sri Lanka'. He maintains that surveillance techniques, intelligence collection, detailed briefings and vigorous follow-up operations were areas that the commandos refined on Nanavatty's watch. Pathak observed that 'Nanavatty was a great "diarist", too, and would note down every action, good or bad.' He remembered him on one occasion, 'moving just behind the scouts in a search and destroy operation we conducted on Delft Island, carefully noting their use of the ground. His observations were not a scribble but notes rewritten deliberately in a print-like hand at the first opportunity.'[11]

A few weeks after Nanavatty had established his Task Force, he received a call from Lieutenant General Bipin Joshi, the DGMO. His message was terse: 'Get Prabhakaran.' Nanavatty responded, 'Intelligence is the key and very little is forthcoming.' Subsequently, during a visit to 54 Inf Div by Lieutenant General Depinder Singh, the GOC-in-C of the Pune-based Southern Command and the Overall Force Commander of the IPKF, Nanavatty mentioned the need to exploit the rival Tamil Groups such as the Eelam People's Revolutionary Liberation Front (EPRLF), People's Liberation Organization of Tamil Eelam (PLOTE) and a few others to acquire intelligence of the LTTE. Summoned to the Headquarters IPKF in Chennai a few weeks later to a closed-door meeting with representatives of India's external intelligence agency, the Research and Analysis Wing (R&AW), Nanavatty was briefed in the presence of Lieutenant General S.F. Rodrigues, the Vice Chief of Army Staff, on an intelligence operation involving operatives of a rival Tamil group.[12]

It was around Christmas 1987 that Major John De Britto, a Tamil-speaking commando from 9 PARA Cdo, heard of his brother's demise. He had barely returned to the unit from a successful 'snatch operation' that resulted in the capture of 'Ranjit', the bodyguard of the LTTE ideologue Anton Balasingham, when he had to board a flight at Palaly airfield to rush to Chennai to attend his brother's funeral. Before heading to Chennai, Britto's CO, Colonel Tej Pathak, told him that he was off the battalion beat and that he had to report to Nanavtty, who was in Chennai, planning a covert operation with R&AW codenamed Operation CAPRICORN. The day after the funeral, at five in the morning, Britto met with Nanavatty at the Area HQ in Chennai and headed for a R&AW safe house where Nanavatty asked him to interview and pick five operatives from a group of anti-LTTE insurgents who would join Brito's intelligence gathering team in CAPRICORN. In the meantime, Nanavatty had also alerted Tej Pathak to put together a strike force from 9 PARA called Tiger Troop, which would lean on the intelligence provided by Britto's team; Captain Anil Nayyar would lead this force.

Britto recalls, 'I spent a whole day with the anti-LTTE operatives and chose five of them with "Robert" as the leader. Robert was smart and asked me what he could call me. I told him to call me "Michael". R&AW got us into CRPF uniforms, and our motley group with Nanavatty boarded the same IAF courier flight from Chennai and landed at Palaly.' It was New Year 1988, and even months after the Indian Army had declared a premature victory over the LTTE in the Jaffna Peninsula, Prabhakaran and his cadres were nowhere to be seen.

'We had no clue as to what was happening. I programmed these guys to scout around for information about the LTTE, its leadership and organization, and where they were regrouping. Within two weeks, we had a fair idea that the LTTE was not on the run and was regrouping and reorganizing—where, we did not know. Nor did we know who the leaders were apart from Prabhakaran,' recalls Britto.[13] He reported to Nanavatty daily. 'We got along well, and he trusted me. The most striking recollection of these interactions was that we would sit in front of a huge map board as he visualized things for hours. He had no needs and did not like people hanging around, and it was all business or, at best, a few words of dry and cryptic humour that we found hard to understand.' Operation CAPRICORN has been under wraps till now, and Britto reckoned that 'if there was an occasion to unwrap it, there was no better place than in a biography of the soldier who conceived it and then executed it with great finesse'.

After several minor apprehensions and seizures, including a successful ambush, CAPRICORN's first significant success was a spectacular raid on the fishing village of Myliddy, some two kilometres to the east of the port of Kankesenturai (KKS) and due north of Palaly airfield by a few kilometres. Following a steady stream of information from Robert and his men that some members of the leadership and their accompanying LTTE cadres were holed up in Myliddy, Britto planned a conventional night operation that had to be aborted because the village dogs started barking when the team approached the village. The following day, Brito suggested to Nanavatty that an approach from the sea in inflatable Gemini Boats would be a better option. Agreeing to the plan immediately, Nanavatty requisitioned two Gemini Boats from the Indian Navy's IMSF, which were transported from KKS by road to a secure location on the coast, where an Indian Army Mechanized Infantry Battalion was operating. Launching the operation the next night, the two boats with Britto's Intelligence Team and Nayyar's Strike Troop silently approached Myliddy from the high seas without alerting the village dogs.

The plan was to walk directly to the door of the house harbouring the LTTE, knock on the door, identify the targets with the help of Robert and his team, quickly gag them, tie them up and spirit them in the dead of night to a planned location where another team was waiting with vehicles. The plan worked like clockwork, and within minutes, eleven LTTE operatives were apprehended from ten safe houses and taken to Palaly in a copybook 'snatch Operation'[14] even as Britto and his team exited Myliddy with the IMSF team in the Geminis. He had been hoping to catch a few hours of sleep, but Britto's buddy woke him up, saying that one of the captured LTTE cadres wanted to talk to him immediately.

Seventeen-year-old Jyothi was the lynchpin of the LTTE's communications network and argued with Britto for three hours that the IPKF should be assisting the LTTE and not fighting it. Using the Tamil card and spilling the beans that he was Prabhakaran's radio operator, he urged Britto to consider helping them out, saying, 'Why are you fighting us? You are our friends and supposed to help us out.' Britto played along and gradually learned about the entire global structure and organization of the LTTE in Chennai, Sri Lanka, Singapore and Europe. Quickly writing a three-page report on the operation, he rushed it to Nanavatty, who was 'thrilled' and directed Britto not to divulge the information to anyone and to continue to work on Jyothi.

Jyothi continued to operate on the radio waves as if all was normal for the next three days and set up a meeting between Brito and several members of the LTTE leadership at a place called 'Akka's House (Akka in Tamil is sister)'. Three top LTTE leaders confirmed their attendance at the meeting: Mahattya, the LTTE's deputy leader and its leading military commander; Susai, the number three in the hierarchy; and Anton Balasingham, the ideologue. Nayyar's Strike Troop was in position for the stakeout, but the 'snatch' never took place as, half an hour before the meeting, 54 Inf Div inadvertently referred to the ongoing operation in a hastily put-out Press Release about the capture of Jyothi!

'CAPRICORN had Nanavatty's stamp all over it, and had he stayed with us longer, we would have achieved greater success in intelligence-driven operations,' Britto asserted. Nanavatty was modest in his assessment. 'The significant lessons from CAPRICORN indicated the need for patience and perseverance in intelligence operations.'[15]

Nanavatty was all praise for 9 PARA Cdo establishing effective links with the leadership in the rival Tamil groups, for methodically collecting and collating intelligence, and for executing intelligence-driven operations. CAPRICORN had a long gestation period, but it was worth the wait and after the first 'textbook' ambush by Captain K.A. Mohan from 9 PARA Cdo in the Vanni region, there was no looking back. Pathak is quick to acknowledge that it was because of Nanavatty's efforts that Britto and Nayyar set up an intelligence network in Mullaitivu District that would later prove to be of immense help when 9 PARA Cdo moved south in support of 4 Inf Div.[16]

Nanavatty was determined that Major Britto receive due recognition for his outstanding contribution to Op CAPRICORN. Accordingly, he forwarded a citation to the HQ IPKF recommending him for the award of a Yudh Seva Medal (YSM), a military decoration for distinguished service in war. Suspecting that the HQ IPKF and the Indian Army's Southern Command had paid scant attention to the brief citation, Nanavatty felt compelled to write to Lieutenant General S.F. Rodrigues, the Vice Chief of Army Staff, a whole year after leaving Sri Lanka, requesting the Vice Chief to consider the matter. He wrote, 'I suspect his citation was rejected at Southern Command. I am not surprised. They did not know what CAPRICORN was all about. If you recall, it was between you, the GOC IPKF, a gentleman of a civilian government agency and me at that stage. I could not divulge the operation's details in a citation at that time and assumed that HQ IPKF would understand. I recognize that every individual action cannot be rewarded for services rendered, but in his case, my conscience will not allow me to let matters rest.'[17]

By November 1987, the semi-conventional operations and battles in the Jaffna Peninsula were over. The LTTE may have been bested, but the outfit was not finished. They had vanished into thin air. 54 Inf Div believed they had dealt the adversary a severe blow and thought that the area down to Elephant Pass, except possibly for the area of Vaddamarachchi, a Prabhakaran stronghold, was rid of the adversary and relatively secure. The near-simultaneous arrival of 4 Inf Div in Vavuniya and its deployment south of Killinochi was reassuring and may have dissuaded the division from pursuing their adversary across the lagoons.

Nanavatty and his COs thought otherwise. His armed aerial reconnaissance sorties in a 'Ranjeet'—a Cheetah (Alouette II) utility helicopter locally modified to mount twin 7.62 mm medium machine guns—revealed long lines of people and every conceivable form of transport moving south out of the Jaffna Peninsula. There were two-wheelers, cars, buses, lorries and the ubiquitous tractor trolleys, moving cross country along rough tracks and an assortment of inland watercraft to negotiate the lagoons and avoid Elephant Pass. That meant only one thing: the LTTE cadres, cleverly 'secreted' amidst the hordes of unarmed Tamil refugees, were exfiltrating south to concentrate and regroup in their jungle base areas in the Vanni (the area broadly comprising the districts of Mannar, Kilinochchi, Mullaitivu and Vavuniya) with the hope, indeed, of returning to their heartland one day.

Major Nayyar, of 9 PARA Cdo in Sri Lanka, wrote of Nanavatty's prescient operational assessment in an article in the March 1994 issue of the *Counter Insurgency and Jungle Warfare Journal*: 'After the clearance of Jaffna Town by the IPKF, there was a general air of euphoria as many felt that the "Tigers" had been crushed, but Colonel Nanavatty felt otherwise. He appreciated that the Tigers had retreated to the Vanni to regroup and return to fight another day. Little was known about the LTTE leadership at that juncture, and intelligence was dark. Nanavatty also felt that the IPKF would get involved in a long-drawn battle with the Tigers.'[18]

Whilst HQs IPKF and 54 Inf Div were fixated on clearing Vaddamarachchi, deemed the last bastion of the LTTE on the Jaffna Peninsula, Nanavatty was convinced of the need to pick up the trail of the LTTE south of Elephant Pass as soon as possible and commenced planning an operation called Operation NYLON. Not surprisingly, the views of the formation headquarters prevailed, and a weeklong brigade-sized 'search and destroy' operation, which included all of 10 PARA Cdo, was launched in the Vaddamarachchi area. It resulted in very little of consequence and brought home the realization that the 'Tigers' had disengaged in a masterly fashion. The commandos cheekily deemed it Operation WILD GOOSE CHASE. It delayed the launching of Op NYLON.

Though Nanavatty mentions that Op NYLON, the first major operation conducted by the IPKF south of the Elephant Pass and outside of the Jaffna Peninsula, was planned with the concurrence of HQ 54 Inf Div, Awadhesh remembers otherwise, maintaining that the operation was planned and executed by the PARA Cdo Task Force alone.[19]

The operation aimed to 'gain and maintain contact with the LTTE and disrupt their attempts at regrouping in the Vanni areas to the South and East of Killinochi'. The operation was planned over ten days and, if the opportunity presented itself, also aimed to trap the LTTE cadres and box them in Kilinochchi and several hamlets such as Chorikenkulam, Parantan and Kandavalai. The strategy was to surround them with a sizeable composite force and seal all escape routes. It involved infiltration on foot; insertion by helicopters into unmarked dropping/landing zones; the establishment of temporary commando bases in the jungle; surveillance of civil habitation from where the LTTE could draw their sustenance; collection of intelligence of the terrain and routes taken by LTTE cadres; destruction of targets of opportunity; and domination of the assigned areas of responsibility. Interestingly, 10 PARA Cdo established contact with the LTTE on the first day of the operation itself. Appendix B features handwritten guidelines for the conduct of Op NYLON.

During the operation, Nanavatty established his command post at a patrol base of 5 MARATHA LI, protecting a communications tower on the Killinochi–Vavuniya axis. He maintained contact and shared information and situation reports with his units on a need-to-know basis. Weather permitting, he also used a RANJEET helicopter for 'armed recce' and airborne command and control sorties. Op NYLON was the first operation of its kind in the impenetrable jungles of the Vanni and experienced several small successes and many 'misses'. Perhaps, the best thing that happened with the PARA Cdo units was the realization to quote Colonel Freddie Spencer Chapman that the 'jungle is neutral'—it is on the side of the soldier who will make the best use of it.[20]

According to Tej Pathak, Op NYLON 'was quite an experience, and we all gained much from it'. His words would ring true in the bitter fighting in the Mullaitivu area where 9 PARA Cdo, under the command of Colonel Hardev Singh 'Hardy' Lidder, Tej Pathak's successor, was to distinguish itself.

Op NYLON was also the end of the road for Nanavatty in Op PAWAN. In his Sri Lanka diary, he mentions that 'Sukhi Mann appeared, unannounced, at my location, and said he was there to relieve me! I was disappointed. There was so much more to be done, and we were just about hitting our straps. However, I was glad it was Sukhi, my compatriot in the SF Study. No one ever explained why the changeover happened, but I suspect it was a matter of the cap badge—Sukhi was a paratrooper and a commando to boot, and I, a Gorkha!'

In Nanavatty's mind, his recall was as unfair as it was untimely. He had established a good working relationship with General Sardeshpande, the GOC 54 Inf Div, and had liaised with Major General J.N. Goel, GOC 4 Inf Div and his staff as they settled in at Vavuniya. Ostensibly, he was recalled barely four months into his assignment to pursue the implementation of the recommendations of the SF Study. Dalvir, too, was surprised at the move. He had all the respect for Mann, a fellow commando, but opined, 'Had Nanavatty stayed with us during the entire duration of the IPKF operations, the performance of the PARA commando units would have been significantly better.'[21] General Sardeshpande was to write to Nanavatty a whole year later when the latter was commanding the Siachen Brigade: 'I missed you so often! May god bless you in your tough new assignment.'[22]

Nanavatty's departure from Palaly was unceremonious. He regretted that he was leaving without even half-finishing the job he had been sent to do. Nevertheless, he considered himself privileged to have served in operations alongside two of the finest units in the Indian Army. He summed them up thus: '9 PARA Cdo was a skilled, highly trained unit possessing excellent battlefield discipline, battle drills and a quiet air of confidence in its abilities.10 PARA Cdo were tough, bold, resolute and aggressive—ever willing to do battle. Together, they truly set the pace for Infantry operations in Op PAWAN in Sri Lanka.'

And what did the commando say of the 'intruder' in their midst? The remarks of Lieutenant General S.S. Tinaikar, then a young lieutenant in 10 PARA Cdo, duly paraphrased by the author, perhaps sums it up best: 'He was a thoroughbred Gorkha: methodical, systematic and proper, insisting on putting military teaching into practice depending on each situation—the hallmark of a professional soldier. He enjoyed soldiering, was committed to the task and drew the best out of his force of two battalions. He left his mark on them. It was a brief but memorable association.'[23]

Nanavatty reckons that his best recognition for his efforts in Sri Lanka was from his colleague and friend Brigadier R.R. Palsokar, the commander of 7 Infantry Brigade in Mullaitivu operating in the heart of 'Tiger' country. In his book, *Ours Not to Reason Why: With the IPKF in Sri Lanka*, Palsokar wrote, 'I am convinced that it was the sound foundation laid by Rostum Nanavatty for special operations in Sri Lanka which were then built upon and resulted in the excellent operational performance of all three battalions. ... Rostum was clear that the para commandos should set operational standards which the infantry should then graduate to and in turn should set even higher standards.'[24]

Three months later, Rostum was back in Delhi. Suniti and the boys were at the airport to receive him as he returned on a commercial flight. His elder son, Rushad, vividly remembers his father's return from Sri Lanka: 'Accustomed to always seeing him impeccably dressed and groomed, we were struck by his appearance. He was gaunt, sunburned and dirty and had lost much weight. The disappointment at an early recall from a combat zone was evident even though he spoke little about his experiences in Sri Lanka. He had left for Jaffna with a single Berghaus rucksack and returned likewise—I still have that rucksack. It was nice having our father back for a while, and I enjoyed the little time we spent together on the terrace of our flat in Arjun Vihar knocking the football around and having him correct my forward defensive stroke.' Veer, Rostum's younger son, was seven years old, and recollects that he missed his father terribly, as all military kids do when their fathers head into the field.

The pangs of separation for Suniti and the boys, albeit for only three months, were accentuated by the fact that the family had spent the preceding three years together in the United Kingdom in peaceful surroundings. At Warminster, Rostum shared the housework with Suniti, bathed the boys, read stories to them, and tucked them into bed. Strict, insisting on decorum and propriety, witty with a dry sense of humour when relaxed, wise in that he could immediately detect if someone in the family was unhappy, quick of temper but never abusive—these were some parenting traits that Veer distinctly remembers. 'Is there something bothering you? If you do not want to share it with me, tell your mother,' is what Rostum used to tell the boys. On her part, whenever the boys pushed Suniti to the limits of her patience, she only had to say, 'If you do not stop this, I am going to tell your father.'

Back at work in Army HQ, Nanavatty was posted as the Director Cdo Cell located on the musty mezzanine floor in the congested space housing the military operations directorate—he and Sukhi Mann had switched chairs. In the next six months, he would share that space with three colleagues from 9 PARA Cdo: Colonel (later Lieutenant General) Hardev Lidder, Colonel K.C. Padha and Colonel K.D. Pathak, all in turn and one at a time, in pursuit of the task of implementing the recommendations of the SF Study. The distinguished scholar-soldier Brigadier (Later Lieutenant General) V.R. Raghavan would be at work quietly next door. He would interject and bring his younger colleagues in line when things got rowdy in the Cdo Cell. Little did Nanavatty know that the latter would be his GOC a few months later.

But first things had to come first. Even though no one had called for an 'After Action Report', Nanavatty felt obliged to render one and set to the task immediately. He was keen that the GOC IPKF, the Colonel of the Parachute Regiment and the three PARA Cdo units draw valuable lessons from this experience. Offering a candid critique, Nanavatty indicated that the units were proficient at executing tactical commando operations but were far from being versatile SF capable of Spl Ops. He argued that it would be useless to lament this lack of capability unless it emerged within the army leadership to set out operational requirements clearly and then painstakingly develop the necessary operational capabilities. Nanavatty acknowledged the units' spirit and motivation and their ability to adapt rapidly to the operational environment in Op PAWAN.

Of the important suggestions made by Nanavatty in a report submitted to Lieutenant General Kalkat, the GOC, IPKF and several other agencies, including the DGMO at Army HQ, several would be incorporated by the PARA Cdo units in the months that went by and to good effect. In his report, he concentrated on six themes: 'Command and Control', 'Grouping and Allotment', 'Liaison and Advice', 'Capabilities', 'Tasking and Employment' and 'Attitudes'.

On 'Capabilities', he assessed the three units as capable of carrying out tactical commando operations in their prescribed areas of operation. However, he reckoned they were far from being the versatile SF they were imagined to be. It is this gap between idea and reality that he felt commanders needed to remind themselves while tasking and employing these units constantly. Commending the teams' adaptability, spirit and motivation levels, he identified their controlled aggression, high endurance standards, mental and physical robustness and resilience as critical positives. Assessing the units as highly proficient in adapting to rapid mobility by air, sea and cross-country by day and night, among the areas that needed improvement were battlefield discipline, combat techniques and battle drills at the sub-unit level, and junior leadership at the JCO/NCO level. While officer leadership was robust and typically of the 'follow me' kind, there was a tendency to over-supervise, which curbed the initiative of the junior leaders.

On 'Tasking', Nanavatty highlighted the aspirational (Priority 1) and the doable (Priority II). Priority 1 tasks comprised covert operations involving civilianized dress, vehicles and captured weapons; direction and control of rival group operations; and Pseudo Gang

Operations. Pseudo Gang operations were first experimented with by the Rhodesian Army against anti-apartheid militant groups in South Africa and involved government forces and guerrilla defectors portraying themselves as insurgent units.[25] Though some attempts were made to head in that direction, the absence of clear direction and policy, inadequate intelligence support and the lack of adequate training, skills and experience meant that the PARA Cdo units, in consultation with HQ OFC IPKF and intermediate formation headquarters (divisions and brigades) concentrated on Priority II tasks—'Snatch Operations', Deep Surveillance, Ambush and Strike Operations.

On 'Attitudes', Nanavatty's observations were clinical and prescient. He wrote, 'All officers almost without exception led from the front. Carried too far, it could prove counterproductive and lead to over-supervision and curb the initiative of subordinates.' Identifying a propensity towards a 'gung-ho' and cavalier approach and cowboy attitudes, which Dalvir corroborates in his email to the author, Nanavatty emphasized the need to imbibe correct professional values and view weapons, equipment, and advanced skills in their proper perspective.

A fair and concise summary of the early days of PARA Cdo operations in Sri Lanka was embedded in the report as Nanavatty wrote: 'Though the results achieved during the period from 19 November 1987 to 3 February 1988 were by no means spectacular, their operations served in more ways than one to set operational trends. This is as it should be and is only to be encouraged with specialized units graduating to the more difficult tasks as conventional infantry units take over. More importantly, the units (PARA Cdo units) themselves were continuously honing their skills and visibly gaining in confidence and expertise.'[26]

In a letter and a copy of his report on PARA Cdo operations in Sri Lanka, he wrote to Lieutenant General V.K. 'Tubby' Nayyar, GOC-in-C Western Command and Colonel of the Parachute Regiment, Nanavatty was forthright in saying that 'the decision to switch commanders unless warranted on the grounds of incompetence was wrong. Apart from continuity in operations, the human aspects of understanding, mutual trust and confidence in command relationships in combat are all important and must not be overlooked.'[27] Tubby Nayyar was magnanimous in his response on 11 April 1988, complimenting Nanavatty: 'It is a well conceived and balanced report, and I was happy to note your frank and candid approach.'

Scathing in his assessment of how the infantryman was equipped during the early days of the IPKF's deployment, Nanavatty wrote to Lieutenant General A.S. Kalkat, the Deputy Overall Force Commander, IPKF on his return from Jaffna: 'It was galling to see the Sri Lanka Army and, in some areas, even the LTTE better equipped than our infantrymen. To the protagonists of the "high tech" approach, it must be said that at least they should pay equal attention to the vital issues of personal weapons, combat clothing, equipment, and rations. Our infantry soldier deserves better.'[28]

With his 'After Action Report' out of the way, Nanavatty, with the help of his PARA Cdo colleagues, got to grips with the detailed implementation plan, a tedious and time-consuming exercise. However, with the appointment of General V.N. Sharma as the COAS in June 1988, the SF study came under fresh scrutiny. Nanavatty remembers making at least two presentations on the SF Study to the Chief, and after each presentation, he could not help but feel that they were going nowhere.

In a demi-official Letter (DO) to Bipin Joshi, the Director General of Military Operations, Nanavatty suggested closure to his association with the SF. He wrote, 'There is a prevailing impression that you are committed to creating a brigadier's appointment for the SF to absorb me in the post, on promotion. Even if you feel the functional need to upgrade and expand the Cdo Cell, I am convinced it should remain the preserve of PARA Cdo officers. Quite obviously, we are not ready for the change. Perhaps a more deliberate approach allowing for gradual evolution is desirable. As we have seen, the units themselves need to consolidate, concentrating first on theatre-level tactical tasks and only then on strategic military Spl Ops in war and peace.'[29]

Notwithstanding the enthusiastic start, the project began to stutter long before coming to a dead end. In hindsight, Nanavatty feels that de-affiliating the SF from the Parachute Regiment based on the

Government of India letter of August 1987 without meaningful internal discussions, particularly involving the Parachute Regiment, contributed in good measure to the subsequent abandonment of the proposal.[30] Nanavatty remains firm in his belief that 'Essentially, SF are forces that are capable of Spl Ops. Spl Ops demand special knowledge and skills. They are generally small in scale but can have an impact at the operational and strategic levels. They may be overt, covert or clandestine.' In the IA, the evolution of SF over the decades continues to be a slow and painful process—one step forward and two steps back. The lid was finally put on the matter in 2023 when a decision was taken to designate all battalions of the Parachute Regiment as Special Forces (Airborne), subtly differentiating them from PARA SF, a move that Nanavatty argues does not do justice to the concept of SF.

Nanavatty reckons that the brilliant General Sundarji was and ever remained an ardent proponent of the 'big battle'. Consequently, he paid little attention to counterinsurgency and the 'vicious and dirty fighting' that took place during Operation BLUE STAR and PAWAN. The LTTE, according to Nanavatty, was the most efficient guerrilla outfit the Indian Army has ever encountered. They were masters of guerrilla warfare tactics and the use of Improvised Explosive Devices. They were technologically savvy, disciplined, committed and ruthless. Underestimating the LTTE and committing the army to operations in Sri Lanka in haste, without adequate preparation, was a serious politico-military error of judgment. Reflecting in a letter on the eve of Nanavatty's retirement from the Indian Army in 2003, Colonel S.S. Tinaikar (later Lieutenant General), then CO of 10 PARA Cdo and a lieutenant in 1987–88 with the same unit in Sri Lanka, highlighted Nanavatty's leadership role in making the Para Cdo units more combat-effective. In the letter to Nanavatty, Tinaikar wrote, 'Young, inexperienced and given to a cavalier approach to soldiery (soldiering), your professionalism was electrifying. That first impression is undying, indelible and has remained a perfect guide, a lodestar to follow. Lucky are those who served and grew with you in service.'[31]

In August 1988, Nanavatty was posted on promotion to the rank of Brigadier, at his request, to command 102 Infantry Brigade in Operation MEGHDOOT in the Siachen, ending his two-year-long association with the SF. He realized that he would always be an 'outsider' within the SF community notwithstanding his expertise and that it was time to explore fresh challenges. He nevertheless continued to engage with the subject of Special Forces and Special Operations in one way or another until he retired and even after. But for now, the narrative ascends towards the icy heights of the Saltoro Range, an off-shoot of the Great Karakoram Range that looks down on the Siachen Glacier.

7

ON THE SALTORO RANGE

'Here, great courage and fortitude is the norm'

—An often-used phrase coined by Nanavatty

Nanavatty received official intimation of his approval for promotion to the rank of brigadier in March 1987. In all these years, missing out on the fighting in the 1965 and 1971 wars had continued to gnaw at his gut. He resolved to do everything in his power not to let such a thing happen again. In April, he wrote to the Military Secretary through proper channels requesting 'if found qualified and fit in all respects' to command 102 Infantry Brigade in Operation MEGHDOOT in Siachen in Ladakh. Suniti never really forgave him for doing so without informing her! Delighted that they had a volunteer, Military Secretary's Branch wasted no time sending him to HQ 102 Infantry Brigade at Partapur on 1 September 1988 as the commander designate with a month to familiarize with his new assignment.[1]

The Siachen Glacier lies between the Saltoro Range to its west and the Eastern Karakoram Range to its east and is separated from the Shaksgam Valley to its north by the Great Karakoram Range. Shaksgam, a high-altitude valley in Jammu and Kashmir which experiences very little precipitation, was ceded to China by Pakistan in 1963. Indra Col and Turkestan La, acting as its 'northern sentinels' lie in relative proximity to each other on the Great Karakoram Range at the very head of the Siachen Glacier.

The Saltoro Range, with the towering Saltoro Kangri rising to over 25,000 feet, is an off shoot of the Great Karakoram Range starting from the area of Sia Kangri. It dominates the western flank of the Siachen Glacier. Sia La, Bilafond La and Gyong La are the only three recognized passes on the Saltoro Range. It constitutes the watershed between the Saltoro River basin to the west and the Nubra River basin to the east.

From the area of Indra Col and Turkestan La the Great Karakoram Range runs eastwards circuiting the Teram Shehr Plateau to the Karakoram Pass. The Eastern Karakoram Range starts from the Teram Shehr Plateau and continues along the Eastern flank of the Siachen Glacier all the way down to the junction of the Shyok and Nubra rivers and constitutes the watershed between the two.[2]

The Teramshehr Plateau is a unique phenomenon—a vast snow and ice covered plateau at an average height of 6000 metres. It is ringed by magnificent peaks: the Teram Kangri group (I, II and III) and the Apsarasas group (I, II, III and IV) to the north and the Rimo Group to the east and southeast. To the southwest of the plateau is Padmanabh (7000m plus), climbed for the first time in 2002 by an Indo-Japanese expedition led by Harish Kapadia, of which Rushad was a part. Nanavatty recalls a brief conversation he had with Harish using a satellite phone. Operation PARAKRAM had commenced, and since tensions were running high between India and Pakistan, Harish wanted to know whether the team should call off the expedition. Nanavatty said to him that he was in the best place under the circumstances and should continue with the expedition, and the war, if it broke out, would be over by the time they got back to civilization![3]

The southern tip of the Saltoro Range is a geographical reference point NJ 9842, the area up to which the Ceasefire Line (CFL) (and since 1972 the LoC) between India and Pakistan was delineated in 1972 before the signing of the Simla Agreement. 'It is a Grid Square comprising a twisting, tumbling knot of high mountains on the north bank of the Shyok River near Chalunka and Bugdang villages some distance northeast of Turtuk,' recalls Nanavatty.[4]

Hand-drawn sketch by Lt Gen. Nanavatty

India's stance is that northwards of NJ 9842 the LoC, now termed the Actual Ground Position Line (AGPL), based on the widely accepted watershed principle, should head northwards along the Saltoro Ridge upto Sia Kangri whereas Pakistan believes that the LoC northwards of NJ 9842 should constitute a straight line 'as the crow flies' joining the latter with the Karakoram Pass. And, therein lies the reason for conflict.

Lieutenant General M.L. Chibber, the Indian Army's Northern Army Commander from October 1982 to August 1985, conceived and executed Operation MEGHDOOT (Op MEGHDOOT), the Indian Army's stunning high-altitude operation to prevent Pakistan from occupying the Saltoro Ridge and the Siachen Glacier. Given a free hand by India's army chief, General Arun Vaidya, Chibber, along with Lieutenant General P.N. Hoon, the corps commander of 15 Corps in Srinagar, brainstormed over the plan from late 1983 onwards with Colonel Narinder 'Bull' Kumar, the Indian Army's mountaineering pioneer, describing the area with hand-drawn illustrations and maps, which he co-related with his climbing expeditions in the area. Pakistan, though, had displayed tactical nimbleness. They had dispatched a small force in the winter of 1983 to occupy Bilafond La or Sia La, two of the highest passes in the northern sector of the glacier. The force turned back due to inclement weather and logistics constraints.[5] Had this operation succeeded, Pakistan may have occupied large portions of the Saltoro Ridge, as access to it from the west is much easier than it is from the east.

Chibber decided that the only way to ensure control over the area was by heli-landing troops on the two pivotal passes of Sia La and Bilafond La in the northern section of the Saltoro Ridge. A decisive Prime Minister, Indira Gandhi, gave the go-ahead sometime in early 1984 and thus began Operation MEGHDOOT. The area, totally devoid of human habitation except for the occasional mountaineering expedition, lay within the jurisdiction of 26 Sector commanded by Brigadier Vijay Channa, GUARDS with its HQ at Partapur. The two units under him, 4 KUMAON and the Karakoram Wing of Ladakh Scouts, were acclimatized to the region, having patrolled the area up to Sia La and

Bilafond La in the summer of 1983. Channa did not know about the plan till March 1984, when he was summoned to the Corps HQ in Srinagar and briefed by Lieutenant General Hoon, the corps commander. Hoon left the choice of the teams and the date for the assault to Channa within the window of 1 to 30 April. Channa chose 13 April as it was Baisakhi—a holiday to mark the harvest in Punjab, also celebrated in Pakistan—which he reckoned would provide the surprise element.[6]

A handful of pilots were chosen for the Helicopter Task Force from four units of the Indian Air Force and Army: 114 Helicopter Unit, 131 FAC Flight, 662 and 663 AOP Flights. The Task Force, comprising six to eight Cheetah helicopters and about fifteen pilots, was led by Wing Commander C.S. Sandhu, with Colonel G.S. Ghuman, the senior-most army pilot, acting as the Force Commander. After a quick aerial survey of the possible landing areas around Bilafond La and Sia La along with officers from 4 Kumaon and Ladakh Scouts on 12 April 1984, a company from 4 Kumaon led by Captain (later Lieutenant General) Sanjay Kulkarni secured Bilafond La in a high risk joint heliborne operation on 13 April. Braving casualties and isolated on Bilafond La for four days because of a blizzard and inclement weather, it was when Kulkarni radioed for a casualty evacuation sortie that the Pakistan Army realized that the heights they coveted were in Indian hands. When the weather cleared on 18 April, the sub-unit of 4 Kumaon was reinforced and their casualties were evacuated.

That same day, exploiting a window of good weather, Major A.N. Bahuguna and his company of Ladakh Scouts with two Mi-8 helicopters carrying ammunition and supplies from Thoise lending them logistics support occupied the area of Sia La.

Subsequently a Forward Logistics Base (FLB) and additional staging camps were set up to lend support to the localities at Sia La and Bilafond La. Throughout the period 1984 to 1988 the areas of Sia La and particularly that of Bilafond La were contested with the Pakistan Army making desperate attempts to gain a foothold on the ridgeline even as both sides consolidated their positions for the long term.

Nanavatty, a tough soldier in every respect as a forty-six-year-old brigadier, was not a military mountaineer of repute like his predecessors, Brigadiers Jal Master and Chandan Nugyal. Not comfortable with heights, he had constantly sought to challenge himself and now, he had an opportunity to soldier in the high mountains to overcome his fears.

Brigadier Chandan Nugyal, the man Nanavatty would replace, was an outstanding soldier with an enviable reputation as a military mountaineer. Commissioned into the Sikh Regiment, it was a twist of fate that saw him assigned to command the Siachen Brigade. Posted to take over command of a brigade in the mountains of Uttar Pradesh in mid-1984, Army HQ rushed him instead to command the Sikh Regimental Centre at Ramgarh and restore normalcy following the mutiny of Sikh troops in the aftermath of Operation BLUE STAR. After spending two years there, he assumed command of 102 Infantry Brigade in Siachen in mid-1986. Nugyal is modest about his tenure as the brigade commander, which saw some of the biggest successes of the Indian Army, particularly on the Northern Glacier around Bilafond La.[7]

Nugyal, according to Nanavatty, was a man of few words, practical, forthright, possessing great stamina, strength and courage. He was a man you would not want to cross swords with, as Brigadier (later General and then President of Pakistan) Pervez Musharraf was to learn at some considerable cost. In a conversation with the author, Nugyal explained: 'I presume you know that Brigadier Pervez Musharraf was the brigade commander on the Pakistan side when I was commanding 102 Infantry Brigade. You may not know that he was relieved of his command of the 323 Infantry Brigade at Dansam for failing to dislodge our boys from any of the posts in the Northern Glacier Sector. That is why Musharraf writes so little about his tenure as a brigade commander in his autobiography, *In the Line of Fire*.'[8]

Nugyal recollects that it was a tradition during the early years of the Siachen Conflict for the outgoing brigade commander to recommend who his likely successor could be to his superiors. By a strange coincidence, Nanavatty was Nugyal's choice. Nanavatty was unaware of this recommendation till the author mentioned it to him. Nugyal signed off the conversation by saying, 'Nanavatty was a fine soldier and did an excellent job in command of the Siachen Brigade.'

Nanavatty had the entire month of September as the commander designate to familiarize himself with his command and understand his responsibilities. Chandan Nugyal had planned his schedule carefully. A series of staff briefings at the headquarters was followed by introductory visits with the commander to various units, a few important forward localities and observation posts. After that, he spent ten days at Base Camp at the snout of the Siachen Glacier—the roadhead and the source of the Nubra River. Here, he would familiarize himself with the complex operational, training, and logistics support activities that went into keeping the show on the road. He would also use the opportunity to do some essential training.

Nanavatty was fortunate. In Subedar Mangla Rai, 7 GUARDS, he had an outstanding JCO Instructor of the Siachen Battle School (SBS) as his 'personal trainer'! Every morning, Nanavatty went through his paces in the glacier snout training area to understand the correct use of special clothing and mountaineering equipment and the basics of living, moving and surviving in the mountains. Little did he know that one day, several months later, he would learn from the daily Situation Report (Sitrep) that Mangla Rai was killed in a fall while descending an ice wall on the lower slopes of the Saltoro Kangri massif—a grim reminder that the mountains can be 'unforgiving' even of the best.

His familiarization and 'education' would be rounded off with an opportunity to attend the annual Joint Army–Air Force logistics support conference at HQ AOC J&K in Udhampur, where the supply tonnages required to be lifted and delivered by the Air Force were finalized. The conference helped Nanavatty comprehend the sheer enormity of the air logistics support task in Op MEGHDOOT and appreciate the importance the Air Force attached to meeting their tonnage targets month on end.

On the last day of his command, Nugyal left a note for Nanavatty, saying, 'There couldn't be a better man I could hand over to. 102 is indeed lucky.'[9] Nanavatty formally assumed command of 102 Infantry Brigade on 18 October 1988. His mission was unambiguous: 'to ensure the sanctity of the AGPL at all costs.'

The command of 102 Infantry Brigade in Operation MEGHDOOT was distinctive in several ways. First, the area of responsibility (AOR) was vast, bound by the magnificent Karakoram Ranges to the north and east, the Ladakh Range to the south and the Saltoro Range to the west. It encompassed the Nubra River basin, including the Siachen Glacier, its tributary glaciers, and the Shyok River Valley from Khalsar to Turtuk. Second, it was a sizeable composite formation with an order of battle (ORBAT) of five infantry battalions; three artillery regiments—one each of light, field and medium artillery—and a flight of Army Aviation Cheetah (SA 315-B Lama) helicopters, together with the usual complement of other arms and services under command. Third, units deployed on the glacier extensively depended on air logistics support. Fourth, there was a constant turnover of units and personnel owing to restrictions on the duration of continuous service in high-altitude areas. To give the reader an idea, Nanavatty had 18 Infantry battalions turnover during his command period of approximately two years and three months. Fifth, the formation was responsible for imparting pre-induction training to all its units and personnel deploying on the glacier. Sixth and finally, it boasted a unique ad-hoc facility called Base Camp, accountable for a range of vital functions. Nanavatty never could understand why the one brigade in the entire Indian Army that was a mountain formation in every sense of the word was deemed an Infantry and not a Mountain Brigade!

Base Camp was a facility that combined operational, training and logistics functions. It was a beehive of activity from dawn to dusk and often well into the night. It provided for an ad-hoc air traffic control organization; heliborne support operations facilities separately for medium lift and light helicopters to include the inevitable special breakfast for aviators—the 'Siachen Omelette'; an Artillery Fire Direction Centre and field and medium gun positions. Base Camp also housed the headquarters of the Central Glacier Sub Sector battalion; the rear headquarters and B Echelon of the Northern Glacier Sub Sector battalion; a reinforced medical aid post cum advanced dressing station; and an EME field workshop under a dynamic Officer Commanding (OC), Major Arvind Sinha—a wizard at improvisation for whom no task was impossible. Making up the dense composition of units was a detachment of the Snow and Avalanche Studies Establishment, Manali, and other logistics support facilities, particularly for the units deployed in the Northern and Central Glacier Sub Sectors. Base Camp was also where the Siachen Battle School (SBS) functioned, and Base Camp was where visitors would often stop and stare at the monstrous snout of the glacier and quickly return to where they came from to be able to say, 'I have been to the Siachen!'

Flying activity was intense in the mornings as An-32 medium-lift transport aircraft, Mi-17 and Cheetah helicopters made a beeline for the drop zones and helipads on the glaciers and gradually tapered off as the temperatures rose. Load management and prioritization was crucial and flying in and out of Base Camp demanded close coordination with the guns in the location.[10]

The diverse activities of sundry units and sub-units at Base Camp called for the closest possible cooperation and supervision. The hectic pace of events also necessitated the appointment of an ad-hoc officer commanding (OC) Base Camp. During the better part of Nanavatty's tenure, Major (later Lieutenant General Harjot Singh Sehgal), the second in command (2IC) of the Medium Regiment and an experienced aviator to boot, would perform this unheralded but vital role with great aplomb. He would infuse every man-jack in Base Camp with a marvellous 'can do, will do' spirit.

In Headquarters 102 Infantry Brigade, to the rear, the routine workload was substantial. Apart from the large span of control, the oversight of ongoing operations, and the in-situation conduct of pre-induction training of units and personnel deploying on the glacier, the HQ had to contend with a constant 'churning' as units came and went. Annoying peacetime administrative procedures hampered operational effectiveness. With the movement of personnel in and out of the theatre primarily by air, ad-hoc transit facilities were established at the brigade HQ and Base Camp. Air logistics support, being the mainstay of troops on the glacier, inter-service matters demanded the closest coordination and cooperation between the IAF base commander at the Thoise airbase and the brigade staff at Partapur. While Air Headquarters prioritized the achieving of set tonnage targets, the army sought flexibility in the type load from time to time to provide need based support.

A continuous stream of officers on temporary duty, particularly artillery OP officers, medical officers and 'volunteers' had to be interviewed on arrival and reported on when they departed. And, there were the inevitable visitors ranging from staff officers of higher HQs, student officers on the NDC and the Higher Command Courses and journalists who needed to be accommodated and treated with the deference they deserved. Many a visitor tossed into the cold, forbidding high altitude environment, sitting in front of a bukhari while listening to a briefing, would nod off, inviting the staff to constantly remind their 'enthusiastic' commander to 'keep it short'. Nanavatty would recall one instance where, at the end of a detailed briefing, a senior staff officer from HQ Northern Command, on his first visit to the formation, said, '*Achhaa, woh sab theek hai; ab yeh bataon ki Siachen Medal kaise milta hai?* (All that is fine; now tell me, how does one get a Siachen Medal?)'[11]

As a first-time formation commander, Nanavatty quickly realized the value of qualified and competent staff officers. Because of them, he could spend as much time as he did with his units in the field. During his tenure, the staff would turn over at least once, but without exception, he found his principal staff officers to be hard-working, efficient and trustworthy. His mantra for the staff was, 'Your job is to assist the units under command, not to obstruct or find fault with them. You have every right to say "Yes" to their needs, but the prerogative of saying "No" and admonishing a unit or its CO is mine and mine alone.'

In Operation MEGHDOOT, all flying, except in an emergency, was restricted to the forenoon for two reasons: an increase in 'clear air turbulence' as the day wore on and a decrease in the carrying capacity, or the 'useful load' of the aircraft, as the ambient temperatures rose. Accordingly, Nanavatty's average working day took on a specific pattern: early morning starts with aerial reconnaissance tasks followed by visits to sub-units on the AGPL and in Base Camp in the forenoon and office work in the headquarters at Partapur afterwards. Evening supper was usually at a reasonable hour. It provided a short but welcome interlude where the 'sparrow' (the Signals Officer) would regale all with his never-ending stream of jokes, after which the key staff officers would invariably return to their offices and burn the midnight oil. And, whenever the situation required that Nanavatty spend two or more days on glaciers, he would often stay in Base Camp or with the unit concerned instead of returning to Partapur.

For Nanavatty, the immediate priorities were twofold. First, to gain a thorough understanding of the terrain and the nature of operations on the Actual Ground Position Line (AGPL); and second, to improve the quality of pre-induction training at the Siachen Battle School (SBS).

It was Brigadier Nugyal who established the SBS to provide pre-induction training to units, sub-units and individuals assigned to serve in Operation MEGHDOOT. However, given Nanavatty's passion for operational preparedness, upgrading the training at the SBS was one of his Key Result Areas (KRAs). He resolved to formalize the training and improve it qualitatively. To begin with, he decided that the SBS would be the responsibility of his reserve Infantry Battalion, which remained on the ORBAT of the brigade for two years, including a six-month tour of duty in Operation MEGHDOOT. Accordingly, he requested Lieutenant Colonel Raghbir Sanghera CO 7 GUARDS to suggest a suitable officer to act as the OC SBS. The CO's choice, Major Basil Hobkirk, a tough, earthy, no-frills soldier, was the ideal man for the job, and he and the commander got along very well together. Other officers, JCOs and NCO Instructors qualified on the Mountain Warfare Course at the High-Altitude Warfare School, Gulmarg, were identified and 'borrowed' from the various units in the formation and the Ladakh Scouts unit in the sector.

The training was organized straightforwardly in two three-week capsules. The SBS would train the Unit Training Team (UTT), which arrived at the location with the unit Advance Party and the UTT, under its own CO, would train the unit with the SBS staff ensuring close and continuous oversight. The syllabus was carefully crafted to include the correct use of clothing and equipment and acquiring basic military mountaineering skills in the first two weeks, followed by specialized training based on individual aptitude on support weapons and equipment such as the Grad-P SBRL, .50 HMG and snow scooters and the training of Special Teams with responsibilities for route opening, rescue and recovery tasks. All practical training was carried out either on the snout of the Siachen Glacier or in a field firing area on the east bank of the Nubra River directly above the Base Camp.[12]

Just before a visit by Admiral Nadkarni, Chief of Naval Staff (CNS) and Chairman Chiefs of Staff Committee (COSC), it struck Nanavatty that it would be a good idea to give the visitors an understanding of the range of skills an infantryman must acquire to live and fight on the glacier. Accordingly, Hobkirk organized a sharp and slick lecture-cum-demonstration, which was very well received by the Admiral and is in vogue to this day with very few changes, if any! 'Yes,' said Nanavatty, 'SBS is an institution I look back on with great satisfaction and pride. I had recommended Hobkirk for the award of a Vishisht Seva Medal, which he richly deserved but, sadly, never got.'

The Indian Army sent up various weapons to try out on the glacier. Some were not designed for high altitude operations, such as the Anti-Tank Guided Missiles or ATGMs, while others, like the Heavy Machine Guns (HMGs) and Grad-P Rocket Launchers, were tried out on the firing range and in live shoots with mixed results. The main challenge for the infantryman was coping with the jamming of the 7.62 SL Rifle and the LMG in the bitter cold while the AK-47 with the Pakistan Army seemed to function satisfactorily.[13] While the 'Gunners' had to experiment with and modify their firing tables the problem with infantry small arms was simply to get them to work. Every ruse had to be used to ensure small arms did not 'freeze' and under the circumstances it was no surprise that the M4 84 mm Carl Gustaf turned out to be the infantryman's weapon of choice.

Nanavatty systematically visited his troops deployed on the AGPL in defended localities and posts, protective patrol locations and observation posts with a bias initially towards the Northern Glacier Sub Sector. In the process, he would familiarize himself with the terrain and the identifiable enemy locations in each area. Typically, a visit entailed a direct fly-in (with a bag full of fresh green vegetables—even chillies if nothing else—clearly being the all-time favourite) and 'drop off' at the most convenient helipad; a trudge—or a snow scooter ride if he was lucky—to one or more forward locations or OPs before returning. This would be followed by a pow-wow with the sub-unit commander and a chat with the men.

On the return, after a helicopter pick-up, it was standard practice to try to confirm the terrain features and enemy locations from the air. This informal interaction with sub-unit commanders, artillery OP officers, medical officers (MO) and the men on the posts was invaluable. It gave him an excellent idea of their problems, needs but, most importantly, their morale.

During his tenure, Nanavatty spent at least one night in every company HQ location on the AGPL and covered every surface route on the glacier, either on his feet or on a snow scooter, at least once. He said, 'Often I would "cheat"—fly in and walk out!' Nanavatty was convinced that sharing in the privations of his men in those harsh conditions was essential—good for him, his officers and his men. He said that strange things happened on these trips. Reminiscing about a night in Sia La, he said, 'It was the height of winter and "snow scootering" into Sia La during the day I spent the afternoon visiting a few outposts on foot. Looking forward to a night's rest, I was ushered into a prefabricated (prefab) shelter buried some twenty feet deep in the snow through a combined trench cum tunnel. Sitting down on the floor of the hut and removing my boots and socks, I heard what I thought was the unmistakeable "quack-quack" of a duck and, sure enough, there was this beautiful wild male Mallard nosing about in the hut amidst all the men without a care in the world. It seemed a flight of migrating ducks was passing overhead, and this "individual", probably exhausted, fluttered down onto the post. The men instinctively took it under their wing, and now they had a genuinely unusual mascot.'

Nanavatty's commanders in the chain of command likewise made every effort to visit the posts. Lieutenant General B.C. Nanda, the GOC-in-C Northern Army Command, was punctilious. He would visit at regular intervals like clockwork to ask if there were any problems and spend time with the troops in the forward locations. He would invariably be accompanied by the GOC 15 Corps, Lieutenant General D.S.R. Sahni, and the GOC 28 Infantry Division, Major General V.R. Raghavan.

As time passed, Nanavatty became increasingly familiar with the area of operations and the enemy's dispositions. He soon realized that enemy locations and routes were more easily identifiable in the pristine white conditions of winter; and, that the angle of the sun could play a significant role in detecting and identifying objects in the snow. 'The enemy's reaction to our aircraft loitering over their positions was to use artillery air burst ammunition to drive us away, particularly in the Central Glacier Sub Sector. And yet only once did he manage to straddle one of our helicopters with a three-round salvo. Luckily, there was no damage to men or material,' said Nanavatty. With a largely static battlefield and given the regularity with which Nanavatty flew over his AOR, he often was best placed to familiarize pilots, post commanders and OP officers with enemy dispositions, tracks in use and targets on the ground! He was not being immodest when he said he knew the area like the back of his hand.

Midway through his tour of duty, Headquarters Northern Command issued instructions for an aerial recce at periodic intervals over the Shaksgam Valley area. To begin with, Nanavatty seldom missed the opportunity. In his words, 'The experience was exhilarating. With a single passenger, the Cheetah, its engine straining every sinew and orbiting in tight circles to gain height over the massive Teramshehr Plateau, would climb to 22,000 feet. Suddenly, beyond the peaks that formed a rim around the plateau, you would get a breathtaking view of parts of Tibet—a sight that looked like a limitless brown ocean with gigantic waves and patches of white—as far as the eye could see. And on the other side of the Great Karakoram Range, which petered out towards the Karakoram (KK) Pass, you would suddenly come upon a wide, almost gentle valley with little or no snow or ice and a faint track running East to West along its bottom. However, there was "Nothing to report" in the Shaksgam Valley at that time.'

Following his visits to the units on the AGPL, he realized there were barely five locations, all in the Central Glacier Sub Sector, where the enemy had a toehold on the Saltoro Ridge; and, there were about eight locations on the AGPL where the enemy was within the range of small arms—primarily medium machine gun—three each in the Northern and

Central Glacier Sub Sectors and two in the Southern Glacier Sub Sector. Much of the indirect fire of artillery and mortars was 'harassing' in nature and essentially of nuisance value. Despite several sub-unit commanders on the AGPL bringing to his notice the restrictions and, therefore, delays in engaging targets of opportunity, he got the distinct impression that both sides were content with the existing status quo, forgetting that the status quo almost always allowed one side or the other to take the initiative and make it difficult for the opponent. He also realized that the lie of the land and the terrain facilitated the use of porters and animal transport (AT) to a much greater extent by the enemy and that the latter seldom had the need to take recourse to maintenance by air. The only time Nanavatty saw an enemy helicopter was when he was on a trans-LoC reconnaissance to 'look' into the Baltoro Glacier across the Saltoro Ridge, where the enemy reportedly had a high-altitude camp cum training facilities. What looked like an enemy utility helicopter was a few hundred feet below them, hovering over the northern most enemy post at Conway Saddle.

Pondering over his tactical options, Nanavatty concluded, 'We were paying a high price by way of air logistical support and casualties owing to weather, altitude and terrain for the one singular advantage of occupying the high ground all along our claim line, the Saltoro Ridge.' And yet, while satisfied with their posture and domination by observation, there was little advantage being extracted from it. Nanavatty was convinced that his brigade had to at least dominate the enemy by fire too, even if that meant stirring the pot. And, in the circumstances, it was a job that the artillery could accomplish best.[14]

In 102 Infantry Brigade, placing artillery units under command was an issue that every Commander Artillery (C Arty) 28 Infantry Division—and there were three whom Nanavatty served alongside—would unfailingly take umbrage to. They would argue that it violated the fundamental principle of the employment of artillery in a division that called for centralized control of resources. Countering it by saying

it was an 'operational necessity' did not suffice. Nanavatty's solution was to appoint the CO of the Light Regiment, whose 120 mm Mortars were deployed in troop mortar positions across the length and breadth of the glacier, as the *ad-hoc C Arty 102 Infantry Brigade*, and that seemed to mollify the senior 'Gunners' somewhat. Colonel Nevis Braganza, the CO of the Light Regiment during much of Nanavatty's tenure, was 'on call' and a mere two-hour drive away from the Brigade HQ. He would assist in framing relevant policies, orders and instructions, and fulfilled his assigned role admirably.

Explaining its rationale, HQ 102 Infantry Brigade laid out a simple policy for the engagement of targets. It essentially said, 'Interdict all observed enemy activity within range by direct and indirect fires.'[15] Since targets were often fleeting, the authority to open fire was delegated down to sub-unit commanders and artillery OP officers up to the amount of ammunition specified at each level.

At one point, a battery of Bofors 155mm FH 77 towed guns, relatively recently acquired by the Indian Army, was moved to Base Camp. Subsequently, Northern Command ordered the formation to select and conduct a trial engagement of an enemy target. After some discussion, Nanavatty decided to target an enemy locality called New Bunker in the Bilafond La area, on the western slopes of the Northern Shoulder of the pass and closest to Indian positions anywhere on the AGPL. The OP for the shoot positioned himself on the forward slope of the pass and planned a shoot at first light the following morning. Nanavatty, along with the 2IC of the Medium Regiment and the OC Base Camp, Major Harjot Sehgal, crept into the OP location before first light and were treated to a spectacular display of accurate shooting. Later, the Army Commander complimented the regiment's excellent shooting that morning. Nanavatty likes to believe that this was perhaps the first time that the Bofors 155mm FH 77 towed gun had fired in anger at an adversary anywhere in the world!

On another occasion, he was at an OP location in the Southern Glacier Sub Sector. When scanning the area, he observed a large column of the enemy moving on foot along a track towards his Lake Camp location in the Central Glacier Sub Sector. The OP officer engaged the target, but the results were difficult to gauge. The enemy, to his credit, responded quickly and accurately, targeting the OP location with airburst ammunition. In another incident, again in the Southern Glacier Sub Sector, a link patrol of the enemy was targeted effectively, resulting in casualties. In a typical example of the unwritten code of conduct that prevailed between the two armies on the AGPL, the Pakistan Army would complain, presumably via the 'hotline', that we had not allowed them to pick up their casualties! General Raghavan would censure Nanavatty, and he would respond by saying, 'All they had to do was show us a white flag,' and so it would continue rather like the trenches of the First World War! Nanavatty was forever egging his sub-unit commanders and OP officers to look for new OP locations; he said, in the mountains, even a few hundred metres left or right, up or down, could make a difference. Eventually, he had the satisfaction of establishing four new OP positions, two each in the Northern and Southern Glacier Sub Sectors.

When the author asked Nanavatty to single out one unit out of all the infantry battalions that served under him, he declined and said, 'As always, what determined a unit's performance was simply the quality of leadership that the CO and his officers provided at various levels at the time.' Nevertheless, one battalion, the 7th Battalion of the Brigade of the Guards (7 GUARDS), by a strange coincidence, always figured in the author's conversation regarding operations on the Siachen Glacier. Two commandants at the National Defence College (NDC), one when the author was doing the course in 2010 and the other when the author was the President's Chair of Excellence in 2022, were members of this unit in Operation MEGHDOOT when Nanavatty commanded 102 Infantry Brigade. Lieutenant General Prakash Menon was a company commander as a Major, and Lieutenant General Manoj Kumar Mago, the Adjutant, was a Captain. Finally, two long conversations with the CO of the unit at the time, Brigadier (then Lieutenant Colonel) Raghbir Sanghera (Retired), prompted the author to incorporate their story here.[16]

According to Sanghera, allowing him to command his unit in operations as a half-colonel was a sign of the commander's faith in his abilities. Almost thirty-five years later, Sanghera considers it an 'honour for the battalion to have served in Operation MEGHDOOT under then Brigadier Nanavatty. He was a man of few words but possessed intellect, depth and courage. He was unsparing of professional laxity and kept himself fully abreast of operational matters through his constant reconnaissance and visits to the forward troops. Spartan in his habits, Nanavatty, on his visits, would "rough it out" at night, sharing whatever accommodation was available, and quietly go about his work preparing for the following day.' Commenting on Nanavatty's superb fitness, Sanghera recollects one long trudge around Sia La at over 20,000 feet after a heavy snowfall. Trailing Nanavatty most of the way, when they stopped, he said reassuringly, 'Raghbir, I come from 9,000 feet at Partapur. I have a greater reserve of oxygen than you, who stays at 15,000 feet! Take your time, and do not worry.'

Encouraging his battalion commanders to speak out and voice their concerns on operational issues during visits by senior officers, Sanghera recollects that on one occasion, distressed at his inability to evacuate his casualties speedily owing to the weather, he requested the GOC-in-C for additional snow scooters and was promptly rewarded with the immediate release of a few machines.

Sanghera also recalled instances where Nanavatty quickly appreciated his officers' initiative and innovation. One such instance was the fabrication of the 'Mago Trolley'—a rudimentary device fabricated by Captain Mago, the Adjutant, using a snow scooter engine and gearbox, a parachute skid-board, ropes and pulleys—to deliver forty-kg loads to the Bana Post and thus avoid the use of 'fighting porters' for the task. Until then, Bana Post was a good kilometre away and was resupplied by a human logistics chain at an incline of 80 degrees from the posts Amar and Sonam. The Pakistanis often spotted the chain from a lower position and disrupted it with mortar and artillery fire.[17]

By the end of the winter of 1988–89, Nanavatty was more than satisfied with the degree of ascendancy achieved over the enemy in the Northern

Glacier Sub Sector. It was time to turn his attention to the Central and Southern Glacier Sub Sectors. He systematically quartered the area opposite the Central and Southern Glacier by conducting several aerial reconnaissance flights to identify targets. In one such sortie recommended by an enthusiastic young pilot of 666 Air OP flight in Partapur, he flew over the AGPL in the Gyong La area to try and locate the enemy camp in the Chumik Glacier that possibly sustained the two enemy posts (the Indians called North OP and South OP) on the Saltoro Ridge, one each to the North and South of the difficult pass. The oval-shaped camp neatly 'tucked in' at the base of the Saltoro ridge was hard to miss in the pure white snow and presented an attractive target. As the aircraft turned around, Nanavatty said to himself, 'Another good test for the Bofors Battery.' Following the post-sortie de-brief in Base Camp, he ordered an air OP shoot targeting the Chumik Camp at the first opportunity. A few days later, an attempt was made, but the shoot was ineffective because of the 'dead ground' (blind spots that adversely impact calculations in shoots, particularly in complicated terrain), and further attempts were called off.

Shortly thereafter, on 24 March 1989, Nanavatty proceeded on thirty days of annual leave. His Deputy Commander, Colonel J.K. Sharma, a paratrooper and seasoned veteran on the glacier who had performed well in the operations in 1987–88 and was nearing the end of his term in Operation MEGHDOOT, was in charge.

Towards the fag end of his leave, the Nanavattys made a 'social call' on Lieutenant General and Mrs Ramesh Kulkarni at their residence in Delhi. General Kulkarni, the previous GOC 28 Infantry Division, mentioned to him that all was not well in Siachen. Taken aback, Nanavatty said he had no information whatsoever. Driving home with his wife, he said to himself that 'things must be under control; otherwise, the formation would surely have contacted him, and, if that were so, he did not think it was proper to interfere. After all, what were officiating commanders meant for?' A few days later, on the termination of his leave on 22 April, he was back in Partapur, and as luck would have it, Lieutenant General D.S.R. Sahni, the corps commander, was returning after a visit to the Base Camp. True to form, Sahni was calm and said to him, 'The situation is under control; there is no cause for worry. Take your time, and don't rush there in a hurry.'

That afternoon, the deputy commander and the staff organized a briefing cum discussion on the ongoing operation. During the briefing, Nanavatty learned that Sharma had ordered yet another attempt to engage the Chumik Camp towards the end of March, with the same result. Soon, there were intelligence reports of the enemy inducting reinforcements, including a Special Service Group (SSG) Company, into the area. The move set the alarm bells ringing. Sharma assessed that the enemy would attempt to occupy Point 6400, the highest feature on the Saltoro Ridge in the Central Glacier Sub Sector, to dominate the entire area by fire and observation and make things increasingly difficult in the Gyong Glacier area and beyond.

Sharma consulted with Raghavan, the GOC 28 Infantry Division, and decided to pre-empt the enemy by securing Pt 6400 (later christened Dogra Hill). The operation code-named Operation IBEX (Op IBEX) was approved by the commanders in the chain of command and assigned to the 2nd Battalion of the Dogra Regiment (2 DOGRA), which had barely completed taking over the operational responsibility of the Central Glaciers Sub Sector from the unit it relieved.

By 6 April, Sharma had mobilized a team of skilled military mountaineers from the Karakoram Wing of the Ladakh Scouts at Partapur and placed it under command 2 DOGRA for route opening tasks. The operation to secure Pt 6400 commenced on 8 April and was completed, unopposed, by 15 April. The feature comprised the top with a convenient, relatively flat 'shelf' a little below the top on the reverse slope, which would serve as a helipad and restricted administration area. From the top, the Saltoro Ridge continued in a southwesterly direction, first dipping to form a small saddle and then rising again to form yet another bump that obscured the view beyond. Between 15 and 22 April, 2 DOGRA stabilized the surface routes from the Company HQ in the Gyong Glacier to the Support Base in the glaciated basin below and east of Pt 6400 to the objective. Army Aviation aircraft established a tenuous air bridge, inserted an artillery OP party, and completed the first relief of an officer and a section plus of the infantry. The race to the top had seemingly been won![18]

Nanavatty knew the area well and was not particularly pleased with the decision to occupy Pt 6400. He said, 'It gave us no real advantage except to boast of the occupation of yet another dominating feature on the AGPL.' The long and tortuous surface routes to the objective forward of the tri-junction—the area where the three tributary glaciated basins in the Central Glacier met to form the main Gyong Glacier—were already under the observation of the three existing enemy posts on the Saltoro Ridge. Consequently, all routine moves ahead of the tri-junction were carried out in the hours of darkness in any case and, in the long term, the occupation of Pt 6400 would have meant yet another 21,000-foot post to be maintained by air. Unsurprisingly, the occupation of Pt 6400 by the enemy would not have allowed him to observe the areas beyond the tri-junction, either because of intervening features. And, that is perhaps why, in all these years, he had made no attempt to occupy the feature. But the die was cast, and Nanavatty knew that this was neither the time nor the place for recrimination. He decided to proceed to Base Camp early the very next day.

In Base Camp, he hitched a ride on the first Mi-17 drop sortie to the Support Base DZ, where the surface route started the steep 1000-plus metre climb to the objective. He then had detailed discussions with the CO 2 DOGRA, the OC Base Camp and the FDC. Realizing the importance of establishing a proper support base, stabilizing the surface routes and pushing up stores, he called for a temporary halt to all training at the SBS. The personnel of the 20 SIKH UTT (the battalion training at the SBS at the time) were attached to the CO 2 DOGRA as fighting porters to assist in the collection of stores on the DZ and the stocking up of the base and the post.

Around the end of April, the first reports were received of the enemy inserting a small detachment, presumably of the SSG, on the Saltoro Ridge SW of Point 6400. In a desperate, ingenious and courageous move, each Pakistani soldier was transported 'under-slung' by helicopter and deposited in the snow beyond the saddle and the second bump on the Saltoro Ridge itself. On the night of 30 April/1 May, this detachment

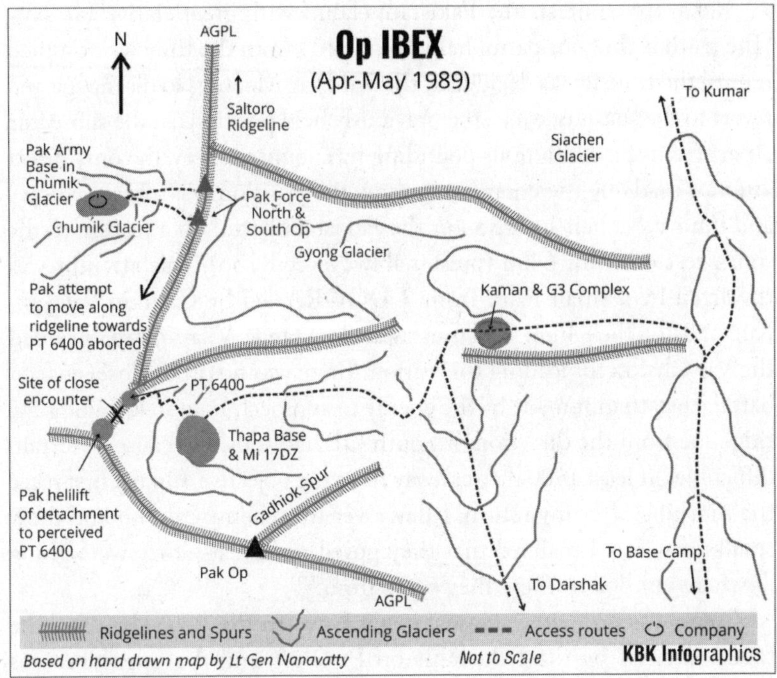

probing forward encountered a protective element of 2 DOGRA forward of Pt 6400. In the ensuing firefight, the enemy suffered casualties and left behind two AK-47 rifles and a Commando dagger, which the Dogras recovered.

The Pakistani narrative not surprisingly is different. In an account of Operation CHUMIK, as it was called in Pakistan, Lieutenant Colonel Syed Ashfaq Ali narrates a tale of equal courage and daring in his book *Fangs of Ice.*[19] Ali writes about the audacious helicopter assault on Naveed Top (presumably the second bump on the ridge southwest of Pt 6400) and uncorroborated firefights that forced the Indians down from Pt 6400. According to Kevin Fedarenko—the first Westerner to be given access to both Pakistani and Indian posts—three teams of Pakistani soldiers attempted to reach the summit to thwart the Indian operation but failed.[20]

Nanavatty contests the Pakistani claims with great clarity. He says, 'The truth is that our patrol held Point 6400 from the time we occupied it until the time it was decided at the 3rd Flag Meeting to disengage and revert to the status quo, i.e., the previously held positions in the subsector. Apart from the continuous pounding by enemy artillery, the only direct attempt made by the enemy to occupy the position was after the brave and innovative heli-insertion of the Pakistani patrol on a feature to the southwest of Point 6400 (presumably Naveed Top). This attempt was thwarted by a small team from 2 DOGRA led by Captain Vijayant Kumar using the 84mm Carl Gustav at close range. Vijayant was awarded the Vir Chakra for leading this action. There was no other close-quarter battle. The attempt made by the enemy to approach Point 6400 along the ridgeline from the direction of South OP had stalled because of terrain difficulties at least 1500 metres away from the objective. On my first recce the morning after my return, I flew over this enemy column and drew small-arms fire. I realized that they posed no threat—they were going nowhere but down where they came from.'[21]

There was no further close contact between the two sides after the failed attempt by the Pakistanis on Pt 6400, and the operation was reduced to an artillery slugfest. Even artillery fire other than airburst ammunition was less than effective because of the terrain configuration, the reverse slope positions and the soft snow conditions. What artillery did manage to do was to trigger massive avalanches, which devastated the surface routes. Besides the artillery, the IAF and Army Aviation flew tirelessly through April and May in an exceedingly hostile environment and played a sterling role in the operation. While the Air Force remained responsible for all the supply drops in the Support Base DZ, Army Aviation was responsible for carrying out all the sundry intimate support tasks.

Indeed, the After-Action Report singles out the Army Aviation as 'the most important agency that helped sustain the operations'. Its pilots, ably supported by their ground crew, executed multifarious missions to include surveillance, observation and direction of artillery fire, vital replenishment and casualty evacuation, notwithstanding the risks of operating off a tiny makeshift helipad at 6,400 metres with a unidirectional approach and no margin for error. The inevitable happened at one stage during a critical phase of the operation when a helicopter malfunctioned and had to be abandoned after being pushed precariously to a side to enable minimal essential flying operations to continue.[22]

Group Captain (later Air Vice Marshal) Harpal 'Harry' Singh Ahluwalia, the commanding officer of 129 Helicopters, and his crew flew non-stop to support Op IBEX and simultaneously deliver supplies elsewhere on the glacier as scheduled. Ahluwalia flew thirteen sorties on 22 April 1989 in support of Op IBEX. Recalling the operation, he said, 'We loved it—flying, switching off, refuelling, loading, dropping and back again. We made up for the winter shortfall in that one month.' Ahluwalia recollects that enemy artillery and mortars would begin firing as soon as they heard the helicopters and sighted them in the tri-junction area heading towards the Support Base DZ, forcing them to take different evasive measures. Summarizing his experience on the glacier, he said, '1988–89 were particularly tough years, and Nugyal and Nanavatty were tough guys and great soldiers.'

By 4 May, the situation on Dogra Hill had become critical—the surface routes to and from the Support Base had all but been destroyed. The Army Aviation helicopter was awaiting repairs and recovery on the tiny helipad, and wounded personnel were awaiting evacuation. Later, Nanavatty was to learn that one of the wounded was the Artillery OP officer himself, who had refused to pass on the information for fear that the enemy was monitoring their transmissions.

On 5 May, the GOC-in-C, corps, and division commanders were in Base Camp. The mood in the makeshift operations room shelter was sombre. Nanavatty was blunt and did not waste any time. He said that the situation on Point 6400 had become critical and 'either we call for a ceasefire or else be prepared to accept the loss of our men on Pt 6400'. For a moment, the ops room went silent. The GOC-in-C looked at his corps and division commander in turn, and then, his mind made up, he suggested to Major General Raghavan that he speak to the DGMO.

A series of Flag Meetings with his opposite number, commander 323 Infantry Brigade, Pakistan Army, followed quickly, all in the Kargil Area. In the first two, Nanavatty would meet with Brigadier Asif Riaz Bukhari and in the third and last, it would be Brigadier Yasub Ali Dogar, Bukhari's relief. All three meetings were civil and business-like. According to

Nanavatty, Bukhari was a typical public-school product, sophisticated and professional. On the other hand, Dogar was the archetype Pakistani officer in the Zia-ul-Haq mould with Islamic fervour, who took regular prayer breaks during the meeting and remained aloof and frosty during his interaction with Nanavatty. Initially, it was agreed without much ado to enforce an immediate ceasefire. This enabled the evacuation of the wounded and the in-situation repair and recovery of the aircraft from Pt 6400, which was flown out on a wing and a prayer by two of 666 Flight's best pilots.[23]

Unfortunately, the ceasefire would come a day too late for the JCO and six other ranks of 2 DOGRA who were manning the Support Base. In an early morning call from the CO 2 DOGRA, Nanavatty, who was in Kargil and leaving for the Flag Meeting, would learn that they had all perished in an avalanche with the JCO making his last call to his CO saying, '*Sahib, hum yahan se nikal nahi payenge: sab ko hamare Ram Ram keh dena* (We won't be able to get out from here. Give our best to everyone).' In the second meeting, Nanavatty was instructed by the Command Headquarters 'to demand the withdrawal of the Pakistan Army from the Chumik Glacier in return for our falling back to the positions previously held'. Nanavatty thought the demand was preposterous but did as he was told. Bukhari, too, was rendered speechless by the untenable demand. He quietly put his papers away and left the meeting without a word.[24] In the third and final meeting, better sense prevailed, and both sides agreed to return to positions previously held, ending the whole episode. The meetings were videographed, and Raghavan, while suggesting that they be discussed on the Higher and Senior Command courses at Mhow for instructional purposes, would pull Nanavatty's leg about his 'acting' abilities.

Op IBEX resulted in five officers and eight other ranks killed in the Pakistan Army as against one JCO and seven other ranks killed in the Indian Army. Though the fighting was nowhere as ferocious as combat in the Northern Glacier Sub Sector in 1987–88, it was climatically and topographically challenging, as the following extract of a letter from Nanavatty to Lieutenant Colonel P.S.R. Hallikeri, the CO of the Karakoram Wing of the Ladakh Scouts, would suggest: '... Your personnel were employed in opening the surface routes from the

Company HQ in the Gyong Glacier to the Support Base and then to Pt 6400 and establishing the defended post in that location. Several of them, demonstrating superb mountaineering skills, incredible strength and stamina, completed several trips over the tortuous route involving an eight-hour climb ...'[25]

Nanavatty, even today, maintains that the Op IBEX was 'triggered by a misreading of intentions by both sides. Our intense aerial reconnaissance activity, repeated attempts to engage the Chumik Camp with artillery, and the large-scale movement of troops through the Gyong Glacier as 2 DOGRA relieved the previous unit in the Central Glacier Sub Sector at that time will have alerted the enemy. And his legitimate response of moving in reinforcements will have troubled us. When two sides are pitted against each other over a prolonged period, any sudden departure from the norm, if detected, can have severe and unintended consequences.'

Nevertheless, the speedy acceptance of the decision to disengage suggested that neither side wished to expand or prolong the face-off. According to Raghavan, the disengagement and return to previously held locations was an indirect acknowledgement and acceptance of the Saltoro Ridge as the dividing line between the two countries, and this is what severely discomfited the senior leadership in the Pakistan Army.

Nanavatty has had his share of critics for not holding on to Pt 6400, with one individual who commanded the formation later stating that 'Nanavatty may have ceded the initiative in the area to the adversary.' But there is little evidence to suggest that is true. Nanavatty, in his mind, is clear: 'The elevation of the feature apart, it had little or no tactical significance; our ability to administratively support the post was uncertain; and there was the question of the safety of our men—I am sure we did the right thing by seeking a ceasefire.'[26]

Nanavatty is effusive in his praise of the aviators irrespective of whether they wore Air Force 'blue' or army 'olive green'. He firmly believes that, in Operation MEGHDOOT, nothing could have been achieved without their support. Broadly, the division of the air support tasks between the

Army Aviation and the Indian Air Force was clear without having to be spelt out in black and white. While the Air Force concentrated on air logistics tasks, Army Aviation carried out various other intimate tasks supporting the troops on the ground. Casualty evacuation, however, was one task that was responded to with zeal by whosoever was on hand.

Air logistics support would be provided in three ways by the IAF—parachute drops by AN 32 fixed-wing aircraft confined to the Northern Glacier Sub Sector, parachute drops by Mi-17 helicopters, and landed delivery of loads by Cheetah helicopters on posts above an altitude of 19,000 feet. Perhaps worth mentioning here is that artillery pieces for the glacier gun positions were dropped in parts by Mi-17s during the early phase of Operation MEGHDOOT, and the guns were then assembled on site—a stupendous feat by any yardstick. For obvious reasons—aircraft speeds, the height of the drop, and prevailing wind speeds—drops by fixed-wing aircraft proved to be rather wasteful. Besides, locating and retrieving stores dropped in challenging crevasse-ridden terrain where DZ clearance teams were often 'roped up' was backbreaking and extremely dangerous work. A herculean retrieval effort by one battalion alone, 7 GUARDS, is worth mentioning in the Northern Glacier Sub Sector, which resulted in the retrieval of vast quantities of kerosene oil otherwise deemed lost.

In Air Vice Marshal Dushyant Singh, AOC (J&K), the Air Force had a hard taskmaster whose single-minded goal was to ensure that it achieved its set tonnage targets. The army found that annoying at times when the situation demanded some flexibility in task execution. Dushyant Singh would always remind Nanavatty of the need to try to reduce the number of Cheetah-dependent posts for good reason. He was delighted when the army proposed a Southern Glacier Sub Sector rifle company convert to a Mi-17 drop-dependent locality. Talking of inter-services cooperation, Nanavatty was sure of one thing: 'It improved as you came closer to where the shooting was!'

During Nanavatty's command tenure, there were two major 'incidents' involving Cheetah aircraft in addition to recovering the Army Aviation helicopter from Pt 6400 in Op IBEX. First was the recovery of an aircraft after a 'hard landing' in the Saser La area; and second was the repair and recovery of an Air Force aircraft from a post at 20,000 feet in the Bilafond La area.

As a commander, aviation was a boon and provided him essential mobility. It allowed him to be everywhere—to interact with his command and know his Area of Operations. He particularly enjoyed the frequent Trans-Saltoro and Karakoram aerial reconnaissance, target identification and fire direction sorties using Army Aviation Cheetah helicopters. During these sorties, he would make a special effort to familiarize Artillery Observation Post officers with targets in their respective areas of responsibility. According to Nanavatty, air operations in Op MEGHDOOT called for 'nerve, courage and exceptional flying skill as there were several occasions when the Pakistan Army would attempt to deter our aerial reconnaissance sorties using air-burst artillery munitions. There was no margin for error and even less hope of recovery.' Reminiscing again, he said to the author, 'What can one say of our aviators—the Ahluwalias, Baths, Goles, Randhawas, Chauhans, Whigs and Gills—they gave new meaning to the expression "to fly by the seat of your pants". Routinely pushing man and machine beyond all known limits, they are, truly, our magnificent men in their flying machines.'[27]

Nanavatty would recall a few issues that defied a satisfactory solution during his time in Siachen. They were the issue of special clothing, the disposal of waste, and the 'mapping' and updating of avalanche sites. At the end of an individual's tour of duty, all special clothing was washed, cleaned and produced before a condemnation board, following which the serviceable items were reissued! Considering that the clothes were hand-washed and cleaned by the troops themselves in the hot springs at Panamik, the standards of cleanliness left much to be desired. Just the thought that such clothing, some of it of a very personal nature, used by person A for three to six months in unimaginably severe conditions, could be reissued to person B was simply unthinkable. Considering the overall costs of Operation MEGHDOOT, it was a penny-wise, pound-foolish attempt at achieving economy. Nanavatty recalled that the problem persisted till his return in 2001 to the same theatre of operations in a different capacity. It was the subject matter of the last letter he would write to the Raksha Mantri before retiring from service, and it took a George Fernandes to sort things out.[28]

The disposal of waste on the glacier at scale was an insurmountable problem. There was no way you could dispose of waste. In the winter, nature helped by covering everything with a deceptive blanket of snow and ice, but come summer, the inhabited areas, particularly the larger camps, were an eyesore. Nanavatty recalls a visit by Dr Raja Ramanna, the eminent scientist and then the Rajya Raksha Mantri (Minister of State for Defence)—the only politician to visit Operation MEGHDOOT during his command. Turning to him in the helicopter with a horrified look on his face as they approached the HQ of the Northern Glacier Battalion located on the medial moraine of the main glacier, he remarked, 'What is this? Aren't you the commander here? Can't you do something about this filth?'

Nanavatty waited till they had landed, and the aircraft engine had been switched off, and then said, 'Sir, this is a battalion headquarters with upwards of 60 all ranks in this location. The DRDO, in all these years, has recently managed to install one toilet with an incinerator here. I believe they are working on the problem. Do you know we even have mice that come down by parachute with the rations? And we could add to the gene pool of mice because their tails drop off with the cold here. We simply pretend the rubbish does not exist and get on with our job. At least the cold takes care of the stench. I am afraid, in my mind, there is no solution to waste management at scale on the glacier short of vacating it.'

Avalanches were another cause of terrifying accidents in Operation MEGHDOOT. Though the Snow and Avalanche Studies Establishment, Manali, had a detachment in Base Camp, they were only capable of predicting and issuing warnings of the likelihood of avalanches in the general area. What was required was a careful periodical survey and mapping exercise of avalanche sites and the periodic 'proving' of routes and campsites on the glacier, and that kind of effort was just not available. Nanavatty would recall two incidents. In the first incident, following Operation IBEX in 1989, on a request from Nanavatty, a team of the High-Altitude Warfare School, Gulmarg, led by the commandant himself, had opened a new route along the Zingrulma Glacier in the

Central Glacier Sub Sector, which was protected from enemy observation and fire. Traversing the route subsequently, Nanavatty and his two-man escort stopped for a short break at a small staging post manned by an NCO and three men. Sipping his tea, he could not help but notice a menacing mass of ice poised dangerously near the campsite and wondered if it was a threat. Continuing their journey, he would put the thought away, saying that the HAWS team would have considered the matter. A few days later, the hanging glacier broke, wiping out the staging camp and its occupants. In the second incident, a glacier troop gun position that had been dormant for a long time was activated, consequent to the relocation of an OP. A few effective shoots later, the gun position was buried in a massive slab avalanche, though in true gunner tradition, the CO with a rescue party was on the spot in the shortest possible time. All three guns were recovered and promptly set right, but sadly, the small contingent was lost to a man.

In 1990, following six years of combat and acute privation in truly extraordinary conditions, Army HQs decided to analyse the various factors that determined combat performance in Siachen for the first time. The questionnaire was passed on to personnel in eight infantry battalions and five artillery regiments that were either serving on the glacier or had recently completed their tenure. The questions related to fear, leadership, combat effectiveness and motivation. Responses were sought from persons in their individual capacity and collected and collated centrally at HQ 102 Infantry Brigade in Partapur.[29]

The findings were interesting. Death, disablement, effects of cold and loss of respect and self-esteem were all considered equally important causes of fear. In the early stages overcoming *fear* was the most important objective during pre-induction training. While complex and complicated leadership paradigms found little traction in the survey, officers and men alike considered physical and mental robustness and the ability to plan and coordinate actions as crucial leadership attributes. Officers and JCOs leading by example, sound training and good equipment occupied pole position when assessing positive contributors to ***combat efficiency***. An interesting revelation was that 'mixed-class' infantry units coped as well, even better in comparison with 'one class' units. An example was 20 JAT with an equal percentage of Jats, Marathas, Garhwalis and Rajputs, part of a short-lived experiment instituted by General A.S. Vaidya, a former COAS after Operation BLUE STAR. Nanavatty, however, attributed it to the quality of leadership in the unit at the time. Nevertheless, honour of the unit and regiment was the most important factor in ***motivation***. The soldiers' oath to serve the nation and the righteousness of India's cause came next. The absence of any ideological animosity towards the Pakistan Army confirmed the apolitical nature of the Indian Army. Two factors—speedy casualty evacuation by air and robust pre-induction training scored higher than issues such as compensation or increased allowances in motivating troops.[30] In this context, Nanavatty's focus on improving pre-induction training in the Siachen Battle School at Base Camp paid rich dividends.

For the better part of Nanavatty's tenure as Commander of the 102 Infantry Brigade, Major General V.R. Raghavan was his GOC (division commander). He fondly remembers him as a fine, clear-thinking, and erudite commander in the soldier-scholar mould. Very calm and deliberate in his demeanour, he was non-interfering but would not hesitate to convey his views firmly where necessary.[31] At one stage, Nanavatty realized that the SAM-7 Surface-to-Air Man-portable air defence system (MANPADS) allocated to the brigade was untested at high altitudes. To test the weapon in live conditions in the Sia La area, he cleared the engagement of an enemy helicopter within range of a SAM-7 team even though there existed an unwritten and unspoken norm of both sides avoiding targeting each others' helicopters as they were literally the lifelines at several higher posts. Fortunately for Nanavatty, the shoulder-fired weapon missed the target and prevented a possible escalation. Raghavan promptly reminded Nanavatty that the Indian Army was more dependent than the enemy on helicopter-based maintenance operations and that he should think twice before escalating matters. However, in the years ahead, both armies would bring down enemy helicopters on a few occasions.

Another area where Nanavatty had a mild difference of opinion with Raghavan involved Annual Confidential Reports. Raghavan conveyed in a letter that Nanavatty was a trifle too liberal in some of the reports he had raised.[32] Responding to the letter, Nanavatty respectfully wrote back, 'My decision to give officers an outstanding overall rating was a conscious and deliberate one after much thought. I felt it necessary to elevate an officer whose operational performance was worthy of note in a sea of "7s" and "8s." You will, I think, find that such individuals have almost without exception been recommended for distinguished service awards, too. It has been against my instinctive reporting trend, and I have been guided solely by what I saw of the individual officer during his tour of duty. In a "Battle Report", I think that is how it should be.'[33]

Ironically, in later years, Nanavatty acquired a reputation for being a 'tough' reporting officer. MS Branch in Army HQ would selectively incorporate what was known as the 'Nanavatty Factor' to moderate his strict grading policy. Nanavatty confessed that he did not grade anyone above eight throughout his career unless they were actively involved in operations.

Brigadier Rostum Kaikhushru Nanavatty's last visit to a forward post on the Siachen Glacier was on 19 December 1990 after two years and three months in command of 102 Infantry Brigade in Operation MEGHDOOT in Siachen. The day previous he had formally handed over command of the formation to his relief Brigadier Ajay Masih but was required to continue in station in accordance with extended handing/taking-over norms then prevalent. That morning the CO of the Southern Glacier Battalion had reported that his post at Rewari was being shelled with unusual severity and was out of communication with his HQ. Seeing that Masih was indisposed Nanavatty sought his acquiescence and flew to the post to take stock of the situation. Even as desultory shelling continued the Cheetah helicopter barrelled in, delivered Nanavatty and departed without missing a beat. Nanavatty met with the post commander and the troops, reassured them and commended them for staying strong; and, an hour or so later after satisfying himself that the situation was under control was 'plucked' out by another helicopter. Miraculously there were no casualties. The second-in-command (2IC) of the Light Regiment in the Southern Glacier mischievously called it the enemy's '100-gun salute' to the outgoing commander![34]

Responding to an email in 2014 from Nitin Gokhale, the veteran journalist and the author of the earliest Indian combat narratives of the Siachen Conflict, *Beyond NJ 9842: The Siachen Saga,* Nanavatty was emphatic that his command experience with 102 Infantry Brigade between September 1988 and December 1990 was arguably the best command assignment in his career. An operational command in a unique environment that involved direct control over artillery units and the conduct of joint operations with the Indian Air Force presented immense physical and mental challenges. Highlighting the 'satisfaction of spending a night at every forward company headquarters; visiting every single post, standing patrol and observation post, and traversing (on my flat feet!) every surface route on the glaciers at least once (if not more often) during my tenure,' Nanavatty added, 'I am not being immodest in claiming that I knew the sector like the back of my hand.'[35]

When Gokhale asked about the most memorable moments during this tenure, Nanavatty listed several that remain etched in his mind as reflecting the Siachen Spirit. The Artillery OP officer on Dogra Hill (6400m), who, conscious of the fact that the enemy was monitoring radio traffic, refused to divulge that he was grievously wounded and continued with his mission until a lull in the battle made it possible to evacuate him by air. The soldier from the 7th Battalion of the Brigade of the Guards (7 GUARDS), who fell several hundred feet and lay immobilized and exposed on the forward slopes of Bana, the highest post on the glacier, greeting the young officer who mounted a perilous rescue with the words, '*Sahib, mujhe pata tha ki aap aoge* (Sir, I knew you would come).' The sad and poignant moment was when a Junior Commissioned Officer (JCO) of 2nd Battalion the Dogra Regiment (2 DOGRA) in charge of the advance support base, even as avalanches were crashing down about him, refused to abandon his post and calmly signed off—forever—saying to his CO, '*Sahib, main yahan se nahi nikal paunga: sab ko mere Ram Ram bol dena* (I will not be able to extricate myself from this post: my good wishes to you all).'[36]

The resolution of the Siachen Conflict has been among the most vexing and intractable issues in India–Pakistan relations since 1984. As a thinking soldier, it occupied much of Nanavatty's mind throughout the rest of his service career and for almost a decade after his retirement. In

2007, in a presentation to the 'Group of 12'—a group of distinguished retired civil servants and officers of the Armed Forces officers presided over by Air Chief Marshal S. Moolgaonkar and Lieutenant General E.A. Vas—in Pune, Nanavatty argued much against the prevailing hawkish perspectives of retaining significant deployment on the glacier. 'The Siachen Area is of limited military significance. Its importance lies in the fact that it is a mountaineer's dream world with numerous peaks above 24,000 feet, and it encompasses the Nubra River basin, which joins the Shyok River to flow into Pakistan. There is a propensity to overthink the threat across the Saltoro Ridge and from the Shaksgam Valley across the Karakoram Range into the Siachen Glacier. The climate, terrain and altitude do not lend themselves to large-scale military operations. India and Pakistan continue to contest the area solely for national and military prestige. A resolution to the conflict is possible and indeed very desirable. However, it is hostage to a resolution of the larger Kashmir issue and the continuing adversarial relations between India and Pakistan.'

Control of the Siachen Glacier continues to occupy significant bandwidth within India's strategic community considering that east of the glacier across the Eastern Karakoram Range lies the vast high-altitude desert plains drained by the Shyok River that the Indian Army calls Sub-Sector North (SSN). The eastern part of SSN along the Line of Actual Control (LAC) which abuts the Aksai Chin region saw much action in the 1962 India–China War and includes the Indian Advanced Landing Ground (ALG) of Daulat Beg Oldie and the Depsang Plains. These areas have seen numerous face-offs in the recent past between Indian and Chinese patrols. India has recently objected to the Chinese building roads and associated infrastructure in the Shaksgam Valley of Pakistan Occupied Kashmir (PoK), terming it as 'illegal attempts to alter facts on the ground.'[37]

The stalemate over Siachen continues, and unless there is a Black Swan event in the form of a natural calamity, the status quo could remain for the foreseeable future, draining resources and taking lives over what is akin to a 'struggle of two bald men over a comb'.[38]

After Rostum left for Siachen, Suniti and the boys continued to stay in Arjun Vihar, awaiting the allotment of Separated Family Quarters. At Suniti's insistence, Rostum applied for and obtained a temporary civil telephone connection for the family. Suniti waited anxiously for the telephone to ring. On the seventh day, the Brigade 'Sparrow' or Signals Officer, deeming it high time that the new commander spoke to his family, connected Suniti on a call. Wholly preoccupied with his new assignment, Rostum absentmindedly thanked Suniti for her call. Ha! As though she knew his military number! That was the last time that the Sparrow put a call through of his own volition. The three continued to commute to Modern School—Suniti and Veer to the Junior Wing and Rushad separately to the Senior School, for a year.

Three landmark family events occurred while Rostum was in command of his brigade—the arrival of Boomer the basset hound, the joint Navjote ceremony of Rushad and Veer, and Rushad's departure to boarding school. Boomer arrived in a dog container from New York, a gift from Suniti's sister. He was a wonderful distraction and soon became a much-loved family member. His serious training only began when Rostum came home on leave.

Learning the Zoroastrian prayers and preparing for their Navjote required a fair deal of effort. To help the boys understand the faith, Suniti took the boys to the scholarly Pilloo Jungalwala, the author of several children's books on Zoroastrianism. The prayers were learned at home with the aid of books and cassettes.

One of the prevailing jokes at Partapur was that whenever the commander took leave to go home, the weather packed up! The Navjote date, place and time had been fixed, train bookings to Pune confirmed and leave granted. But, true to form, the weather played truant on the glacier. With Rostum delayed, the family caught the train from Delhi to Pune, minus the head of the family! Fortunately, Rostum had given himself a cushion of three days and made it there in the nick of time. It was a simple, private ceremony at the grandparents' home, with two priests initiating Rushad and Veer into the Zoroastrian faith. The boys were faultless in the chanting of the prayers.

Soon, it was time to start preparing the keenly motivated Rushad for the highly competitive Doon School entrance exam. Suniti helped in the preparations for the exam, which Rushad cleared successfully. Rushad's little trunk was packed, and it was time to leave for Dehradun. The family awaited Rostum's arrival. As usual, Rostum got delayed due to inclement weather. On 31 March, the three took a bus to Dehradun, uncertain of Rostum's whereabouts.

Surprise, surprise! In the wee hours of the following day, there was a tap on the windowpane. Rostum had made it in time to take Rushad to boarding school for the first time. The family posed for a photograph to mark the momentous occasion. However, the normally effervescent Veer completely lost his smile. Upon being questioned, his angry reply was that his parents ought to have 'born' him earlier so that he could have gone to boarding school at the same time as his brother.

Aware of the risks of commanding 102 Infantry Brigade, Suniti looked forward eagerly to Rostum's weekly calls. During his second winter on the glacier, there was telephone silence for three weeks. Naturally, anxiety levels were high. One night, Suniti vividly dreamed about Rostum having an affair with a beautiful nurse named Margaret, posted in the field hospital in neighbouring Hunder! For a long time after that, Rostum teased Suniti about Margaret.

She also recalls Rostum's set of rules for leave and acclimatization: one for himself and the regular one for the others. He would insist that everyone took their full quota of sixty days of annual leave and twenty days of casual leave, while he hardly took a month off every year. Taking undue advantage of his exceptional fitness levels, when it came to acclimatization, he would rush off to the heights while insisting that everybody else who returned from leave did their mandatory stay at lower altitudes.

Very much a city girl interested in the arts and fond of music concerts and plays, Suniti learned to adapt to a husband fond of the outdoors and the two adventurous boys who wanted 'mama' to come along on their small expeditions. Rostum's prolonged absence while Rushad and Veer were growing up brought Suniti very close to them. Many years later, when Rostum asked the boys whether they felt his absence during their growing years, they said, 'Not really, because we knew that mama represented you in every way.' There, indeed, was a strong woman in the background who held the family together!

Suniti remembers Major General Raghavan kindly, given that her husband would not endorse the thought of families spending the summer at Partapur. Overriding his brigade commander's reservations that the presence of families would disturb the operational equilibrium and that it was not a picnic they were on, Raghavan allowed families to come to Partapur for a few weeks in the summer of 1990. Among the several fond memories Suniti has of that summer in Partapur with Rushad and Veer, visiting Ladakhi homes and being highly impressed by their enlightened way of life were among the highlights. There were several long walks, starlit nights, treks to a waterfall that disappeared and their experiences with a frisky ibex, which had become the brigade's mascot.

The story of this ibex is heartwarming and begins one morning—a year since Rostum had been in command. Aware of his keen interest in nature and his love for animals, the villagers brought him a very young ibex. A young goatherd, out with his flock, had found him abandoned by the ibex herd. Perhaps the mother had died. The commander willingly adopted him; however, feeding him proved to be a challenge as he rejected both fresh and powdered milk. Yak's milk did not suit him, nor did that of a dzo. A foster mother had to be found. Fortunately, a pregnant mountain goat proved to be the ideal foster mother. The little fellow began to thrive and grow. Within three months, mama goat gave birth to her kid, and the ibex accepted his foster brother with equanimity.

Initially given a free run through the camp, the trio wasted no time raiding the kitchen garden in the Mess with its precious, short-lived crop of fresh vegetables. Very reluctantly, Rostum ordered that they remain confined to one of the two animal enclosures in the camp.

The ibex soon grew very fond of the brigade commander, and in return, he got special privileges. Whenever the commander was at home, the ibex was let loose. He would head straight for the hut, approach the nearest open window, spring onto the sill, and cautiously enter. He never deigned to enter through the door! On his return, as his helicopter would land on the helipad, the three would rush for the quadrangle outside his office. As he drove up in his jeep, they would present a perfect guard of honour. Seeing was believing![39]

When the family came to visit, the ibex befriended them quickly. However, he began to ignore Rostum almost as though he was jealous. By then, the ibex had grown to half his full size. His curved horns had grown alarmingly, but he was infinitely gentle. Twelve-year-old Rushad would curve his hands above his head to form a pair of horns as an invitation to the ibex to butt him, which the ibex did—but so gently that they knew he would never hurt him. Watching the ibex and the boys indulge in this mock fight was a rare pleasure. The ibex was wary of Veer, the younger boy, who was somewhat more boisterous in his approach and usually declined to play with him.

Reflecting on the quality of the time that Rostum spent with his sons, particularly during his operational tenures, Rushad reckons that it was a mix of complete involvement interspersed with distraction. 'He could be relaxed and witty with a repository of wisecracks directed spontaneously, but also distant when preoccupied—I was very fond of the outdoors and wished I could have spent more time with him doing things like trekking and climbing.' Now in his mid-forties, Rushad reckons he makes an extra effort to commit himself 100 per cent whenever his children ask for his time. Rushad's reflections mirror the feelings of most children of service personnel.

Ten-year-old Veer, perceptive and observant, would wander around the brigade headquarters for hours together, exploring the streams and fascinating rock formations before dropping into his father's office. Being the youngest, he was the only one given the license to intrude into Nanavatty's office space. Veer recollects that his father had rearranged his office, positioned his table next to the window, and always left it open for the ibex to enter. On his part, the ibex would jump through the window onto the table like a ballet dancer and navigate his way into the room without toppling or disturbing anything on the table.

As the time drew near for the end of Rostum's tenure, the future of the ibex began to perplex him. He had three options: to release him into the wild, give him to a zoo or leave him where he was. After much thought, he decided that the ibex would be the safest and happiest where he was. The other officers assured their commander that the ibex would be well looked after. Unobserved, one even photographed the commander, bidding him a quiet goodbye. That was the last time Rostum saw the ibex. But he did not forget his gentle companion. He continued to enquire after him and learned that the ibex had mated with a goat. The result was a pair of 'gobex' kids. What an enchanting thought that was. About three years later, the Nanavattys heard that the ibex had passed away. Suniti writes poignantly: 'None of us will ever forget him. We have many wonderful memories of the ibex and the summer of 90. We can feel his gentle presence whenever we recall those times. We know his spirit dances at will on the craggy mountaintops of Ladakh.'[40]

8

INTERLUDE BETWEEN OPERATIONS

'The military leader lives simply and within his means. He asks no personal favours, seeks no privileges and ensures there is no misuse of resources.'

—Nanavatty speaking at a Leadership Seminar at NDA on 14 January 2009

It was October 1990. Nanavatty and his division commander, Raghavan, were in a helicopter visiting a forward locality in the Southern Glacier Sub Sector. At one point, Raghavan turned to Nanavatty and, above the chatter of the rotors, said that he was sorry that Nanavatty hadn't made the cut for the prestigious National Defence College (NDC) Course commencing January 1991. Raghavan was solicitous, expressed his concern and suggested that Nanavatty represent through proper channels against his non-selection for the course. Nanavatty was unaware and unfazed. His immediate response was 'it does not matter': he was thoroughly enjoying his command and there was no question of his representing against a decision of a selection board at Army HQ. This was perhaps the first significant setback in his career, and he took the news, like a good soldier, on his chin. To put the matter in proper perspective, being nominated for the NDC course in the Indian Army is a matter of pride and for some, even a matter of life and death. It is a reward for a consistently above average professional performance hitherto, and possibly a 'ticket' to a two- and three-star rank. The author knows of many officers throwing in the towel after not being nominated for the course—but not Nanavatty. Suniti recollects that she did sense disappointment but never noticed any despondency. She reckons that there might have been a 'Plan B' but saw no signs of any flagging in his commitment to soldiering and the army.

Unknown to Nanavatty, in June 1990, a little prior to these events, Lieutenant General B.C. Joshi, by then the GOC-in-C Southern Army Command and the future army chief, had wanted Nanavatty as his Brigadier General Staff (Operations). However, Army HQ rightly insisted that the latter complete his two-year tenure in command of the brigade as they felt he was certain to make it to the NDC Course in 1991. When Nanavatty did not make the grade, Army HQ decided to post him to the Defence Services Staff College after his Siachen tenure. It was then that Nanavatty requested a posting close to Pune on compassionate grounds. His father had suffered a series of debilitating strokes and his mother, the only caregiver on-hand, could do with some family support. In November, Joshi wrote Nanavatty a letter saying, 'I made a second attempt to get you as my Brigadier-in-charge of Administration (Brig A) after the NDC list was finalized but was told that it was too low grade a job for an officer of your talent. I have made another attempt invoking the Military Secretary (MS) with a view to see if you could be placed at Belgaum. Once again, the main reason against it seems to be your "high career profile". Let us see what comes of it. As a last resort, you will have to grin and bear it.'[1]

Dr Akshay Joshi, General Joshi's son, a former commander in the Indian Navy and now a senior bureaucrat in the National Security Council Secretariat, recollects that his father regarded Nanavatty highly and often spoke of the need to resurrect his career as the army could ill-afford to see such an outstanding officer fall by the wayside.[2] It is in the backdrop of these developments that Nanavatty was posted as Commander, Platoon Commander's (PC) Wing at the Infantry School, Belgaum. Nanavatty was delighted at the opportunity to evolve, teach and practice infantry small unit tactics—his forte—at his alma mater and looked forward to the task.

Driving to Belgaum from Delhi via Mhow, with Rushad and their basset hound Boomer for company, was a pleasant 'boys only' journey. Unfortunately, they met with a nasty accident at dawn an hour or so out of Mhow. Blinded by the lights of an oncoming truck on the narrow two-lane highway, Nanavatty was late in spotting a bus that lay on its side half-way across the road as a result, apparently, of a mishap the previous day. Despite 'standing' on his brakes, there was a mighty collision. Rushad, asleep in the co-driver seat slid, into the well of the car and was cushioned by Boomer at his feet and Nanavatty hit his head against the windscreen and cracked it! Both father and son were relatively unhurt. The front of their 1982 Volkswagen had been driven in but German steel had saved the day.

When the dust settled, both father and son realized that Boomer had vanished. Rudely awakened, completely disoriented and frightened out of his wits, the dog had shot off and disappeared in the semi-darkness into the fields and beyond. It took the duo a while to track him down, calm him and coax him back to the car. Locking the car, the three of them thumbed a lift in a passing truck and backtracked their way to the nearest police station. Using the police communications network Nanavatty spoke to his good friend Brigadier Ravi Palsokar, then an instructor in the Senior Command Wing in the College of Combat and sought his assistance. Settling Rushad and Boomer in the police station, he hitched a ride in yet another truck and returned to the site of the accident. By midday, an insurance agent from Indore had visited him; late in the afternoon, he was relieved to see a staff car and recovery vehicle arrive to take them back to Mhow.

At Mhow, Ravi and his wife, Villol were the perfect hosts: they set up calls to family both in Delhi and Pune and fed the Nanavattys. The following day, in the afternoon, a mid-size truck was lined up; the car was loaded onto the truck and with father, son and Boomer squeezed into the cab with the driver, they 'winged' their way to Pune driving through the night.

Between 1965 and 1991, Nanavatty met with four vehicle accidents: the first in 1965 in Nagaland where his Jeep rolled over and for a moment and he thought it was goodbye; the second in 1966 after Dussehra celebrations in Calcutta with the battalion—the bachelor boys out for a drive in a borrowed car after 'Kalratri' well past mid-night slammed into a truck full of Bangla Bandhus outside Fort William (Nanavatty is not sure which of the two lots were the more inebriated!); the third in 1984 at Warminster, in a British Army Staff car head-on collision; and the last one described above. Save for the one just outside Warminster, Nanavatty was the culprit—the driver. He reckons, 'I would never have made it beyond the first aircraft accident if I had been a fighter pilot!'

Thus far, Nanavatty believed that small unit tactics—individual, section and platoon level fighting skills, techniques, tactics and drills—was the cutting edge of infantry in battle and the subject was simply not receiving the attention it deserved. Here was a god-sent opportunity for him to try and do something about it. He started by carefully reviewing the PC Course syllabus and improving the quality and content of the central lectures and lecture demonstrations. Through networking at the personal level, he made good use of the excellent but somewhat underutilized Maratha Light Infantry Regimental Centre field firing ranges. And he commenced work on a revised Platoon Commanders Handbook—a pet project that he could never really complete to his satisfaction.

Lieutenant General Joshi in Pune however, had other things in mind. Tipped to replace General Sunith Francis Rodrigues as the next army chief, he embarked on an ambitious study on the reorganization of units in the arms and supporting arms. Nanavatty was picked to lead a small team to look at the 'Reorganization of the Infantry Battalion'. Joshi asked his study group members to be transformative and bold in their approach. He demanded that the infantry study group carefully examine the idea of an infantry battalion with three rifle companies instead of four. The study group came up with three distinct infantry battalion organizations—an infantry battalion Type 3, Type 4A and Type 4B. Among a host of other recommendations common to all was the conversion of the erstwhile Pioneer Platoon into a 'Commando platoon', an idea Nanavatty had experimented with in his unit as the CO. The platoon, while retaining its pioneer and explosive handling skills, was to be capable of reconnaissance, sniping, and military mountaineering skills. While the study group recommended the name 'Reconnaissance' or 'Pathfinder' for the platoon to avoid overusing the term 'Commando', it was Joshi who came up with the nom de plume 'Ghatak', a name that has now stuck. The Type 3 battalion with three rifle companies had advantages but also the one obvious disadvantage—the loss of one rifle company. This proved too revolutionary a concept for the wizened infantry fraternity and what was approved was the infantry battalion Type 4B. The study demanded frequent trips to Pune where the members met periodically. This was disruptive and impacted his work and plans for the PC Wing, but it couldn't be helped.

Following the reorganization study, Lieutenant General S.K. Pillai, the Director General Infantry, was enthused by Nanavatty's suggestion that a comprehensive review be carried out of infantry small unit tactics. Barely had the study group been formed under Nanavatty and preliminary work started when the latter found himself on the list for the National Defence College Course beginning in January 1992. This unfortunately put paid to the study, too. Nanavatty departed the PC Wing in the Infantry School, Belgaum, with mixed feelings. It had been a hectic year. While satisfied with the work on the reorganization of the Infantry battalion, he was disappointed that he could neither do full justice to the task of improving the PC course nor properly undertake and complete the Infantry small unit tactics study.

After Rostum took over command of the PC Wing in Belgaum, Veer joined the military school there as a day scholar. This time, it was Rostum's turn to work with Veer to help him prepare for The Doon School entrance exam. The family had to travel to Pune for Veer to sit for the exam, which he easily cleared. And, while Rostum was posted in Delhi for the NDC, Veer left for Doon. From then on, for the first week after the boys returned to boarding school after the holidays, Suniti and Rostum spoke very little. Suniti feared that she would burst into tears at the slightest provocation, and Rostum maintained a stiff upper lip.

The NDC was to be an altogether different experience: an opportunity to listen to 'wise men' and domain experts and do some serious reading in the excellent library. During the course Nanavatty wrote his dissertation on the 'Use of the Armed Forces in Aid to Civil Authority: Problems and Prospects'. An abridged version of the paper appeared in the NDC Journal Volume XV, November 1993, and caught the attention of the national press. It was a subject that he was to be closely associated with for the final ten years of his career as a soldier. Somewhat detached and quietly observant through the course, he earned the moniker '*Chhuppa* (Hidden) Rostum' for not asking even one question during the innumerable central lectures and presentations—a matter of great amusement to Suniti and the boys. Air Chief Marshal Krishnaswamy, then an Air Commodore and Nanavatty's compatriot on the course, recalls him as 'a fine officer who spoke little but, whenever he did, demonstrated great knowledge and depth'.

It was towards the end of the course that Nanavatty learned officially that he was approved for promotion to the rank of Major General in the command and staff stream. As was his wont, he sought command of a division in Operation RAKSHAK in J&K. He wrote to Lieutenant General D.S.R. Sahni, his former Corps Commander and then the GOC-in-C Northern Command. Sahni acknowledged his letter promptly and stated that it was unlikely there would be a vacancy for a division commander soon in his command. Nanavatty persisted in his efforts and sought an interview with Lieutenant General V.K. Singh, the Military Secretary (MS) who had been his ADG PP for a while after General Joshi. At the meeting, the MS heard what Nanavatty had to say, smiled tolerantly and said, 'You've done your bit in the Siachen: we are thinking of sending you to an offensive strike formation in a peace station where you can train them properly for war.' Nanavatty said he was simply mortified at the prospect of commanding a formation in a peace station; with that, the conversation ended with the MS graciously saying, 'he would see what could be done'.

On annual leave in Delhi after the NDC Course, it was in January 1993 that Nanavatty received his posting orders as the Major General General Staff (MGGS) (B), HQ Northern Command at Udhampur. It was a new appointment, created presumably to share the increased workload of the erstwhile MGGS, now to be referred to as MGGS (A). The latter appointment was held by Major General Sethi, an experienced, efficient and capable artillery officer who had commanded 25 Infantry Division and enjoyed the full confidence of the GOC-in-C. He was in no mood whatsoever to share his workload. In their very first meeting, he made it clear to Nanavatty that his responsibilities would be confined to matters concerning staff duties, weapons and equipment, education, and IT; the latter about which Nanavatty knew very little. Under no circumstances was he therefore to interfere in intelligence, operational and training-related matters!

Nanavatty used his time gainfully, familiarizing himself with areas south of the Pir Panjal, thc 'Valley', and parts of Ladakh he was unfamiliar with. Four months later, in early June 1993, fate intervened. Major General Inder Verma, GOC 19 Infantry Division, a fellow Gorkha and a good friend, was seriously wounded during an encounter in the Baramulla sector; and, thirty-six hours later, Nanavatty was on his way to assume command of the division.

9

COVERT WAR IN BARAMULLA

'Offensive Counter Anti National (CANE) Operations will be pursued against all militant groups without prejudice or discrimination, and the focus must be on pro-Pakistan militant groups.'

—Nanavatty, in his first address to all Staff officers at HQ 19 Infantry Division, 25 June 1993

From the icy heights of the Siachen Glacier and two years and six months of less-intense soldiering, it was back to a command assignment in strife-torn Baramulla, a bustling town in North Kashmir where the situation in mid-1993 was one of near anarchy. Major General Nanavatty assumed command of 19 Infantry Division as the General Officer Commanding (GOC) on 12 June 1993, immediately after his predecessor was shot at and injured during an encounter with Anti-National Elements (ANE) in a village close to Baramulla. Of interest to the reader would be that all insurgents and militants in the state of J&K before 1994, including Pakistan-trained militants (PTMs), were officially classified as ANE but will mostly be termed as terrorists in the chapter. It is only after the widespread introduction and consolidation of Jehadi groups, such as the Harkat-ul-Ansar (HuA) and the Lashkar-e-Taiba (LeT), as the vanguard of Pakistan's covert war in J&K, that the Indian

Army officially started terming them as 'terrorists.' Nanavatty's command tenure as GOC 19 Infantry Division (19 Inf Div) between June 1993 and December 1994 was during the peak of turmoil in J&K. A brief recall of the security situation in the Kashmir Valley from the late 1980s to the early 1990s provides a backdrop to his stint as a division commander.

The Jammu and Kashmir Liberation Front (JKLF), led by the UK-based Amanullah Khan and operating out of Muzzafarabad, the capital of Pakistan Occupied Kashmir (PoK), was the first militant group to present a serious security challenge to the Indian state in the early 1980s. Its choice of Muzzafarabad was symbolic: in October 1947, during Operation GULMARG, the tribal Lashkars had launched their offensive into Kashmir from there. In 1984, the JKLF drew first blood when they kidnapped and executed an Indian diplomat in Birmingham, UK. The act invited a swift response in India. Maqbool Butt, a senior leader of the JKLF, tried and convicted for acts of terrorism in India, was executed. The consequent expulsion of JKLF cadres from Britain led to the group concentrating in PoK. Following this turn of events, large numbers of Kashmiri youth started crossing over into PoK to be trained as Mujahideen or Islamic guerrilla fighters.

The 1987 election in J&K was a watershed event in which the National Conference (NC) party and the Congress alliance came to power after a highly fractured and reportedly rigged mandate. Several JKLF leaders, who campaigned for the Jamaat-e-Islami and the Muslim United Front against the NC–Congress alliance, were disillusioned by the widespread rigging of the vote. They were drawn increasingly to the secessionist agenda.[1] The JKLF, however, was not driven by Islamic ideology alone. Neither did it necessarily subscribe to the 'Kashmir Banega Pakistan' idea. Instead, its cadres were committed to '*Azadi*' (Freedom) and drew inspiration from the Palestine Liberation Organization (PLO). Even so, General Muhammad Zia-ul-Haq, the military dictator of Pakistan, sought to seize the opportunity and directed the Inter-Services Intelligence (ISI) to extend support to the JKLF.

The ISI had honed its skills under the CIA. It was well-versed in the art of covert war and black operations and was ready to expand its operations into J&K. However, in the early 1990s, the JKLF fragmented following the death of its first military commander, Ishfaq Majeed

Wani, in an encounter with the Indian security forces (SF). That and the ISI's decision to cease support to the JKLF hastened its collapse, and Amanullah Khan's dream of an independent Kashmir evaporated.[2] Several J&K-based JKLF cadre exfiltrated into PoK and joined different pro-Pakistan Islamic Jihadist groups that were being trained to infiltrate into J&K.[3]

The ISI had several irons in the fire but chose to sponsor the Hizbul Mujahideen (HM) with Syed Salahuddin, a one-time fiery student leader, as its head. Some years after this, several prominent former members of the JKLF, including Yasin Malik, attempted to join the political mainstream as part of what came to be known as the All Party Hurriyat Conference (APHC). However, by the mid-nineties, the HM, owing to their predominantly indigenous Kashmiri character, also found themselves out of favour, paving the way for violent pan-Islamic Jihadist Groups such as the Lashkar-e-Taiba (LeT) and Jaish-e-Mohamed (JeM).

The encounter that brought Nanavatty to Baramulla was instructive and offered him a chastening perspective of the prevailing situation. A patrol from 15 PUNJAB based in the town of Baramulla had isolated three terrorists in a house in the village of Sheel Kangal (near Sopore), resulting in a firefight. The situation called for using an 84mm Rocket Launcher (RL) to do the job clinically. Incredible as it may sound, the 'rules of engagement' at the time called for specific clearance by an officer of the rank of GOC of a division before using an RL. Major General Inder Verma, who dutifully descended on the scene of the incident as rapidly as he could to 'see for himself' and assess the situation, suffered a grievous gunshot injury to his arm. Worse still, the Colonel GS (Ops) designate who was accompanying him was killed. This incident perhaps was the first of its kind, but sadly, it was not to be the last.[4]

The Valley was in turmoil. Large-scale public demonstrations were the order of the day. The demand for '*Azadi*', though few could explain what they really meant by the word, was on everyone's lips. Terrorists of foreign extraction were *mehmaan* (guests). Terrorists neutralized by the security forces in operations, irrespective of their nationality, were *shaheed* (martyrs). They were accorded public funerals, which often resulted in mass hysteria: and, Kashmiri '*daam*' (pretense and exaggerated display) was on full display. Terrorists sought to establish their presence in urban and semi-urban areas, particularly Srinagar, Sopore, Baramulla and Handwara. They would carry out stand-off attacks, which were, by and large, ineffective, and resort to indiscriminate firing of small arms to demonstrate their presence and cock a snook at the security forces. In the Indian context, the security forces as referred to in this chapter comprise of the Armed Forces, the Central Armed Police Forces and the J&K state police.

Grenade attacks in congested areas to provoke SF retaliation and inflict unintended civilian casualties were common, as were attacks against isolated vehicles using mines and improvised explosive devices (IED). Mass murders of members of the minority community and the targeted killing of suspected 'informers' resulted in an environment of fear. Fidayeen actions, suicide attacks and the use of IED in tandem were yet to come. A Fidayeen action differed from a suicide attack in that well-trained terrorists would carry out and pursue a planned operation even if it meant a fight to the finish. Suicide attacks, on the other hand, are primarily driven by ideological, religious and political motives, performed outside the context of conventional war in which assailants are prepared to commit suicide to destroy others.[5]

While the Indian Army intercepted and inflicted significant casualties on terrorists infiltrating across the Line of Control (LoC) in the initial phases, counterterrorism (CT) operations in rear areas (interior areas away from the LoC) were generally of the 'hit and miss' type large-scale 'area domination', 'cordon and search' (C&S), and 'search and destroy' missions with poor returns. A well-thought-out and flexible CT operations grid in rural areas comprising sub-unit operating bases would only come about towards the end of 1993.

Major P.K. 'Royal' Mehrishi, the GSO 2 (Operations), has clear recollections of a summer morning on 12 June 1993 when Nanavatty assumed command of 19 Inf Div. He said, 'A youthful-looking Major General with a khaki beret got down from the divisional commander's Jonga (jeep) with a black leather bag slung over his shoulder. He brushed off requests to carry the bag and remarked, "This is my bag, and I will carry it." Walking into his office, he noticed the "furnishings" and articles adorning the desk. Turning to Royal, he said, *"Sab hata do"* (remove everything); we are in the field and operations—no "bells and whistles" in the office, please.'[6] Colonel K.S. Aithmian, CO 15 PUNJAB, recollects that all battalion and brigade commanders in the division knew that Nanavatty's standing in the Indian Army was 'rooted in truthfulness, honesty, good intentions, professional excellence and self-belief. Impartial and independent-minded officers perceived him as being genuinely interested in the good of the organization. This approach had a pronounced effect on everyone during his command tenures.'[7]

There is an interesting story here about the khaki beret. Until Field Marshal Manekshaw became the army chief, all officers promoted to Colonel rank and above wore a khaki beret. Nanavatty had bought himself a couple of good-quality khaki berets in the UK, assuming he would make it to at least full Colonel's rank before retiring. He was reluctant to discard them when the dress orders changed and continued wearing the khaki beret during his command assignments in the field. Was there a hidden rebellious streak within!

At the time, terrorism was primarily confined to the 15 Corps area of responsibility (AOR) in the Kashmir Valley north of the Pir Panjal Range. However, isolated terrorist-related incidents were reported south of the mountain range, too. With its headquarters in Srinagar, the corps had a force level of three infantry divisions and two independent infantry brigades. 19 Inf Div, with its HQ at Baramulla, comprised two infantry brigades and a sector HQ with an infantry and BSF battalion under command, all deployed on the LoC. In addition, an Independent Infantry Brigade in the rear areas of the division managed counterterrorist (CT) operations. Subsequently, in July 1993, an additional infantry brigade was allotted for CT operations for approximately six months in the Rafiabad area north of the Jhelum River. 19 Inf Div was a dual-tasked formation at the time responsible for conventional operations against Pakistan in the event of war and CT operations to include counter infiltration and exfiltration operations in its AOR.[8]

After the customary initial briefings by the staff and his brigade commanders at their respective headquarters, Nanavatty gave himself two months to get to know his staff officers, formation commanders and COs down to the unit level—'two down' as they say in the army; identify with the troops; get familiar with the terrain and AOR; observe and learn from the conduct of ongoing operations—and, was forever asking questions. Next, he set about doing what he termed as 'tidying up the AOR'—restoring the order of battle (ORBAT); rationalizing—reducing if not eliminating attachments and detachments; reviewing the tasking of formations and units; and redrawing boundaries where necessary.

A firm believer in FM Rommel's dictum, 'one look is worth a hundred reports', Nanavatty, according to Royal, would have walked the entire frontage of the division and visited every platoon locality on foot in the sector at least once during his tenure. He was perfectly at ease interacting with the men, sitting on the ground and sharing a mug of tea or a meal from the *langar* (community kitchen). Royal clarifies, 'These events were not orchestrated in any way. It simply was his way of doing things.' On one such 'walkathon', Royal remembers that he managed a peek into Nanavatty's sling bag—his signature piece of equipment from his days as a brigade commander. In it was an immaculately maintained .45 Colt Pistol of 1905 vintage gifted to him by his father, a pair of binoculars and a magnetic compass. 'Also in the bag was a neatly folded map of the sector, a notebook, water bottle, a packed meal, and a bar of chocolate—three pora rolls (thin Parsi-style omelettes wrapped in roti) was the "haversack meal of choice" when Suniti was around!'[9]

Curious to see how units conducted their operations, he accompanied 15 PUNJAB on a 24-hour operation over the Kazinag Dhar, a mountain range across which terrorists infiltrated into the Rafiabad Area. Joining the unit in the late afternoon and seeing him take his place quietly in the order of march with his 'buddy', the irreverent Sikh troops watching, mischievously quipped, *'Ki gal hai; aaj te tradesmen bhi aye si operation vich* (How come a tradesman is out on operation with us today)?' since the only non-Sikhs in the unit were tradesmen—cooks, barbers, *dhobis* (washermen), and the like causing a poker-faced Nanavatty, who was not amused in the least, to icily pronounce, 'I am your GOC and I want to see how you work!' putting an end to the good natured ribbing. Keeping pace with the lads through the night, not uttering a word, quietly observing their drills and procedures, the Punjabis were reassured. As dawn broke and the leading elements approached a village on the edge of the forest, there was a flurry of shots fired in the distance, presumably sounding a warning. Suddenly there was a commotion, and a torrent of troops bore down the slopes shouting *'pajjo, pajjo'* (run, run in Punjabi), almost sweeping Nanavatty off his feet—silence, field craft, and battle craft be damned! The only good thing was that they were running towards where the shots came from and not away! Much like in Sri Lanka, Nanavatty's acceptance by his officers and men was because he was willing to put himself in harm's way along with them, not to score points but to observe and learn.[10]

Nanavatty would arrive at a few broad conclusions at the end of his familiarization period. First, CT operations would, of necessity, be his priority. Second, the Pakistan Army (PA) deployed on the LC must 'pay' for the support they extended to terrorists. Third, effective counter-infiltration operations demanded that special attention be paid to 'turning' or neutralizing guides and dominating the 'Receiving Areas'—areas where infiltrating groups linked up with inland guides and Over Ground Workers (OGW). Fourth: Baramulla town, the district headquarters, must be rid of the menace of terrorism. Fifth, intelligence was the key to effective CT operations in the rear areas. Sixth, the army and police needed to work in 'sync'. And, lastly, role and area-specific pre-induction training under formation arrangements was necessary for new units.[11]

The HQ staff quickly settled into a routine with their new GOC. When in his headquarters, the day would commence with 'morning prayers'—a review of the operational situation along the LoC and in the rear areas of the division in a conference discussing essential matters and conveying decisions. Nanavatty encouraged his officers to air their views freely. He felt it promoted self-confidence, instilled a sense of participation and ownership, and helped the individual's all-round development. He had what he termed a 'nasty' habit of drafting all his directives, orders, instructions, policies and demi official letters—always only using a pencil and eraser. Nanavatty would then invite comments from the staff before their finalization and dispatch. He was to follow this practice throughout his career and did so because he was particular about what he wished to convey, how he wished to do things, and because it saved time. Staff officers were encouraged to work to laid-down timings irrespective of whether the GOC was in office; he would invariably skip lunch and work through the day. After work, it was always a grim battle with his ADC, Mukesh Gurung, on the squash courts—a contest the latter invariably won, but not without a fight.

The District Security Committee meeting, which Nanavatty chaired, was held once a month in the GOC's office and whenever there was a specific need. The District Commissioner (DC) and the District Superintendent of Police (SP) attended. Though there were several BSF units dotted about in sub-units and detachments primarily to protect vulnerable areas and points (VAs & VPs) in the divisional AOR, the BSF representatives would do pretty much as they pleased: their chain of command was distinct, and the less said, the better about the 'coordination of effort', a fundamental principle of internal security operations. Nanavatty insisted on a round table for the meetings, so no one was sitting at the so called 'head'! It was not uncommon at the time for senior army officers who outranked their civilian peers to send a junior officer of appropriate (equal) rank to represent them if meetings were held elsewhere. It was a silly matter of protocol which had no place in an operational situation.

When Nanavatty assumed command of 19 Inf Div, several changes in the higher command organization were in the offing. General B.C. Joshi was appointed the army chief. Not surprisingly, he visited 15 Corps on his first official tour outside Delhi accompanied by Lieutenant General Surender Singh, the Northern Army Commander designate. Apart from the corps staff, the three divisional commanders were also required to be present. After the briefing, the chief sought to expand on his plans for the raising and induction of Rashtriya Rifles (RR) formations and units into Operation RAKSHAK, the ongoing CI and CT operations in J&K since 1990, for the express purpose of relieving the infantry of the responsibility for CT operations in the hinterland. Before doing so, he turned to Nanavatty; and presumably harking back to their differences over the concept of RR in the PP Directorate, looked him in the eye and said, 'You will *not* utter a word on this subject' smiled and looked away. Eighteen months later, as Nanavatty's tenure came to an end in December 1994, the first RR Sector HQ and its units would deploy in Baramulla.[12]

Soon after the army chief's visit, Lieutenant General Surender Singh was appointed the GOC-in-C, Northern Command. Briefing the GOC-in-C at his headquarters in Baramulla on his first visit to 19 Inf Div, Nanavatty began by stating that 'the conduct of CT operations in the divisional sector is my priority'. It caused a flutter and drew the GOC-in-C's strong and immediate reaction. Asked to explain, Nanavatty said, in his opinion, 'Pakistan was only likely to resort to conventional operations if we should fail in our CT operations effort.' Later, the Army Commander would visit again and stay the night during a two-day divisional war game conducted by Nanavatty for his officers. Major Bipin Rawat (later India's first ever Chief of Defence Staff), serving with his battalion in the division, would help him put the exercise papers together.[13]

Lieutenant General S. (Paddy) Padmanabhan assumed command of 15 Corps in Srinagar around the same time. According to Nanavatty, Paddy was of pleasant disposition, had a razor-sharp mind, excellent communication skills, and a great sense of humour. Calm in crises, he asked searching questions and listened carefully but seldom interfered. It is to Paddy, ably assisted by Brigadier S.P.S. Kanwar, the commander, Srinagar Sub Area at the time, that credit must go for the successful handling of several delicate incidents and restoring temporary control in Srinagar city. On Srinagar, Nanavatty argued with Paddy that however successful the Indian Army was in securing the peripheral areas, the centre of gravity of the secessionist movement was and would remain Srinagar. He strongly opined that the army should grasp the nettle and assume complete responsibility for the security of the state capital. 'Clearly, this was a political decision, and no one was willing to bite the bullet,' he said. Nanavatty was also severely critical of the static 'bunker' based method of deployment of the police and para-military forces in the city. At every opportunity, he strongly recommended the adoption of an urban CT Grid based on fortified police stations from where patrols with specific tasks could have sallied forth. While the former deployment method was static and predictable, the latter would have been mobile and unpredictable.[14]

Whenever summoned to the corps headquarters, and fortunately, that was not often, Nanavatty was invariably privileged to have a quiet meal with the Padmanabhans in their home. The two men talking shop would exasperate the hostess, and led Mrs Roopa Padmanabhan to remark to the author, 'He was always prim and proper, like those German Wehrmacht Generals of the Second World War. Polite and formal, he never made small talk with me about family and other things, and I always asked Paddy afterwards why he was so stiff, and Paddy would laugh and say, "That is the way he is."'[15]

The one aspect that was plain to Nanavatty during his familiarization was that 'we seemed to have no answer to the Pakistan Army (PA) for aiding, abetting and supporting, in every which way, the infiltration and exfiltration of terrorists across the LoC. They denied any support whatsoever, and there seemed to be nothing we could do about it. It was frustrating. I was convinced that we had to extract a price and make the PA pay for their hostility. No longer was it acceptable to have a PA soldier in his tracksuit sunning himself atop his bunker and shouting a hearty *"Kyun saathi, kya haal hai?* (How are you, my friend?)."'[16] The rules of engagement on the LoC spelt out in policy letters from Army Headquarters were outdated and irrelevant in the current circumstances. Perhaps no one at Army Headquarters had the time or inclination to review what may have seemed to them a trifling matter.

Nanavatty decided he would change the rules of the game and dominate the enemy and 'no man's land' in his sector. He cleared units to engage and destroy all opportunity point targets, specifying the type of targets, the weapons that could be used, and the ranges up to which targets could be engaged without reference to higher headquarters. Since his instructions were at variance with orders from higher formations, he felt obligated to put them down in writing to protect his subordinates. Not all his commanders were overjoyed, though. A 'hot' LoC would also demand greater battlefield discipline from their own troops, and there was bound to be retaliation by the PA. Nanavatty, on the other hand, was seeking to loosen the reins and allow commanders down to the company level the freedom to act without continuously looking over their shoulders. 'We had to message the regular PA soldier that simply "denying" any knowledge and support to terrorists was not going to be enough.'[17]

Recognizing that the PA was bound to respond, 19 Inf Div started examining and preparing for fire assaults and 'shallow penetration' offensive tasks across the LoC—the next step on the escalatory ladder. Uppermost was the need to achieve and maintain moral ascendancy over the enemy, for he firmly believed that 'we had the necessary strength, wherewithal and staying power'.

The aim of Nanavatty's CT operations policy was simple: 'To suppress terrorist activity and restore normalcy to enable the civil administration to assume its legitimate role.' Balancing offensive action with responsible and restrained military-civic action, the policy advocated 'ruthless and efficient conduct of counter-infiltration/exfiltration operations along the LoC and vigorous and relentless conduct of offensive CT operations to neutralize the terrorist organizations in the rear areas of the 19 Inf Div AOR'. Complementing the above were clear instructions to commanders to provide adequate assistance to the civil administration including the police, adopt correct custodial treatment of terrorists during detention and interrogation, and ensure exemplary conduct of the troops towards the civilian population.[18] Directing all his formations to pay special attention to mundane but essential defensive CT operations tasks such as road opening, convoy protection, layered protection of vital assets (VAs and VPs) and protection of isolated detachments, the policy laid out clear guidelines for developing alert and inquisitive soldiers in the division with high standards of situational awareness.[19]

There were three main avenues of infiltration in the 19 Inf Div Sector. First, the densely forested areas between Gulmarg and Mandir Buniyar that led to Rampur and the villages bordering the Kandi north of Gulmarg. Second, past the notorious village of Kamalkote on the North Bank of the Jhelum, along the Kazinag Dhar and into the Rafiabad bowl; and third, through the Lipa Valley and astride the inter-formation boundary with 28 Division, the adjoining division, leading into the densely forested areas of Handwara.

The modus operandi of infiltrating groups usually followed a pattern. The group would first assemble at a 'launch pad', without exception a PA post on the LoC. At the launch pad, they would 'marry up' with their guides to study the terrain, weather and Indian Army (IA) activity on the LoC, and would carry out their surveillance and reconnaisance of routes to the extent possible. In the second stage, a guide(s) would lead the group across the LoC to a rendezvous with Over Ground Workers (OGW) in the 'receiving area'. Here, the group received succour and replenishment after their arduous crossing before moving on to their areas of operation, the second stage, clearly being the most challenging part of the process. Guides were a select lot. They were usually from the Gujjar, Bakkarwal and Pahadi communities and were familiar with the terrain and weather. Blessed with remarkable eyesight, sure-footedness, endurance and instincts, the Gujjar moving through rugged terrain reminded Nanavatty of the feline grace of a leopard. Guides were in the dangerous 'game' simply for the money. Formations and units on the LoC were encouraged to identify and 'turn' them by whatever means possible. The best counter-infiltration results, by far, were achieved using 'turned' guides who could lead a group into an ambush. Additionally, a determined effort was required to be made to cultivate sources in the 'Receiving Areas'.

Second Lieutenant Rajesh Raman (now a senior serving officer), commissioned into 5 RAJPUT, is a second-generation officer. Raman was pitch-forked into intense counter-infiltration operations in the Rampur Sector—an area preferred by the 'fat cats' of various terrorist *Tanzeems* because of the shorter 'trudge' and the proximity of receiving areas. Commanding an isolated post in the upper reaches of the Pir Panjal, Raman established a lower patrol base to dominate the 'Receiving Areas' in a section of the Kandi bordering a village.

On that fateful day, based on credible information that a group of terrorists might attempt to infiltrate through the area, Raman was leading a section strength patrol to reconnoitre the area. Working their way carefully through broken terrain and dense cover, the scout detected and signalled suspicious movement, quickly causing the patrol to go to ground and into an opportunity ambush. In a neat and clean operation, the patrol accounted for the entire group of five infiltrating terrorists, including Abdul Majid Dar, the leader of the Muslim Mujahideen Tanzeem. The patrol recovered several small arms, ammunition and warlike stores, and seven lakh rupees in currency to boot. Raman recalled the incident: 'It was one of those rare occasions where everything went right.'[20]

For Nanavatty, who was constantly encouraging his officers and men to 'fight clever: fight small' and to fight like a 'shikari, not like a chowkidar'; this was a copybook encounter where 'he who sees first, shoots first, and he who shoots first wins'. Later, he would summon the patrol to the divisional headquarters for a 'shabash'. A few weeks later, to Raman's surprise, he received a letter from his father informing him that Nanavatty had written about his son's exploits. Recommended for a Shaurya Chakra, Raman was awarded a Sena Medal. Several months after the unit had moved out of the theatre, Raman was touched when he received a letter of congratulations from Nanavatty.

Nanavatty recalls that 5 RAJPUT had seemed to make a habit of pulling off such operations regularly. Earlier too, a 'turned' guide had led another group of infiltrators into a 'dhok' and their destruction in a pre-planned ambush. The lessons learned in that operation proved critical during subsequent operations. With 'turned' guides leading them, the infiltrating terrorists soon became wary of letting them out of their sight even for a moment, so the game of ruse and counter-ruse would continue. Recounting the incident to the author almost thirty years later, Raman said, 'Nanavatty's attention to detail, sterling qualities of leadership, his ability to relate to and meaningfully engage with young officers and troops, and his relentless operational focus make him a tough act to emulate.'[21]

In July 1993, an additional infantry brigade, commanded by Brigadier Trigunesh Mukherjee, was allotted to 19 Inf Div for CT operations in the rear areas. A welcome addition, the brigade deployed astride the Class 9 road between Baramulla and Handwara, and over six months, it systematically and efficiently stabilized the situation in the Rafiabad

The author with
Lt Gen. Nanavatty,
Dehradun, Jan. 2023.

EARLY DAYS

Rostum's parents, Kaikhushru and Dhan, marry in Rajpipla, Gujarat in 1937.

Kaikhushru Jehangir Nanavatty, Inspector General of Police, Bombay State.

IMA, Panipat Company 31st Course 1st Termers. Rostum standing middle row, fourth from right.

Gentleman Cadet Sergeant Rostum Nanavatty with the Sword of Honour. Flanked by his mother and sister after the Passing Out Parade.

Dec. 1962, a family portrait prior to joining 2/8 GR.

2/8 GR

April 1966, Fort William, Calcutta: Havildar Nand Lal Thapa, George Cross, with (from left to right) B.C. (Rony) Sarma, A.P. Singh, Rostum and Sub. Major Kul Bahadur Gurung.

1967, Fort William Calcutta: Introducing the battalion football team representing the Bengal Area to Lt Gen. S.H.F.J. Manekshaw, MC GOC-in-C Eastern Command.

Jan. 1973, outside the South Block, Army Headquarters: Field Marshal S.H.F.J. Manekshaw inspecting the Guard of Honour provided by the battalion while bidding farewell to the army.

25 Feb. 1981, Cooch Behar. Photograph of officers and JCOs in the battalion at the time of Handing Over Command to Lt Col. Behram Panthaki (seated to Rostum's left).

With his Student Sponsor, Captain Wayne Porter, and his wife, Pat.

Receiving the Distinguished Allied Graduate Award on Course IOAC 1-72 from Lt Gen. R.G. Stilwell, DCOAS Operations.

Allied Students attending IOAC 1-72. Rostum standing front row third from left.

HQ Staff, School of Infantry, Warminster. Brig. Ian Mackay, MC, CBE seated at the centre; Rostum seated fourth from left.

With his ubiquitous sling bag.

With a young Observation Post (OP) officer on the reverse slope of Bhim Top.

With Col. Raghbir Sangera, CO, 7 Guards at Bilafond La.

The Commander and his Ibex.

Pep talk to troops after a raid rehearsal.

With Mr Shiv Sahai, the Superintendent of Police, Col OPS Chauhan, Dy Cdr 79 Mtn Brigade, and an 'over-protective' ADC Mukesh Gurung at the site of an encounter in the Rafiabad Area.

Inspecting captured weapons with Col K. Aithmian CO 15 PUNJAB.

Changki! Welcome home.

With Boomer the Basset and Kartoosi the Bear at the water point.

On a makeshift range at an Assam Rifles post in Manipur.

Receiving Shri George Fernandes on his first visit to the Northeast as the Raksha Mantri.

Receiving the Param Vishisht Seva Medal from President K.R. Narayanan, 2001.

Taking over Northern Command.

With troops in 14 Corps along with the corps commander, Lt Gen. R.B. Singh.

Visiting 9 DOGRA in Drass Sector, accompanied by the CO, Col Ranbir Singh.

'We meet again, sir!' Welcoming the Raksha Mantri, George Fernandes to NC.

At Daulat Beg Oldie with the magnificent Eastern Karakoram Range in the background.

Civilian mine casualties at the LoC, a reality—Jaipur foot to the rescue.

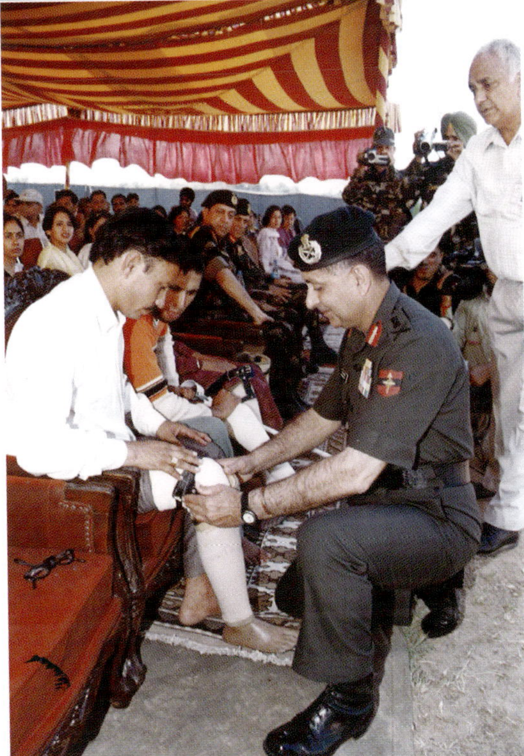

With next of kin of gallantry award winners killed in action.

'Shooting Straight' with the archers of the Gorkha Regiment.

Bidding 'au revoir' to General S. Padmanabhan, the COAS. Nanavatty would follow in his footsteps three months later.

Last Barakhana, 2/8 GR style, at Base Camp.

Bidding goodbye to Northern Command and the army.

We have right to strike but end alienation too: J&K's top Army officer

ONCE again, the Govt seemed to be in two minds over Kashmir, the problem and the solution.

While the seniormost Army commander in the state said India reserved "every right to take military action" against Pakistan but the real challenge was to fulfil the people's aspirations, the MEA's junior minister said the issue was not political but military.

Speaking at a Jammu University seminar on the future of the state, Lieutenant General R K Nanavatty, GOC-in-C, Northern Command, said that the situation now wasn't "entirely dissimilar" to the one in 1965 when Pakistan had forced India to go for "limited conventional operations" in Haji Pir Pass.

But, he added, the challenge now before India was to restore normalcy in Jammu and Kashmir by persuading Pakistan to withdraw its support to militants in the state. And the only way to do this, he added, was by fulfilling the aspirations of the people and reduce their sense of alienation.

This, Gen Nanavatty said, could be done through an improvement in the centre-state relationship, rehabilitation of militants, isolation of foreign mercenaries and economic regeneration.

Nanavatty's statement was an echo of what Defence minister George Fernandes said four days ago in Mamun Cantt when he stressed on the need for a political solution to the Kashmir imbroglio.

However, speaking at the same function, MEA minister of state Omar Abdullah said he disagreed with those who call Kashmir a political problem. "Kashmir is not a political issue but a

CONTINUED ON PAGE 2

Army to Pak: Stop terrorism or else...

BY OUR SPECIAL CORRESPONDENT

Srinagar, Oct. 31: Even as the skirmishes at places along the Line of Control in Jammu and Kashmir continue to shatter peace, the chief of Northern Command on Tuesday chose to sent a direct warning to the Pakistani Army against carrying out any hostile act.

Lt. Gen. R.K. Nanavatty, General Officer Commanding-in-Chief of the Northern Command, said at a seminar held in Jammu University that any hostile act from across the border will be dealt with severely and the enemy taught a lesson.

He said "I've a message for the Pakistani Army opposite the state of Jammu and Kashmir and I'm hoping that media will get it right," he said.

And the general's message was, "We're committed to restraint on Line of Actual Control, the Line of Control which includes the actual ground position line on the Siachen glacier and International Border in Jammu and Kashmir. If, however, the Pakistan Army or terrorists supported by it continue to carryout hostile acts to include sabotage, infiltration, raids or intrusions in a clear violation of the Shimla Agreement we reserve the right to take military action against the Pakistani military and terrorist targets as deemed appropriate."

The Northern Command chief's warning came a couple of weeks after his men claimed smashing about a dozen Pakistani forward posts in Mendhar and Akhnoor sectors along the LoC as a "punitive action" for helping militants to sneak into the Indian side. The Indian action was followed by a series of clashes along the de facto border and International Border in Jammu and Kashmir leaving a number of soldiers and civilians on either side dead and wounded.

The seminar on "Jammu and Kashmir — The way ahead" was organised by the Political Science Department of JU.

. Speaking on the occasion, minister of state for external affairs Omar Abdullah also assured the audience and the world at large that "we'll be as restraint as necessary but at the end of the day where it is necessary we'll act in whatever way we think is essential."

He added, "We'll also protect the lives of our people and the sovereignty of our country at any cost."

Mr Abdullah said that the military option to tackle with what he called was proxy war unleashed by Pakistan was always open.

"The military aspect is and will remain open as long as Pakistan is involved in terrorism on our land," he asserted.

Meanwhile, reports received here said that in fresh clashes between the facing armies in Kashmir Valley's Gulmarg and Uri sectors, one Indian Army trooper was killed and half a dozen wounded on Tuesday.

Reports said that the Pakistani artillery started hitting the Indian positions and villages in the Haji Peer area between Uri and Gulmarg. The shelling continued for an hour before Indians retaliated in "appropriate fashion."

The casualties, if any, caused by this on the other side of the LoC could not be known immediately.

Situation in J&K similar to '65, says Nanavatty

JAMMU: An Army commander Wednesday warned Pakistan that India reserved the right to take military action against its army and terrorist groups if it continued to carry out "hostile acts" against the country like sabotage and infiltration.

In an unusually combative address at a seminar here, Lt-Gen R K Nanavatty, GoC-in-C, Northern Command, said the "blatant aggression" being witnessed now in Jammu and Kashmir was not "entirely dissimilar" to that in August 1965 when India was compelled to undertake limited conventional operations against Pakistan in the Hajipur Bulge.

"The nuclearisation of the subcontinent may have altered the situation but space still exists for limited conventional war. While every effort must be made — politically, diplomatically and economically — to deter Pakistan, we must remain prepared to exercise the military option," Gen Nanavatty said in his address at a seminar on "Jammu and Kashmir: the way ahead."

In an unusually forthright speech, he said, Pakistan must be made to realise that it could only persist with its gross interference in India's internal affairs at its "own peril." (PTI)

Indian Army General sends aggressive war signa

JAMMU, Oct 31—India and Pakistan are close to the situation that existed before their 1965 war, India's army commander in Kashmir said on Wednesday, warning that if pushed to the edge, New Delhi could choose military action against Pakistan's army and Islamic guerrillas.

In the most aggressive war signal in years by a military commander, Lt Gen R K Nanavatty, head of the Indian army's Northern Command, said India must remain prepared for military action, and that the capture of Pakistan-controlled Kashmir was achievable.

"The nuclearisation of the subcontinent might have altered the situation, but despite that, the stage exists for a limited conventional war," Nanavatty said, referring the Indian and Pakistani nuclear arsenals developed after 1998 tests. "We must remain prepared to exercise the military option as well."

"In August 1965, the situation was not entirely dissimilar to what it is today when we undertook a limited, conventional war in the Haji Peer area," Nanavatty said. The Indian assault on the 9,000-foot (2,700-metre) Haji Peer Pass was the first major campaign by Indian troops in the 1965 war.

Nanavatty, who commands the more than half a million soldiers in Jammu-Kashmir, was speaking at a seminar in the state's winter capital of Jammu. His troops guard the international border in southern Kashmir established after the 1971 war and the 20,000-foot (6,000-metre) Siachen Glacier, the world's highest battlefield.

There was no official comment from the Pakistani government on the general's remarks.

Prime Minister Atal Bihari Vajpayee has indicated that the army is set to take tough action to end the 12-year insurgency by Islamic guerrillas in Kashmir - a violent campaign that has claimed tens of thousands of lives. The militants want independence, or merger with Pakistan, for the only mostly Muslim region in Hindu majority India.

A Defense Ministry spokesman said the general's comments assessment of the situation was "theoretically correct. On the ground we are maintaining strict vigil and restraint. In case any action beyond this is required, it will need the will of the nation and a decision by much higher authorities," P K Bandopadhyay, the Defense Ministry spokesman, said.

Nanavatty said India stood for peace, but it would take drastic action if Pakistan did not end its backing for the militants, who strike at military targets and explode bombs in civilian areas. "We are committed to restraint on the Line of Control, (and the) actual ground position on the Siachen Glacier," the general said. "If, however, Pakistan's

Indian paramilitary personnel stand guard under the Chinar tree in Srinagar. In the most aggress war signal in years by a military commander, Lt. Gen. R.K. Nanavatty, general officer commanding the Indian army's Northern Command, said India must remain ready for war, and that the capture Pakistan occupied Kashmir was "achievable."

army and terrorists continue to cause trouble, including sabotage ... we reserve the right to take action against the Pakistani military as deemed appropriate."

Two-thirds of the region is with India, the rest controlled by Pakistan, and both sides claim it in its entirety. Nanavatty said India was able to take back the area controlled by Islamabad, and parts of Pakistan's North West Frontier province.

"The reclamation of Pakistan occupied Kashmir and the no ern territories is achievable it demands strong conviction single-mindedness of purp on the part of the whole natic Nanavatty said.

Media coverage on Nanavatty's keynote address at a seminar on 'Jammu & Kashmir: The Way Ahead' organiz by HQ 16 Corps at Jammu on 31 October 2001.

Rostum and Suniti: A private wedding ceremony at Suniti's parents' home.

Pleased as punch after the ceremony.

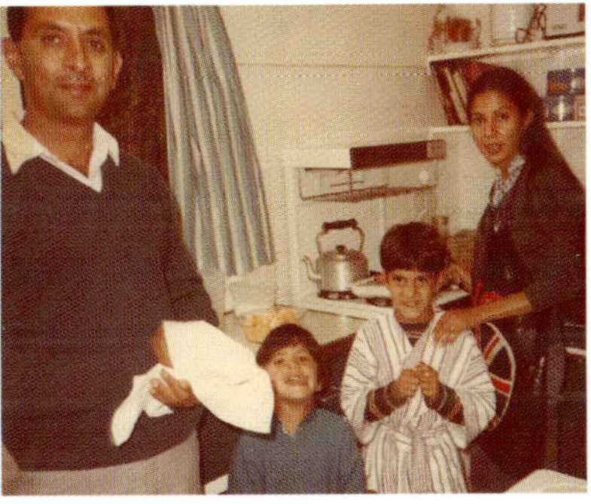

Warminster: all hands in the kitchen!

Relaxing with the boys in Nubra Valley not far from where Col Chewwang Rinchen won his first Maha Vir Chakra as a seventeen-year-old Nubra Scout in 1948.

Veer and Rushad with Rostum and their grandmother at a private jashan (thanksgiving) for Rushad's engagement to Kate.

A last foxtrot at the Officers' Institute in Udhampur.

Goa 2023: Rostum and Suniti flanked by Rushad, Kate and Veer and a family friend, with grandsons Kiyan and Cyrus.

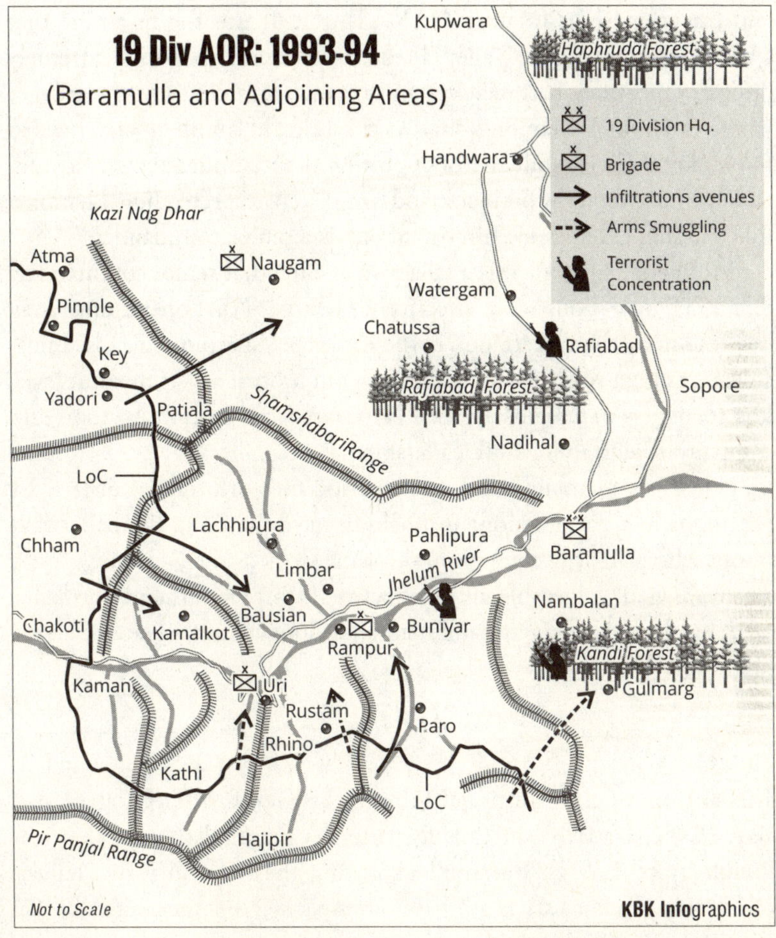

bowl. Mukherjee understood CT operations and functioned with the minimum of interference.

Mukherjee recalls, 'We were on Rostum's ORBAT for about six months. I am sure he welcomed additional boots on the ground, considering that his division was stretched. He was a great guy to work under, and his contribution to our efforts was subtle yet immense. Our brigade had a big handicap as one of my three battalions was a Jammu and Kashmir Light Infantry (JAK LI) unit. It was the first time that JAK LI operated in the Valley. Their troops found operating extremely difficult since they had relatives and friends, sometimes in the villages where operations were ongoing. As the brigade commander, I needed to employ them carefully without putting their families at risk. Rostum clearly understood my problems and completely respected how I handled this battalion. That made him stand out as a senior commander.'[22]

Mukherjee suggests it is a fallacy to assume that senior commanders direct CT operations more effectively. He argues that operations rarely involved more than a battalion in the Kashmir Valley, and success almost always resulted from good intelligence and proficiency at the unit level. His focus resonated closely with Nanavatty's on section, platoon and company-level training and leadership.

Nanavatty maintains that over a period the performance of JAK LI battalions in CT operations in Kashmir gave the lie to the belief that troops who primarily come from the same stock as the locals are grossly disadvantaged, vulnerable and ineffective. In his view, the performance of JAK LI units, adequately trained and motivated, has been of a very high order indeed.

The settling of the additional infantry brigade in the Rafiabad area allowed Nanavatty to shift his focus to the Baramulla town. The river Jhelum runs through Baramulla, splitting the town into two halves. Old Baramulla consists of storied houses packed together in traditional mohallas with narrow winding streets not wide enough to permit vehicles. The principal mosque cum madrassa, and the town's water supply point nestle against the forested lower slopes of the Kazinag Dhar to the north of the river. The new town is less congested and lies south of the river. The offices of the District Commissioner, the Headquarters of the District Superintendant of Police and Police Lines, the HQ 19 Infantry Division and other military establishments are all located south of the river. New Baramulla also has the St Joseph's Franciscan Convent (now the St Joseph's Catholic Church), which the Pakistani tribesman ravaged during the Kashmir Operations in 1947–48,[23] educational institutions, bus stations, banks, shops, markets and residential areas. In those days, the town had three major entry points: one each from Handwara, Srinagar and Uri, all three Class 9 roads. A bridge over the river connected the two halves of the town, and little 'dongas' and boats were constantly ferrying people to and fro across the river.

On arrival, Nanavatty learned that Old Baramulla was virtually a No-Go Area. 'Terrorists and their supporters mocked the security forces using loudspeakers at the mosque, even occasionally lighting up the evening sky with tracer,' Nanavatty recalls. 'They "held court" there and dispensed their brand of justice. I was dumbstruck by the impunity with which they were consolidating their presence right under our nose, and I was simply appalled by the situation. "Why has so little been done to restore normalcy in Baramulla?"' Nanavatty asked his staff soon after assuming command of the division. The team told him that it would call for a brigade-size operation and that civilian casualties could result. Elsewhere, 8 Mountain Divisions, responsible for CT operations in the rear areas, faced a similar problem on an even larger scale in Sopore. There, they discussed the probability of street fighting and house-to-house clearance operations.

Nanavatty studied the layout of Baramulla and paid a surprise visit to the mosque and the madrassa, where the maulvis seemed edgy but were courteous enough. He examined the options and discussed the matter with Brigadier Niranjan Hegde, his coursemate at the NDC and now commanding the Independent Infantry Brigade, and the latter's live wire deputy, Colonel O.P.S. Chauhan, who had an excellent aptitude for intelligence work. Together, they decided that 19 Inf Div would do things differently.[24]

Nanavatty's aim was to clear the town of overt terrorist presence and deny reversion to the present situation: inflicting casualties on the terrorists was of secondary importance. The task was to be carried out by 15 PUNJAB—the only unit available in town occupying the lines directly opposite the divisional headquarters. The broad plan was to establish Permanent Vehicle Check Points (PVCP) on the three main arteries at the entry points to the town; and redeploy the unit in an urban CT operations grid comprising company and platoon operating bases with precise areas of responsibility (AOR). Cultivating intelligence sources at the sub-unit level and dominating their respective AOR using a variety of urban operating techniques—multiple patrols; Pedestrian (P), Vehicle (V) and Boat (B) checks; and small unit offensive operations based on specific intelligence.

The operation was carried out in two phases. In Phase I, New Baramulla, seemingly the easier of the two tasks, was tackled using all four rifle companies from 15 PUNJAB; and, in Phase II, having learned several lessons, the more difficult task of securing Old Baramulla was addressed, leaving sufficient forces to persist with a somewhat diluted operating grid on the South bank. In new Baramulla, several derelict Kashmiri Pandit homes from where their occupants had been forcibly evicted provided the opportunity to fortify the premises and set up secure operating bases. In Phase II of the operation, the Water Point in Old Baramulla and the mosque area at the western edge of the town were ideally placed to serve as locations for two company operating bases.[25]

When Nanavatty first outlined his plan to the brigade commander and CO 15 PUNJAB, he was met with disbelief and wry smiles. He reassured the commander and the CO that he would allow them sufficient time for reconnaissance, preparation and training to understand and assimilate the unfamiliar urban operating techniques. On 28 June 1993, addressing the officers and men of 15 PUNJAB, Nanavatty highlighted the challenges of operating amongst people, which called for self-discipline and the use of 'appropriate' force. He urged them to fight in small teams, ensuring surprise and deception, and cautioned them against monotony, fatigue and staleness. He urged officers to lead and conduct small unit operations by night, be mindful of collateral damage and resort to subtle interrogation techniques.

Nanavatty clarified, '15 PUNJAB was a fine all-Sikh unit with a committed, courageous and hardworking Commanding Officer. I told them that this test would be a question of the Paltan's izzat (honour) and that they must be mindful of the sensitivities of ordinary citizens, especially women. I explained that the operation's objective was not necessarily to eliminate terrorists but to secure Baramulla and its people. To their credit, I did not get a single report of any misbehaviour by 15 PUNJAB.'

Writing to the author, Colonel Aithmian spelt out what he made of Nanavatty's approach: 'His strategy was to free this urban centre of terrorism initially, then prevent the return of terrorists to the area and, after that, fan out to clear the rural areas. Once the OGW and rebellious population realized the futility of their actions, military civic action programmes to win the hearts and minds of the local population would follow.'

Multiple patrol techniques involved the deployment of several small five-man patrols 'scouting' and surveilling their area of responsibility, looking for suspicious signs and activity, carrying out spot checks. In the event of a 'contact' the patrols would converge rapidly to the point of contact. A brief standardized 'contact report' that conveyed the 'who, what, when and where' of an incident triggered coordinated action by the 'multiples' with the seniormost patrol leader quickly establishing an incident command post and taking charge. This procedure proved to be far more effective than employing large columns. Aithmian maintains that Nanavatty's 'empathy, patience, conviction and attention to detail encouraged them and gave them the confidence to operate in small teams'.[26]

Lieutenant General V.R. Raghavan, then the DGMO and Colonel of the Punjab Regiment and Nanavatty's former boss on the Siachen Glacier, was visiting 15 PUNJAB at the time and expressed his reservations and concerns about deploying Sikh troops near the civil population. Unfortunately, Nanavatty was not in the station at the time of his visit. On his return, he took pains to explain to the Colonel of the Regiment that he had carefully considered this matter, spoken to the officers and men, and that the unit enjoyed his complete confidence and trust. The Deputy Commissioner, Mansoor Hakim, a well-meaning and sincere officer of the State Cadre, was also worried about the consequences of the Army's deployment in the town. He dashed off a letter to Nanavatty that reflected similar fears and demanded that the army return to their barracks and desist from occupying areas adjacent to civilian housing.

On 20 November 1993, Nanavatty wrote to Mansoor Hakim assuaging his fears: 'I aim to suppress militancy in Baramulla town to create a climate where your administration can function without serious interference. We chose Baramulla town because it is the seat of the district administration. The achievement of our objective will be a clear and unmistakable signal of our resolve to restore normalcy. Between 23 October and today, there has been a determined attempt by the militants to establish their ascendancy over a new Border Security Force Unit in the town. There have been 14 militant shootings and grenade-throwing incidents that have resulted in 9 security forces casualties. I am determined to reduce this menace by intensifying operations. We have had to patrol the town day and night, carry out pedestrian checks, and conduct selective searches. In the same period, we killed 5 ANE (terrorists) and apprehended 12. Some people may have been inconvenienced in the bargain, and some individual freedom was sacrificed. But these are abnormal times calling for abnormal measures. Inconvenience, I am afraid, is but a small price to pay.'[27]

Assuring Mansoor that he was aware of the shortcomings of his troops and had no intention of protecting them when they were wrong, Nanavatty explained, 'My message to them is clear: hunt the militant, find him and destroy or apprehend him, but treat the public with firmness, fairness and courtesy. As a soldier, nothing would please me more than to hand over the responsibility for conducting operations against the militants to the District Administration and the state police and mind my own business. Still, we both know that this is not a feasible proposition. Tomorrow, inshallah, if we are successful, your administration will enjoy its rightful position of pre-eminence in the governance of your beloved state.'[28] Moving into and fortifying abandoned buildings and the burnt-down homes of Pandits who fled Baramulla in 1990, the Punjabis systematically set up an effective urban counterterrorism grid. They developed contacts from amongst the local population and engaged with the town elders to convince them that they were there to ensure peace.

Explaining the measures taken to root out terrorism from Baramulla Lieutenant Colonel (later Lieutenant General) J.D.S. Rawat, posted as Nanavatty's GSO-1 (Intelligence), highlighted the effectiveness of squeezing information out of OGWs. The three PVCPs at the major entry points required elaborate arrangements. There was signposting with instructions, caltrops and other arrangements to prevent vehicles from breaking away, measures for identification and interrogation of suspects, and arrangements for sources to pass on information without raising suspicion. On one occasion, the finding of a single AK-47 cartridge in the boot of an Ambassador car during a routine check eventually helped to blow the cover of a network of OGWs, which transported arms and ammunition to various groups in the area. Setting up a medical clinic was a master stroke and helped in gaining the confidence of the populace. In several ways, this operation was the antithesis of the dominant counterinsurgency strategy of using maximum force to secure ANE-dominated areas like Sopore, where a more kinetic approach was assessed as the need of the hour.

Rawat terms the securing of Baramulla as one of the most systematic and scientifically executed operations during the early years of the insurgency in Jammu and Kashmir. Rising in later years to head the Indian Army's Intelligence Corps and School, Rawat reckons that 'serving under a brilliant commander who conveyed his mindset and intent very clearly down the chain of command and respected the value of intelligence-driven operations was a defining moment in his career. Staff officers and commanders in the Division had to be dead sure of what they wanted to convey to him and that there was no room for faffing around.'[29]

Alert to media distortion in counterinsurgency operations, Nanavatty responded quickly to an article in *The Tribune* of 25 August 1994 by a fellow Gorkha and distinguished retired Major General-turned-scribe, Ashok Mehta. Mehta suggested that the situation in Baramulla necessitated a heavy-handed approach by the security forces like the one employed a few months earlier by 8 Mountain Division in Sopore. Nanavatty wrote: 'Baramulla town is well under SF (security forces) control, with overt militant activity effectively suppressed since November 1993, allowing a return to normalcy. This was achieved during September–November 1993 without fuss, bother or publicity using a single Infantry battalion—15 PUNJAB, operating in an urban counterinsurgency grid and adopting various small unit operations techniques. This was a significant "first" in the Valley, and it is a pity you could not visit us. I could have shown you around.'[30]

Clearing Baramulla with a single battalion from his division with minimal loss of life and minimum kinetic force, with proactive support from the J&K police, is a memory that gives him great satisfaction even today. That campaign reflected the growing maturity of the Indian Army in dealing with complex semi-urban counterinsurgency and counterterrorist operations. Reporting from Baramulla in *The Times of India* on 4 January 1994 about attempts by 19 Inf Div to restore normalcy in the town, Dinesh Kumar wrote: 'The Army is launching systematic operations with clinical precision and minimum force to clear out militants from important townships in the Kashmir Valley.' After describing an operation in neighbouring Sopore that was predominantly kinetic, the article describes operations in Baramulla: 'A similar operation that has remained relatively unpublicized was recently carried out in this district headquarters, which has long remained a stronghold of dreaded militant groups such as the Hizbul Mujahideen. In fact, the army has experimented with establishing an entire battalion in select town locations for the first time. The tactics, as explained by Brigadier Hegde, a brigade commander in 19 Inf Div, were the brainchild of Major General R.K. Nanavatty, who has considerable experience tackling the LTTE in Sri Lanka.'[31]

Given the assorted terrorist groups and their inter-factional rivalry in the field, this was also a time when ideas regarding unconventional operations surfaced. General Padmanabhan and Nanavatty had several discussions about a surrender policy for terrorists, 'turning' and using captured terrorists and forming 'Counter Groups'. Enterprising COs with keen young officers were already experimenting with the use of 'civvies' and civilian vehicles on their own initiative. Some were foolhardy enough to even attempt pseudo-gang operations with dangerous portends. According to Luise White in her book, *Fighting and Writing: The Rhodesian Army at War and Post War*, 'In pseudo operations, security forces and loyal local people some of whom may have been former insurgents, track down gangs of real insurgents and capture or kill them. In so doing, pseudos earn great praise for their subterfuge and daring.'[32]

While covert operations were disallowed in 19 Inf Div in neighbouring 28 Inf Div a 'half-baked' attempt at a pseudo-gang operation had gone horribly wrong and the Army Commander ordered HQ 15 Corps to appoint Nanavatty to investigate and draw lessons from the incident. It was a case of an overconfident young company commander with a good operational record thus far and his even younger deputy on a company operating base in the Haphruda Forest area attempting a pseudo-gang operation without adequate preparation. Here, Nanavatty believed the formation HQ bore direct responsibility for what transpired.

It was the eve of the first-ever Infantry Day recently instituted in the army. The formation HQ decided on a 'social evening' in the brigade Officers' Mess. The two officers, both talented musicians, were to perform at the event. Instead of declining the invitation, given their tricky mission the following day, they departed their post having issued a perfunctory warning order and returned after the 'festivities' late that night. The next day, the patrol set out and established contact with a terrorist group on the outskirts of a notorious village, Lachhampur. In a brief verbal exchange that followed their cover was blown and a fierce firefight erupted almost immediately. Suddenly, there was a lull in the firing, and the two officers, thinking they had the measure of the terrorists, ventured forward without taking adequate precautions to take stock and see if they could retrieve any weapons. Unfortunately, they walked straight into a trap. Both the officers were captured alive, murdered in the most gruesome manner, and their corpses defiled and displayed in the Handwara area. Leaderless, the patrol disintegrated, and individuals were left to their own devices to return to their unit—in each case, it was a harrowing experience.[33]

Nanavatty's analysis led him to believe that covert operations by regular infantry battalions were not sustainable because they invariably led to overreach in an ugly race for kills, apprehensions, arms hauls, honours and awards. 15 Corps immediately suspended pseudo-gang operations on Nanavatty's recommendations. Even at that early juncture, it had crossed Nanavatty's mind that counter-groups ill trained, ill disciplined and inappropriately handled could become a law unto themselves, a nuisance to the lay public, and prove downright dangerous. He firmly believed that unconventional operations demanded a clear policy that clearly spelt out responsibility, authority, preparation and effective command and control. But, it would be a few years before he returned to the scene as the Northern Army Commander to try and set things right with only 9 PARA (SF) being authorized to carry out pseudo-gang operations.[34]

Nanavatty did not have much to do with the civilian population in his Division AOR. Being the early stages of CANE operations his focus was kinetic and stabilizing operations. However, he encouraged several innovative measures to manage civic action after an army operation. With the help of the civil administration and the police, he formed composite teams to set up day-long civic action camps to administer to people's needs and treat livestock, ponies and mules. These initiatives also offered opportunities to engage with the existing pro-security forces operatives within the civilian population and talk to people about their grievances and problems. Detailed instructions were issued for the conduct of military-civic action following kinetic operations based on the cardinal principle 'help the people to help themselves'. Some early initiatives involved supporting schools, restoring the water and electricity supply, selectively adopting families, providing limited transport support, and the implementing of village cooperative and community projects.[35]

Acutely aware that intelligence was the key to effective CT operations, Nanavatty accorded it the highest priority. Having failed to coax and convince his deputy GOC to assume the additional responsibility of intelligence operations in the division, he was delighted when Lieutenant Colonel (later Lieutenant General) J.D.S. Rawat was posted as the GSO-1 (Int.). In Nanavatty's words, Rawat was one of the best intelligence officers he had ever worked with.

Rawat reckons that one of Nanavatty's most significant contributions to CT operations in the early stages was to systematize the intelligence process—its collection, collation and dissemination—at all levels company command upwards. 'The scene in the Valley was chaotic. Apart from the HM, the main Pakistan Trained Militant (PTM) group, there were at least a dozen other Locally Trained Militant (LTM) groups operating, prominent among them being the Al-Barq, Al-Jehad and the

Muslim Mujahedin, and the Army was busy "chasing after them" without intelligence.' Nanavatty insisted that formations and units organize their intelligence work to focus on the terrorist leadership in their respective AOR, plot their movement on 'leader tracking maps' with dates, timings and nature of incidents to establish patterns and try and second-guess where the leader and his group would appear next. A systematic drive to cultivate sources and informers and continuously shadow OGW, particularly the 'white collar' variety, even to the point of 'harassment', resulted in increased information and successful operations.

The second major initiative that Nanavatty initiated was to create data-driven predictive analysis of terrorist and CT operations activity. Rawat was responsible for developing a model that identified parameters and sub-parameters that linked various actions by terrorists and SF, the location, the frequency of their occurrence and results to estimate the overall effectiveness of CT operations. Different types of terrorist activity—grenade attacks, stray firing, stand-off attacks, drive-by shootings, suicide attacks, Fidayeen attacks, ambushes and IED and IED in tandem attacks were meticulously collated on maps to determine broader trends and emerging areas of interest.

As the intelligence process improved, so did operational techniques. Thus far, cordon and search methods involved cordoning an entire village, herding the villagers outside their homes, segregating the men and the women, and then searching the whole area. Terrorists within the cordon would often disappear into ingeniously prepared hideouts and either wait out the operation, emerging after the coast was clear, or spring a surprise and fight their way out, often inflicting avoidable casualties on the SF. Try as he might, Nanavatty was unable to coax the Remount Veterinary Corps (RVC) to train local dogs to locate and 'point' hideouts where terrorists had taken refuge. The RVC had a simple argument: 'Indian breeds are "un-trainable"—yet you only had to look at a mongrel at every post to realize their true worth.' Large-scale C&S were a severe inconvenience to innocent villagers, a very sore point with the populace and a source of serious angst against the army. With improved intelligence, the modified technique required people to remain confined to their homes while searches based on information and intelligence were conducted in specific houses. 'Within a few months of Nanavatty taking over the division, C&S of entire villages in 19 Inf Div stopped completely,' recalls Rawat.[36]

By mid-1994, the influx of foreign terrorists (FT) into the densely forested areas of North Kashmir (Baramulla, Kupwara and Sopore), once a trickle, had turned into a tide. The Harkat-ul-Ansar (HuA), its affiliate the Harkat-ul-Mujahideen (HuM), and later the LeT and JeM were the main FT *Tanzeems* (organizations) operating in North Kashmir until the end of 1995. Comprising well-trained and radicalized Pakistani and Pashtun terrorists, the groups also included a sprinkling of Chechen, Uzbek and Arab fighters trained by Al-Qaeda and the Taliban. Veterans of the fighting in Afghanistan were a different 'cup of tea' and posed a significant challenge to the Indian Army.

After carefully studying trends, Nanavatty came to four conclusions, which he shared with his command. First, the LeT would emerge as the preferred tool of the ISI in its covert war in J&K. Second, it would not be long before the LeT expanded its area of operations to include South Kashmir. Third, LeT, being Kashmir-centric, and not yet involved in terrorist attacks in other countries[37] the fight would be India's alone. Lastly, the LeT was capable and more than willing to execute Fidayeen attacks. Consequently, the mandate given to the troops as the fighting turned vicious was to eliminate FTs during encounters. It did not pay not to be ruthless.[38]

Nanavatty believed that operational planning aside, every formation commander was responsible for ensuring that his formation's approach to battle was sound. Training specific to the enemy, terrain and nature of operations formed an essential element of this approach. Reminiscing about his command of the 102 Infantry Brigade in Operation MEGHDOOT in Siachen, he believed that, time and space permitting, pre-induction training for impending operations under formation arrangements was invaluable.

Whereas the Nagrota-based 16 Corps was establishing its own Battle School, 15 Corps relied on an ad hoc training facility under the Command Headquarters in the erstwhile Transit Camp location at Ramban. With 15 Corps having little or no say in the matter, it was an unsatisfactory arrangement. When terrorist tactics and techniques were constantly evolving, a battle school simply had to interact continuously with the formations and units in the field. Nanavatty, with the limited means at his disposal, had already started working on the idea of a divisional battle school and discussed the matter with Padmanabhan. The latter liked the idea and asked Nanavatty to give him a brief note with the essentials on the subject as soon as possible. Nanavatty gives full credit to Paddy for establishing the 15 Corps Battle School in Khrew in 1994. Several years later, the facility was to reach its zenith when Colonel John de Britto, 9 PARA (SF), volunteered and ran the facility in 2002–03 when Nanavatty was the Army Commander.

'You must talk to Shiv Sahai, an officer from the Indian Police Service (IPS) who was the District Superintendent of Police (SP) in Baramulla during the first year of my tenure. Initially, there was a bit of chafing between the army and the police, which was soon smoothened out. Shiv did well and was marked for higher assignments,' said Nanavatty, during a discussion with the author on the role of the J&K police in stabilizing Baramulla.

The police initially were a little worried about being 'marginalized' by the army, and there were turf-related issues to be sorted out. Despite that, Nanavatty and his deputy forged a good working relationship with Sahai. A former Additional Secretary with the National Security Council Secretariat (NSCS) and an officer who, over his career, established a good rapport with military commanders in J&K, Sahai was the first officer from the IPS to be posted as SP Baramulla in mid-1992. 'The killing of several policemen between 1989 and 1992 by terrorist groups such as the Hizbul Mujahedeen had resulted in a serious erosion in the morale of the police force, and it was a challenge to reverse this trend, particularly in sensitive areas such as Baramulla, Kupwara and Sopore,' Sahai recollects.

On the scene, barely an hour after Major General Inder Verma, Nanavatty's predecessor, was shot and injured, and a Colonel killed during a cordon and search operation that went bad, Sahai reckons that the unfortunate incident took place because senior officers entered the arena prematurely. He replays their first meeting. 'Nanavatty and I had a few things in common—my father was a retired army officer, and I knew that his father had been a respected police officer from the Bombay State Indian Police (IP) Cadre, the forerunner to the IPS. When we met for the first time, he asked me, "What are you doing in the police?" and I retorted, "What are you doing in the army?" I remember him as a professional, straight-talking, perceptive and no-frills kind of soldier who was keen to take the police along, both in operations and during civic action after operations, to assuage citizens' concerns and help during stability operations.[39]

'We broke bread for the first time over Wazwan at home—an elaborate Kashmiri meal traditionally partaken sitting around a large community plate on the ground with everyone eating with their hands—which Nanavatty enjoyed immensely. Always dressed in his army combat dress, he would drop in occasionally for a meal with minimum fuss, accompanied by just one escort vehicle. During these meals, he shared several ideas with me and listened to what I had to say about the situation in town,' recalled Sahai.

Minor differences between the army and the police on custodial procedures and human rights notwithstanding, Sahai stated, 'Nanavatty was balanced and a good listener, but I remember one public spat I had with him during a Townhall Meeting that he had called for,' says Sahai. Surprised that the police were put in a tight spot by Nanavatty about issues such as laxity in handling the judicial custody of suspected militants with all members of the District Administration in attendance, Sahai pushed back firmly in public when Nanavatty asked him, 'Whose side are you on?' However, resolving the differences behind closed doors did not take long. Sahai commented on the impact of joint operations, 'Overall, however, I think the J&K police turned around in Baramulla during that period, and I must give credit to Nanavatty for including several of my good policemen in active and challenging kinetic operations around Baramulla.'[40]

Sahai recollects one such operation soon after Nanavatty took over hen a large group of HM militants were running amok in the Gulmarg ndi area because the road from Baramulla to Gulmarg had collapsed was taking long to repair by the State Public Works Department)). Since Gulmarg was in the AOR of 19 Inf Div, the absence of nnectivity allowed the HM to dominate the area until Al-Barq, another terrorist group comprising hill tribesmen, which was losing control to the HM, decided to approach the J&K police with information on the location of the large HM group in return for protection. The Indian Army termed such groups as 'counter groups' when they turned against the major *Tanzeems.* With Baramulla town in fair control, 15 PUNJAB was chafing at the bit and looking to recommence offensive CT operations in the rural areas around Baramulla. Acting on the tip-off from the J&K police, troops of 15 PUNJAB swung into action on 27–28 August 1994. Along with the J&K police, they manually lifted several small Maruti 800 cars across the damaged portions of the road making it appear like the police was assisting stranded civilians. They then mounted a swift operation that eliminated a large HM group of 10 militants in a single encounter in the village of Shirapura in the Gulmarg Kandi. Writing to Sahay on 6 September 1994, Nanavatty called it 'a fine example of cooperation between the state police and the Army and an enormous step toward integrated functioning'.[41]

Nanavatty's operational leadership style as a divisional commander was enabling and empowering. Reading the 'big picture', strategizing continuously with his commanders and staff, he rarely interfered in their operations after passing orders. On decision-making, Rawat recalls, 'There was no hesitation and dithering at all; he was meticulous, deliberate and decisive. To cite an example, one day, when a counter group approached 15 PUNJAB at 1630 hours with actionable information, and the brigade commander informed Nanavatty, the latter was on the spot within the hour. After a brief discussion, while the counter-group leader and the CO favoured immediate action, Nanavatty advised that the counter-group representatives be detained, and the operation be launched after a sufficient pause to eliminate the possibility of running into a possible ambush. This pause confirmed the intent of the counter group and resulted in a successful operation the following morning.'[42]

On risk-taking, Rawat reckons that the strategy to clear Baramulla was tricky, considering that such a deployment of the army amidst hostile civilians could have easily turned sour with even one untoward incident.

Nanavatty did not think so because he had carefully considered it and concluded that the risk was worth it. Highlighting that operational patience is imperative in covert operations, Nanavatty recalls an operation in October 1993 in close coordination with the apex intelligence outfit in Northern Command. The operation had a long gestation period and involved the release on bail of three senior leaders from the Al-Jihad Group who had ideological differences with the HM. Tried for the first time since the start of militancy and secessionist activity, the initiative to drive a wedge between competing terrorist groups resulted in direct and indirect payoffs that degraded the capabilities of the local Kashmiri terrorist groups such as the HM; however, it failed to affect the political process since the ISI quickly replaced the HM with groups such as the LeT and JeM to keep the 'pot boiling'.[43]

Colonel (later Brigadier) Sushil Negi, Nanavatty's Colonel-in-Charge (Administration) or Col Adm, recalls his divisional commander as 'kind-hearted and considerate to all, but strict and ruthless while dealing with deliberate and serious breaches of discipline'. Managing cases involving ethical and moral transgressions in divisions on active operational duty can be a nightmare for staff officers because of several contradictions and dilemmas often used as mitigating factors, but not in Nanavatty's case. Negi recalls the clarity with which, early on in his tenure, Nanavatty ordered a Court Martial and awarded 10–12 years of imprisonment to offenders who were charged with attempted rape. This stern action set an example; no such incident was repeated in the Division AOR. Following this award, the District Collector of Baramulla remarked, 'It would have taken 10–12 years in civil courts to settle, and maybe the accused would have been acquitted.'[44]

Towards the end of his tenure, Nanavatty was dismayed that some of the units under him were misrepresenting facts, inflating kills and seizures, and concocting After Action Reports. Nanavatty cautioned his commanders in September 1994 that he generally possessed first hand knowledge of an incident because of his wanderings. He urged them to reflect on whether, in the race for honours and awards, both individually and collectively, we were losing our sense of self-respect. He made it plain that he 'would view any attempts at exaggeration extremely seriously and added that such indiscretion would debar an individual or unit from an honour which otherwise might justly have been well deserved'.[45]

Major General Nanavatty's diary-like real-time reflections as a division commander in an intense operational environment are surreal in their neatness, compactness and honesty. It almost appears that these loose sheets measuring 5 x 7 inches, bound together by a neatly tied shoelace and stacked together as a 'bahi khata' (a traditional Indian account ledger), were waiting to be read by someone all these years. That it took almost two decades after his retirement to unravel is a gift and a treasure for a military historian. Though Nanavatty has such compilations for all his command assignments, the easiest to contextualize are his recordings of events during the early years of the Indian Army's Counter Anti-National Elements (CANE) Operations in J&K in the early 1990s, also called Operation RAKSHAK. The jottings are brutally honest and cryptically analytical, a vital facet of Nanavatty's persona. A selection of entries from the diary is featured in Appendix C.

Personal and family affairs occupied very little bandwidth in Nanavatty's scheme of things during his divisional commander's tenure, and there was little he could do to stem the sharp decline in his father's health. Enfeebled by a series of strokes, Kaikhushru Jehangir Nanavatty passed away on 17 December 1994, a day after Nanavatty reached Pune.

Wrapping up his recollections about his father, Nanavatty unearthed an article in the *Afternoon Despatch and Courier*, a Bombay newspaper, by Julio Ribeiro, the legendary Mumbai and Punjab Director General of Police, who had worked as a young Assistant IG of Police under Kaikhushru in the Maharashtra police. Written as a part obituary and part reflection on the state of India's police forces on 13 February 1995, a few months after Kaikhushru passed away, Ribeiro writes: 'Kaikhushru Jehangir Nanavatty belonged to that breed of gentlemen police officers fast becoming extinct. "Keki", as he was called by his wife of 57 years, did have those qualities that many police leaders of today do not seem to value—honesty and integrity of the highest order. He was a man of honour. Keki never favoured particular officers, harboured no ill-will towards others, and judged men and matters squarely according to his conscience and understanding.'[46]

Suniti recalls, 'Rostum's posting to command 19 Division came suddenly and unexpectedly, and he had his bags packed even before his posting order came. The timing could not have been less inopportune. Rushad and Veer were on their way home from The Doon School for their two-month summer vacation. But Rostum was gone before they reached Udhampur.' Thereafter, it made little sense for Suniti to stay alone in Udhampur, so Rostum applied for SF accommodation in Dehradun. As soon as he could take leave, Rostum and Suniti drove down from Udhampur to Dehradun, where Suniti had been allotted accommodation in remote Birpur. Here, too, Suniti insisted on a civil phone connection. Rostum offered to buy her a toy phone instead, giving the propensity of Dehradun phones to go dead at the mere hint of a breeze!

For Suniti, it was reassuring to know that the boys were just a twenty-minute drive away and that she could visit them every Sunday with homemade treats for them and their friends. Boomer invariably accompanied her to visit them and received significant attention from the boys and their friends.

The family saw little of Rostum. Rushad and Veer's little successes and achievements, like missed milestones, went by. As soon as she was settled, Suniti joined to work as a volunteer at Raphael, an NGO with which she remained connected for the rest of her life. Raphael's mission, as enunciated by its founders—the legendary Royal Air Force ace from World War II, Group Captain Lord Leonard Cheshire, VC, OM, DSO**, DFC and his wife Baroness Sue Ryder—is simple yet all-encompassing: 'the relief of suffering'. It strives to achieve its goals through three thematic programmes: the detection and treatment of tuberculosis (T.B.); the identification, assessment, education and rehabilitation of children with intellectual disabilities; and the life-long care of persons with disability with simply nowhere to go.

Suniti became a familiar sight on the twelve-kilometre route, driving her white diesel Volkswagen to and from work. This was her first interaction with the intellectually challenged. Deeply affected by their condition to start with, she grew to think of them as different but as normal as the so-called 'normal'. When they moved to Pune, on Rostum's next posting, it was natural for her to volunteer to take charge of ASHA, the Army Wives Welfare Association School for special children. Throughout their twenty-month stay there, Suniti devoted much time and attention to the school. It proved to be an enriching experience for her.

Nanavatty's tour of duty with 19 Inf Div ended abruptly on 14 December 1994, only nineteen months after assuming command of the formation. There was much work yet to be done, and he had hoped for atleast a two-year tenure in command. That was not to be. He stood posted as the MGGS, HQ Southern Command, Pune, once again relieving his friend, Inder Verma. On reporting for duty in HQ Southern Command, the first assignment that Nanavatty undertook was to make a comprehensive presentation to the officers and a few academics and intellectuals on J&K. On 30 January 1995, Nanavatty offered a compelling assessment of the ground situation to a select audience at Pune University through the lens of multiple stakeholders. He suggested that North Kashmir was a 'war zone' with intense military activity, a sullen populace that was accustomed to violence and, despite the combat, trying to lead normal lives. There was a sense of alienation and deprivation among the people, nepotism and corruption across layers of government and a sense of helplessness that offered an excellent opportunity for Pakistan to enter the fray with a war-by-proxy strategy. Following almost five years of concerted and effective operations by the Indian Army, the people were disenchanted with Pakistan, realized that '*Azadi*' was unattainable and were waiting for a 'Messiah' to lead them out of their troubles. Nanavatty cautioned that the army had done all it could and that it was time for the government and the civil administration to step in and swiftly move the peace process forward.[47]

Nanavatty served under three GOC-in-Cs as the MGGS in Southern Command: Lieutenant Generals Moti Dar, V.P. Malik (later the army chief) and H.M. Khanna. Pune was Nanavatty's home station, and the posting allowed them time to catch up with family and friends. General Malik recalls Nanavatty as his 'Devil's Advocate' and said, 'Rostum did stand apart in many ways: professionally, he was high grade, and his outstanding character qualities were even more exemplary than that. He was diligent and hardworking and spoke his mind, never couching his words behind niceties when asked for an opinion. Suniti came across as charming and knowledgeable, but both Rostum and she kept to themselves and were not very social in the traditional army way.'[48]

It was around the middle of 1996 that Nanavatty was officially informed of his approval for promotion to the rank of Lieutenant General in the command and staff stream. His request for the command of 15 or 16 Corps, both in J&K, was turned down by Army HQ, and he was posted as the Chief of Staff (COS) in HQ Western Command (WC) at the behest of the army chief, General Shankar Roychowdhury, considering the 'exigencies of service'. Seeking an interview with the chief, the latter told him that he would have to wait for the command of a corps and that it may not be a corps in an active operational zone. The chief, however, acknowledged Nanavatty's request to command 3 Corps in the North-east if 15 and 16 Corps were unavailable. Nanavatty's tenure as COS WC was brief and uneventful as he waited for another field command. Finally posted to 3 Corps, Nanavatty with Prem Singh, his 'sahayak', and Boomer, his basset hound—the latter only with the special permission of an indulgent pilot who gave the 'funny looking dog with enormous ears' a thorough once over—boarded an IL 76 Courier flight to Guwahati and reported to the Corps HQ in Dimapur on 31 August 1997.[49]

10

RETURN TO THE NORTHEASTERN CAULDRON

'Societies that shun violence must experience the benefits of doing so.'[1]

—LIEUTENANT GENERAL NANAVATTY IN A LETTER (DRAFT) TO HQ EASTERN COMMAND, 7 AUGUST 1999

HQ 3 Corps was raised in 1985 at Rangapahar on the outskirts of the township of Dimapur in Nagaland. Lieutenant General Bakshi Jogender Singh, an outstanding soldier of the Jat Regiment was the first GOC. Its raising fulfilled the perceived operational need of a suitable HQ in location to exercise command and control over army and Assam Rifles formations and units operating in the insurgency ridden states of the North-east—Nagaland, Manipur, Mizoram, Tripura and parts of Arunachal Pradesh. It served as an intermediate HQ between Eastern Command in Calcutta and the governments in the various states. 8 Mountain Division—'forever in operations'—the repository, in many ways, of the army's expertise in counterinsurgency operations, was a crucial part of the corps until its departure for the J&K theatre in 1989.

Lieutenant General Sarabjit Singh Grewal, the former commander of 8 Mountain Division in J&K around the same time that Nanavatty commanded 19 Infantry Division in neighbouring Baramulla, was the GOC 3 Corps. He wrote to Nanavatty saying, 'You will be taking charge of affairs here at a time which is critical and epoch-making not only for Nagaland but the entire NE States, and I dare say even the country. Towards this end, I believe you are a befitting choice. Under your leadership and dedication, perhaps peace will return to Nagaland after more than five decades of turmoil.'[2]

During Grewal's tenure, the most powerful and influential of the anti-India Naga groups, the National Socialist Council of Nagaland (Isaac & Muivah) (NSCN (IM)) had been put under severe military pressure. This had 'upped' the infighting within the rebel groups causing great discomfort to the people and encouraging the already deeply divided Naga factions to pull in different directions. Sensing an opportunity, the army chief, General Shankar Roy Chowdhary, urged New Delhi to sieze the moment and extend an olive branch to all the Naga insurgent groups. The Government of India (GOI), for reasons best known to it, did not involve the state government in its parleys and acting, presumably, on the advice of the central intelligence agencies, extended the offer to the NSCN (IM) alone. The NSCN (IM) was quick to seize the opportunity and thereby not only gain a respite from kinetic operations but also reinforce, in the eyes of the people, their claim to the leadership of the Naga underground movement.[3] The Ceasefire (CF) between the GOI and the NSCN (IM) came into effect on 1 August 1997 exactly a month and ten days before Nanavatty assumed his responsibilities on 10 September 1997.

While Nanavatty's previous command experience was in intense operations against terrorists in a covert war environment, in 3 Corps it was different. The situation demanded dexterous handling at the politico-military levels and required Nanavatty to focus on building working relationships with Governors, Chief Ministers, Chief Secretaries and the heads of state and central police forces alike.

He recalls a brief meeting in HQ Western Command with General V.P. Malik then the Vice Chief. Malik had Nanavatty's back all along. When Nanavatty missed out on the early placement of corps commanders despite being the senior most officer approved for promotion in his batch, he made a special effort to see that his erstwhile MGGS was assigned to an operational corps. Reassuring Nanavatty of the command of 3 Corps he summed up things pointedly 'you will now be dealing extensively with political leaders and bureaucrats and will have to tread carefully'.[4]

Interestingly, in a chat with the author Nanavatty had expressed a contrarian and macro perspective of the fundamental reasons for the never-ending discord in the northeastern parts of India. He said, 'I have often wondered whether we did wisely by "clubbing" the states in the region, several severely troubled, under the over-arching term "North-east" (NE). We seem to forget that each state in the region, irrespective of its size, is different; the people are different, their past is different, their present problems are different and, so are the solutions to their problems. Clubbing them under the umbrella term NE, to my mind, only reinforces the argument that Delhi does not know and does not even care to know and understand the region and its people. The use of the term NE may only have served to unify them in an anti-central government stance and encouraged them to follow the example of others in the region, often down the wrong path.'

This chapter does not seek to offer the reader a holistic and comprehensive understanding of discord in the northeastern region of India or dissect the entire landscape of internal security challenges posed to the Indian state by various insurgencies or secessionist movements. However, it will continuously offer context through the strategic and operational lens of a military commander who understands the region and its people.[5]

In September 1997, when Nanavatty assumed command of 3 Corps, the areas where the army and Assam Rifles were assisting the state governments in maintaining public order (as opposed to mere *law and order*) were Nagaland, Manipur, Tripura and South Assam. Mizoram was the only state on his beat which, after years of turmoil, was relatively 'normal'.

In Nagaland, while there was a ceasefire between the SF and the NSCN (IM), operations against the NSCN (Khaplang) (NSCN (K)) were ongoing. S.C. Jamir, the Chief Minister, an Ao Naga himself and known to be sympathetic to the NSCN (K) was clearly nursing a deep grudge against the GOI for having been left out of the decision-making process leading upto the CF; and for not simultaneously extending the CF to the NSCN (K). That translated into the state government, not surprisingly, adopting an indifferent, hands-off—none of our business approach towards implementing the CF.

Manipur on the other hand was a tinder box. The state was faced with a severe law and order problem following bloody clashes between Kuki (Kuki National Army) and Zoumi (Zoumi Revolutionary Army) factions seeking to protect their respective communities in the Churachandpur District. On the other side, the CF between the GOI and the NSCN (IM) and as a result of the subsequent clarification by the GOI that the CF applied to the 'group and was not restricted to the geographical limits of Nagaland alone', the Meitei—politicians, state government officials and common man alike—were fearful that the GOI would arrive at a settlement of the Naga problem at the expense of the territorial integrity of Manipur. With a distracted and uncertain state government in place the predominantly Meitei 'Valley Based Insurgent Groups' (VBIG) were on the rampage bringing the population particularly in urban and semi urban areas virtually to their knees with their extortion and violent criminal activities.

The state in Tripura, all this while, was dealing with a low-grade insurgency which drew its sustenance from large sections of the disaffected tribal population. Whilst it was capable of tackling the problem effectively with the forces that were available, it was forever crying 'wolf' and seeking the help of the army. It simply did not understand that the need of the hour in Tripura was to uplift the tribal population politically, socially and economically. And, in the Haflong District of South Assam, it was the Dima Halam Daogha (DHD) having links with the NSCN (IM) that needed to be brought under control.

3 Corps under Nanavatty was stretched owing to the situation in J&K. The Inspector General Assam Rifles (North) (IGAR (N)) with his HQ at Zakhama (near Kohima) commanded a division-size mixed force of army and Assam Rifles and was responsible for operations in Nagaland. GOC 57 Mountain Division with his HQ at Leimakhong had a similarly mixed force and was responsible for operations in Manipur. In addition, a Sector HQ and four battalions of the newly raised Rashtriya Rifles were split between Nagaland and Manipur. The artillery brigade of the division was detached and was responsible for operations in the Haflong District of South Assam. Tripura and Mizoram both had brigade size

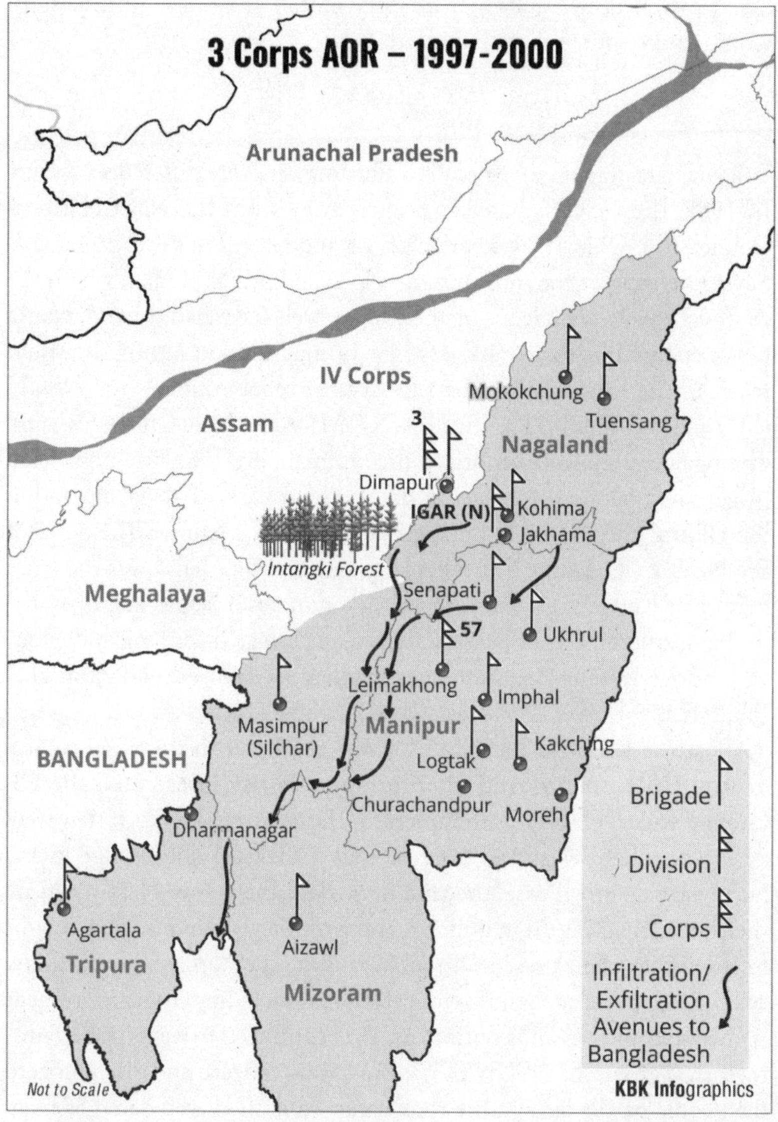
3 Corps AOR – 1997-2000
Arunachal Pradesh
IV Corps
Assam
Mokokchung
Tuensang
Nagaland
3
Dimapur
IGAR (N)
Kohima
Jakhama
Intangki Forest
Meghalaya
Senapati
57
Ukhrul
Leimakhong
Imphal
Masimpur (Silchar)
Manipur
Kakching
BANGLADESH
Logtak
Churachandpur
Moreh
Dharmanagar
Brigade
Division
Corps
Agartala
Tripura
Aizawl
Mizoram
Infiltration/ Exfiltration Avenues to Bangladesh
Not to Scale
KBK Infographics

independent Assam Rifles Sectors with Tripura frequently seeking and being assigned an additional infantry battalion from within Eastern Command resources based on need.

The Naga insurgent movement has a history of severe differences within. In 1988, the NSCN that had broken away from the Naga National Council (NNC) in 1980 experienced yet another rift in the organization. Severe fighting of the most bitter, vicious and brutal kind, in which the central Indian intelligence agencies may well have had a hand, would break out within their ranks leading to much blood letting. It would result in the formation of the two distinct rebel entities—the NSCN (IM) and the NSCN (K). The NSCN (IM) led by Isaac Chishi Swu and Thiungaleng Muivah comprised predominantally Tangkhul and Sema Nagas and operated generally in the southern parts of Nagaland and in the Ukhrul and Mao-Maram areas of Northern Manipur. The ranks of the NSCN (K), led by S.S. Khaplang, on the other hand was made up mainly of Konyaks, Aos and Hemi (Myanmarese) Nagas and operated in the northern parts of Nagaland (Mokokchung, Tsuensang and Mon) and the overlapping Naga-inhabited regions of Myanmar and Arunachal Pradesh.

Post the CF with the NSCN (IM), the latter in the absence of a neutral CF enforcing and monitoring authority interpreted the CF Ground Rules (CFGR) as they pleased. The cadre behaved as if they were a law unto themselves and believed that if they did not indulge in any hostile act against the SF, they did no wrong. They moved freely outside their prescribed camps in uniform and with their weapons. They sought to strengthen their presence in urban and semi urban areas to facilitate 'tax collection'—a euphemism for extortion—including from government agencies, employees and contractors. They continued to wage 'war' against their rival group the NSCN (K) causing great concern and discomfort to the people particularly in the rural areas. And, they even dared to mete out justice of a rudimentary kind to the people.

Nanavatty had no doubts in his mind; in the circumstances prevailing in Nagaland he saw his primary task as that of 'enforcing the Ceasefire'.

He was convinced that the CF provided an opportunity for a peaceful solution to the problem and was in the best interest of the people of the state. Scrutinizing the CF Ground Rules (CFGR), Nanavatty noted several inadequacies in the text. Though he was to spell out clarifications and suggest amendments, he realized it was too much to expect their admissibility and incorporation at this late stage. He decided that HQ 3 Corps would take the initiative, interpret the CFGR as best as it could and assume the responsibility for enforcing it in as fair a manner as possible.

He emphasized the need to ensure the highest standards of battlefield turnout and discipline; strict measures for the security and protection of his troops even as the army consciously reduced its visible presence; and, simultaneously a focus on intelligence collection and preparedness to recommence operations at short notice. In the event of the CF collapsing he had no intention of being caught unprepared.

Next on his list of priorities was facilitating the maintenance of law and order in the state and the mobilizing of public opinion in favour of the peace process.[6] The immediate challenge was to 'discipline' the NSCN (IM), confine their cadres to their camps and restrict their free movement in uniform with weapons. The task involved 'messaging' the NSCN (IM) leadership 'in subtle and not so subtle ways'; identifying their camp sites; establishing SF posts and checkpoints on approaches to and from such sites; and maintaining an unobtrusive SF presence in vulnerable areas. This sustained pressure eventually would compel the NSCN (IM) to uproot their HQ from the outskirts of Dimapur to a new location called Camp Hebron in the Peren District.

With the Nagaland police and CAPF lacking direction from the top and standing disinterestedly and idly by, 3 Corps was mainly concerned with two types of unlawful activity the Naga underground groups were indulging in that could, if not countered immediately, disturb the peace and threaten the CF itself. First, 'tax collection' particularly in urban and semi urban areas; and second, violent inter-factional clashes between the NSCN (IM) and NSCN (K). At one stage, there was a sudden and noticeable exodus of the non-Naga business community from Dimapur because of the jostling between the NSCN (IM) and NSCN (K) to gain effective control of the town—the state's financial hub. Under the circumstances, HQ 3 Corps was compelled, notwithstanding the CFGR, to occupy temporary operating bases and 'demonstrate' the Army's presence in the town. This move had an immediate sobering effect on the factions and promptly brought businesses back.

Regarding the SF intervening in inter-factional clashes there were two views. First, was the rather cynical view that inter-factional clashes between rebel groups did no harm to the SF: indeed, they helped the SF indirectly and that, should they occur, the latter should merely 'look the other way'. The other view was that inter-factional clashes were an example of the protagonists taking the law into their own hands and 'disturbing the peace'. It was unlawful and threatened the lives of people who were mere onlookers. Nanavatty decided inter-factional clashes would not be tolerated. There were two occasions where the SF had to intervene directly in inter-factional fights to prevent a dangerous conflagration from spreading. In the first instance Brigadier P.C. Bhardwaj, commanding the brigade in Mokokchung intervened in a clash in the Mokochung-Wokha area earning plaudits and a written appreciation from the CM himself for his presence of mind, courage and professionalism. And, in the second such incident it was the IGAR North, Major General R.B. Singh, who stepped into the breach and established order this time in the Tuensang District. In both instances, it was the NSCN (IM) trying to dominate the NSCN (K) and expand its areas of operations and influence.

Initially, the CF with the NSCN (IM) was declared for three months. However, with elections to the State Assembly just around the corner in February 1998, Nanavatty, when asked for his opinion, had no hesitation in recommending to Army Headquarters an extension of the CF for a further three months. Simultaneously, he advised the state government on the need for greater involvement and participation of the civil administration, the state police, and the Central Armed Police Forces (CAPF) in the maintenance of law and order if the polls were to be conducted peacefully.

Politicians, bureaucrats, police officers, civilians with factional loyalties and several other constituencies made up a heady cocktail of personalities with whom Nanavatty engaged as the corps commander.

S.C. Jamir, the CM, was a wily, veteran politician and a staunch member of the Congress Party to boot. He played his cards close to his chest but never failed to remind Nanavatty every time they met—and they met often and regularly—that the CF should be extended to the NSCN (K) too. Jamir believed that the GOI had made an error in inferring that the NSCN (IM) could assume the mantle of leadership of the Naga people.

On this one issue Nanavatty concurred with the CM whole heartedly. He believed that the GOI 'default' policy for far too long was invariably to drive a wedge between differing factions within a hostile organization. While such a move often paid encouraging dividends in the early stages it seldom resulted in a final solution to the problem. He felt strongly that the offer of a CF should have been extended to all the groups that had taken up arms against the state in Nagaland. To begin with, the government could have held discussions with the various groups separately and in camera; and, then slowly brought them around at the same table, all the while emphasizing that a CF and a peaceful solution was in the best interest of the people of Nagaland. He felt that such a move would have unambiguously conveyed to the NSCN (IM) that they alone did not represent the entire Naga population in the state.

In pursuit of the above goal, Nanavatty, sometime later, sought a meeting with Khetovi Sumi, a Sema Naga and an important leader of the NSCN (K) in the Mokokchung Area. He sought to convince Khetovi and through him, Khaplang, to accept a CF with the GOI. The meeting took place despite two nasty incidents in the areas of Mokochung and Tuensang where the SF had been bested in both resulting in serious casualties. The prevailing tension notwithstanding, Khetovi readily agreed to a meeting with Nanavatty reflecting the faith a Naga has in the spoken word of even an adversary he can trust. It took a long time for the wheels to turn and for a formal CF between the NSCN (K) and GOI to happen but come about it did during the tenure of Nanavatty's successor, Lieutenant General T.S. (Maun) Shergill.[7]

Nanavatty was aware that the NSCN (IM), despite being a party to the ceasefire, had warned political parties and the people at large against participating in the elections, even threatening those who chose to defy the ban with 'capital punishment'. As a counter, 3 Corps issued a press release, which was shared with Army HQ, urging 'the NSCN (IM) to refrain from vitiating the peaceful atmosphere. Indeed, we wish them to extend their whole-hearted support to holding the elections in the true spirit of Naga democratic values.'[8] A relatively peaceful and incident-free election took place on 23 February 1998, returning S.C. Jamir and his party to power in the state.

After the elections, Nanavatty wrote a short memo to HQ Eastern Command offering a bleak but accurate outlook for Nagaland.[9] His assessment highlighted the possibility of non-cooperation, obstruction and undermining of the state government by the NSCN (IM); the probability of greater inter-factional violence within various Naga groups with the NSCN (IM) making a determined bid to gain mass support; and, most alarmingly, attempts by the state government to subvert the CF with the assistance of the NSCN (K). These views would be vindicated in the decades ahead as Nagaland lurched from crisis to crisis in search of an elusive peace.

Nanavatty narrated an incident involving the CM that very nearly proved his assessment right. A cat with nine lives Jamir had survived several assassination-attempts during his long career, including one during his tenure. In the habit of spending his weekends at his farm in Sukhovi (near Dimapur), he would return to the capital, Kohima, every Monday morning—a cardinal error which the state police should have taken note of.[10] On one such weekend trip on 29 November 1999, his convoy was ambushed on his return journey. Jamir survived, scared but unhurt. His police escort suffered casualties, including two killed. While the evidence at the site pointed clearly to the NSCN (IM) and its C-in-C, Hansi Tangkhul, the first question the Director General of Military Operations in Delhi asked Nanavatty was, 'Are you sure it was not stage-managed?'—such was Jamir's reputation! Given the fatal and other casualties suffered by his escort, Nanavatty thought it absurd to think it was stage-managed, but later he wasn't so sure![11] Was it a singularly well thought out and planned operation involving the NSCN (K) to scuttle the CF is the question that runs through his mind even today?

Would this mean the abrogation of the ceasefire was the question on everyone's lips, including that of a news reporter who cornered Nanavatty at the site of the ambush. 'Not necessarily; the police will, I am sure, treat the incident as a serious crime and investigate the matter. We will take stock and then arrive at a deliberate decision,' was his answer. The police had to be 'encouraged, coaxed and pushed' to issue a lookout notice for Hansi Tangkhul and announce a reward for information. For a while after this incident, the security forces upped the ante against the NSCN (IM) and in one instance, a quick witted Hansi Tangkhul, spotting an Assam Rifles Vehicle Check Point ahead deftly stepped off the vehicle he was travelling in and escaped 'falling into the bag'.

Nanavatty recalls the visit of the Union Defence Minister, George Fernandes, to Nagaland in April 1998, soon after the polls.[12] 'I found Fernandes to be a man of tremendous energy and endurance and hit it off well with him. It was a pleasure having him visit. There was no posturing and no "bandobast"; he ate the food from the *langar*, picked up his thali, stood in line with the troops and sat down on a bench in their midst. The linguist that he was, he could converse in several languages. There was no stirring "Not an inch of our territory ..." type of speech when he addressed the troops. He would sit through briefings wide awake and make his own notes. I never once saw him droop off, even for a few seconds.'

Continuing his impressions of Fernandes, Nanavatty said, 'He possessed immense stamina. Let me explain. On one occasion, he took off from Delhi in a service aircraft at 0500h and having to fly avoiding Bangladesh air space arrived in Agartala about noon and went straight into an hour-long briefing by the commander of 21 Sector Assam Rifles. He then visited an Assam Rifles post and had lunch with the troops; "helicoptered" to a BSF post, returned to Agartala at about 1700h, had a chat with me and wound up with dinner at the governor's residence, which finished at about 2330h. The following day, he was at the airfield for departure at 0630h. He would take immediate action on matters over which he had complete jurisdiction. On one occasion, when Fernandes was told during a visit that officers and men of 3 Corps found it difficult to connect with the weekly Indian Air Force courier from Guwahati to Delhi, he immediately authorized connecting flights from places such as Dimapur and Agartala.'

As Nanavatty accompanied Fernandes around parts of Nagaland, Manipur and Tripura, he noticed the excellent rapport that the latter established with the troops. Endowed with a razor-sharp memory, George Fernandes asked Nanavatty: 'Did you have a relative in the Bombay police? I recollect someone by that name who lifted me bodily from the railway tracks in the 1950s when I was agitating as a union leader in the Railways.' When Nanavatty replied that it was his father, Fernandes laughed. The two were to meet frequently again when Nanavatty moved to Northern Command as the GOC-in-C.[13]

The Governor of Nagaland for most of Nanavatty's tenure was Om Prakash Sharma, a distinguished retired police officer of the Punjab Cadre. He was punctilious, correct and very supportive of the army. Nanavatty would meet with him regularly and keep him abreast of developments. The state's chief secretary, Achyut Madhav Gokhale, a Padma Shri awardee, was a thorough gentleman. Reserved by nature he consciously steered clear of most conflict-related matters, minded his own business, worked essentially from home, and pursued his hobbies; he was a great naturalist.

The only part of Manipur that Nanavatty had set foot in 1963 was the district of Tamenglong as a nineteen-year-old subaltern in 2/8 GR. The area then was inhabited by the relatively peaceful Zeliangrong Naga tribes; one of the more illustrious members of the tribe was the feisty 'daughter of the Hills', freedom fighter 'Rani' Gaidinliu, awarded the Padma Bhushan in 1982. He had much to learn about Manipur the land, its people and their aspirations. Manipur, the 'abode of jewels', the land and its people are both blessed and blighted. Endowed with nature's bounty, it is perhaps the most beautiful part of India but is torn apart from within because of factionalism and bitter conflict.

Before Nanavatty had settled into his new assignment, Churachandpur (Lamka), the second-largest town in Manipur in the southwestern part of the state, erupted in an orgy of violence over leadership issues between two communities of similar origins—the Kukis and the Zoumis. Despite a Church-induced 'ceasefire' as recently as July 1997, the violence in September was a repeat and had the state government again standing by as a mute spectator. A lone Rashtriya Rifles battalion was valiantly trying to act as a buffer between the two warring communities and prevent the situation from worsening. The internecine quarrel would continue to fester for another year until yet another Mizo Church–sponsored agreement would settle matters in September 1998.

Summoned to Delhi at short notice after his two-day visit to the district, Nanavatty accompanied the Vice Chief of Army Staff, Lieutenant General Chandra Shekhar and the DGMO, Lieutenant General Inder Verma, to a hurriedly called meeting at the residence of the Home Minister, the veteran Communist Leader Indrajit Gupta. The trio was ushered into the minister's bedroom to find him reclining on his bed, apparently indisposed, with half a dozen civil servants—paper pads and pens poised—seated on chairs around him. The DGMO introduced Nanavatty to the gathering, saying that the corps commander had just returned from a visit to the district and perhaps they would like to hear what he had to say firsthand.[14]

Nanavatty explained the district's dire situation and reiterated that the state government had completely abdicated its responsibilities. He cautioned the assembly of the dangers of ignoring Manipur even as efforts were being made in neighbouring Nagaland to ensure free and fair elections. The minister, taken aback by Nanavatty's remarks, thanked the vice chief and turned to his staff as the army officers excused themselves and quietly departed. It was here that Nanavatty first encountered G.K. (Gopal) Pillai, then a joint secretary (later the home secretary) in the Ministry of Home Affairs, and said to himself that here is a civil servant who knows the NE and the problems of the states therein. It was the start of a professional relationship between the two that lasted his term and one from which he benefitted greatly.

Attributing the Churachandpur incident to the abject apathy of the state administration, Nanavatty wrote a firm letter to Chief Minister Rishang Keishing, before the latter demitted office at the end of his second term. Interestingly, Keishing, a veteran Congressman, was a Tangkhul Naga who fully supported the concept of Greater Nagaland or Nagalim. Yet, he was much respected by the various communities in the state for his administrative abilities and capacity to diffuse inter-factional tensions in the past. In his letter, Nanavatty stressed that Kuki-Mizo-Chin vigilante groups—the KNA and ZRA—were getting out of control of the moderate leadership of their communities. Pointing at the lack of will in the Manipur police and other Central Armed Police Forces (CAPF) to control, coordinate and direct operations, Nanavatty rejected a call from the Director General of the state police to 'hand over operations in the Churachandpur District to the Army'. He wrote, 'I wish to state most emphatically that the civilian government authorities may not abdicate their responsibility of administering and governing the district, and the Army "will not take it over." The law does not provide for it. The situation in the state calls for urgent political initiatives, a reconciliation between the communities and an assertion of will by the state government, even to the extent of resettling the people to facilitate their security, protection and administration.'[15]

With elections to the Nagaland Assembly in February 1998 done and dusted and the CF holding satisfactorily in Nagaland, Nanavatty turned his attention to Manipur. After visiting his formations and units, consulting with his commanders and staff, and reviewing the conduct of ongoing operations in the state, he came to the following six conclusions:

Firstly, the state largely comprised four groups of people of Tibetan-Burmese origin: Meiti, Naga, Kuki and Zoumi. A fifth group, Meiti Pangal, were Bengali Muslims who had migrated from Sylhet (now in Bangladesh) first in the eighteenth century.

Secondly, the state was riven by internecine conflict and factional infighting, the primary cause invariably being the possession and ownership of land. It compelled communities to organize and support vigilante groups and 'private armies' for their survival. The looting of weapons from police armouries in times of trouble was a recurring feature of violence in the state. In 1998, reports indicated that even the relatively small Pangal community was beginning to hoard arms. These groups were not necessarily anti-national. However, they presented a serious threat to law and order and *public order*.

Thirdly, only the Meiti insurgent groups—the People's Liberation Army (PLA), United National Liberation Front (UNLF), People's Revolutionary Party of Kangleipak (PREPAK), Kanglei Yawol Kanalup (KYKL) and others—were initially driven by ideological goals and sought secession from India. They were deemed Valley Based Insurgent Groups (VBIG).

Fourthly, the VBIG had now abandoned their secessionist ideology and were directly involved in organized crime: extortion, kidnapping for ransom and selective killings. For the young Meitei, it was a lifestyle choice. They had the people, particularly in urban and semi-urban areas, reeling.

Fifthly, in 1998, reports from various central intelligence agencies suggested that the VBIG were attempting to form a political front called the Revolutionary People's Front (RPF). HQ 3 Corps noted the issue but discounted the possibility because no single leader seemed the sort that could preside over and hold the flock together. However, if the intelligence agencies were correct and the VBIG were to succeed in their attempts to merge and form the RPF, the threat from the VBIG would be considerably magnified.

Sixthly, the recent clarification by the GOI that the CF with the NSCN (IM) was with the group and not area-specific was very timely indeed. It would allow a hard-pressed 57 Mountain Division to thin out troops from the Naga hill areas and reassign them to the Valley districts to counter the threat from the VBIG.

Nanavatty's mind was clear: 57 Mountain Division's task would be to downgrade the VBIG with a focus on the Valley districts of Imphal East and West, Thoubal, Kakching and Bishenpur to include 'the phumdis' (floating islands) on the Logtak Lake. He outlined a simple three-pronged strategy, part doable and part aspirational, that signalled a whole-of-government approach, which he shared with HQ Eastern Command and the MO Directorate at Army Headquarters:

- Suppress and neutralize the VBIG to include the vast Over Ground Worker (OGW) network.
- Empower and uplift the Meiti population.
- Fulfil the genuine aspirations of the other minority subnational groups in the State—Naga, Kuki and Zoumi—without prejudice to safeguarding Meiti interests.[16]

The strategy envisioned first gaining positive control over the Valley districts. Next was extending the security forces' domination to the villages in the nearer hill areas around the valley and, finally, ensuring preparedness to launch offensive operations across the International Border to destroy insurgent infrastructure and camps in Myanmar. The emphasis was on small unit operations based on actionable intelligence, especially targeting white-collar OGWs. Units were briefed to strictly adhere to the law and avoid confrontations and physical contact with agitating mobs and demonstrators. This was a comprehensive strategy on the surface. However, it relied on minimum support from the state police, objective reporting by the local media and meaningful engagement with civil society, which would hardly be forthcoming during Nanavatty's tenure.

Emerging from this complex interplay of tribal and ethnic strife and casting a shadow over Manipur was the demand for 'Nagalim'—a Nagaland that included all the Naga inhabited areas in the neighbouring states of the Union and Myanmar. For the Meitei, on the other hand, it resulted in the deep-rooted fear that the GOI might seek a resolution to the conflict in Nagaland by transferring a portion of the Naga-inhabited hill districts of Manipur to help create Nagalim.[17] Nanavatty's stance on Nagalim was consistent. He felt that the GOI could have got around the Nagalim stumbling block in the Naga peace talks by drawing the affected states of Manipur, Arunachal Pradesh and Assam into the dialogue and testing the waters to see if a negotiated settlement was possible at all.[18]

The readjustment and redeployment of forces to concentrate in the Valley districts and the conduct of intense small-scale offensive counterinsurgency operations had an immediate effect. While the South Asian Terrorism Portal would reveal only two major incidents during 1998–99—one a Naga–Kuki clash, and the other an ambush by the UNLF in which seven CAPF personnel were killed—Nanavatty's diary notings from December 1997 to April 1998 reveal that the situation was grim before stabilizing in the latter half of 1998. There were four ambushes, nine encounters, sixteen shooting incidents and nine IED attacks. Losses suffered by the security forces included 29 personnel killed, 50 wounded, and 18 weapons lost. The corresponding figures for the VBIG were 38 killed, 319 apprehended, and 128 weapons recovered.[19]

Nonetheless, what was of concern to Nanavatty was that in the environment obtaining in Manipur at the time, the VBIG were increasingly being perceived 'as defenders' of Meitei interests and enjoying the support of not just the Meitei population but of Meitei politicians, civil servants including the police, the judiciary, academics and the local media. Widespread demonstrations, violent agitations and virulent propaganda vilifying the security forces were symptomatic of the nexus.' At one time Nanavatty seriously considered publishing a newspaper by 57 Mountain Division to counter this propaganda. However, looking at the logistics and costs of such a venture, it was decided that a better option would be for the formation to proactively put out a 'fact sheet' giving the 'who, what, where, when, why and how' of each incident irrespective of whether the media carried it or not.

On 16 April 1998, the VBIG, under the RPF banner, urged the state's people through the Imphal Free Press, Manipur's most widely read newspaper, to 'eschew all interaction with the Indian Army & its personnel in Manipur'. Reflecting the hold of the VBIG in the Valley districts, the RPF went on to brazenly announce 'that it would stop any social or public activity organized by the Army or its personnel'. The RPF said these steps were necessary to prevent the army from 'duping the people into going along with their designs despite the intense public movement against their atrocities and violation of human rights'.[20]

Responding almost immediately, a hard-hitting Press Release from HQ 3 Corps on 'Human Rights and the Security Forces' reflected

Nanavatty's combative approach and willingness to try and occupy the moral high ground. Stressing that the security forces in Manipur were fighting the menace of armed insurgent groups seeking secession and the subjugation of rival ethnic groups through the illegal and violent use of force the release argued that 'their actions pose a direct threat to the integrity and security of the nation and the state. In this, the insurgents are encouraged by an apathetic and cowed populace that permits terrorism and insurgency to thrive.' Bringing to light the role of the Meira Paibis (literal meaning 'torch bearers': women activists), who severely compromised the effectiveness of the security forces by obstructing, hindering, assaulting and forcibly preventing them from discharging their duties, the press release described this as a new phenomenon for the SF in the North-east.[21]

Countering the malicious and fabricated narrative over human rights violations, the Press Release highlighted that in January and February 1998 alone, the SF had apprehended 164 insurgents, of whom 59 had sophisticated and lethal weapons at the time of their arrest. In every case, the report emphasized that the individuals were dealt with strictly by the law and handed over to the police within the time stipulated. In comparison, the same two-month period saw 11 of the 18 soldiers killed in the line of duty being murdered and burnt alive as they lay helpless in their upturned vehicle after meeting with an accident without a whimper of protest from the champions of human rights. About misdemeanours by the Security Forces, the Press Release revealed that in the preceding five years, seventeen cases were investigated, and punishments were meted out in seven cases ranging from administrative action to dismissal from service and imprisonment.

Nanavatty was emphatic when he said, 'Every alleged aberration during my tenure was carefully investigated, and the guilty were swiftly brought to book. I was very particular about human rights aberrations and ethical and moral misconduct in operations in the public glare. Some of my toughest administrative decisions were made during my tenure as GOC 3 Corps. These included the removal from command of a much-decorated brigade commander and commanding officers of three battalions.'[22]

Like Nagaland, Manipur threw up interesting personalities for Nanavatty to reckon with. Of the two Chief Ministers he dealt with, Rishang Keishing was a Tangkhul Naga, a seasoned politician, and a tough nut to crack. This was not his first time as CM, and Nanavatty enjoyed working with him. Things changed when Keishing was replaced as CM by W. Nipamacha Singh, a Meiti who was a 'wishy-washy and slippery politician' and extremely parochial. The Governor of Manipur for the first half of Nanavatty's tenure was O.N. Shrivastava, who hardly interacted with him. However, he often met with Shrivastava's successor, Ved Marwah. Marwah was an accomplished police officer with a stellar track record as the Commissioner of Delhi Police and Director General of the National Security Guard. According to Nanavatty, Marwah was 'well connected and intellectually inclined but past his prime and ill-suited for the rough and tumble of CI in Manipur. Though we were on the same page on several issues, he hardly offered me any advice. He was hospitable though and had me over for a meal often. Relations soured a bit after he accused the Army of "tapping" his phone—an accusation I thought was absurd and said so.'

Of the two division commanders of 57 Mountain Division, the first, a fellow Gorkha, was 'keen as mustard, rode his subordinates hard, and had a heap of HR issues to deal with during his tenure. Things improved when Major General Arvind Sharma commanded the division. Calm and controlled in crises, he was a mature and experienced officer who adapted well to the vagaries of operations in Manipur.'

Sharma offered his nuanced understanding of Nanavatty's leadership in 3 Corps in a profile that he shared with the author in late January 2024. He wrote, 'My first official meeting with him was instructive. After confirming whether I had asked for this command given that I was the Military Assistant (MA) to the Vice Chief, he said, "You have the most complex command of a division in the Indian Army today." I realized straight away that he would be a hard taskmaster.' Recognizing the complexities of the dirty and vicious fighting in Manipur, Nanavatty demanded professionalism and accountability from subordinate formations. Though Nanavatty gave a long rope to his commanders, he came down hard on military incompetence, ethical violations and negligence in dealing with human rights violations.

Confirming the complexities of soldiering in a 'no-war-no-peace' situation that involved days of 'nothing to report' and then a sudden transition to short but intense encounters, Sharma recalled an incident wherein he had to come down heavily on combat negligence that resulted in serious casualties. He wrote, 'While on leave in Calcutta for my daughter's marriage, I learnt that one of my battalions was ambushed by Manipuri militants and suffered eight fatal casualties. The ambush was due to complacency that had set in amongst the troops and was in gross violation of the laid down Standard Operating Procedures. When I sought answers from the CO, he was not only evasive, but blamed the company commander for the mishap. After further enquiry, I came to know that the CO never spent a night at a company post but visited them once a month! After due deliberation, I requested the corps commander that the CO be posted out prematurely, as he was not fit to command in the prevalent counterinsurgency environment. Consequently, the CO's posting order was issued. The CO got in touch with his contacts in Delhi to have his posting order rescinded. However, Nanavatty would have none of it and stood his ground, the CO had to go; his decision was the hallmark of a commander who did not buckle under pressure from his superiors.'[23]

During the Kargil Conflict in mid-1999, 57 Mountain Division was pulled out from 3 Corps and redeployed in the Western Theatre for its conventional role during wartime. Nanavatty, with a skeleton Headquarters 3 Corps, was moved to Northern Command in anticipation of the conflict expanding. Major General R.B. Singh, the IGAR (North), assumed responsibility for conducting CI operations in Nagaland and Manipur with the Assam Rifles. While the Assam Rifles units remained deployed in the hill areas to ensure the CF with the NSCN (IM) was undisturbed, 3 Corps had to hand over CI operations in the Valley districts of Manipur to the state police and the Central Armed Police Forces (CAPF).

On the termination of Operation VIJAY in Kargil, 57 Mountain Division reverted to Masimpur in South Assam, its permanent station, for a 'rest and refit'. In Nanavatty's mind, this was an error in judgment, and it took him some time to convince HQ Eastern Command to revert them to Manipur for CI operations. By then, much ground gained in operations against the VBIG by the Security Forces had been lost.

Major Ashwini Channan (later Major General), the BM in HQ 9 Sector, a part of 57 Mountain Division combating the Manipur insurgency, served in the area for two years from 1997 to 1999. 9 Sector, one of the largest brigade-size sector, had eight battalion-sized units on its order of battle and was responsible for CI operations in the Imphal and Thoubal districts. Speaking to the author on 3 January 2023, he said, 'I will gladly give you my honest perspectives of those two tough years if it is for a biography of General Nanavatty. He took several tough and clinical calls during his stint as the GOC, even if they irked Army HQ.' Describing Nanavatty's leadership as a 'no-nonsense, no-frills and hands-off' style, Channan also recollects an excellent connect that Nanavatty established with young officers and men whenever he visited the brigades and battalions in his AOR.[24]

On one occasion, Nanavatty walked away from an Assam Rifles unit he was to inspect because he was accorded a red-carpet welcome despite having passed instructions that none of these trappings were acceptable to him in a war zone. Instead, he went to the Sector HQ close by and sat through an impromptu briefing by Channan since the brigade commander was away. Channan said: 'He listened intently and asked a few probing questions—his demeanour that morning left a lifelong impression on me that I matter.' It was not uncommon for Nanavatty to land at a helipad unannounced due to inclement weather and chat with the men at the helipad. One commanding officer of a battalion told Channan a few years later that he owed his career progression more to a few impromptu conversations that Nanavatty had with his troops than what his Brigade Commander said of him in the Annual Confidential Report (ACR).[25]

Closing his candid recollections of Nanavatty with an incident in February 1998, Channan described the contours of a thirty-seven-day lockdown in Manipur during which the Indian Army was on the backfoot with several of its operating bases and camps under siege by thousands of locals. With no help forthcoming from the state authorities, Nanavatty flew into Imphal and spoke to the Chief Minister, W. Nipamacha Singh and the Director General of the Manipur police. He warned them, 'I am ordering the Indian Army in Manipur back to their barracks if you do not disband the ongoing agitation in the next twenty-four hours. Good luck to you in managing your problems.'[26] The coercion worked even as the Manipur police swung into action, even lathi-charging the mobs and assisting in several encounters with insurgents the following day.

Tripura completed the troika of troubled states in the 3 Corps zone but with a difference—it was a state where the security situation was on the mend. The conflict dynamics too were different, with only two protagonists, tribals and non-tribal migrants from neighbouring Assam, Bengal, Bangladesh, and a small but rising number from Bihar. Before Independence, Tripura had a ruling family with tribal linkages, whereas educated Bengalis entrenched themselves in most white-collar and government jobs. Over the years, a role reversal crept into Tripura's political landscape, creating the inevitable conflict between those who held power in the present (non-tribal immigrants) and those who had held power in the past but were now disadvantaged (tribals). The insurgency in Tripura evolved as the two wings of the Tripura National Volunteers (TNV). The National Liberation Front of Tripura (NLFT) had a secessionist agenda, while the All Tripura Tiger Force (ATTF) demanded the deportation of illegal migrants and the finalization of the Tripura merger agreement. The NLFT armed wing raised the ante in 1990 by starting a low-grade insurgency and commenced regular attacks on the police and Central Paramilitary Forces (CPF) but generally steered clear of the army.[27]

Soon after Nanavatty took command of 3 Corps, he impressed on the state government that what they now were faced with was a severe militancy-related law and order problem with political and ethnic overtones and not an insurgency. Intelligence reports suggested that the armed groups no longer demanded secession or sought to destabilize the legally constituted government. However, what exacerbated the militancy was that the NLFT and ATTF, with safe sanctuaries in Bangladesh, enjoyed political patronage from the tribal-dominated Indigenous Nationalist Party of Tripura (INPT), which by the mid-1990s had become the principal political opponent of the Communist Party of India (Marxist) (CPI (M)). Complicating matters was the United Bengal Liberation Front (UBLF), which sought to protect the interests of the migrant population and enjoyed the protection of the CPI (M) government.

With elections to the State Assembly around the corner in February 1998, there was pressure on the state administration and the Security Forces to get their act together to ensure they were free and fair. Jotting some thoughts down in his diary before including them in a formal concept that 3 Corps was working on, Nanavatty put the overall picture in the correct perspective as he wrote, 'The militant groups (ATTF and NLFT) are engaged primarily in criminal activity and intimidation through terror. Violence is generally either politically motivated or because of the existing tribal/non-tribal ethnic divide. Incidents against the security forces have been sporadic and isolated.' He assessed, 'In the run-up to the election, we are likely to witness an increase in politically motivated violent incidents, particularly by the NLFT. The opposition, mainly comprising the Congress and the INPT, appear disunited, and it is likely that the ruling party, the CPI (M), will be returned to power.'[28]

Nanavatty spent much time in Tripura in the first few months of his tenure. He said, 'The Chief Secretary, Mr Thulasidas, was difficult to get along with. The first time I wanted to call on him, he requested I meet him at home. I realized that working from home was very much the practice in the North-east—perhaps officials felt safer at home than in their offices. I refused the next time and insisted we meet in his office! When I spoke of the need for unity of effort in CI operations, he assumed the army sought to disrobe him of his powers and insisted that he alone was answerable to the CM for law and order in the state. Consequently, the senior military commander in the state, the brigadier commanding 21 Sector AR, who should have been sitting at the same table with the chief secretary and the DG Police to coordinate CI operations in the state, was generally given short shrift.'

Unfortunately, operational responsibilities between the state police, including the Tripura Rifles, the BSF and 21 Sector Assam Rifles (AR) with four AR battalions, were not clearly defined. After Nanavatty's first visit to the state, it was decided, in consultation with HQ Eastern

Command and Army Headquarters, that Major General S.D. Mahanti, the Chief of Staff HQ 3 Corps, would be positioned in Tripura to provide the necessary heft to the Commander 21 Sector. Unfortunately, like so many ad hoc arrangements, that did not work well, either.'[29]

In November 1997, with the elections to the State Assembly approaching, a nervous CPI (M) government and civil administration anticipating, as in the past, a further deterioration in the law-and-order situation, bid for the deployment of the army. Nanavatty opposed the idea and instead urged better civil-military liaison and coordination of efforts. He wrote to the GOC-in-C Eastern Command, 'I do not see the need for additional army units in Tripura. Indeed, we have long believed that the state is affected by an acute law and order problem partly of its own making. I, therefore, find it ironic that we should talk of an increase in force levels in the state when elsewhere, in areas worse affected, we vehemently oppose the idea.'[30]

Elections in Tripura were conducted successfully and in a free and fair manner despite the threat of a boycott of the polls by militant groups, isolated attacks on non-tribal villages, an ambush on the Tripura State Rifles and stray instances of violence.[31] Manik Sarkar, a progressive and relatively young CPI (M) leader, was elected the CM. Nanavatty enjoyed interacting with Sarkar and reckoned that he was easier to get through to than the chief secretary. Sarkar asked questions and listened carefully. He acknowledged that 'understanding the legitimate aspirations and concerns of the tribals was the only way to prevent violence between the two communities,' said Nanavatty.[32] Determined to root out militancy in the state, Sarkar took firm charge, bringing fresh ideas and thinking to the table that went a long way in bringing peace to the state, albeit slowly. Some of that credit must go to Nanavatty for urging the CM during his discussions to develop a 'whole of government' approach to counter militancy.[33]

At the top of Sarkar's agenda was improving civil-military synergy. Of the four states in the 3 Corps Zone, Tripura had the most suitable formal structures for coordinating the CI effort. These included the State Level Coordination Committee (SLCC) and the State Level Operations and Intelligence Group (SLOG). The trouble was the clash of personalities and the sheer dominance of the Chief Secretary, which discouraged the exercise of initiative at lower levels. There was much correspondence between HQ 3 Corps and the Chief Secretary that dealt with hierarchy, reporting chains, status and protocol in the functioning of these groups. It required a fair push from both Sarkar and Nanavatty with the active involvement of the army chief, General V.P. Malik, and the DGMO, Lieutenant General Inder Verma, to get things moving.

By facilitating the training of Tripura Rifles and the State Armed Police contingents at the Counter Insurgency and Jungle Warfare School (CIJWS), Vairengte, with the help of Army Headquarters, police morale and efficiency were restored. With HQ 21 Sector paying serious attention to military-civic action directed at the upliftment of the tribals despite its minimal resources, there were rumblings and serious misgivings within the government that the army was being partisan and overly sympathetic to the tribal cause and the INPT. This led to avoidable adverse publicity in the media. According to Nanavatty, 'We had a task to perform, and I told my sector commander, Brigadier Basant Ponwar, a dynamic officer full of initiative and aggression, to be careful and fair to both sides. It took me some time, but I managed to get through to CM Manik Sarkar and mollify him on this account.'[34]

In addition to combating militancy in Tripura, 21 Sector Assam Rifles had to contend with yet another security-related problem, which was not of the making of the militants in Tripura. Intelligence reports suggested that the NSCN (IM) continued to use the corridor astride the Mizoram–Tripura border to move in and out of Bangladesh. This was a clear violation of the CFGR, and 3 Corps could not possibly disregard such developments. With the Tripura police taking on greater responsibilities, it was possible to redeploy Assam Rifles's units. Accordingly, HQ 21 Sector Assam Rifles in Tripura was ordered to redeploy an AR unit in the Langai River corridor and the areas where refugees of the Bru tribe had set up their temporary camps after being driven out by the Mizos. The aim was to deny infiltration/exfiltration through the area. It was not long before a large group of NSCN (IM) cadres was ambushed in the area, resulting in serious casualties. This action infuriated the NSCN (IM), who cried 'Foul' in the media, quoting the CFGR. They quietened down when shown the fine print and even sought 21 Sector's assistance to perform the last rites of their cadres killed in the ambush, support which was readily provided.

'We had made progress in Tripura by the time I handed over command of the Corps. The state police were quite capable and needed encouragement and better training, which the army provided at CIJWS at Vairengte in Mizoram,' said Nanavatty as he wound up the discussion on Tripura during an exhaustive interview with the author on his tenure in 3 Corps.[35]

After joining her husband in Hashimara when he was Commanding 2/8 GR in a peacetime location, Suniti Nanavatty saw little of him during his subsequent operational commands in Siachen and J&K. Although parts of 3 Corps were not entirely at peace, families were permitted in Rangapahar. The corps commander, of course, had an official residence called *Spear Top*. With both their sons, Rushad and Veer, in college and boarding school, Suniti joined Rostum in Rangapahar. At Spear Top, the Nanavattys inherited a menagerie that included a full grown black bear called Kartoos. One day, when Kartoos was unwell, the veterinarian was called in and and after one look at the bear, the good doctor pronounced '*Yeh Kartoos nahi Kartoosi hain (The bear is female).*' The corps commander was wont to feed her jam with a spoon through the mesh of her enclosure. Kartoosi also enjoyed having her back scratched, and going out every evening on a walk outside the compound using a collar and leash. She and Boomer, the basset became friends and every now and then you had barking deer and the odd Red Jungle Fowl pottering in the garden in the mornings and evenings.

Narrating her first experience in Rangapahar, Suniti wrote in an email to the author, 'Soon after taking over command of 3 Corps, Rostum had a visit from a delegation from Changki dressed in traditional gear led by the gaon bura (village headman). Little did the HQ staff know of Rostum's relationship as Adjutant 2/8 GR in 1965 with the people of Changki. Delighted to learn that "Nanabatty" was back in Nagaland, after giving him a ceremonial welcome, they invited him, along with his family, to come and spend a day with them in Changki. Rostum was happy to acquiesce and planned a visit during Rushad and Veer's holidays.'

A day prior to the proposed visit to the village, the family drove up to the Madras Battalion HQ and spent the night in their guest rooms.

Early the next morning, the visit began with the villagers tying vines to the front fender of Nanabatty's vehicle and pulling him into their village, with much pomp and ceremony. Suniti and the boys walked dutifully behind the vehicle.

A raised platform had been erected at one end of the village square. Every able-bodied villager was present there. The Naga people have a tremendous sense of ceremony and there is an appropriate speech for every occasion. It turned out to be a memorable day. Speeches, presentation of gifts, songs, dances and a grand feast were the order of the day. A group of middle-aged women—young women of yesteryear—danced to the accompaniment of a song that had 'Nanabatty' in its refrain. Suniti and the boys basked in reflected glory. The visit indicated that in India's borderlands, the locals valued their relationship with officers and men of the Indian Army who understood their customs and traditions, empathized with their predicament and made genuine attempts to help them.[36]

Staying in Rangapahar was an opportunity for Suniti to see Rostum's deep involvement with the North-east, a region that had offered him his first lessons in soldiering. It was now an area that he understood very well. At a personal level, being a corps commander's wife in a conflict zone came with its share of responsibilities: visiting soldiers in hospital, providing support to bereaved parents and widows of soldiers killed in action, conducting Teachers' Training Workshops in Army Schools, and trying to improve living conditions for the troops and their families. Given the prevailing security situation, families were not permitted to leave the confines of the Military Station. Suniti worked towards providing facilities inside so that breaking bounds would be less tempting.

Rostum encouraged Suniti to communicate with the Next-of-Kin (NOK) of soldiers killed in action. Soon, a system evolved whereby Suniti wrote a letter of condolence and established contact. She then informed them of their entitlements and how to avail of them. They were urged to contact her in case of any problem they confronted. In Northern Command, Suniti continued with this practice until Rostum's retirement. Always on the lookout to upgrade her professional skills, Suniti squeezed in a course in Guidance and Counselling for Children from IGNOU, for which she had to travel to Kohima to take the exam.[37]

For Suniti, a stark introduction to the violence in Manipur was Nitu Channan's horrifying experience, narrated to Suniti by Nitu after she recovered from her injuries. Travelling in a convoy with her husband, Major Ashwini Channan, and three-year-old son, the six-month-pregnant Nitu was caught in the crossfire of an ambush. Despite numerous bullet injuries, her presence of mind and her calm and courageous conduct won her the Governor's Gold Medal for 'valour in the most unusual circumstances'. Suniti was deeply moved by her courage and positivity and felt compelled to write 'Nitu's Story' for the AWWA journal.[38]

In Residence at St Stephen's College, Rushad made the best of his three years there, dividing his time between academics, sports, debating and acting. Every weekend, he would catch a bus to his maternal grandmother's home to enjoy being pampered and fussed over. His friends were always welcome, too. In 1999, towards the end of his third year, he began to focus on a career in the army, but then finally decided to explore other opportunities.

Altruistic by nature and strongly influenced by his maternal grandmother's steadfast community service, Rushad graduated from St Stephen's College, did a year-long postgraduate course in Humanitarian Law, Human Rights and Refugee Law run by the International Red Cross, followed by his post-graduation in International Relations at the School of Advanced International Studies (SAIS), Johns Hopkins University, Washington, DC. During one of his summer breaks, he travelled to Afghanistan to help build and rebuild its schools. And it was at SAIS that he met and fell in love with his future wife, Katharine (Kate) Bernsohn. Among other professional accomplishments in humanitarian work, environmental issues, and sustainable development, Rushad is an avid mountaineer who climbs Alpine style.

Veer displayed fine motor coordination, creativity and artistic talent very early. He was selected to represent The Doon School at inter-school debates in his final years at school and was awarded the prize for Best Actor as well as Best Sculptor. Keen to pursue a career in architecture, he had no hesitation in selecting the subjects he needed. At about the same time Rushad finished college, Veer completed his schooling and applied to various architecture schools. Fortunately, he got his first choice:

The Centre for Environmental Planning and Technology (CEPT) in Ahmedabad. The next five years were spent there, interspersed with a year on exchange in Switzerland.

Among the few dissonant voices regarding Nanavatty's leadership style comes from his Chief of Staff (COS) in 3 Corps, Major General S.D. Mahanti (Retd). In a candid conversation with the author, Mahanti suggests that his placement as COS in 3 Corps came about at the behest of the army chief, General Shankar Roy Chowdhury. Roy Chowdhury felt that Mahanti's experience of commanding a brigade in Nagaland in the 1990s would come in handy and help Nanavatty find his feet quickly as a corps commander in an area where he had last served in the early 1960s. Mahanti soon found himself at odds with his boss on several issues and reckoned that it was possible that the 'highly egoistic' Nanavatty felt that Mahanti was undermining his authority. Mahanti's views on Nanavatty's leadership style offer a contrarian view that merits some reflection. Divergent from the majority opinion is Mahanti's perspective that leading by example and presence, as Nanavatty did, was not inspirational and functional enough as a corps commander. Critical of Nanavatty's 'Gorkha parochialism' and over-reliance on his powers of observation and notes, Mahanti bore the brunt of Nanavatty's strict assessment and did not make it to three-star rank despite being cleared earlier.[39]

Nanavatty's observations, analysis and prognosis about the Nagaland and Manipur problems are striking. He felt there was too much constitutional propriety in the conflict resolution process that did not adequately consider regional and sub-regional aspirations, such as the spread of the Naga population and how the state would address it. Writing to the GOC-in-C Eastern Command, Lieutenant General A.S. Kalkat, the following prescient observations made by him in 1999 apply even today, twenty-four years later:

- Post-CF developments in Nagaland pointedly suggest that the GOI is unlikely to arrive at a long-term settlement of the Naga political problem through negotiations with the NSCN (IM) alone.

- Nanavatty urged New Delhi to recognize the destabilizing power and potential of regional satraps like Chief Ministers S.C. Jamir in Nagaland and Rishang Keishing in Manipur and their ambivalent attitude towards the CF.
- Even though the NSCN (K) and its affiliates of the United Front (a grouping of minor Naga factions, including some in Myanmar and Manipur who owed their allegiance to the K Group) were a headache for the Indian Army, Nanavatty felt that the only way forward was to include them in the CF, however difficult it would have been to orchestrate.
- Nanavatty did not shy away from pointing out that the Tangkhul (Manipur-based) Nagas would be the most challenging constituency to satisfy when it came to solving the problem of scrapping the concept of Nagalim. The next challenge he envisaged was drawing the Manipur State Govt. and the Meitis into the dialogue to find a lasting solution to the problem.[40]
- Considering that the first instances of covert foreign involvement in India's internal affairs occurred in this region, the GOI cannot ignore this aspect.

Nanavatty's tenure at the helm of 3 Corps, which he termed as 'complex and difficult', exposed him to the perils and complexities of modern conflict, which involved the intersection of politics, culture, societal faultlines and complex interpersonal relationships with subordinate commanders. Insights into his leadership style in 3 Corps are placed at Appendix D. Coupled with his prior command experiences in Siachen and Baramulla, this period saw the emergence of a well-rounded Indian military commander who understood the nuances of contemporary warfare and statecraft and was well-prepared for more significant responsibilities as an Army Commander.

11

A MINEFIELD CALLED NORTHERN COMMAND

'This old soldier sends his good wishes to you all to fight without hate or anger, with extraordinary courage and tenacious determination to win. Terrorism must be uprooted both physically and ideologically.'

—Lieutenant General M.L. Chibber, in a letter to Nanavatty, 27 May 2002[1]

After commanding 3 Corps for almost three years, Lieutenant General Nanavatty spent seven months as the Chief of Staff (COS) HQ Northern Command (NC) before assuming the appointment of General Officer Commanding-in-Chief (GOC-in-C) NC on 1 February 2001. His stint as COS allowed him to understand administration and logistics within the command and would stand him in good stead during a period that saw a revival in Pakistan's covert war in J&K. Though he had kept a close track of happenings in J&K during the six years since he left Baramulla, he had not entirely grasped just how militarized the state had become.

Responding to a congratulatory letter from a former GOC-in-C, NC, Lieutenant General M.L. Chibber, among the most cerebral of the Indian Army generals during the 1980s, Nanavatty offered his initial perspectives on the situation in J&K. He wrote, 'With Islamic mercenary and terrorist forces in Pakistan continuing to pursue an aggressive policy on Kashmir with the support of the Pakistani establishment; a central government unwilling to spell out the contours of a possible politico-military solution(s); a state government incapable of providing the good governance that its people yearn for; an army driven by a compelling need to dominate its adversary and; a sensitive and volatile people caught between the devil and the deep blue sea—how are we going to 'win hearts and minds'? And yet, this war will not be won if we don't.'[2]

NC at the time comprised three corps with distinct geographical Areas of Responsibility (AOR). The newly raised 14 Corps, with its headquarters in Leh, had two divisions and an independent brigade. The two divisions were 3 Infantry Division, responsible for the Line of Actual Control across the entire region of Ladakh, and 8 Mountain Division, responsible for the Line of Control east of Zoji La. The independent brigade (102 Infantry Brigade) continued to be responsible for the Siachen Glacier area. Lieutenant Generals Arjun Ray and R.B. Singh were the two corps commanders who served alongside Nanavatty one after the other.

15 Corps, with its headquarters in Srinagar, had on its order of battle (ORBAT) two divisions (19 Infantry Division and 28 Mountain Division), two independent brigades and two division-size Rashtriya Rifles (RR) formations, Counterinsurgency Force (CIF) Kilo and Victor (commonly called Kilo Force and Victor Force). While the infantry divisions and independent brigades defended a long stretch of the LoC from Zoji La to Gulmarg, they were also responsible for counter-infiltration operations on the LoC and counterterrorist (CT) operations in their respective rear areas. The two CIFs were responsible for CT operations in the hinterland in the Kashmir Valley. 15 Corps southern boundary with 16 Corps ran along the Pir Panjal Range from Gulmarg to Banihal and beyond. Lieutenant General John Ranjan Mukherjee, followed by Lieutenant General Vinayak Patankar, commanded the corps during Nanavatty's tenure.

The third and largest corps in NC was 16 Corps, headquartered at Nagrota near Jammu. It was commanded first by Lieutenant General J.B.S. Yadava, followed by Lieutenant General T.P.S. (Tippy) Brar. It

Northern Command AOR: 2001-2003
Xinjiang
CHINA
Area Ceded to China by Pakistan
Tibet Autonomous Region
Karakoram Pass
Pakistan Occupied Kashmir (PoK)
AGPL
Siachen
Aksai Chin
LoC
NJ9842
LAC
PAKISTAN
Kargil
Dras
Leh
Srinagar
INDIA
Ladakh
Indus River
HQ NC
Udhampur
Nagrota
Jammu
Corps Hq.
Division Hq.
IB
Pathankot
Not to Scale
KBK Infographics

Northern Command 2001-2003
(15 & 16 Corps AOR)
Kupwara
Sopore
Shamshabari Range
Baramulla
CIF K
Srinagar
Uri
Gulmarg
Pahalgam
PoK
Awantipora
Pulwama
CIF V
Op Sarp Vinash
Poonch River
Poonch
Shopian
Hil Kaka
Krishna Ghati
Surankote
Anantnag
Mendhar
CIF R
Bhimber Gali
Thanamandi
Banihal
Rajouri
Kishtwar
LoC
INDIA
Pir Panjal Range
Naushera
CIF U
Patnitop
Doda
Katra
HQ NC
CIF D
Akhnoor
Udhampur
Nagrota
Jammu
Corps Hq.
Division Hq.
Infiltrations routes
Max. Arty engagements
Secessionist activities
IB
Pathankot
Not to Scale
Deployments approximate
KBK Infographics

comprised four infantry divisions deployed along the LoC and the International Border (IB) from North to South in the order: 25, 10, 26, and 29 Infantry Division, two independent armoured brigades, and two independent infantry brigades. For CT operations in the rear areas, 16 Corps had under its command 39 Mountain Division and two RR CIF, Delta and Romeo. In 2003, a third RR CIF, Uniform, would relieve 39 Mountain Division of its CT operations responsibilities. The 16 Corps AOR encompassed the towns of Poonch, Rajouri, Nowshera, Akhnur, Jammu and Pathankot. Subsequently, during Operation PARAKRAM (Op PARAKRAM), HQ 3 Corps with 6 & 27 Mountain Division would also be part of HQ NC, and 1 Corps ex Mathura would be concentrated 'in location'—within the territorial jurisdiction of 16 Corps.

In addition to these forces, several battalions of the Central Armed Police Forces (CAPF), such as the Central Reserve Police Force (CRPF), Border Security Force (BSF), Indo-Tibetan Border Police (ITBP), and the Jammu and Kashmir State Police, were present. It was, by any yardstick, a highly-militarized environment with probably one of the densest deployments of security forces anywhere in the world.

The vicious fighting in Kargil in 1999 had left the Pakistan Army sullen in defeat and the Indian Army dissatisfied with a 'pyrrhic victory'. Both armies struggled to come to terms with the large number of battle casualties.[3] Peace was nowhere on the horizon. After overthrowing the civilian government of PM Nawaz Sharif in October 1999, General Pervez Musharraf, the Pakistan Army (PA) Chief and architect of the Kargil intrusions, was firmly entrenched as the military dictator of Pakistan. Pakistan's lack of enduring military successes against India in 1965 and 1971 and the Siachen and Kargil conflicts, in which Musharraf had participated in different capacities, left him with a deep-rooted dislike for India.

A professional soldier with a devious strategic mindset, Musharraf realized that Pakistan's only way of keeping the Kashmir pot boiling was to continue with President Zia-ul-Haq's strategy of 'Bleeding India with a Thousand Cuts', albeit with a more nuanced and sophisticated 'Covert

War' strategy interspersed with peace overtures to keep India guessing. Atal Bihari Vajpayee, India's Prime Minister from 1998 to 2004, was at the helm of affairs when the India–Pakistan relationship reached its nadir with the Kargil Conflict and the subsequent peaking of the covert war. After over a decade of violence and counter-violence in J&K, there emerged a growing realization within the GOI that the resolution of conflict in the state lay beyond the mere use of force. Encouraged by signs from the ground and inputs from intelligence agencies that there were widening differences between moderates and hardliners within the Kashmiri separatist movement, Vajpayee saw the potential to create political alternatives before the State Assembly elections that were scheduled in 2002.

An idealist, Vajpayee attempted to stitch together a rapprochement with Musharraf by easing the tension along the LoC as a prelude to a more concrete peace initiative. To achieve this, he announced an initiative on 27 November 2000 to coincide with the month of Ramzan, called Non-Initiation of Combat Operations (NICO). The broader aim of NICO was to isolate the Foreign Terrorists and their handlers, the Pakistani Deep State, from the people of J&K and encourage support for a peaceful resolution of the Kashmir Conflict. Pakistan played along by announcing restraint on the LoC on 1 December 2000, a move that encouraged Vajpayee to announce three successive extensions of NICO through May 2001.[4] NICO demanded that the Security Forces cease all offensive CT operations and only resort to the use of force in self-defence.[5]

The corps commander of 15 Corps, Lieutenant General John Ranjan Mukherjee, was closely involved in the operationalization of NICO with other government agencies. He recounted to Nanavatty after he took over as the GOC-in-C as to how he was working with disaffected elements to try and 'turn' them. According to Mukherjee, he even had some elements shelter in his household! Nanavatty recalls his predecessor, Lieutenant General H.M. Khanna, asking him as the Chief of Staff in NC what he thought of the NICO proposal. 'Having come from 3 Corps, my gut reaction was that there was no harm in trying it,' said Nanavatty.[6]

Lieutenant General John Ranjan Mukherjee, an extremely diligent, hardworking and conscientious officer with vast experience in CI operations in the NE, served under Nanavatty for almost a year in NC. They shared a mutually respectful professional relationship marked by a nuanced understanding of J&K. No one contextualizes the situation in Northern Command at the time better than Mukherjee, who wrote in his highly credible book, *A Soldier for Life: My Story*, that by early 2001, 15 Corps and Northern Command had severely eroded the combat capability of Kashmiri terrorist groups such as the Hizbul Mujahideen (HM) and brought them to the negotiating table—achieved through a combination of effective counterterrorist and counter-infiltration operations that saw the Indian Army neutralizing the maximum number of terrorists since the late 1980s.[7]

Instead of eliciting a genuine response from across the border, the duplicitous Musharraf-led Pakistani strategic establishment engaged New Delhi on twin tracks. The first track was preparing for the Agra Summit between PM Vajpayee and President Musharraf, scheduled for July 2001. The second covert track sought to exploit the opportunity that NICO provided to infiltrate foreign terrorists—the Lashkar-e-Toiba (LeT) and Jaish-e-Mohammed (JeM)—into J&K. These groups had taken a heavy hit at the hands of the Indian Army in the post-Kargil period and reinforcements were an imperative if the covert war in Kashmir was to continue.

After Nanavatty took over as the GOC-in-C, he realized that NICO was not working because the Pakistan Army was not a party to the agreement and continued its support to the terrorists as if nothing had changed. Seeing that his troops were seriously disadvantaged in such an environment, he issued orders to recommence offensive CT operations based on intelligence without waiting for a decision on NICO. Soon after, in April 2001, during the commanders' conference in Delhi, he explained the situation to General Padmanabhan, the army chief and the Director General of Military Operations (DGMO). Nanavatty argued that apart from the hit that the Foreign Terrorists had taken, the reason for the PA to welcome NICO was the severe casualties it had suffered because of the artillery engagements during the period August–November

2000, wherein the Indian Army's engagements were twice as intense as the PA's (approximately 18,000 vs 9,000 rounds). Additionally, the casualties suffered by the PA during low-level trans-LoC operations, duly moderated, were four times as heavy as IA casualties (165 versus 42). He also pointed out that even though there was a marginal reduction in the number of infiltration attempts during NICO, a larger number of encounters had ensued, resulting in a greater number of infiltrators being killed. He would also point out a shift in the infiltration spread to areas south of the Pir Panjal Ranges. Finally, he pointed out that considering that the number of violent incidents during the period of NICO only showed a modest decline in the areas of both 15 and 16 Corps as compared to a corresponding period during pre-NICO times (301 versus 294 in the 15 Corps zone and 246 versus 164 in the 16 Corps zone), the scepticism of military commanders about the effectiveness of NICO was correct.[8] He strongly recommended that NICO be revoked—and the sooner, the better.

On his return from Delhi, Nanavatty advised his commanders to anticipate a 'stalling of the J&K Peace Initiative'; to be prepared to adopt a Declaratory Punitive Policy to deter Pakistan from continuing overt and covert support to terrorism; and simultaneously, ensure adequate reserves to cater for escalation. Revising several existing orders, including those dealing with dominating the enemy by observation and fire on the LoC, the objective was straightforward: the PA had to pay the price for their continuing support to the terrorists and for the actions of their BAT (Border Action Teams). Soon, the Indian Army would commence the use of artillery south of the Pir Panjal Ranges in the 16 Corps Zone—a self imposed embargo till then.

Under pressure from his commanders and recognizing that India had given Pakistan the space and time to recalibrate its covert war strategy in J&K, General Padmanabhan, the army chief, urged the GOI to suspend NICO on 23 May 2001, two months before the Agra Summit.[9] The gloves were off again after a brief flirtation with a 'phoney' peace.

'We all agreed on the issue, and the COAS instructed the DGMO to allot additional forces for CT ops, particularly in the 16 Corps zone, in anticipation of NICO being scrubbed. These forces were de-inducted after three months or so,' recalls Nanavatty. Even though NICO and the uncertainties associated with it lasted almost six months, it was in 2001 that NC recorded the highest number of terrorist casualties. The three years 2000 (1708), 2001 (2345) and 2002 (1758) statistics as recorded in the South Asia Terrorism Portal (SATP) are telling.[10] Unfortunately, the proposed Declaratory Punitive Policy was never promulgated. Nanavatty recalls, 'I think the view was that it would make no difference to Pakistan. I thought it would, and not just to Pakistan but the rest of the world, too.'[11]

Given the fate of NICO and notwithstanding media expectations and the hopes of peaceniks within the strategic establishment who marvelled at Musharaff's 'body language', in Nanavatty's mind, the failure of the Agra Summit was a foregone conclusion.

In June 2001, Nanavatty urged his Chief, General Padmanabhan, to authorize NC to prepare for a series of limited battalion-size operations to seize and hold key areas across the LoC. This punitive strategy aimed to redefine the LoC and coerce Pakistan to cease support to the ongoing covert war in J&K. 'Why not brigade size? Are you well placed to cater for escalation? We will do something, and they will do something,' said Padmanabhan. Nanavatty's reply was, 'Sir, I am confident that we have the size, the strength and the resilience to outlast the PA and to "go a bit further".' 'Will you hold the ground that you capture?' asked Padmanabhan. Nanavatty said, 'Yes, we should, unless ordered otherwise.' Approved in principle by the army chief but subject to final political clearance, NC commenced preparation for Operation KABADDI (Op KABBADI) in July 2001.[12]

Op KABADDI envisaged a departure from NC's operational philosophy as it pushed the envelope of proactive deterrence. Objectives were carefully selected either to deny terrorist launch pads or to improve the defensive posture, thereby redefining the LoC. Forces for the operation were allocated from command and corps reserves without upsetting the counter-infiltration posture or the CT operations grid in the rear areas.[13] The operation envisaged measured, deliberate, controlled and localized retaliation to hostile actions by the Pakistan

Army, infiltrators and terrorists at a time and place of NC's choosing. While Nanavatty suggested 1 November 2001 as the date for readiness to launch Op KABADDI, the army chief desired NC to be prepared by 1 October 2001.[14]

Nanavatty's observations regarding Op KABADDI scribbled in his diary, probably before he addressed his formation commanders, are illustrative: 'I am not happy with what I have seen of contingency planning. Everyone but the person directly responsible for execution is doing the planning. Plans must be made by the individual directly responsible for the operation, but not below the level of a unit commander (meaning the battalion commander).'[15]

Some brigades, though, were well prepared to launch their offensives as early as July 2001. Brigadier (later Lieutenant General) H.S. Panag, commander of a mountain brigade, was well-prepared to capture objectives in the Chorbatla-Shungroti sub-sector. He even had artillery (75/24 howitzers deployed at 16,000 feet) to support his plans. After being briefed by Panag in the presence of GOC 14 Corps, Nanavatty hopped into a helicopter to see the selected objectives, quizzing Panag on whether the brigade was sure of success. '100 per cent, Sir,' replied Panag, and that was it. Calling the plan audacious because of its spread across the LoC, Panag remembers Nanavatty as a 'farsighted general who was very sure of himself'.[16]

In hindsight, Op KABADDI was a bold option. It fitted well into the template of a carefully calibrated limited conflict in J&K. However, given the reconciliatory political climate in India towards Pakistan at the time, there was an element of overreach in Nanavatty's plans. He thought Paddy would convince the government to change the rules of the game and introduce a new punitive paradigm in the conflict. Perhaps he should have realized that only a very provocative trigger initiated by Pakistan may have convinced the Vajpayee government to 'go for it'. That trigger would not take long to materialize, and the next chapter would give readers an idea whether India was adequately prepared to respond.

Then, the 9/11 terror attacks on the Twin Towers by Al-Qaeda happened. With the US President George Bush declaring the Global War on Terror (GWOT) and with Musharraf falling in line and supporting the US in Afghanistan, things got further complicated for India. If India were to act unilaterally, it would be perceived as an irresponsible state even as Pakistan was aiding the world in the GWOT. The window for coercive action thus closed. Though several formation commanders expressed disappointment at not being able to punish Pakistan, Nanavatty believes that calling off KABADDI was the right decision in the given circumstances. He confessed, 'I was unsettled by Pakistan's pronouncement that it would not support terrorism and felt that the time was not suitable to settle scores.'[17]

Speaking at a seminar on 'Jammu & Kashmir: The Way Ahead' organized by HQ 16 Corps at Jammu on 31 October 2001 offered Nanavatty an opportunity to send a stern message to Pakistan. It was also an opportunity to engage with diverse stakeholders in the J&K peace process, such as politicians, academia, civil society, diplomats and the media. 16 Corps sent Nanavatty a draft keynote address that he put aside and wrote his own. He thought it was about time and felt the need to speak his mind to the political leadership on the state of affairs in J&K. 'I did not clear my talk with anyone, but I said what I wanted to and sat down,' remembers Nanavatty.[18]

His keynote address was crisp and lasted no more than fifteen minutes. Nanavatty stated that the 'conflict in Jammu and Kashmir arguably presents the most serious challenge to the security of our nation. With time, Pakistan's role has dwarfed that of the Kashmiri separatists. We are now faced with a relentless covert war, in the guise of a freedom struggle planned, organized, directed, coordinated and controlled by Pakistan.' Candid as always, he admitted that it was a conflict arising from the nation's failure to meet the aspirations of a section of its people and exploited by Pakistan to serve its geostrategic ends. Much to the chagrin of the Minister of State for External Affairs, Omar Abdullah, who parroted the line of his father that attributed the chaos in J&K solely to Pakistan's meddling, Nanavatty highlighted that the breakdown in governance over decades in J&K must be concurrently addressed with the use of force. He also urged the media not to sensationalize and distort happenings in the strife-torn state.

Delivering a clear message to Pakistan, he said, 'We are committed to restraint along the LoC and the International Border in J&K. If, however, the Pakistan Army or terrorists assisted by the Pakistan Army continue to carry out hostile acts to include sabotage, infiltration, raids or intrusions in violation of the Shimla Agreement, we reserve the right to take military action against Pakistani military and terrorist targets as deemed appropriate.'

Addressing the contentious issue of reclaiming occupied territories that military commanders thus far had stayed away from in public forums, Nanavatty did not mince his words as he offered a reality check. 'The reclamation of occupied territories—Pakistan Occupied Kashmir (POK) and the Northern Areas—however, is quite another matter. It is achievable but would demand extraordinary synergy of political, diplomatic, economic, intelligence and military effort, and an uncharacteristic single-mindedness of purpose.'[19]

He concluded his talk by addressing the people of Kashmir, Kashmiri separatists and the Pakistan Army, 'In no democratic state can a section of its people be permitted to take recourse to the use of force and violence to achieve political objectives no matter what their grievances. The task in J&K is straightforward: dissuade Pakistan, fulfil the people's aspirations and restore normalcy. The campaign will be long and hard, but let no one mistake our will, resolve and ability to prevail.'

Speaking at the same seminar, Omar Abdullah, then Minister of State for External Affairs, the rising star in the Abdullah family and a future Chief Minister of the state, naively dismissed Nanavatty's assertion that J&K was a political and governance problem, saying, 'Kashmir is not a political issue but a military problem as Pakistan is aiding and abetting terrorism in the state. The present turmoil is often interpreted as an outcome of electoral malpractice, unemployment or non-fulfilment of people's aspirations.' He justified his arguments by suggesting that other Indian states, too, experienced similar problems but did not have a 'Pakistan' to deal with. The *Indian Express* commented, 'Sounding at times more as a spokesperson for his father's political party, the National

Conference, than a cabinet minister (at the Centre), Abdullah sought to justify a common (and widespread) charge made against the National Conference that rigging in the elections had given rise to militancy in the state.'[20]

Remarking to Nanavatty over lunch, the Foreign Secretary, Salman Haider, commented, 'General, the wheels will start turning in Washington, D.C.' The media's response to Nanavatty's talk went 'viral'. The press was buzzing over the next five days with twenty-five national and regional newspapers, including ones in Hindi, interpreting Nanavatty's remarks in news reports and editorials; all these reports are meticulously preserved in a folder.

Some of the varied responses are highlighted below:

- *The Indian Express* (01 November): 'We have right to strike but end alienation too: J&K's top Army officer.'
- *The Asian Age* (01 November): 'Army to Pak: Stop terrorism or else…'
- *The Tribune* (01 November): 'Seminar throws up conflicting views.
- *The Hindu* (01 November): 'We reserve right to military action. Pak sees a disparity between the government and the army.'
- *The Times of India* (01 November): 'The situation in J&K is similar to that in '65, says Nanavatty.'
- *Hindustan Times* (01 November): 'Nanavatty warns Pakistan against backing terrorism,' 'Sore with Media over "Distortion," But Why?'
- *Kashmir Times* (01 November): 'India can opt for Military Action: Gen Nanavatty,' 'Speakers favour political solution.'
- *The Times of India* (02 November, Editorial): 'War with Words.'
- *Kashmir Times* (03 November, Editorial): 'Ominous War Clouds.'[21]

Alerted by the widespread comments in the media, Army HQ asked for a transcript of Nanavatty's talk. Sanguine that he had said nothing beyond plainspeak and mirrored the views expressed by India's defence minister, George Fernandes, at a military cantonment four days before the Seminar, Nanavatty was vindicated when the Public Relations Officer (PRO) in the Ministry of Defence told the media that 'Nanavatty's presentation should be seen in the spirit of the remarks that the defence minister himself has made in the last ten days. This, however, does not translate into any concrete instructions being passed to the military command.'

In hindsight, had 9/11 not happened, this speech of Nanavatty's could have been a precursor to Op KABADDI. Unfazed by the flurry of comments after the talk, Nanavatty reckons that the seminar was a turning point in his own practitioner-intellectual's journey towards putting together a 'Strategy for the Resolution of Conflict in J&K'. Having spoken his mind, Nanavatty also decided that for the remainder of his tenure, he would stay clear of the media as it would detract from his primary responsibility. In May 2003, a few weeks before he retired, Nanavatty recalls, 'New Delhi asked Major General Ashok Mehta (Retired), a fellow Gorkha and prolific writer and columnist, to bring a team of senior journalists to interview me. Unfortunately, Robin Raphael, the US Assistant Secretary of State for South Asia and a frequent India baiter, was on a sudden visit to Delhi, causing the visit to be cancelled at the last moment; my time was coming to an end, and I refused to reschedule.'[22]

Reflecting on his interactions with the CM, Farooq Abdullah, Nanavatty said, 'Going by past practice in dealing with civil governments in internal security situations, I dutifully called on him immediately after assuming the appointment of GOC-in-C NC. The first question he asked me was whether I played golf. I said "No" and that I did not intend to start, either! After that, it was all downhill.' A larger-than-life figure who wore his patriotism on his sleeve, Abdullah loved the limelight and made it as if he had all the answers to the Kashmir imbroglio.

As far as he was concerned, Pakistan was responsible for all the trouble in Kashmir. Sometimes it was '*General Saab, Pakistan ke saath to bas "dhaard"* (a good thumping is what Pakistan needs)' and on other occasions it was 'the Government of India must talk to Pakistan'. He showed no inclination to discuss issues of importance with Nanavatty. Instead, he would 'pass him on' to Ashok Jaitley, the incumbent chief secretary and an experienced civil servant, who enjoyed the CM's confidence and on whom Abdullah depended greatly. That might have worked except that Jaitley departed the scene in April 2002, and the person who relieved him, I.S. Malhi, a thorough gentleman, did not have the same standing or clout with the CM.

Nanavatty's assessment was not incorrect. In the decades ahead, whenever the Abdullahs were out of power, they would urge the government to engage in talks with the pro-Pakistan Hurriyat People's Conference and with the Government of Pakistan over Kashmir. In the above circumstances, the person Nanavatty would interact with regularly was the Governor, Girish Chander Saxena, a distinguished police officer with a sound understanding of Pakistan's covert war against India. 'Quiet and reserved, he was very supportive and appreciative of the work being done by the armed forces and always thanked me for keeping him informed,' said Nanavatty.

Lieutenant General V.K. Ahluwalia served under Nanavatty for two years as the brigade commander of the Rampur Brigade. An artillery officer (colloquially called 'Gunners'), Ahluwalia opted for the General Cadre in the Indian Army as a brigadier, which allowed him to command an infantry brigade. Posted in the MS Branch of Army HQ (the branch that deals with promotions, postings and HR issues), when Ahluwalia opted to command a brigade in NC, a colleague took him aside and told him, 'Are you sure because Nanavatty is shortly to take over NC and no one wants to serve under him.' Ahluwalia had no such fears and took over the Rampur Brigade a month before Nanavatty became the Army Commander.[23]

A patient listener during briefings by formation commanders, Nanavatty would offer space for dissent and contrarian views and always wait till the end of a presentation before asking questions. Ahluwalia remembers briefing Nanavatty about the task assigned to his brigade in Op KABADDI and recommended it be changed in favour of an option that offered better value with the likelihood of incurring fewer casualties. Decisive in his operational instructions and giving a long rope to his brigade commanders during trans-LoC operations and punitive engagements, particularly after terrorist attacks, Ahluwalia remembers, 'We gave the Pakistanis hell after the Parliament Attack. All my guns, including the Bofors, opened fire over several nights, and the only cautionary we got from NC was to engage military and terrorist targets and avoid civilian casualties. During this period, Nanavatty constantly advised us not to conduct speculative shoots and only shoot to destroy.'

Ahluwalia recollects that military bearing, turnout, physical fitness, mental agility and moral courage were essential markers of how Nanavatty assessed officers across all ranks. He reckons that it was unfortunate that many officers feared him because they could not live up to his expectations.[24] 'Were you aware of your reputation as a taskmaster and that, apart from respecting you, there were many who feared you?' the author asked Nanavatty during one of his interviews. 'Yes, I was, but this did not trouble me one bit. NC was an active theatre—it was a combat zone as far as I was concerned, and I had no time for professional incompetence or poor leadership.'

Apart from preparing for punitive operations across the LoC, the period from June to November 2001 was marked by relentless and vigorous CT operations resulting in unprecedented terrorist attrition, particularly in the areas south of the Pir Panjal Ranges. Addressing the 44th National Defence College Course during a talk on 20 October 2004, Nanavatty said the next logical step was to 'deny terrorist bases in the fringe areas of the Pir Panjal and Shamshabari Ranges in the arc extending from Bandipora through Lolab, Rajwar, Baramullah Kandi to Hill Kaka. The time had come to extend our areas of effective control and bust the boastful terrorist-speak, "*Makki hamari, barf tumhari* (The corn is ours and the snow is yours, meaning we have the upper hand in the summers and you in the winters)."'[25]

Lieutenant General S.K. Saini, who retired as the Vice Chief of Army Staff in February 2021, was a colleague of the author on the faculty at the National Defence College, New Delhi, during the years 2015–17. He was the CO 7 JAT on the LoC in the Mendhar Sector during 2000–02. He recalled that the army policy of retaliation on the LoC until the year 2000 was rather 'aimless—we responded to small arms fire with light weapons and to little effect, and for some strange reason, there was an unstated embargo on the use of artillery in the 16 Corps zone'. However, all that was about to change: after the abrogation of NICO, the NC policy called for deliberate and planned fire assaults against PA in response to any infringement and violation of the LoC to include the obstruction of villagers from performing their chores, attempts at infiltration and any other aggressive action.

Saini cites an incident on 15 October 2001 as an example. In response to a major infiltration bid by terrorists assisted by the PA in the Mendhar Sector of 16 Corps AOR, a night-long fire assault was carried out against PA posts suspected of aiding the terrorists. The media unfortunately sensationalized the engagement and needlessly linked it with extraneous geopolitical developments, such as the 9/11 attacks: 11 bunkers and fortifications destroyed, and 14 terrorists killed became, '11 posts destroyed, and 30 terrorists killed.'[26]

Saini remarked, 'Nanavatty visited my battalion twice, and I found him to be a commander who stood out for his clarity of thought and leadership qualities. He was always well-prepared with maps of the area he visited and had cue cards ready for all the ridgelines within visual observation. On one occasion, Nanavatty was discussing offensive plans from our brigade viewpoint with brigade commanders and the division commander of a Dual-Task Formation (DTF) that had come from the east. I was hanging around as the battalion commander from the adjoining battalion and had the opportunity to observe him closely. When Nanavatty found that the commanders were unsure of matching the terrain and their plans, he turned around and asked if anyone wanted to chip in. Since I was familiar with the area, I piped up, suggesting that seizing one of the two planned objectives was wasteful and that the second objective met the requirement of dominating the area by observation and fire. Nanavatty listened to me carefully and suggested to the others present to factor in my assessment while recalibrating their plans.'[27]

Always with an ear for his men and young officers while on field visits, a heartwarming letter from Captain A.J.L. Gomes, the RMO of 2 DOGRA, says it all. Gomes writes, 'We had put forth a request to you for a Village Public Telephone (VPT). The VPT arrived a couple of days later, and the morale of the men was high. There was cheer all around the area, from the civilian villagers to the lads on the forward most peaks. It is quite evident that a point noted in your diary never gets erased until the job is done.'[28]

Lest the reader wonder why China does not figure yet in Nanavatty's operational musings as the Northern Army Commander, he was honest enough to admit, 'China at that time was low in my order of priority. Since Army HQ dealt directly with HQ 14 Corps on matters concerning the PLA and the LAC in Ladakh and given that the China Study Group (an informal official group set up in 1975 for advising the government on its China policy)[29]completely dominated decision making regarding the strategic posture and activities along the LAC, I did not want to be distracted. HQ NC was kept informed but did not interfere.'

At one stage, GOC 14 Corps Lieutenant General Arjun Ray had worked up a sweat over the PLA acquiring and deploying new craft on Pangong Tso, which outperformed anything his corps possessed. There was a flurry of activity to include advice and assistance from the Indian Navy. Nanavatty's advice to 14 Corps was to keep their eyes and ears open and not overreact. In due course of time, the matter died a natural death.

During the same meeting with the Chief and the DGMO in April 2001, Nanavatty had also touched in outline about India's defensive posture in Eastern Ladakh—of where its main defence lines should lie and what its infrastructure development policy should be. Notwithstanding all that has occurred along the LAC since 2014, he still believes vis-à-vis the Chinese that India must:

- Distinguish between the areas it must 'defend' and areas that it must 'police'.
- Infrastructure must be developed accordingly (and NOT necessarily to match that of the Chinese).
- In Eastern Ladakh, he believes that India's defences must lie along the Eastern KK Range and the West Bank of the Shyok R to Darbuk, then along the South Bank of Pangong Tso to Chushul and then along the Kailash Range to Demchok.
- Ahead of its main defences, he argues that 'we must police the area up to our Claim Line using the SFF, Ladakh Scouts and the

ITBP with the latter being placed under the operational control of HQ 14 Corps'.

- India must seriously consider how we can deny China the use of the area between our Claim and Defence Line(s), i.e., use the area for Field Firing, including by the IAF; selective mining and even controlled and organized grazing of livestock duly escorted in the summers.

Rounding off his assessment of China, he suggests, 'Above all, we must decide on an LAC that is mutually acceptable to both China and India and the sooner the better. We cannot continue with this business of "our perception" and "their perception". This is a matter of the highest importance and demands a national political consensus, as indeed do all problems that relate to national security, irrespective of whether they are external or internal.'

12

ALMOST WAR AND ADIOS

'Trust in god and keep your powder dry.'

—Oliver Cromwell

On 13 December 2001, terrorists from the Lashkar-e-Toiba (LeT) attacked the heart of the Indian Republic, the Parliament in Delhi. Prime Minister A.B. Vajpayee called for an urgent Cabinet Committee on Security (CCS) meeting following the attack. The three service chiefs were required to be present. Since General Padmanabhan was away on an official visit to Chennai, the Vice Chief of Army Staff, Lieutenant General N.C. Vij attended the meeting. Nanavatty recollects[1] that he received a call from Vij after the event to say that the mood at the assembly was grim and one of despair.

Apparently, Air Chief Marshal S. 'Kichcha' Krishnaswamy, India's air chief, was the first to respond during the meeting and indicate that he was ready for either a limited response against targets in POK or a conventional response across multiple sectors in J&K, Punjab, and Rajasthan.[2] The naval chief, Admiral Sushil Kumar, indicated likewise and in the case of the army it was pointed out that its views would be conveyed to the government soonest on the return of the chief. Nevertheless, the meeting terminated with an abrupt political directive to the armed forces to 'mobilize for war'. What immediately struck

Nanavatty was that, as 'first movers', in our haste, we seemed to have forgotten the biggest lesson of the India–Pakistan War of 1971—'in thorough preparation lies the key to victory'.

By the third week of December 2001, even though the Union War Book—'a classified voluminous document which lays down the exact role each government machinery will play in times of war',[3] an essential prerequisite for the nation to go to war—had not been invoked, India's Armed Forces had commenced mobilizing with Operation SANGRAM, the code name for the mobilization serving as a quasi-formal government sanction to go to war. Southern Command (Gujarat–Rajasthan theatre), Western Command (Punjab theatre), and Northern Command (J&K and Ladakh theatre) with their three Army Commanders, Lieutenant Generals Gurbaksh Sihota, Shamsher Mehta and Rostum Nanavatty, would be directly involved. Nanavatty recalls, 'Paddy told Gurbaksh, Shamsher and me to disengage from everything else, reshape plans and be ready for conventional operations by the end of December.' Taking Nanavatty aside, Paddy conveyed that he intended to change the narrative and commence offensive operations with a primary offensive in the NC theatre to make purposeful gains in J&K before the inevitable ceasefire. He had previously approved the broad aim of capturing key areas to redefine the LoC to India's advantage.

Back in his headquarters, Nanavatty took stock of the situation. The lack of time for preparation for an offensive by 3 Corps was of grave concern to him. He apprised the army chief that seven of his nine divisions were fully committed to intense CT operations on the LoC and in the rear areas. They would have to disengage and reorient themselves to their conventional war-fighting tasks. 3 Corps allotted to NC for a major offensive in the J&K theatre was an ad-hoc strike corps. It comprised two dual-task divisions from diverse commands and a reserve division from NC that was committed to CT operations in the 16 Corps Zone. Lieutenant General V.K. Jetley, the GOC 3 Corps, had assumed the appointment as recently as 5 October 2001 and had no time to familiarize himself with his conventional war tasks in NC. Indeed, this was his first exposure to the formation as a corps commander from the Eastern theatre. Lastly, weather and terrain at that time of the year restricted major offensives to the areas south of the Pir Panjal Range, which limited

NC's options. Nanavatty was emphatic in his communication to the army chief that 3 Corps needed at least three weeks for preparation in location before their launch into operations. And, on that score, he was not willing to make a compromise.

It was not what Paddy wanted to hear, but Nanavatty reckoned that the chief would understand his compulsions given his experience as a corps and Army Commander in NC.[4] Brigadier (later Lieutenant General) Rajan, a trusted staff officer to the Chief, would recall a visit to Udhampur to discuss operational plans wherein an exasperated Padmanabhan would turn to him in the car and say, 'Who does Rostum think he is? Monty?' (Monty was the nickname of the British Field Marshal Montgomery, who garnered the reputation of being meticulous and deliberate in launching offensive operations in the Second World War.)[5]

Vijay Jetley, GOC 3 Corps, was a good friend and colleague of Nanavatty's from their days together in the Perspective Planning Directorate in Army Headquarters. He had commanded the Siachen Brigade in Op MEGHDOOT with distinction a few years after Nanavatty. Jetley took umbrage to the fact that he was presented with a fait accompli—an outline plan of attack that laid down the aim, objectives, force levels, direction of attack and details of fire support—on arrival. He justifiably desired the flexibility and space to plan his operations given the aim and objectives.

'I empathized with Vijay, but we simply did not have the time,' said Nanavatty. Lieutenant General Nagaraj, who later commanded South Western Army Command, was the Major General General Staff (MGGS) under Nanavatty. He worked closely with Jetley and explained to him that 'Army HQ had already approved of the broad plan and that his recommendation of an offensive along multiple thrust lines was impossible owing to the paucity of artillery.' As things turned out, after the initial flurry, the armed forces were in for a long wait.[6]

In May 2002, NC was jolted once again by a horrific terrorist strike in Kaluchak, where seven bus passengers and twenty-three family members, including children of army personnel, were killed in their married quarters. Nanavatty issued orders to standby to execute one of NC's contingency plans involving a division-size force and sought clearance from Army HQ since he was sure it would trigger the outbreak of a general conventional war.[7] Lieutenant General Mohan Pande, then a Major General commanding 26 Infantry Division in the 16 Corps zone, recalls that his division was the pivot in the area through which NC would launch the offensive operation and confirms that it was the closest they came to the balloon going up during Op PARAKRAM.[8]

After the Kaluchak incident, the likelihood of a general conventional war between India and Pakistan receded with every passing day. Nevertheless, with elections to the J&K Assembly in the offing later in the year, India could ill afford a change in its forward posture, and NC continued in their efforts to dominate and punish the PA on the LoC.

During this period, the Leh-based 14 Corps quietly set about improving its defensive posture by securing and occupying ground of tactical importance on the LoC without adding to their already considerable logistical difficulties. In May 2002, 19 JAT secured and occupied Point 5070 (16,600 feet), a winter vacated PA post on the LoC with a commanding view of the Gultari Nala and the approaches to the LoC from the PA logistics hub at Gultari. In a letter to the CO, Nanavatty wrote, 'It has been an inspiring example of military mountaineering skills, grit, courage and determination. I am fascinated by your salutation, "*Balwan Pakarenge, Sahib* (We will get Balwan, sir)." It is most apt and very original. Now we must ensure "*Balwan Rakhenge* (We will keep Balwan)"; from what I see, I am sure you will.'[9]

9 DOGRA, another battalion in 14 Corps had plans to capture Pt 5353, an utterly dominating feature on the LoC that the PA had surreptiously occupied in Operation KOH-E-PAIMA in 1999. The objective had been on Nanavatty's radar for a while and 56 Mtn Bde had over a period systematically softened it up. Colonel (later Lt Gen.) Ranbir Singh, CO 9 DOGRA recalls, 'We had excellent support from 56 Mtn Bde and launched a withering fire assault for days on Point 5353 that involved BMPs (the Indian Army's Armoured Personal Carrier)105mm, 130mm and the 155mm Bofors guns. Air Defence guns too were dismantled and carried to Indian posts that flanked Pt

5353.' The sustained and accurate fire assault exerted much physical and psychological pressure on the enemy. It softened the enemy's defences and by late May 2002 we were fully prepared to attack and capture the objective. Disappointingly for the Dogras, they would have to stand down at the last moment for the fear of unintentionally triggering a wider confrontation in what was a 'hair trigger' environment.[10]

In July 2002, 15 Corps detected and reported an intrusion by the PA in the Machhil Sector of North Kashmir. The intruders were promptly evicted in a joint Army and Air Force operation involving Mirage-2000s. It was the first incident after the Kargil Conflict where offensive air power was used in a minor operation on the LoC without fuss or bother. It challenged the traditional thought process that desisted from using air power in operations other than war and would set a precedent for the subsequent employment of offensive air power against a JeM training camp at Balakot in February 2019.[11]

In the 16 Corps zone, where the 3 Corps offensive was planned, the emphasis was on punishing the PA without giving away their intentions. However, even as Op PARAKRAM wore on and despite peace overtures by Pakistan and the increasing involvement of the US in its attempts to diffuse the volatile situation, serious terrorist-related incidents continued. In September 2002, Pakistan-based terrorists, having infiltrated across the International Border (IB) with the assistance of the PA post at Sukmal, carried out a strike in the Hiranagar (Kathua) area, killing a total of 12 civilians. In response, 29 Infantry Division carried out a fire assault on the Sukmal locality the following night, inflicting several casualties and causing severe damage to the post.[12]

During the closing stages of Op PARAKRAM and after, the army chief would ask Nanavatty on two separate occasions whether he would reconsider a change in the NC punitive policy on the LoC. Convinced that the PA was hurting and was bound to seek a CF at some point in time in the future, he would recommend 'no change' on each occasion. Sure enough, on 23 November 2003, Musharraf not only asked for but declared a unilateral CF on the LoC, leaving India with no option but to accept the offer.[13] And, India would squander yet another opportunity to promulgate a punitive policy declaring that 'India reserves the right to take military action as deemed appropriate in response to any infringement of the LoC in a manner and at a time and place of it's choosing.'

Nanavatty is aware of the talk that spread after PARAKRAM suggesting that it was his reluctance to 'rush' into battle that stalled the operation. He dismisses it as an afterthought. However, he acknowledges the fact that his inputs may have been a factor in deciding whether to launch operations or not but is sure in his mind that the army chief would have overruled him if it was necessary, and that would have left him with only two options—comply or resign. And resignation at that juncture was simply not an option.[14] Lieutenant General Nagaraj concurs entirely with Nanavatty. Nanavatty remains firm in his assessment: 'this was our war of choice; we were to decide the "where, when and how". In NC, I asked for the minimum essential time for preparation for an offensive by an ad-hoc strike corps.'

He cautions that the designation and earmarking of formations for multiple tasks and switching them from one theatre to another, or 'dual tasking' as the Indian Army terms it should not, in any way, imply that such formations do not require time for preparation. It needs to be understood that while the formations may be the same, the units and individuals that constitute the formation are constantly changing. And, no commander worth his salt is prepared to 'open a drawer, pull out a plan made by someone else, dust it off, and issue orders for its execution even though it may have been war-gamed several times in the past'. Carl Von Clausewitz may have said, 'Every plan is a good one—until the first shot is fired,' but that is no reason to ignore adopting a sound approach to battle and proper preparation.

In the author's assessment, the Indian strategic establishment missed a trick or two by going ahead with a general mobilization of India's Armed Forces in Op PARAKRAM. Without properly thinking it through, this one step closed the door on exercising a limited but appropriate punitive option that would have ensured 'escalation dominance and control' subsequently. After the attack on the Parliament, NC could have integrated the IAF and exercised the Op KABADDI option, especially since the CAS had indicated that he was ready to hit targets in POK. This latter action could have been an appropriate response to the attack on Parliament or even the Kaluchak incident without necessarily crossing any of Pakistan's stated red lines, which could have triggered a general conventional war.

Under the circumstances, it could have proved to be India's best option of a limited and yet substantive reply. Instead, India's general mobilization resulted in the Pakistan Armed Forces doing the same. India eventually lost the first-mover advantage even as tensions built up, causing alarm bells to ring across the West. It was then only a matter of time before US pressure and the prospect of a vast financial burden would confront both countries and lead to a mutual de-escalation.[15] Nanavatty, pondering over what the author said two decades later, remarked, 'I had never thought about it then, but in hindsight, yes, that was a possibility. However, remember in the tense atmosphere prevailing, even a limited action could have precipitated an escalation.'[16]

Browsing through the manuscript of this book as one of its early reviewers, Lieutenant General Hooda, a former Northern Army Commander and then a Lieutenant Colonel actively involved in building logistics for Op PARAKRAM, endorsed Nanavatty's assessment that India was unprepared to wage a general war. In 2006, replying to a friend, Major General S. Jatar (Retd), Nanavatty assessed that Pakistan and the international community—the US in particular—did view India's mobilization and preparations for war during Op PARAKRAM seriously. Though India's military mobilization was not intended to be an act of coercive diplomacy, it may have turned out that way. Op PARAKRAM was a mobilization to wage a proactive war of choice. The conditions for success should have been deliberately created, plans for achieving surprise should have been made, and the timing should have been worked out carefully since India had the initiative.[17]

Based on his Op PARAKRAM experience, Nanavatty believes India is deceiving itself if it can prosecute a unilateral 'war of choice' in today's world without creating the right conditions. Even today, looking back, Nanavatty often wonders whether, at the very apex political level, a deliberate decision 'not to go to war unless forced to do so by the adversary' was the best-kept secret of Op PARAKRAM. If that be true, it was a masterstroke that helped save many lives and enormous financial costs for both sides.

On 22 August 2002, despite the ongoing Op PARAKRAM, the Election Commission of India issued the notification of elections to the J&K State Assembly. The elections were planned in four phases from 16 September to 8 October 2002. While this should have ended the eight-month-long perilous standoff between India and Pakistan, neither side was willing to trust the other, and the armies continued to stay locked in a grim embrace.

NC's immediate task was to create an environment that encouraged the electorate to vote without fear or favour. To enable such conditions, CT operations focused on inhabited areas—towns, villages and hamlets—with the aim of compelling terrorists to vacate such spaces and give confidence to the common people to join the electoral process. Speculative operations ceased, particularly those that the people found particularly irksome. Curfews, searches and checks were avoided, and the tried and tested tactic of swiftly occupying a temporary election support grid of operating bases purely for the duration of voting in any given area was carried out with good results.

The voter turnout was a satisfactory 43.7 per cent considering the situation. The J&K National Conference (NC) emerged as the single largest party, followed by the J&K Peoples Democratic Party (PDP) and the Indian National Congress (INC). The elections were conducted in the glare of the international community. They were free and fair according to international and national observers and the people of Kashmir. The US lauded the elections. According to several discerning political observers, the historic elections were a victory of the ballot over the bullet and a reversal of the 1987 Assembly elections.[18] After Nanavatty's brief, less-than-fruitful association with Dr Farooq Abdullah, he had looked forward to the possibility of working with his son, Omar Abdullah, the NC candidate for the post of the Chief Minister, for the few months that he had left. However, that was not to be.

Following the Assembly elections, the PDP and INC came together to form the government, and Mufti Mohammad Sayeed of the PDP assumed the appointment of CM for the first three years. Nanavatty sought a 'one-on-one' meeting with the Mufti. The latter appeared diffident and uncomfortable dealing with the military and had to be coaxed and persuaded to agree to the meeting. At the meeting, his daughter, Mehbooba Mufti, the architect of the PDP election campaign and the person to whom Mufti owed their success, was present. After his briefing, the only point the Mufti made was a request to ease restrictions during the month of Ramzan. That was quickly done, and Nanavatty wondered how much of what he had said had registered with the CM.

After his 'swearing in' as CM on 2 February 2003, Nanavatty insisted, and the Mufti agreed, to a formal briefing by HQ NC in the Secretariat in Jammu. Unfortunately, on the morning of the briefing, an article appeared in the press suggesting that the army wanted to take charge of the CT campaign in J&K. Halfway through the briefing by the MGGS, Major General (later Lieutenant General) K.K. Khanna, the Mufti interrupted the proceedings and in an angry outburst accused the army of undermining civilian control. Nanavatty recalls, 'I was forced to intervene, take him aside and tell him bluntly that he should allow us to finish our presentation without any disturbance or else we would call off the meeting. Later, I would write a letter to the CM and brought his conduct to the notice of the Governor.'[19]

After the above incident, Nanavatty had little to do with the CM, as the chief secretary, came to the rescue of civil-military relations in the state. In the few months that Bloeria and Nanavatty worked together, they got on very well. They organized a helpful Civil-Military Liaison Conference held after a lapse of several years in the state and created favourable conditions for operations in the notorious area of Hilkaka in the Poonch District.

After the eventful October 2001 Seminar in Jammu, Nanavatty first thought of writing a paper on a comprehensive strategy for resolving conflict in J&K and raised the subject with the COAS. On 29 November during the Army Commanders' Conference, Paddy gave him the thumbs up, saying, 'Go ahead. Be brief and ensure there are no accusations and no recrimination.'

Nanavatty set to his task with the assistance of Colonel (later Lieutenant General) Sanjeev Langer, then a staff officer in HQ CIF (D), and submitted the 'exploratory and recommendatory' paper suggesting a 'whole of government approach' for the resolution of conflict in J&K to Army HQ on 13 April 2002.[20]

Nanavatty's paper suggests that internal conflict in J&K is as much a result of the people's alienation, poor governance and lack of development and employment as it is a by-product of Pakistan's covert war and its support for terrorism. It highlights the need for a long-term, coherent, comprehensive, all-encompassing strategy that is enduring and flexible and delineates tasks between the centre and state. The strategy aimed to restore normalcy in the state, 'normalcy' being the point where 'democratic institutions, including those responsible for law and order, can function unimpeded'. The essentials of the strategy are direct and unambiguous and comprise nine conditions, reproduced verbatim below:[21]

- Persuade, dissuade, and, if necessary, deter Pakistan from pursuing its strategy of covert war and support for terrorism in J&K.
- Seek a peaceful resolution of the conflict within the framework of the Constitution of India.
- Fulfil the legitimate political and economic aspirations of the state.
- Ensure the sanctity of the Line of Control (LoC) by including the Actual Ground Position Line (AGPL) and the International Border (IB) in J&K.
- Suppress and neutralize all terrorist groups.
- Prevent the spread of conflict to the unaffected areas of the Ladakh region and Jammu division.
- Synergise the functioning of the governments at the centre and the state and the various instruments of government within the state.
- Improve administration and governance within the state.

- Mould public opinion in support of a peaceful resolution of conflict.

In his closing address at what would be General Padmanabhan's last Army Commanders' Conference in October 2002, the COAS acknowledged the NC effort, saying, 'In the past, we may have discussed several issues contained in the paper at different times, but never has our strategy to restore normalcy in J&K been put down as holistically and pointedly as has been done by the Northern Army Commander. I find the paper worth sharing with the government.'[22] And yet, there was no official response to the paper—not even an acknowledgement. Mystified by the lack of interest, he often wonders whether the tumultuous events of 2002 left people—politicians, civil servants and soldiers alike—so drained that they had no time for serious introspection and study. Fearing that it would be filed and lost forever, he decided to send it to individuals in the government who mattered, starting with L.K. Advani, the home minister and deputy Prime Minister. Not surprisingly, only two individuals, Jaswant Singh, the minister for External Affairs and N.N. Vohra, who, having retired as the Principal Secretary to the PM, was a Special Secretary appointed by the GOI as India's interlocutor for carrying out the J&K dialogue, responded. Jaswant Singh invited Nanavatty to a one-on-one discussion with him in his splendid office in North Block, and Vohra did likewise. Vohra, who later became the Governor of J&K, recollects having interacted with Nanavatty on issues related to 'Border Management' and found him to be a General with 'clarity and conviction who was not afraid of calling a spade a spade'.

Then, on 23 March 2003, the dastardly Nadimarg incident involving the gruesome killing of 24 Kashmiri Pandits brought the home minister, L.K. Advani to Srinagar and the GOC 15 Corps, Lieutenant General Vinayak Patankar, insisted on Nanavatty's presence during the visit. Nanavatty recalls being introduced 'enthusiastically' to Advani for the first time by someone in his entourage. It dawned on him that this could be his last chance to put NC views to the establishment, and who could be better than the home minister, the man responsible for internal security in India? He requested Advani to set aside an hour to visit HQ 15 Corps, where he would brief him. He aimed to inform Advani of the

NC paper and discuss some of the salient issues contained therein. The Home Secretary looked at his watch and said they would not have the time. Nanavatty, however, wasn't giving up easily and 'waylaid' Advani at the Raj Bhavan as Advani walked in with the Governor, Girish Saxena, ashen faced after visiting the families of those killed in the massacre.

Nanavatty recalls, 'It was a bit of a shock for him to witness the wailing and breast-beating women and the covered bodies laid out. I highlighted to him the need for decisive political intervention in J&K and the urgent need to institutionalize a formal and regular exchange of views between Army Headquarters and the MHA whenever and wherever the army was playing a lead role in internal security situations in the field.' Then Advani said, 'Please carefully examine the NC paper on the Strategy for the Resolution of Conflict in J&K.' He thanked Nanavatty and left without any response.

The fallout of the home minister's trip was a visit by a Special Group, comprising essentially civil servants of the MHA and senior police officers, to HQ NC just days before he retired. Addressing the group after a formal presentation of the NC paper by the MGGS, Nanavatty forcibly presented his case, saying, 'Pakistan is waging a relentless covert (not proxy) war using a mix of Islamic Jihadi fighters and subverted indigenous youth: employing tactics of terror, supported, albeit increasingly grudgingly and wearily, by a severely alienated population. It is a complex situation that demands an all-encompassing strategy. Unfortunately, and disappointingly, the questions being asked, and our limited interaction, suggest an overriding and continuing preoccupation with just security-related strategy and the micro-management of issues. In the last three years, we have systematically neutralized twice the number of terrorists assessed to be operating within Indian territory at any one time. We are being naïve if we believe that the solution lies in the mere neutralization of terrorists. Conflict resolution demands simultaneous and vigorous implementation of political, social, economic, administrative, psychological and security strategies.'

Nanavatty urged the Special Group to 'reflect' on the NC paper and ended on an ominous note, saying, 'Even though the Army is not best equipped to dilate on matters political, diplomatic, social and economic, we are compelled to do so with the hope of stimulating an informed debate. The paper would have served its purpose if a strategy blueprint had emerged from this debate. Any failure to address the issue holistically will condemn the security forces to manage the conflict indefinitely and at great cost.'[23]

More recently, commenting on the government's politically decisive steps in trying to break the cycle of chaos in Kashmir by splitting the state into two—the state of J&K and the Union Territory of Ladakh and abrogating Articles 370 and 35A of the Constitution that accorded special status to J&K, Nanavatty said, 'It is a bold step, which was long overdue and needs all the support. It could suck the oxygen out of Pakistan's covert war strategy if followed through in letter and spirit with electoral legitimacy, good governance and sustained vigilance at the heart of the system.'[24]

All was not over yet. Nanavatty's parting shot in NC was going to be an operation to 'clear, secure and hold' the area of Hilkaka North of Surankote. A large densely forested bowl on the southern and southeastern slopes of the Pir Panjal Range bounded in the west by the Ranjati Ridgeline, and in the south by the Suran River, the terrain was rugged with innumerable ridges, spurs and nalas. In the summers, it supported a migratory population of Bakarwals and Gujjars from the surrounding villages and beyond who would graze their livestock in the region. It was pockmarked with temporary shelters—dhoks and bahiks. The area was completely void of locals in the winter. Lying a couple of days march east of the LoC at the crossroads leading to Pulwama–Anantnag in the Kashmir Valley to the north and Doda–Kishtwar south of the range, it had become a haven for terrorist groups infiltrating and exfiltrating in and out of J&K. The graziers would provide them sustenance, information and early warning of troop movements and act as their guides and in return be paid handsomely for their services.

Surankote had been on Nanavatty's list of operational tasks since late 2001, but KABADDI, SANGRAM, and PARAKRAM prevented him from launching a major operation in the area. On the termination of Op PARAKRAM in October 2002, Nanavatty decided that an operation to secure Hilkaka was essential and could only be carried out after the winter of 2002–03. The one term of reference was that the seasonal migration of the civilian population with their livestock into the area would have to be disallowed that summer. The CM thought the proposal preposterous, but it was quietly put to him that there would be no operation unless this was agreed to. He was advised that the civil government would have to make suitable alternate arrangements to compensate the population and arrange the fodder supply if he wanted the Hilkaka problem resolved.[25]

HQ NC assigned the task to 'clear, secure and hold' the Hilkaka Area to 16 Corps, who in turn assigned it to CIF (Romeo) under the command of Major General (later Lieutenant General) H.S. Lidder. 'Hardy' Lidder had distinguished himself as the CO 9 PARA (Cdo) in Op PAWAN in Sri Lanka and knew about the terrain and terrorist activity in the Rajouri-Mendhar-Poonch Sector. At a preliminary briefing cum discussion of the operation, it became plain to Nanavatty that the task was beyond the capabilities of RR units in general and the RR Sector in particular because of their existing operational commitments and the nature of the task itself. Therefore, Nanavatty directed that a reserve brigade of 16 Corps, less a battalion, be allotted to CIF (R) to 'clear and secure' the area; an RR battalion ex CIF (D) on road opening duties was 'milked' and allotted to occupy a CT grid of company operating bases and hold the area permanently. A 9 PARA (Cdo) team was assigned special tasks since they knew the area well. At the behest of the GOC CIF (R), the operation was code-named Op SARP VINASH, and D Day was set for 1 May 2003.

GOC CIF (R) set to his task methodically, constructing helipads with IAF support and operational tracks to supply points, ensuring the work-up training of the infantry formation allotted and intelligence collection by the team of 9 PARA (Cdo). The plan was simple. Infantry columns using PARA (Cdo) guides would infiltrate their assigned areas under cover of darkness from three different directions, secure and occupy bases, and then commence search and destroy operations within their assigned areas of responsibility. Lidder also liaised with HQ 15 Corps to ensure the simultaneous establishment of stops and ambushes to cater for terrorists attempting to escape across the Pir Panjal into the Kashmir Valley region.[26]

Lidder recalls that the operation was advanced by a week and completed by 1 May 2003. A total of 66 terrorists were killed in the Hilkaka area, and a further 19 were killed in ambushes laid by units of 15 Corps on the Pir Panjal Range. Though the number of kills claimed by the IA was questioned and contested by a section of the media, Nanavatty clarified that the object of Op SARP VINASH was to 'clear, secure and hold' the area of Hilkaka and, in so doing, deny it to the terrorists. That had been achieved; the 'terrorist sanctuary' had been 'cleaned up' and had not posed a problem since, and terrorist casualties were of secondary importance.[27]

Replying to a question in Parliament, George Fernandes, the Raksha Mantri, set the record straight by saying, 'In Operation SARP VINASH, troops were moved by NC in the last week of March 2003, and the operation in Hilkaka was launched on 21 April 2003. The operation resulted in the elimination of sixty-five terrorists and the arrest of three, the busting of 119 hideouts and the recovery of 79 major weapons and large quantities of warlike stores. During the operations, five army personnel were killed, and five were wounded. Details about the killing of all the terrorists by the Army were reported to the nearest police stations.'[28]

In response to a question by the author about the operations of Special Forces in J&K to Nanavatty, he said that he had two PARA (Cdo) units in NC. Apart from 9 PARA (Cdo) on the order of battle of the command, 2 PARA was under conversion to the commando role and, at the request of the CO, was doing some additional conversion training 'on the job' in the 15 Corps zone.

In Colonel K.A. Mohan, 9 PARA had an outstanding CO who had earned his spurs under Hardev Lidder in Op PAWAN in Sri Lanka. Since the unit was virtually permanently in operations in NC, they would deploy only one of its three teams in operations at any one time to allow for rest, relief, refit and training in rotation and, for the better part of Nanavatty's tenure that team would be based in Surankote and carry out operations in the 16 Corps Zone. Mohan recollects that since late 2001, his unit has carried out several audacious strikes on terrorist leaders in the Surankote and Hilkaka regions and shaped the battle space for further exploitation.[29]

All the operational tasks assigned by NC to 9 PARA (Cdo) were done in consultation with the CO and executed according to the directions of the Army Commander. According to Mohan, 'It was the most exhilarating and rewarding operational tenure in my career, serving under an Army Commander who understood SF operations.'

Like many other Special Forces officers, Mohan would leave the army to take up challenging assignments in the corporate sector and hostile environments abroad that presented the same challenges they faced while in active operations. Pushing files in staff assignments peacefully was not his cup of tea![30]

General N.C. Vij took over from General Padmanabhan as army chief in March 2003 and immediately mooted the idea of a counter-infiltration fence all along the LoC to stem the continued infiltration into J&K. Among those who resisted the idea were Nanavatty, his Northern Army Commander and many from Vij's staff in Army HQ, who felt that commanders on the ground would lose their tactical autonomy and flexibility once the fence came up. Nanavatty wrote, 'With deterrence, not destruction being its effect, the fence deadens the offensive spirit of the fightingman.'[31] However, Vij managed to convince them all to go along. Though much effort and cost go into maintaining and repairing the fence, the linear obstacle has contributed significantly to stemming the infiltration to manageable levels over the last two decades.

Speaking to the author on his relationship with Nanavatty, General Vij said, 'Rostum and I got along fine as we both were leaders who spoke less and listened more. He was as forthright in expressing his professional disagreement over critical issues as in accepting where he was wrong. In the case of the fence, he was gracious enough to tell me over a cup of tea in Pune after he had retired that he was wrong in being sceptical about the operational viability and usefulness of the fence and wrote in his book that "He (Vij) single-mindedly pushed for its creation. He brooked no opposition including from the author and as things turned out he was proven right."'[32]

On operational issues, the two agreed on the need to respond to provocation across the LoC with punitive action, including employing Special Forces to hit high-value targets. General Vij said, 'Northern Command under Nanavatty was more than happy to go along with the freedom to open up with the artillery to protect the fence-laying parties whenever their work was interfered with from across the LoC by the PA.'

When asked why the national security establishment did not leverage Nanavatty's experience post-retirement, Vij reckoned that it may have been because of his inability to adapt and mellow down his straight-talking and direct approach to cater to the requirements of politicians and policymakers. Ending the conversation, General Vij said, 'Straightforward, disciplined, strict in his assessment and meticulous in his approach to soldiering, Rostum and I remain good friends.'[33]

Tara Mount, the Northern Army Commander's residence in Udhampur, was a haven of beauty and serenity. It teemed with wildlife that was deliberately left undisturbed by its inhabitants. The estate was opened every spring for public viewing while the Nanavattys were away from home. Looking back at the three challenging years in Northern Command, Suniti realized that although she and Rostum lived under the same roof, they were moving on parallel tracks.

Most importantly, Suniti continued with the practice of communicating with the Next of Kin (NOK) of combatants who were Killed in Action (KIA) or seriously injured, informing them of their entitlements and encouraging them to communicate with her in case of need. Rostum instructed the NC exchange to put calls from NOK through to her without delay. The rest of her time was spent visiting the hospitals to meet with the injured soldiers, visiting the family lines to meet the families and visiting the schools run by the army. She brought back firsthand information to Rostum. Her visits to the nursery schools were of concern. Not governed by the 'Red Book' issued by the Army Welfare Education Society (AWES) for running Army Schools, the units given the responsibility ran them as best they could.

When Suniti raised this with Mrs Roopa Padmanabhan, the army chief's wife, she was, in return, tasked with formulating the guidelines for running nursery schools in the Indian Army. In the ensuing year, Suniti and her small team of army wives sent a detailed questionnaire to over 100 army-run nursery and primary schools for their feedback. This was followed by a year-long pilot project in the Udhampur Nursery School, running it with the new curriculum of no homework, no tests and no marks. However, plenty of activities within the school and visits to venues as varied as the Military Farm, the Dental Centre, the water purification plant, the airfield and the helipad, among other places sparked the interest of the toddlers. The following year, the Class 1 teachers at the station Army Primary School declared the project a success, as the intake of children from the Nursery School were eager learners. Suniti followed this with a formal presentation to Mrs Padmanabhan in Delhi. The AWES approved the proposal and issued guidelines to all the Commands. That was the vital first step in reforming pre-school education in the Indian Army. Since then, Nursery School education has come a long way.

Lieutenant General Nanavatty retired from service on 31 May 2003. Recognized over the years by the Government of India for his distinguished service both in wartime and peace, he was awarded the Uttam Yudh Seva Medal (UYSM) for his command of the Siachen Brigade; the Ati Vishisht Seva Medal (AVSM) for his tenure at the helm of 19 Inf Div in Baramulla, and the Param Vishisht Seva Medal (PVSM) for leading 3 Corps in turbulent and complex times. On 2 June 2003, before boarding his flight from Delhi to Pune, he would perform his last 'semi-official' assignment. On a special request from Lieutenant General S.K. Sinha, who was transiting from Guwahati in Assam through Delhi to Srinagar, J&K to assume his gubernatorial appointment, they would have a breakfast meeting during which Nanavatty would brief him about the situation in J&K.

Writing to thank the Nanavattys for their hospitality during a visit to Pune in early 2004, Sinha wrote succinctly: 'It is a pity that we did not get an opportunity to work together in Jammu and Kashmir. You left too early, and I arrived too late. We are trying to do our best here and very much appreciate all that you did as GOC-in-C Northern Command at a difficult stage of militancy. I earnestly hope your talent and experience are duly used in the future.'[34] Several well wishers and friends assumed it would be soon that his experience in the North-east and J&K would land him a government-sponsored assignment. Given the internal security dynamics in the country, others reckoned that his expertise would be invaluable in organizations such as the National Security Advisory Board (NSAB).

It is clear from some of the letters that Nanavatty wrote to several senior leaders of the IA and from within the strategic establishment, such as the National Security Advisor, that he was brimming with ideas on Siachen, J&K and internal security that he wanted to share with them. One letter that he wrote to Brajesh Mishra, the National Security Advisor, on 23 October 2003, a month before Pakistan formally offered a Ceasefire to India, is so detailed, logical and proactive that any reader would come away with the impression that 'this guy knows exactly how India should respond to and prepare to exploit this window of opportunity'.[35] Offering a background on what may prompt Pakistan to make this offer, Nanavatty writes, 'In the recent past—in the space of less than two months—the President of Pakistan has, on two separate occasions, appealed for a ceasefire on the LoC. In all honesty, this is a development the Army had foreseen. It would be safe to conclude that it is a result of the punishment the enemy has received because of the effectiveness of our punitive operations.' Advising caution, Nanavatty laid a roadmap that included three tracks, all of which needed to roll concurrently.

The first track called for wide-ranging talks with Pakistan to convey India's commitment to peace and thus occupy the moral high ground. The second track was to promulgate a Declaratory Punitive Policy (DPP) that put the Pakistan Army and the Jihadis on notice that any violation of the CF and continuing prosecution of the covert war in J&K would invite swift retribution. The third track was especially instructive: it laid out a possible escalation control model that would need close monitoring since a DPP was no solution to the problem. 'It would be naïve to imagine that Pakistan will remain a mute spectator to the launch of punitive operations by India,' he said; however, 'to assume also that Pakistan would immediately raise the conflict threshold to that of a conventional general war or worse would be equally incorrect.' Ending his letter on a balanced note, he wrote, 'In the present scenario, given the near parity of forces on the LoC in J&K, Pakistan can match us strike for limited strike; however, it does not have the strength and depth to persevere. We should embark on a DPP only if prepared to step up the escalatory ladder and stay the course. We have the strength, will and determination to prevail.' Predictably, Nanavatty never received a response to his letter!

Though Nanavatty made several lucid presentations at war colleges and think tanks and had a reputation for calling out things as they were on the ground, the national security establishment did not leverage his experience. As the years went by, Suniti and the boys tried their best to motivate Nanavatty to pen down his ideas and experiences in the Indian Army and write a book. Rushad would argue, 'If not a book, at least collect your thoughts and put them together for your grandchildren.'

In September 2007, his friend, coursemate at IMA and former army officer, Professor Gautam Sen, the erstwhile Head of the Department of Defence and Strategic Studies, University of Pune and Major General (later Lieutenant General and VCOAS) S.K. Singh, the MGGS in HQ Southern Command and Colonel 8th Gorkha Rifles convinced him to accept a two-year fellowship as the Chair Professor of the Chhatrapati Shivaji Chair for Excellence—an Army Endowment Chair—at the Pune University. His work during the two years resulted in a fine book, *Internal Armed Conflict in India: Forging a Joint Civil-Military Approach*, published in 2013 by the Pentagon Press, New Delhi.

One perceptive reader says: 'With the benefit of his professional experience, General Nanavatty gives a lucid account of the history, current resources and recommendations for countering the widening problem of internal armed conflict in India. A must-read for anyone wishing to appreciate the complexity of the problem both politically and militarily.'

Another reader says, 'The author has brought his unmatched experience of counterinsurgency warfare in South Asia in writing this book. It needs to be read by all students of COIN warfare not only in the subcontinent but by all countries battling insurgency.'[36]

Gautam Sen reviewed the book in *CLAWS Journal* and wrote: 'Rostum Nanavatty has been a reluctant scholar and a committed soldier's general with his feet on the ground. Iconized by his juniors and respected by his peers, seniors and even by some of the political elites for his actions and views, this book is an undiluted output of the experience and judgment of a soldier that has unwittingly transgressed into the realm of policy relevance.

'Nanavatty's work is based on conceptual analysis supported by observed facts and studied approach rather than taking recourse to strong opinion.'[37] Though the book is recommended for reading on several lists in the Indian Army, it does not get the recognition it deserves, much like its author.

Both Rushad and Veer recollect that post-retirement was the first time they had seen their father frustrated with the sudden vacuum in his life. 'Given the complete focus he had on his work in the army—something that lasted till his very last hour in uniform and perhaps even beyond—he was unprepared for life out of uniform,' is how Veer Nanavatty remembers his father during his first year after retirement. 'All of us could sense his despondency and frustration at not being able to continue contributing to national security,' said Veer.[38] Different from several of his contemporaries, Nanavatty had neither networked nor planned for a life out of uniform except buying a flat in Pune, where he moved in immediately after retiring.

Veer recalls, 'A few months into retirement, Dad got a call from a senior politician in Nagaland saying that he was in the running to come to the North-east as a governor and all he had to do was to go to Delhi and call on the powers-that-be.' Nanavatty recalls a conversation with Imkong L. Imochen, the powerful home minister of Nagaland and a close confidante of the Chief Minister, S.C. Jamir, with whom he was well acquainted. 'He told me he knew Mrs Sonia Gandhi well and would speak to her on my behalf.' In a lighter vein, Imkong suggested that he expected Nanavatty 'to do as he was told', to which Nanavatty said, 'You know me well; I will do what I think is good for the people of Nagaland and the Indian State.' His perspective on such issues was clear: 'If I was wanted, I would have been sounded out.'

When asked whether his father was out of sync with realities on the ground when it came to engaging with the political establishment, Veer reckons that he would have it no other way. 'Ultimately, what may be seen by others as an unbending—perhaps even inflexible—streak in Dad's personality is nothing less than a reflection of his self-knowledge. He is a man who knows himself, knows what he is capable of, has the conviction of his principles, and is therefore able to stand firm in the face of almost anything—good or bad.' 'Not once did I regret not getting an after-retirement advisory assignment, though Suniti would often suggest that I ought to try,' said Nanavatty.[39]

Suniti and Rostum travelled to Africa to visit Rushad, first in Malawi and Tanzania, where he was doing fieldwork with Population Services International (PSI) in the prevention of AIDS and malaria and reduction in mother and child mortality. Meanwhile, having joined the US Foreign Service, Kate managed her first posting in neighbouring Tanzania. And so, it came about that Rushad and Kate were married at Ras Kutani, a beautiful resort outside Dar es Salaam. On a wooden deck jutting over the Indian Ocean, sixty family and friends flew in to witness the ceremony. Both of Rushad's grandmothers were also present in deference to his ardent wish. Continuing with the US Diplomatic Service, Kate has taught at Georgetown University and is currently the Consul General in Amsterdam. Rushad and Kate have two sons, Kiyan and Cyrus, whom Suniti and Rostum adore.

Upon completing his five-year architecture course, Veer took a break and worked for six months in filmmaking in Mumbai, designing the sets for the Aamir Khan starrer, *Taare Zameen Par*. He got back to architecture and took up a short architectural assignment in Dar es Salam, which gave him the opportunity to be with Rushad and Kate and design their wedding. After working in Delhi for three years, lodging with—and giving much joy to—his grandmother, he successfully applied to Yale for his post-graduation; Veer is now an established architect in New York City, where he is a Senior Associate at Leroy Street Studio. He is a carefree bachelor.

Unsettled with apartment living in Pune and yearning for a more laidback lifestyle, the Nanavattys moved to Dehradun in 2012. The move was cathartic for Rostum and Suniti as they plunged into building their dream house with the same passion and attention to detail that Rostum accorded to soldiering in the preceding decades. Despite working full-time in New York, Veer chipped in by painstakingly designing their home.

They named the house 'Saltoro' after the Saltoro Range on which Rostum spent some of the most exhilarating times of his long and illustrious soldiering career.

Dehradun also gave the Nanavattys a new meaning to their lives as they immersed themselves in Raphael. Having volunteered to work with Raphael while staying alone when Rostum was commanding 19 Inf Div, Suniti encouraged Rostum to shift his focus from national security and soldiering to meaningful social work. Several commanders who served alongside Rostum have joined him in this venture, where they work in an honorary capacity. Suniti is now content to be known as a proud mother and grandmother, plus a fiercely staunch 'fauji patni' (military wife).

13

SOLDIERING, LEADERSHIP AND STRATEGY

'A strong mind that can maintain its serenity under the most powerful excitement … strength of character, clear and deep … energy, firmness, staunchness … Above all, a fine and penetrating mind is called for here to search out the truth by the tact of its judgement.'[1]

—CLAUSEWITZ ON THE QUALITIES WHICH HE SOUGHT IN A LEADER TO MEET THE UNCERTAINTIES OF WAR

'What does soldiering mean to you?' asked the author.

'That is a profound question, and you will have to give me some time to think,' said Nanavatty. Weeks later, this is what came in by email:

- I loved 'soldiering'—the method, regimentation, discipline, camaraderie, challenges and sheer 'physicality' of a soldier's life, much of it in the outdoors.
- I had no distant ambitions. All I wanted to be was a good soldier—to do every job that came my way to the best of my ability.

- I was more concerned with what my 'command' thought of me than my superiors. I looked 'down', not 'up' for satisfaction.
- Loyalty to my superiors meant doing my duty to the best of my ability and being honest with them by saying and doing what I thought was right.
- Professionalism means applying one's knowledge and skills according to the situation to accomplish the mission.
- I believed in seeing things for myself—'one look is worth a hundred reports' and 'time spent on reconnaissance is seldom wasted'; in deliberating; in giving clear directions and orders; in delegating authority and responsibility, and standing back, only interfering if the situation is critical or life-threatening. Lessons learned would come later.
- At senior levels I found 'suggestion' the best way to bring subordinates around and accept ownership.[2]

Lieutenant General Nanavatty's papers comprise several reflections and musings on leadership across his command assignments. Included is a carefully bound compilation of speeches on leadership, morale and courage by Field Marshal William Joseph 'Bill' Slim, the iconic British commander of the Fourteenth Army, instrumental in defeating the Japanese during the Burma Campaign in the Second World War. Slim's speeches, delivered in the 1950s to varied audiences when he was the Governor General of Australia, greatly impacted the young Nanavatty.[3] Highlighted in his 'blue diary' is a jewel from Slim's leadership tenets, which the latter shared with cadets at the US Military Academy at West Point. It reads, '*Leadership is that mixture of example, persuasion, and compulsion that makes men do what you want them to do*'—the very essence of the way in which Nanavatty would seek to practice leadership throughout his career.

'What if all these thoughts were to form the framework of a thematic final chapter to the book, Sir: would it not appeal to a wide cross-section of leaders in the military and other walks of life?' asked the author. Nanavatty's reply was typical: 'After all these years, it is easy for me to pontificate and preach, but given the generational shift, my views may no longer be relevant and will likely add little value to your work.' Rushad, Veer and Kate felt otherwise and thought it would be a priceless chapter with which to end the book.

When I came across three sheets written in hand in 1970 tucked away inside the flap of his blue diary with the title 'Young Officer (YO) Briefing', it was a no-brainer. If these were the thoughts of a young infantry Captain on his approach to the profession of arms, there surely would be more as he moved up the ladder.[4] His discussions with Gorkha officers (officers commissioned into the Gorkha Rifles Battalions of the Indian Army) on the Infantry Young Officers' (YO) Course at the Infantry School, Mhow, where Nanavatty was an instructor, reflect the universal and enduring tenets of soldiering and leadership. Simple, straightforward, 'doable' and based on his own experience, the briefings comprised five segments—'Own Attitude, Know Your Men, Characteristics of Gorkhas, Man Management and Day to Day Working'—that constituted the bedrock of his early career as a soldier.

Nanavatty believed that officers and men, being volunteers and professional soldiers, the army needed to invest deeply in their mentoring to inculcate in them the correct values; and training to achieve high professional standards. Nanavatty invariably began his discussions with the YOs with a session on 'personality traits' and 'attitudes' that would stand them in good stead. He would stress the importance of pride in the uniform—being well turned out and carrying oneself well always, being physically fit and mentally robust, and being self-disciplined. He expected young officers to be enthusiastic, show initiative and be calm and controlled in challenging situations. He would caution his wards—'the greatest crime is inaction—nothing is ever not your business. Also, remember, not every mistake demands punishment. Most often, mere correction is enough; you have no extra privileges for the extra duties, responsibilities and risks you take; subservience breeds an inferiority complex, adversely impacting your methods and mannerisms.' Severely critical of group think, he said, 'You don't have to be a part of the herd; do not indulge in self-deprecating talk and the airing of personal grievances that undermine the unit—loyalty means never letting the side down and speak up when you must: not saying yes, Sir—three bags full, Sir.'

'Leading officers and men into battle is the *raison d'être* of the Infantry Officer, and the first step for a YO is getting to know the men they will lead,' he wrote. Drawing heavily from time-tested sociological and behavioural studies but keeping it simple, Nanavatty exhorts his wards to lead by example, to 'muck in' and develop a feeling of oneness and belonging with their men. 'Get to know them as a group and understand the forces that motivate them; this outweighs the knowledge gained through textbooks.'

'Continuous, clear, straightforward communication with the troops is essential to keep them informed and ensure good situational awareness. Junior leaders who keep their men informed are professional leaders,' he would say. Taking things for granted, he told the YOs, was a sure recipe for suboptimal performance, and the only way to avoid this was by inculcating the spirit of enquiry and finding out, even if it meant asking for the help of their subordinates. Finally, he stressed the importance of tried and tested concepts such as playing troop games and engaging in informal conversations with the troops, which offered disproportionately positive outcomes during training and combat.

'We are what we repeatedly do. Excellence, then, is not an act, but a habit,' Nanavatty would say, invoking Aristotle, the Greek philosopher. He would also urge young officers to follow the creed of the Spartan warrior that epitomized the core values of discipline and courage to 'sweat more in peace, bleed less in battle'. He urged YOs to 'Live simply, be truthful and be self-disciplined. Set a good example in your personal and professional conduct at all times.' Together, these core values represented the framework around which Nanavatty developed his leadership skills and passed them on.[5]

Recognizing through his career that young officers were the lifeline of the Indian Army, Nanavatty put them at ease during his visits to forward posts. Probal Dasgupta, now an accomplished corporate leader, military historian and author of *Watershed 1967: India's Forgotten War over China*[6] was a Second Lieutenant in the Fifth Battalion 11th Gorkha Rifles (5/11 GR) when Nanavatty commanded 19 Infantry Division in Baramulla in 1994. Visiting the unit in 12 Infantry Brigade in Uri, Nanavatty stayed the night at the forwardmost post of 5/11 GR called King Post, a thirty-minute climb from the battalion HQ. After listening to a short briefing by Dasgupta on the terrain and tactical situation existing, Nanavatty switched to an informal chat and meal with the men. Afterwards, he moved to Dasgupta's bunker, where he set down his small rucksack, put the rookie at ease and engaged him in conversation about Mumbai, where Dasgupta's home was. 'He was unlike any general I had met thus far in my short career, and I wish you luck in your project,' said Dasgupta at the end of his conversation with the author.[7]

About the Gorkha soldier, this is what Nanavatty says to young officers commissioned into the Gorkha Rifles even today: 'The Gorkha is cheerful, tough and disciplined by nature. He has a keen sense of duty and likes doing the right thing, the right way. He learns quickly and takes pride in being good at his trade. Soldiering comes easily to him. There is not the slightest trace of subservience, servility or flattery in his manner, which, together with his childlike sense of humour, make the Gorkha a delightful companion, especially in the field. For most Nepal Domiciled Gorkhas, the Indian Army is the first career option. Your soldier will watch you and bide his time before accepting you as his leader. Please get to know him, learn his language, participate in his activities, share in his privations and be your true self.'

Going deeper, Nanavatty says, 'Look after him but do not spoil him; be strict but fair; train hard—concentrate on the how to fight skills—marksmanship, field craft, battle craft, fighting techniques and small unit tactics. Treat the soldier with respect; do not be sarcastic; do not nag; do not to use foul language; and do not resort to physical abuse. Punish him if you must, but do not strip him of his dignity.'

Finally, he says, 'You will be privileged to serve alongside the Gorkha soldier. You will learn as much from him as he from you and you will be a better person for the association. He may or may not be the best soldier in the world, but if you can show him the way, he will be what you want him to be.'[8]

Nanavatty is modest when he reflects on his briefings to the YOs at the Infantry School: 'Much of what I have said and what you have quoted in these paras are what one might call eternal truths written and talked about endlessly. I have not said anything original. The challenge before us is their conscious application in real life.'

On a sunny November afternoon in 2022, I chatted with a group of veterans comprising 10 Junior Commissioned Officers from 2/8 GR who served alongside Nanavatty at various stages.[9] Getting a 360-degree view of Nanavatty, the soldier, was essential to arrive at a holistic appraisal of the man.

From the group of Subedar Majors and Honorary Captains, all except one were in awe of Nanavatty for his soldiering skills, physical toughness, leadership qualities and concern and empathy for the troops he commanded. The exception was Subedar Major (Honorary Captain) Barta Bahadur Gurung, who joined 2/8 GR four years before Nanavatty in 1958 and soldiered alongside him till halfway through Nanavatty's command of the battalion in 1979 before transferring to a new raising in the regiment, 7/8 GR. The views and recollections of Barta Bahadur Sahib, who boxed for the battalion, fought at Walong and then survived the retreat from Mechuka in 1962, were more of comradeship and respect. He said, 'Nanavatty Sahib is a tough soldier who leads his troops by example. Being a good soldier meant everything to him; for me, he remains a soldier in every way, even today. He spoke our language, upheld our unit's *tarteeb aur dastoor* (customs and traditions), and refined the interior economy (an all-encompassing term in the army to include training and administration). He involved all ranks in framing policies and procedures that concerned the troops directly. He visited our veterans in Nepal, making his last visit there when he was the CO.'

Others in the group recalled Nanavatty as a relentless taskmaster during training. Packing his own rucksack and carrying his 7.62 mm SL Rifle, he loved being with the men outdoors. Loosening up a bit, one of the younger veterans recalled that Nanavatty had a vast collection of one-liners in Gorkhali, which he used liberally and with a poker face—'*dhukoor* (dumb dove)', '*more ko siyal* (miserable Jackal)', '*Kina kukhura jasto basechha* (why are you sitting there like a chicken)?' if he found someone slouching. He also banned using the word '*Kunnii* (Don't know)' in the battalion. The youngest of the lot, who served with Nanavatty when he was the Northern Army Commander, recollects that he had an intense dislike for '*geru chuna* (meaningless spit and polish)' and how units would scramble to remove vestiges of the stuff before a visit. Unlike some officers the author spoke with, none of the JCOs was intimidated by Nanavatty or his expectations of them because they knew that '*Hamari jaan, unki jaan thi* (Our life was his life)'. 'For us, that was everything, and we would have gone wherever he took us,' said another.

Unconsciously invoking the Bhagavad Gita, India's ancient philosophical text, Nanavatty's leadership style involved careful deliberation over the task, the issue of clear orders and instructions, the delegation of responsibility and leading by example. As one colleague put it, '*Sunnta hain sabki; karta hain apni* (He listens to everyone but does his own thing).' Loyalty to his subordinates was paramount, and 'cancellations and postponements' were an anathema. On the core issue of taking responsibility for one's actions, he urged officers to emulate what is good, guard against going solely by precedence, not be afraid of making mistakes and be prepared to accept the consequences of their actions. Acknowledging that orders that are sometimes hastily passed need to be properly thought through, he urged young officers not to merely pass them down the chain of command, saying, '*CO Sahib ko hukam chha* (CO's orders). Orders to one's subordinates must always go down as your orders.' Clear and decisive communications, he told them, were essential for precise mission execution.

Deeply impressed with the performance of Warrant Officers and Non-Commissioned Officers in the US and British Army, one of Nanavatty's Key Result Areas (KRAs) when in command was to raise the performance levels of JCOs and NCOs to much higher levels than the norm in the Indian Army. Recognizing that the Indian Army is predominantly officer-led and driven, he urged junior commanders to develop their JCOs and NCOs professionally, educate them and get them actively involved in all facets of the unit's operations, training and administration. 'Give them responsibilities; involve them in the decision-making process, guide them but do not interfere constantly; and lend them your support—that is a sure-shot recipe for raising their self-esteem,' wrote Nanavatty in his memos.[10]

Nanavatty's leadership style was flexible and practical because of his 'lived experience' of leading in turbulent times dominated by numerous national security crises that spanned the entire spectrum of conflict, barring a full-fledged conventional war. Acknowledging the diffused nature and unpredictability of subconventional operations, he considered brigade commanders and above merely enablers and facilitators. Nanavatty expected initiatives from his battalion and company commanders to deliver positive outcomes in counterinsurgency and counterterrorist operations. He went the extra mile to acknowledge and appreciate successful small-team operations.

After his experiences in Sri Lanka, Siachen and Baramulla, Nanavatty recognized the importance of the cognitive domain in improving combat leadership skills at the tactical and operational levels. Among the several traits that he considered essential for young leaders to cope with future battlefields, the following feature prominently in several presentations made by Nanavatty:

- Develop a frame of reference to understand the various Army Rules and Rules of Engagement (ROE) in a turbulent environment.
- Exercise initiative and foresight to stay ahead of nimble adversaries.
- Generate higher levels of unit cohesion with an emphasis on small team operations.
- To develop all the above, he urged senior leadership to create a climate of risk-taking, which is a significant enabler of junior leadership.
- Finally, he recognized the need for significantly higher levels of technical competence among junior leaders to understand and exploit the emerging 'tools of war' by embracing new learning paradigms.[11]

A hard-core 'foot slogger', Nanavatty was the archetype of the old-school, conservative but 'thinking' army officer who believed that victory is still 'measured by the foot'. Much of Nanavatty's appreciation of the other arms and services revolved around the proposition that they were essentially 'enablers'. His understanding of manoeuvre warfare was profound and significantly influenced by his course in the US, his tenure as the BM of an Armoured Brigade where the brilliant General Sundarji had a profound effect on his officers and command.

Appreciative of air power, particularly of the non-kinetic roles at high altitudes such as surveillance and reconnaissance, casualty evacuation, and air maintenance in hostile and adverse terrain and weather conditions, there is little to suggest in his writings that he deliberately studied and analysed the war-winning potential of offensive air power in conventional general war beyond that of Offensive Air Support (OAS) to ground forces. To be fair to Nanavatty, he looked at kinetic air power as an attractive coercive option to respond to sensational acts of terrorist violence through the conduct of punitive strikes using ground and air forces, provided there was a distinct technological edge over the adversary and the necessary politico-military will.[12]

Nanavatty was often concerned with the IAF's lack of focus on the use of air power in 'short of war situations'. In a discussion with the army chief, General Vij, on 5 March 2003 at HQ 16 Corps, Nanavatty argued that given the former's highly centralized control, planning and decision making, the Air Officer Commanding J&K (AOC J&K), a two-star IAF officer posted alongside HQ NC found it difficult to fuse or integrate Offensive Air Support either with the Punitive Operations or Limited Offensive Operations. He recalls, 'Air Vice Marshal Limaye was the AOC J&K at Udhampur during my tenure. He was keen, interested and involved in all our operational briefings and discussions. However, unlike other Army Command HQs, we did not have an integral AF staff element. Limaye had little control over AF resources and had to look over his shoulder to WAC for everything.' Nanavatty, quickly added, 'However, I built up a good rapport with Air Marshals "Jimmy" Bhatia and Adi Ghandhi, the AOC-in-Cs of Western Air Command and understood their limitations of balancing resource allocation for independent and joint operations.'

Lieutenant General Arjun Ray, the former corps commander of 14 Corps in Leh when Nanavatty was the Army Commander, is also one of his vocal critics. Ray told the author, 'I have known General Nanavatty since we were majors. We also served together when he was the Army Commander. He is known more for his human qualities than military prowess (*sic*). He is a gentleman, value-driven, and abides by the credo of the Indian Military Academy—country first, soldiers second, me last. In today's times, this means a lot. However, innovation, strategy, big-picture thinking, mental mobility, and foresight are not his strengths. Consequently, he is better suited for tactical battles and positional warfare.'[13] While there is little to disagree with the initial portion of Ray's assessment, it would be interesting for the reader to benchmark the second part of Ray's assessment against Nanavatty's demonstrated performance as an operational and strategic leader and the views of a division commander who served in Northern Command around the same time as Ray.

Lieutenant General Mohan Pande first came across Nanavatty at the Defence Services Staff College, where he was undergoing the course while the latter was an instructor. He later served under him in Northern Command as a division commander. Pande later became the Director General of Military Operations after commanding a corps. An informal student of behavioural science, Pande's evaluation of Nanavatty as an operational commander and strategist is instructive. In an email to the author, he wrote, 'Evaluation of a military leader irrespective of the level of command is best done by evaluating and indexing the performance of his command. Organizational performance in the military is a product of the overall commander's vision, a clear understanding of policy, strategy, planning and vigorous execution by subordinate commanders.'[14]

Pande highlighted the complex landscape in Northern Command—the inhospitable climate and terrain and diverse threats varying from terrorism and insurgency to conventional general war. He argued that 'to ensure cohesion in the complex scenario, obtaining a clear understanding of the operational environment, striking a balance between centralization and delegation, and effective communications with one's subordinates is essential. You had to be physically fit and mentally agile to make the right decisions and be seen by your command to gain their trust and confidence. Nanavatty was all of this.'

When pushed to dwell more on Nanavatty's demonstrated performance, Pande wrote, 'The most striking was his clarity of vision and tasking based on the threat and the resources available. He struck a conscious balance between defence, offensive-defence and unbridled offensive action. Next was the cohesion he imbued through his being physically present amid his formations and units and his ability to communicate across all ranks. It boosted morale and confidence. A good listener with insightful environmental awareness, he encouraged participative operational discussions before embarking on a decision-making process, which was invariably decisive.'

Calm and collected during crises, Pande recollects how Nanavatty handled the immediate impact of the Kaluchak incident by empathizing with his officers and men but desisting from a knee-jerk retaliatory action. Instead, he moved several formations into their concentration areas, readied reserves, communicated a sense of urgency and readiness to New Delhi and waited for the necessary political directive to launch retaliatory attacks, which never came.[15] Pande argues that Nanavatty demonstrated excellent strategic acumen by shaping the operational environment in NC through continuous assessment of the adversary's intent, effective force deployment, resource integration and timely reserve employment.

Reflecting on some other aspects of Nanavatty's leadership, Pande explained that he 'may have been misunderstood at times and seen as an autocratic, hard-nosed leader with a strong sense of discipline, but he was also empathetic and endowed with a wicked sense of humour, which lightened the mood during stressful operational discussions. He was a role model for younger officers being physically fit, emotionally strong, and frugal in his personal needs.'[16]

Pande, who sometimes, during conversations with other division commanders in NC, discussed their Army Commander, said that there was consensus that Nanavatty stood out for 'clearly conveying his politico-strategic vision to his corps and division commanders and giving them the resources they needed and the freedom at the tactical level to dominate and deter the adversary'. Summarizing Nanavatty's leadership traits, Pande wrote, 'he was a "soldiers' general" and had broad shoulders. He understood the predicament of junior leaders in the prevailing "grey zone" environment. Several incidents occurred during his tenure wherein he demonstrated compassion and fairness with no compromise in military ethos.' Ending his analysis of Nanavatty with a flourish, Pande wrote, 'An effective military leader in the complex operational environment of those times had to be a risk taker. He could be "instinctive and bold" or deliberate and calculating in his approach. General Nanavatty perhaps qualifies as the latter.'[17]

Not given to intuitive decision-making, Nanavatty's desire to create an overwhelming asymmetry before launching an offensive during Op PARAKRAM may have frustrated some subordinate commanders, but it upheld a fundamental tenet of strategic leadership that the correct preparation for war and not diving impulsively into it may well lead to the avoidance of war. Closely involved in planning Limited Offensive and Punitive Operations in J&K (Op KABADDI) and Op PARAKRAM, Nanavatty comes across as a deliberate and process-driven commander with a directive style of command.[18]

General V.P. Malik, the army chief for much of Nanavatty's tenure as the GOC 3 Corps, recalls that while 'Nanavatty was honest and conscientious himself, he was rather harsh while assessing people who did not think like him or perform to the high standards that he expected of them. I did advise him to go easy, but he stuck to his point of view and suggested that Army HQ use its discretionary powers to modify the reports they felt did not do justice to an officer's performance.'[19] Some officers recall the 'Nanavatty Factor' that Army HQ applied to 'bump up' some stiff reports he rendered. Others remember an informal list in the Military Secretary's Branch in Army HQ that placed him high up in the order of 'tough' assessors.

Reluctant to explain himself except by saying that he never played the system to protect or promote officers who served with him, Nanavatty relented and offered an opinion only when the author suggested that it was important for military leaders to balance the ethical dimension of military leadership with organizational requirements. He said, 'I was never in the run for being "popular" and did not worry about what others thought of me: my concern was for the organization.' Nanavatty, throughout his later service career, would ponder over trying to nurture a meritocracy using an assessment system structured around objectivity.

The Military Secretary's Branch in the IA is mandated, among several other responsibilities, to manage HR issues related to the Annual Confidential Reports (ACR) of officers across all branches and ranks. A strand of that organization is embedded in Commands HQs, with the Army Commander having a Military Secretary (MS) and an Assistant Military Secretary (AMS) on his staff. Lieutenant Colonel (later Brigadier) Loave Verma, 5 PARA, was Nanavatty's AMS for his entire tenure and had a bird's eye view of Nanavatty's reporting style.

Verma recalls that the writing of appropriate and objective ACRs was a cause of concern to Nanavatty throughout his tenure. 'He could not get himself to be subjective. The general ensured he visited every officer to be reported upon at least twice and, when in doubt, a third time. He painstakingly made notes of his impressions, which he would invariably refer to before putting pen to paper. As his staff, we would usually bring to Nanavatty's notice that while he was "objectively" and "correctly" writing his assessments, the rest of the environment was showering "9s" (officers are graded on a scale of 1-9).' Nanavatty would patiently listen to the views from his staff on his reporting, but did what he felt was right. His approach was simple: 'A good performance merits an award; a good performance with potential merits an award and promotion.'[20]

Verma added, 'Almost a year into the job, the MA and I analysed the promotion boards of Brigadiers and Major Generals to the next rank from among those who had been reported upon by Nanavatty. To our surprise, only some did not make it to the next rank because of Nanavatty's reports. They stumbled either because of intermediate reporting officers' assessments or their poor service record. It was only much later that we realized that while very few "good" commanders may have been adversely affected by his reporting on them, several others managed to get through, only to be "caught out" later.'

The natural reaction of an officer who does not make it to the next rank in the army is to register a complaint as per the provisions of an Army Order. Nanavatty's response to complaints against him as a reporting officer stated that he stood by his assessment. If, however, it was his report that was hindering the individual's promotion, he had no objection to the erasing of the relevant portions of his assessment. Brigadier B.C. Muthana, Loave Verma's boss and the Deputy MS in Northern Command offers his nuanced understanding of Nanavatty's leadership style. He writes, 'As the Northern Army Commander, General Nanavatty was a task-oriented and driven leader but not a typically hard task master. Of his subordinates, he expected full commitment with the highest professional ethics in what was a literal war zone. In his reporting, he was honest, truthful and without malice. The proof of all this was that Northern Command under him did well in the selection boards as well as in the honours and awards list.'[21]

Nanavatty often gave distant observers the impression that, given his involvement in the present, he had little bandwidth for intellectual pursuits and strategic thinking. Several of Nanavatty's critics, including Lieutenant General Arjun Ray, argue that he had little understanding of the 'big picture'.[22] General Malik, the army chief during the Kargil Conflict, then a Brigadier in the Directorate of Military Operations, remembers several discussions on the potential roles of Special Forces with Nanavatty as a participant. Malik recalls that Nanavatty missed the fact that the Indian political establishment would never officially authorize covert operations behind enemy lines during peacetime as a role for the Special Forces, unlike in the West. General Malik suggested that Nanavatty's views were not in 'sync with reality' at the time and that he did not factor in the political repercussions of casualties in covert missions in peacetime. When the author posed this criticism to Nanavatty, he pondered and said without resentment, 'Maybe they were right, but wonder why those who disagreed did not put forth their views. We could have saved a lot of time and effort.'

About strategy, Nanavatty said without any hesitation, 'I was more interested in what needed to be done and what could be done within the difficult framework of what was right and what was wrong in the complex "grey zone" operational environment obtaining in J&K and the North-east. I did not want to be strategic for the sake of being strategic. There were no abstract issues for me to think through. The only time I did some crystal ball gazing was when I wrote the Future Battlefield Milieu on my return from Warminster. I did not receive any feedback from the environment, but I know that the word "milieu" certainly got tossed around and became a part of the army's lexicon. I was satisfied with my effort. Many good men in the army could look at the big picture. They could do the crystal ball gazing while I got on with my job. I do not know whether that was good or bad, but I would not have done it any other way.'[23]

His writings and recollections leave one with an understanding that while he often reflected and wrote on the 'big picture', he was more interested in dealing with the 'now' and the 'near distance' and how he could do things better in his area of operational responsibility. Strategy formulation at the apex level for Nanavatty was not to quote or clone fashionable Western doctrine at the division, corps and army level but to spell out policies that were understood and could be implemented by all. 'Doable and practical' at the operational level, Nanavatty added the 'aspirational and idealistic' whenever confronted with politico-military problems.

While the depth of Nanavatty's observations, analysis, and prognosis about internal security challenges in Nagaland, Manipur, Tripura, and J&K were striking from a politico-military perspective, his personal value system made it difficult for him to see the 'grey' amidst the political chaos. The absence of a bipartisan and whole-of-government approach towards national security at the time made it difficult for him to make inroads and influence policymakers in New Delhi.[24]

'Why did you then spend so much of your time during the last few years of your service writing strategy documents for the resolution of conflict in J&K and the North-east when you knew that there was a high probability that they would fall on deaf ears?' I asked Nanavatty during an interview.

'It was simple,' he said. 'I had a ringside view of events, the kind few policymakers ever have. I felt obliged and duty-bound to write down my thoughts, hoping someone would take note.[25] I circulated my J&K

Strategy paper far and wide within the army and political hierarchy. Besides Paddy, the army chief, Jaswant Singh, the foreign minister and N.N. Vohra, no one looked at it!'

Lieutenant General Panag, who took over as GOC-in-C Northern Command in 2007 when the proxy war in J&K was waning, recollects that the only worthwhile strategy document for conflict resolution in J&K that he dug out in NC was Nanavatty's paper. Calling it 'a clear, bold and contemporary road map for conflict resolution', Panag says that he attempted to build on it significantly and offer constructive advice to the powers that be.[26]

Another example of his strategic foresight and understanding of regional dynamics is his letter to the Manipur Chief Minister, Rishang Keishing, after the 1997 Churachandpur killings. Twenty-five years later, even as Manipur burned, Nanavatty suggested that if the government did not control the heady cocktail of ethnic and tribal strife, and if regional leaders with heft did not share a vision of peace and economic prosperity for the people of Nagaland and Manipur and continued to hunger for power and resort to political opportunism, the region would remain a conflict zone.[27]

Answering a question from a faculty member at the Defence Services Staff College in Wellington on the need for formalized training in military strategy at institutions of Professional Military Education, Nanavatty argued that while formal training in tactics and an introduction to strategy was possible, he did not think it was possible to teach officers formally on how to strategize. Drawing on examples from contemporary Indian military leadership, he suggested that generals such as Manekshaw, Inder Gill, Sagat Singh and Sundarji had much less formal military education than today's officers. And yet, they possessed great qualities of head and heart, extraordinary professional insight, the courage to think freely and the confidence to participate and hold their own in events of national importance, developed no doubt through years of reading and self-study. They further developed the ability to strategize as they acquired self-confidence, maturity, moral courage and experience through participation in policy formulation and decision-making at the highest levels—Manekshaw was a Lieutenant Colonel when he accompanied V.P. Menon to secure the accession of J&K in 1947.

Nanavatty ended his reply by suggesting that one of the reasons why strategic acumen may be missing from the repertoire of skills possessed by a large section of contemporary Indian military leaders was because they are denied the opportunity to participate in policy formulation, strategizing and decision-making at the high table in government. It stunts their professional growth and prevents them from growing into their roles.[28]

Attempting to redefine organizational culture and military ethos within the Indian Army to keep it relevant in the contemporary security milieu that prevails in the country, Nanavatty suggests the need to start at the cradle of military leadership in the Indian Army, the Indian Military Academy (IMA). In an address on leadership to cadets and faculty on 17 October 2007, he suggested a review of the Indian Army's expectations of its officers by arguing, 'The Indian Army's leadership philosophy should emphasize core military values and enduring military virtues. It should be indigenous and secular. It should be contemporary, relevant and practical. It should be based on the concept of an *officer as a leader* instead of the traditional view of *an officer and a gentleman*. Arguably, the qualities of a gentleman—*integrity, dependability, unselfishness, justice, fair play, courtesy and manners*—are, in good measure, the very qualities required of a military leader, and yet there is little that is common in the contemporary image of a gentleman—*a man of means; a man of noble birth*—and that of a military leader. I suggest a subtle shift in emphasis because of the misconceptions that arise over the image of a gentleman. The Indian Army officer should be a *military leader possessing the essential qualities of a gentleman*—and not the other way around—*a gentleman possessing the qualities of a military leader*. This will ensure that the Army officer is viewed in the correct perspective and that military leadership is accorded the priority it deserves.'[29]

'Speaking Truth to Power' was a trait that Nanavatty imbibed from his father. Kaikhushru had built a formidable reputation as a senior police officer in the undivided Bombay State who was not afraid to speak his mind to powerful political 'satraps' of the time, such as Morarji Desai and Y.B. Chavan. Ethically uncompromising and honest in thought and action, Nanavatty observed that these traits did not impede his father's rise within the police hierarchy. He had, therefore, an ethical leadership template to emulate. What did 'speaking truth to power' mean to Nanavatty? After a long pause during an interview, Nanavatty said, 'I was never worried about what someone who asked me a question would feel about my answer or whether something I wrote would go against the grain of current thinking. It was an opportunity to say what I felt and that it would be a shame if I spoke anything but the truth. I never needed to change my approach throughout my career. I rarely received any pushback from the leadership on my views, even if there was professional disagreement.'[30]

Accepting genuine mistakes and errors of judgement and coming clean were issues that Nanavatty appreciated. It formed an essential element of speaking truth to power. Brigadier (later Lieutenant General) Zameeruddin Shah commanded a mountain brigade in Kakching, Manipur, during Nanavatty's command of 3 Corps when the insurgency in Manipur was hot. In a 'snatch' operation at night based on inputs from two 'turned' Meiti guides, the young Captain leading the operation used his discretion to ignore the SOP of not giving arms to informers. Assessing that the guides would stand out in uniform without weapons, he gave them unloaded AK-47s and continued the operation. At one stage, the duo gave their escort the slip and disappeared with the weapons. Woken up at 2 a.m., the loss of firearms disconcerted Shah. As the brigade commander, he was in a quandary about the kind of Situation Report (Sitrep) he needed to send the following morning. A planned visit by the army chief, General V.P. Malik, to his HQs that morning added to the stress. Shah was tempted to report the weapons as 'lost in the Logtak Lake owing to their skiff overturning'. Nanavatty was on-site an hour before the chief and was briefed by Shah on the incident. He laughed when he heard what Shah wanted to do and said, 'Zameer, come clean; rest assured that all will be well.'

The brigade filed the Sitrep exactly as things transpired. Soon after, the local papers in Manipur published photographs of the two insurgents proudly presenting the two weapons to the PLA chief! Shah says, 'Imagine what would have happened if I had reported otherwise? In the event, it was considered a genuine error of judgement and condoned.' Nanavatty distinguished between genuine mistakes and deliberate wrongdoing through all his command tenures. '*Galti sau bar maaf, galat kaam kabhi nahi maaf* (A mistake is forgivable, not wrong-doing),' he would say.[31]

Professional loyalty is another aspect of Nanavatty's persona in some of his letters to his seniors. Nanavatty was 'bewildered and dismayed' when he saw an interview given by Lieutenant General J.F.R. Jacob, the Chief of Staff HQ Eastern Command during the 1971 conflict, to Karan Thapar on the CNBC show, *India Tonight,* on 30 April 2007. In the interview, Jacob downplayed Field Marshal Sam Manekshaw's contribution to India's spectacular military victory and the creation of Bangladesh. Not mincing his words, Nanavatty wrote to Jacob: 'You have already narrated your story of the Indo-Pakistan War of 1971 in your book. Therefore, it isn't easy to understand the purpose of the interview. Two of the principal players whom you mention by name—Generals J.S. Aurora and I.S. Gill—have passed on, and the Field Marshal, even if he were well today, would deem it below his dignity to join issue with you. General, I believe the media has used you. In the interview, you come across as the person in sole charge of operations in Eastern Command, as though Lieutenant General Aurora did not exist; you disparage your seniors and make out as if history has been unkind to you. The country awarded you the Param Vishisht Seva Medal for distinguished service. You were promoted Army Commander and later appointed Governor of Goa and Punjab—apt recognition for your contribution to the nation.'[32]

Concluding his biting letter, he reminded Jacob: 'Many would like to lay claim to India's famous victory in Bangladesh, but if we had lost that war, the nation would have held only one man responsible. Ever generous in his praise for his peers and juniors, he has always attributed his success to luck—kismet, as he calls it. Are we going to grudge Sam Manekshaw his slice of luck?'[33]

When asked whether he encouraged subordinates to express themselves similarly, Nanavatty responded emphatically: 'On a matter of principle, at the sub-unit and unit level, I adhered strictly to the chain of command—the "Orders (O)" group. However, in formulating policies that affected the rank and file, a cross-section of persons affected would invariably participate in the preliminary discussions. Later, at the formation level, every individual required to participate in an event, irrespective of whether it was the "morning prayers" (conference), a specific briefing or discussion, would have an opportunity to "pitch in" if they so wished to. In addition, time and security permitting, policy papers in draft form would invariably be circulated to the addressees for comment before finalization. This was essential to give commanders and staff officers a sense of partnering and ownership, essential for policies and orders to survive.'

Major General Dalvir Singh, now in his mid-seventies and a committed soldier for life given that he still trains commandos from the Rajasthan police, likened Nanavatty to a warrior who was constantly in search of achieving a balance between doing his duty, searching for the truth and pursuing a higher realization without any fuss or personal ambition. Drawing from the ancient Hindu philosophical treatise, the Bhagavad Gita, Dalvir suggests that from his early days, Nanavatty devoted all the energy of his body, mind and soul to soldiering under challenging circumstances and derived immense satisfaction and even enjoyment during that pursuit. Consequently, he asks, are these not the hallmarks of a Karmayogi, a person who, according to the Bhagavad Gita, follows the path of righteousness, a personal philosophy or Dharma, and accepts destiny as it comes?[34] A diverse set of letters from the Nanavatty Papers that reflect his persona are placed at Appendix E.

Srinath Raghavan, arguably one of India's finest contemporary historians, served as a young Captain in NC when Nanavatty was the GOC-in-C. Serving as ADC to the divisional commander in one of the divisions under Northern Command, the Doda-based Delta Counterinsurgency Force (CIF), Raghavan rates Nanavatty as an outstanding soldier and leader for whom the military was a calling, a vocation and not a career. As Raghavan succinctly put it, 'For Nanavatty, the army was a living and breathing institution, and he would do everything within his zone of influence to prevent it from degenerating and settling into a set pattern of functioning that is so typical of a peacetime mindset.[35] What makes Nanavatty an even more exciting leader to analyse is his willingness to go beyond the routine focus on threats and capabilities and walk that extra mile to nurture morale, motivation, creativity and small innovations at the grass-root level as a conduit for building operational proficiency that directly influenced the conduct of war.'

On the more significant issues of war and conflict in modern times and the necessity to always 'keep the edge of the sword sharp' and 'train as you fight' to cater for sudden contingencies, Raghavan reckoned that Nanavatty was mindful of the reality of a proposition offered by the brilliant and prolific British military historian, Sir Michael Howard, who argued that the vocation of soldiering was 'nine parts boredom and one part terror'.[36]

Content with what he is currently doing but remaining connected with the Indian Army and the Gorkha Rifles, this book reflects on Lieutenant General Rostum Kaikhushru Nanavatty's grit, stamina, commitment, intellect and passion for the profession of arms. Unsettled by the unravelling of his life's story but sharing the author's hope that his experience as a soldier known to 'shoot straight' will inspire readers and aspiring leaders across disciplines and domains to live their lives with purpose, Nanavatty, ever the quintessential Gorkha infantryman, marches to the same drum beat at eighty-one with a quiet and steely determination.

ACKNOWLEDGEMENTS

This is the toughest book I have written thus far. It has emerged from perseverance and focus and in that sense, I owe myself a big 'shabash' for convincing Lieutenant General Rostum Kaikhushru Nanavatty to share his fascinating journey through a lifetime of soldiering in turbulent times. Once that hurdle of convincing him was done, words cannot describe General Nanavatty's wholehearted commitment to the project; his flawless recollections of events corroborated with impeccable writings of various kinds that served as primary sources of research—draft papers and articles, diary entries, talking points, personal and Demi-Official (DO) Letters and presentation scripts. Demonstrating a mental stamina that would often seem unreal for an eighty-one-year-old, General Nanavatty patiently sat through over almost a hundred hours of formal interviews, long telephone conversations and frequent email exchanges over two years. Had the gracious and charming Suniti Nanavatty not gently prodded her husband, Rostum, to break free from his cocoon of reticence and privacy to share his experiences of soldiering, command and leadership, this book may never have seen the light of day. Her recollections of life as a 'fauji' wife, mother and an educationist have infused variety into the narrative and livened up the book, giving it a flavour that is not often revealed in traditional and conservative military biographies. Rushad and Veer complemented their mother in convincing their father to 'loosen up' and share his story for posterity. Nanavatty's elder sister, Erna showed remarkable interest in the book and shared some of her insights with me.

The book also coincided with some tough times for both the Nanavatty and the Subramaniam families in terms of relocation, travel, illness and adjusting to change—fortuitously, these changes did not disrupt the book. It only made it imperative for both the author and the central protagonist to buckle down, focus on the deliverables and drive the deadlines!

I am extremely grateful to scores of General Nanavatty's friends, professional colleagues and acquaintances, seniors and juniors, most of them from the Indian Army, the bureaucracy and the Indian Police Service, for sharing their insights, opinions and criticism of this remarkable military leader. I regret I cannot mention all of them individually, but I have been wiser after every conversation I have had with them. Among those who were early readers of the project proposal and manuscript, I must thank Vinay Sitapathi, Srinath Raghavan, and Lieutenant General D.S. Hooda for their encouragement and suggestions. I am deeply grateful to Indra Nooyi, two former army chiefs, General V.P. Malik and General N. C. Vij, Mr N.N. Vohra, Lieutenant General Prakash Menon, Ambassador Syed Akbaruddin, Narayani Basu and Nitin Gokhale among others who saw value in the book and have offered generous endorsements for the book. I am also very grateful to Lieutenant Generals P.N. Ananthanarayanan and Ravin Khosla for their support as the Colonels of the Regiment of the 8th and 5th Gorkha Rifles.

Several anonymous readers including serving army officers gave me a 'thumbs up' about the acceptability of the narrative to a wide-spectrum readership with far-reaching 'leadership and life-lessons'. Their message—'Sir, this book is a must-read for officers of all ranks'—boosted my morale. Team Harper Collins led by Udayan Mitra and Paloma Dutta were supportive and patient through disruptive and challenging times. I am also deeply indebted to my literary agent turned friend, Kanishka Gupta, for his support throughout the writing of this book.

Last but not the least, my entire family has backed me in one way or another—my eighty-nine-year-old mother always enquired how the writing was going; my brother, Shanker, has been a quiet cheerleader for my writing over the years; my daughters Shruti and Meghna, kept track of the progress from overseas and expressed their concern whenever they felt I was pushing myself; and Mowthika, my wife, gritted it out through long periods of loneliness in a new city and tolerated my erratic schedules and idiosyncrasies. However, she peripherally kept track of my narrative, played the 'devil's advocate' about not getting overwhelmed by Nanavatty's persona, and pushed me towards objectivity. This book is for all of them!

APPENDICES

APPENDIX A

(Refer page 35)

EXTRACTS FROM A PAPER WRITTEN BY SECOND LIEUTENANT NANAVATTY IN 1963

IC-13878 2/LT RK NANAVATTY 2/8 GORKHA RIFLES

D-29 Jun 63

During the fighting along our Northern Borders in Oct and Nov 62 we suffered serious reverses at the hands of the Chinese. Why were we beaten by the enemy? What steps do you suggest we take to overcome our shortcomings."

Even by one who was a spectator (a mere onlooker) our having suffered such serious reverses at the hands of the "Little yellow men" can be attributed to a good many causes. Outstanding among them our complete and shocking unpreparedness, right down from morale to material and a remarkable lack of knowledge as to what was going on "On the other side of the Hill". ✓

It was not the "antiquated" Arms nor the insufficiency of ammunition that everybody seems to point at and say – That's the reason. Agreed there probably was not enough at the right place and at the right time – when it should have been at 'A' it was probably at 'B' – But what is this if not fumbling and disorder at the top a complete lack of foresight and planning. Besides right from top to bottom there seemed no will to fight which like everything nauseating is extremely contagious.

I don't think things were so bad.

Taking things right from the start there is no doubt our Army was a mere 'Parade ground', peace time machine. Physically unfit, ill equipped and ill trained with little or no effort made to increase its fighting efficiency we got what we were asking for. All these years since the 2nd War and we were still plodding along with the same arms and tactics, the latter which seem to change from day to day. Nor were we willing to learn from helpful friends. We seemed to have forgotten the well known maxim "Peace is the trg period for War". 'Brilliant' politicians wanted to completely do away with the Defence services. It might have saved us the shame!

Even the Mahatma changed his views after Independence.

Don't be emotional. It is not exactly correct.

(2)

Not very correct

When the enemy ploughed into TIBET and piled up his hard fighting, battle wizened soldiers on our borders we still sat placid and unruffled. The Chinaman exploiting every opportunity pushed in wedges, established posts on land clearly stamped 'INDIAN'. Even to the layman there seemed something amiss. The question is did the men at the 'top' know, if they did not it shows the lack of foresight and faulty intelligence. If they did they slept over it. Intent on trying to disbelieve with knowing fallacy and growing fear what they saw and heard.

There is nothing wrong in doing this so long as you do not neglect your primary functions.

Invariably all international borders are guarded by Police or Border Scouts. Ideal deployment in peace time is to hold your border posts with Police or Semi military force and keep your regular force at a day's striking distance.

Our Borders manned by far flung small police and Assam Rifles post happy and content with their herd of Pigs and poultry which each seemed to rear as if by magic. The few regular battalions, badly emaciated, split up into small units and sub units and scattered about the country, thus forsaking a golden rule, were firmly established peace time affairs. Little or no attention being paid to training, or getting to know their areas of operational responsibility or its people. No effort being made to find out the enemy's approaches or his intentions. In fact everybody living in a cocoon of bliss, with scarcely a thought for the angry world outside, bliss which became eternal for many of the unfortunate ones.

I don't think we were asleep to the extent you make out things.

The Chinaman getting bolder and bolder strikes out again, but Alas! This time he has hit us evidently somewhere where it hurts and there are angry cries of "Throw him out". An insipid attempt is made and the crafty yellow man is quick to push his advantage home. His wide flung intelligence net tells him of our total unpreparedness, it has already subverted and brainwashed the tribals of the border areas. Men whose uncertain loyalties we blindly trusted; men who can be bought with a bagful of salt. Them the Chinaman with all the cunning of his race utilized to decided advantage. He made them guide him along the innumerable short cuts and passes straight to the few and far between posts. The wretched inhabitants seeing the Chinaman in full war regalia step out of the

Tribals may have helped but they equally hated the Chinese also.

(3) blue, ran leaving all but their pants behind.

Gallant efforts were made to stave the onslaught but without a shadow of doubt it was too late. What went wrong?

The Chinese using old and favoured tactics for such terrain, pushed strong columns guided by locals along little used tracks, hitting our defences on all sides and striving to cut off, in almost all cases, the only one way out.

Inadequate patrolling, lack of knowledge about ground and people enabled the Chinese columns striking, what appeared to us cross country to ~~(arrive)~~ arrive almost as if it were out of the blue, causing utter consternation among all ranks and shattering the morale.

Our own troops thin on the ground, moving in dribbles, into virtually unknown ~~(country)~~ and inaccurately mapped country desperately dug in to await the enemy. They hadn't to wait long. Defensive positions were created in a hopelessly inadequate period. Time was the all saving factor. Units were unable in the little fire support available they were unable to patrol effectively and detect, harrass and delay the enemy moves. Aircraft dumped first the men, the rations and ammunition in extremely inhospitable country and climate. There were no routes of withdrawal and neither were there any plans. The whole effort seemed to spell the word haphazard, it was just trust to luck and pray!

The Hopelessness of the situation and helplessness of their commanders did nothing to increase the fighting spirit. Dropped out of the sky, without adequate fire support and in many cases even the will to fight was completely absent.

Commanding officers found themselves holding positions with varied assortment of troops their original company's already engaged on other fronts. The men not ~~(even)~~ knowing their officers and the latter not knowing the men. A Battalion at least must fight as one!

Tactics utilised by the Chinese should not have been knew to us, after all most of our commanders battle tried in Burma were well

These are not correct.

I don't think any many in 2/8th would have run out if this had been the case.

I don't think any garrison had to give up its fight for lack of ammunition.

Good point.

6

(4) versed with the same kind of tactics employed by the Japs. Surely, here too, the most effective form of defence would have been the "ADMIN BOX." With no means available for an efficient and fighting withdrawal, where withdrawal would mean weeks of footslogging over some of the worst country in the world with no administrative arrangements enroute surely the best way would have been to fight back. Had definite orders to hold out been given the Indian soldier with his great fighting tradition, easily the finest soldier in the world would have obeyed it to the letter. He has done it before and would have done it again.

This refers to 7 Ind Div Admin area in the ARAKAN. [illegible] defences on the basis of "admin boxes". Agreed

most words in English language.

Once however the magical word withdraw was uttered, once the infantry dough-boy sitting in his dirty foxhole knew he had been deserted all the man in him must have become mud. Alone and ignorant barely had he trained his sights on the enemy and he is asked to withdraw. There must have arisen a fear almost amounting to hysteria.

we are not an American Army.

Withdrawal just in name, it started off as a retreat and was very soon a rout. Days on end they marched back heading in the direction which they hoped was home, many of them frostbitten and wounded struggling along as best they could. In ones and twos they came back, hungry? exhausted? these are but words for who can describe the hell they went through. The luck and the fit made it but there were the unfortunate ones men who died an inglorious death of starvation and exhaustion. Remnants of what were once fine fighting men. Years of toil on the soil with their inborn toughness had enabled many to come through.

One wonders why we had to throw pockets of our troops out so far from any help? Why did we not instead allow (him) the enemy come rumbling forward, make him extend his L of C, contain him on a front in an area where it was much more feasible to supply and administer our own forces? After holding him to (sk) strike back when the snows clamped down on the passes and thus beat his communication zone in utter confusion.

Because the Army was ordered to hold on to [illegible] ground [illegible] to give [illegible] up when it was militarily desirable to go further back.

Why, when we knew most of our commitments were in country where fighting

(5) conditions were abnormally severe did we [illegible] in the long years before the trouble conditio[n] and acclimatise our men to fight at those high Altitudes?

Can you do it with, [illegible] this training in peace time?

No use, however, crying over spilt milk, we must gird up our loins and put in work!

We must plan now, and build up our defences in an area where we can (~~[illegible]~~) provide easy logistic support. Ahead of our main defences we should have specially trained formations operating well in front, gathering information, doing intensive patrolling and in the case of an attack doing useful work by harrassing the enemy, cutting his communication, and destroying his dumps.

In the event of hostilities breaking out again we must definitely worry the enemy regarding his no [illegible] comn zone, causing him to leave large formations to protect it. On the other hand our comn zone should be in comparatively safe and easy country and [illegible] better developed. Its no use our sticking our necks out too far.

We should train extremely hard, aiming at top physical condition especially the officers. Anyone not coming up to the required standards should be sacked. There are no two ways, one must aim at the best. Troops must be acclimatised in the areas they are likely to fight in. They must have thorough knowledge of the ground and the people. Junior commanders must be trained to use initiative and deal with sudden situations. Above all an offensive spirit to beat the enemy at his own game must be created. The enemy is not invincible.

You will be commanding a battalion soon & [illegible] this!

✓

Special formations based on the commando would be of immense value in gaining information, hitting back at the enemy, creating nervousness behind enemy lines and destroying his extremely vulnerable comn zone.

For men fighting in such adverse conditions equipment must be altered to something more lighter and a form of rations for a one week's manpack basis be manufactured. The

✓ Rations already being produced [illegible] little has been [illegible]

(6) Present rations for a man pack are entirely unsatisfactory, bulky and heavy they completely weigh a man down. With a change in equipment, clothing, and rations to something much lighter the efficiency of the fighting man will go up immeasurably.

Emphasis in (trg) should be laid on long marches off tracks and cross country, troops should be put through survival and endurance tests. ~~(and what is lacking most in ta~~) Troops should be given opportunities of excercising under live fire and they should be given opportunities to carry out field firing excercises. Training should start ~~to~~ right from the individual soldier upto divisional level. So that a spirit of coordination and comradeship be developed at higher levels also. An offensive spirit with the idea of hitting the enemy (~~at~~) given any opportunity must be developed. Also it must be remem
must be given a break, and
their leave regularly otherwise it will definite have adverse effects on morale. At present there is much to much going by the 'book' at lower levels this must be cut down.

To obliterate this, one of the blackest marks in the fighting history of our countr will mean sweat and blood, and when the opportunity arises again we will have to show the world what happened was all a mistake.

Lt NANAVATI

You have not logically tackled the problem. Your every paragraph must contain one idea and these ideas must make up your complete case.

You have brought in too much emotion in your consideration. Cut it out.

Learn the military art of writing and the layout of a military paper.

A fair effort.

[illegible]

1 You are full of ideas and are very keen to see that things improve at a fast rate. This is as it should be.

2 Your style of writing I would describe as "journalese." This will do if you are writing for the Blitz or the Current. But as an officer you have to deal with the subject in an objective manner without allowing the emotions to get the better of you.

3 You can express yourself well. All you have to do is to alter your style to military writing which in simple words is a more direct way of saying things without much verbiage.

4 You must study military history with a little care. To say that holding of 'Admin Boxes' is akin to defence in terrain along our Northern areas shows you are not clear as to what the defence of an "Admin Box" involved.

[illegible]
Brig

9 Sep 63.

Adjt 2/8 Gorkha Rifles

APPENDIX B

(Refer page 129)

HANDWRITTEN GUIDELINES FOR THE CONDUCT OF OP NYLON

OP NYLON

PARA CDO TF OPS

AREA KILLINOCHCHI 3265 EAST

18 - 30 JAN 88 (APPROX)

Sit

1. Enemy.

(a) Notes compiled by 9 PARA Cdo (from 5 MLI at Killinochchi).

(b) Intsum No ________ dt ________

2. Own Tps

(a) 47 Inf Bde (11 MADRAS, 12 GRENADIERS and upto two coys 5 MLI). Search and destroy, search and find, cordon & search ops gen area Killinochchi West to incl Chorikeni kulam 2371 - Paranthan 3171 - Terumurukandi 3254 - Akkarayan kulam 2254 - Vannerik kulam 1154 - Kunchukkulam 1059. ~~From 20 Jan to 27 Jan 88 (approx)~~. Conc Killinochchi - Iranamadu

(b) Concept. Est grid of ~~Coy~~ Tps/pl posts in allotted sectors. Execute ops to dominate AO from secure base.

(c) Timings. Conc completed 20 Jan. Ops commence 20 Jan. Duration 7 days. Ops terminate Codeword BULBUL

(d) Bdy. Between 47 Inf Bde and PARA Cdo TF. Rd EPS / Paranthan - Killinochchi - Iranamadu incl 47 Inf Bde.

(e) Div Tac loc Killinochchi - 20 Jan 88.

Tps

3. (a) 9 PARA Cdo less one team.

(b) 10 PARA Cdo less one team.

Tasks

4. 9 PARA Cdo (a) Tasks in gen :-

(i) (a) Recce and svl in gen areas Terumurikandi, Kokavil (Old) 4157, Vishwamadu kulam 4960, Kuppulan kulam 5561.

(ii) (b) Ambush and direct/offensive ~~action~~ strikes based on int acquired.

(c) Search and destroy ops in areas Vaddakkachchi 4066, Janipanai kulam 4464, Vishwamadu kulam 4960.

(iii) (d) Deliberate cordon and search and search and find ops based on specific int.

(b) <u>Tasks in particular.</u>

(i) Cordon and search Pandian's house sq 4767

(ii) Apprehend 17 pers (names ~~already provided~~) from ~~to~~ area Vishvamadu kulam.

(iii) Recover all unclaimed tractor trolleys and B vehs.

5. <u>10 PARA Cdo</u>

(a) <u>Tasks in Gen.</u> ~~Shadow msn. Insert~~ Limited recce and svl and search and destroy ops in areas Kandavalai 4174 and Dharmapuram 4667 (not on map)

~~(ii) Search and destroy~~

(ii) Deliberate cordon and search and search and find ops based on specific int.

(b) <u>Tasks in Particular</u>

(i) ~~One tp~~ <u>Shadow msn.</u> One tp gen areas 3777 or 5070.

(ii) <u>Insertion.</u> Combination LCU and ft infiltration of one team gen area 5767.

(iii) <u>Fire Force Msn.</u> Team less one tp standby at EPS 3181

(iv) Cordon and search Sachi's House sq 4667.

(v) Recover all unclaimed tractor trolleys and B Vehs.

<u>Concept of op</u> ~~9 PARA Cdo~~

6. ~~(a) Est jungle bases svl and ambushes prior.~~

(a) 9 PARA Cdo carries out deliberate recce and svl in area of op. ~~Est temp~~ Followed by Est of jungle bases ~~svl and~~ ambushes prior insertion of 10 PARA Cdo.

(b) 10 PARA Cdo inserts ~~Shadow msn and~~ team plus one tp using shadow msn and combination LCU and ft infiltration into AO followed by limited recce and svl.

(c) Raids/direct action strikes on specific tgts.

(d) Search and destroy ops in AO followed by deliberate cordon and search and search and find ops based on specific int.

Coord

7. Induction

(a) 9 PARA Cdo. ~~Already~~ Completed 18 Jan 88.
(b) 10 PARA Cdo. Bn HQ and team less Tp
~~area EPS 0600 h~~ (Fire Force msn)
area EPS 0600 h 23 Jan 88.

8. Insertion [to jungle base gen areas Kokavil (old) and Vishvamadu Kulam]
(a) 9 PARA Cdo less Recce and Svl Elements. Infiltration
On ft ~~21/22 Jan~~. Not before 1500 h 20 Jan.
completed 0600 h 22 Jan.
(b) 10 PARA Cdo [to jungle base gen area 5767
(i) Team. combination HCU and
infiltration on ft. Commence 1400 h
~~21 Jan~~ 22 Jan. complete 0800 h 23 Jan.
(ii) Tp Team. Shadow msn. SHBO
area sq 3977. ~~[illegible]~~ 1800 h 22 Jan

9. extraction. On orders Codeword ______
(i) 9 PARA Cdo. On ft area Killinochchi.
(ii) 10 PARA Cdo. By [HCU / combination]. Details later.

10. Fire Force Msn. Standby 2 h notice at ~~QRF~~ EPS wef 0600 h 23 Jan. Dply on orders. Codeword FIRE FORCE

11. ~~Timings~~ Duration of Op. 20 to 27 Jan (approx). op terminated on orders. Codeword BULBUL.

12. Bdy. Between 9 & 10 PARA Cdo. Rd ~~Putto~~ Paranthan 3171 - Murasumoddai 3770 - Puthukuddirupu 6655 incl to 9 PARA.

Adm & Lgs

13. Sups. Self contained for seven days. Emergency resup by helitr. ~~Scale~~ of.
14. Med. Aero med ~~evac by~~ cas evac using daily changing wire code
15. All HP will be marked ~~and~~ secure.

Comd & Electronics

16. HQ PARA Cdo TF ~~with~~ dplys Killinochchi 20 Jan thereafter with 9 PARA Cdo.

APPENDIX C

(Refer page 213)

EXCERPTS FROM NANAVATTY'S DIARY ENTRIES DURING HIS INITIAL DAYS IN COMMAND OF 19 INF DIV

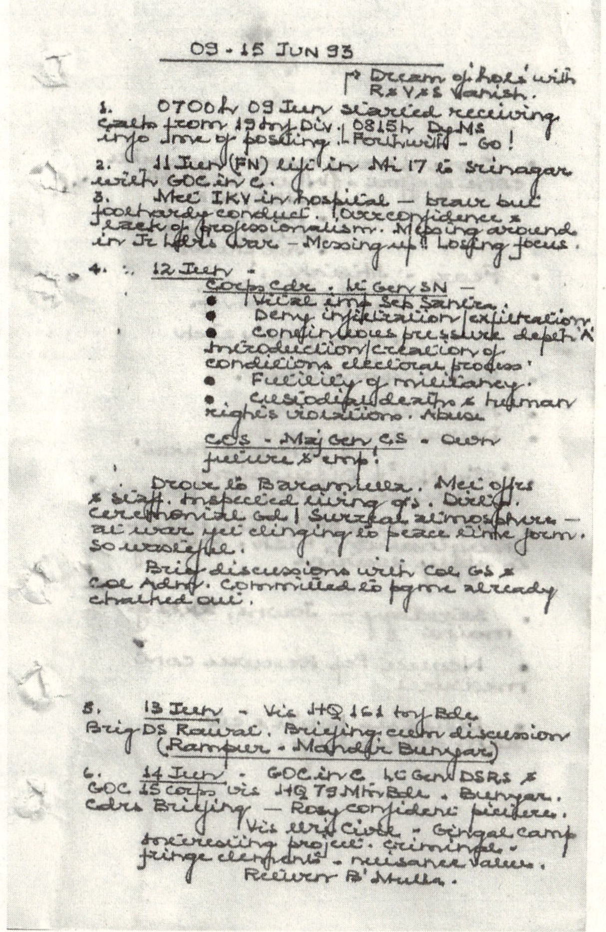

09 - 15 JUN 93

Dream of 'hols' with R & V & S vanish.

1. 0700h 09 Jun started receiving calls from 19 Inf Div. 0815h DGMS info ...ne of posting. Forthwith - Go!

2. 11 Jun (FN) left in Mi 17 to Srinagar with GOC in C.

3. Met IKV in hospital — brave but foolhardy conduct. Overconfidence & lack of professionalism. Messing around in Jt Int's war — Messing up!! Losing focus.

4. 12 Jun -

Corps Cdr - Lt Gen SN —

- Vital area Sep Sanctra.
- Deny infiltration/exfiltration
- Continuous pressure depth 'A' Introduction/creation of conditions electoral process'
- Futility of militancy.
- Custodial deaths & human rights violations. Abuse

COS - Maj Gen CS - Own future & emp!

Drove to Baramulla. Met offrs & staff. Inspected living qrs. Dull. Ceremonial Gd | Surreal atmosphere — at war yet clinging to peace time form. So wasteful.

Brief discussions with Col GS & Col Adm. Committed to pgme already chalked out.

5. 13 Jun - Vis HQ 161 Inf Bde Brig DS Rawat. Briefing cum discussion (Rampur - Mahdi Buniyar)

6. 14 Jun - GOC in C Lt Gen DSRS & GOC 15 Corps vis HQ 79 Mtn Bde - Buniyar. Cdrs Briefing — Rosy confident picture.

Vis ...ff Civil - Gingal camp interesting project. Criminal - fringe elements - nuisance value.

Return B'Mulla.

(2)

7. 15 Jun - Vis Naugam, TMG (Tutmari Gali), Kaiyan Bowl. Overfly Jatti Gali & Satsari (Cdr 16 Sect, 17 JAK RIF, 2 MLI, 11 SIKH). Briefing & discussion

First Impressions! Focus - Today's War

- Centralisation over (COL(GS) the lynchpin) both at Corps & Div.
- Self imposed (inflicted!) restrictions. Lack of freedom of action. COs & YOs chafing
- Comd & cont entity — 79 Mtn Bde Lachhipora Sect & depth 'A'. 17 JAK RIF Jatti Gali, Walargam, Satsari.
  No consolidation
- Concepts — vacuum. Old SPOC strategy "keep them under pressure" & "keep them on the run". Were on the run, fatigue, stale & open to attack. Presence of ops → Br Gds.
- Lack of focus & lack of cont of effort; dissipation of effort, redundant activity continues - NWNP!!
- Dissuasion (deterrence?) through demonstration of highly vis presence. "Stealth, cunning & skill" as always at a premium. Svl tasks.
  Reactive or hit & miss. Little evidence of planned proactive ops
  Lack of res for reaction at anywhere

Dynamism in application of concepts. Persist with outmoded. Phraseology & language.

- Planned Civic Action — unfocussed - Rations, water, k oil, electricity, Medical, Schools, Lin (mosques?)
- Pop Resource Cont - systematic -
- Int effort - Analyse types of attack
- Much "heart" & "sweat" but little method / 1/2 & blood".
- ANE mil capability limited - demo of presence for propaganda mileage/value. Low threat - confused signals lower guard. Distracted from primary aim. Confused response. Wide popular sp complicates sit.
- Absence of civ govt.

APPENDIX D

(Refer page 246)

OBSERVATIONS ON NANAVATTY'S LEADERSHIP STYLE IN 3 CORPS

THE SECRET SAUCE OF LEADERSHIP

Colonel Chandrakant Tembe joined 2/8GR in Fort William on 8 May 1966 when Captain Rostum Nanavatty was the Adjutant. Serving alongside Nanavatty in the battalion at various points of his early and mid-career till 1979 left Tembe with lasting impressions on the value system and leadership style as demonstrated by the former. Almost twenty years later, after commanding 2/8 GR himself, Colonel Chandrakant Tembe ended his career in the Indian Army with a tenure on Nanavatty's staff as the Colonel (MS) in 3 Corps when the latter was corps commander. It was during that tenure that Tembe jotted down impressions and vignettes from Nanavatty's briefings, value system and leadership style, a comprehensive list that he passed down to his son, Abhijeet, who would go on to command the same battalion as his father and Nanavatty. Here then is that list—unfiltered and unchanged:

- Tremendous vision—Peace in the NE, curbing of insurgency and extortion, acceptability by both Naga factions, appreciated by Swaraj Kaushal, GOI interlocutor.
- Interest of the organization paramount—all else subordinate.
- Inexhaustible capacity and time for work (finds that 25th hour in a day) but does not create work.

- Accepts mistakes taken place in good faith and does not baulk from admitting own errors of judgement (rare as they be) in public.
- Cool and unflappable.
- Affords total freedom of action to subordinate commanders and staff with no interference. Total trust in his subordinates.
- Tenacious—never gives up easily.
- Unafraid to face awkward situations—avoided by many—tries to find a solution/resolve differences.
- Positive attitude—no Nos—Staff Officers to provide advice, guidance and suggest solutions.
- Never speaks ill of superiors, peers or subordinates and never ridicules a person even in private for committing a mistake. Never holds a grudge.
- Will not brook unprofessional attitude or conduct—particularly severe in cases of moral turpitude.
- Clear concise expression—will convey in three sentences what others would in 30 and more!
- Genuinely welcomes dissent and views divergent to his own.
- Fair, just and correct—humane and kind—the serious demeanour is misleading.
- Consistent and predictable
- Frugal with regimental and public funds. Control over expenditure—nothing cosmetic.
- Loyal to his subordinates—holds hands of.
- Extremely concerned about subordinates, especially the troops, SOs, guards, escorts and household staff.
- No skeletons in the cupboard & no axes to grind—a rare entity indeed!
- Says what he believes in and does what he says. Expects the same of subordinates, who he appreciates.
- Particular about dress, turnout and saluting at all times. Conscious

of his image, appearance and physical fitness.

- A reasonably good judge of people. Always willing to give another chance.
- Correct in assessing, misread as strict.
- No frills, demands or extra requirements for self or family.
- Abhors over attendance and dislikes people eager to please.
- A socially correct couple—yet very very private, who also respect others' privacy.
- No time for public display of private emotions.

A soldier's general all the way!

APPENDIX E

(Refer page 308)

LETTERS OF INTEREST WRITTEN & RECEIVED BY NANAVATTY OVER THE YEARS

Regd.

J.F.RIBEIRO,IPS.

D.O. No. 173/PA/DGP

Director-General of Police,
Punjab.

Dated Chandigarh, the 5th Oct,1986.

My dear Roston,

Thank you for your letter dated the 21st October,1986 . You have gone to great lengths to retrieve the notes you made during your stay in London to pass them on to me. I am touched by your gesture and the interest you have shown in my fight against the terrorists of Punjab.

2. I have gone through the material very carefully and I intend to make use of the knowledge in our planning. I have made notes and also copied out the material that is relevant (almost the entire material is relevant).

3. I am also writing to my friend Sunith Rodrigues, as you suggested.

4. I am returning herewith your papers, as requested.

warm regards,

Yours sincerely,

Julio

(J.F.Ribeiro)

Col.R.K.Nanavatty,
Additional Directorate General of
Perspective Planning ,
General Staff Branch,Army.H.Qrs.,
DHQ PO,
NEW DELHI- 110011.

Encl:as above.

13837/RKN/DO 01 Jul 88

1. Reference MS Branch letter No 384848/MS(X)/119 dated 10 Jun 88.

2. I am delighted to know that I shall be taking over from you. I have no illusions about the task and though looking forward to the challenge I approach it with trepidation. I shall be looking to you for your wise counsel and guidance.

3. I am aware of the outstanding job of work both you and Brig Jal Master, PVSM,VSM, have done. I pray I shall have the strength and courage to emulate, at least in a small way, your example.

4. Having handed over my job as Dir MO (Cdo Cell) on 10 Jun 88 I remain attached to the Dte Gen MO. Presently I am on 30 days annual leave (from 13 Jun to 12 Jul 88). If on rejoining from leave I find that there may be a significant delay in the issue of your posting order I shall explore the possibility of doing an attachment with HAWS prior to reporting to the brigade. It should help me prepare for the rigours ahead. You do realise that unlike you, I am not a trained mountaineer!

5. I have not served in Ladakh before. I shall be particularly grateful if a member of the staff could fill me up on the necessary details concerning journey and transit procedures, personal clothing and equipment required, use of private arms, personal documentation and, despatch of baggage.

Brig CS Nugyal,UYSM
Cdr
HQ 102 Inf Bde
C/O 56 APO

Field Marshal Sam Manekshaw, MC

Stavka: Springfield: Coonoor

13 July 1988

Dear Rustom.

I have your letter of 5 July for which I thank you: You have my congratulations on becoming a Brigadier and having command of such an important sector. I have little doubt that both you, and the troops under your Command will distinguish yourselves. I know your wife will be disturbed at the thought of the separation as also your being in such a remote part of the world: but if she wants to be the wife of a futute Chief, she will have to bear with these inconveniences ! Give her my love and tell her not to fret. If there is anything I can do for either you or her please do not hesitate to let me know. In the mean time you have my good wishes and the best of luck in your new assignment.

With my warm personal regards,

Yours Sincerely

Sam Manekshaw

To

Lt-Gen R.K.Nanavatty,UYSM,AVSM,
GOC, 3 Corps, C/O 99 APO.

Dear Sir,

I on behalf of Changki villagers extend our best wishes and warm welcome to you on your recent posting as the GOC of 3 Corps. We hope you must also have the feeling of coming back home. The villagers still remember fondly your association with the village during your tenure at Changki as a Captain. We are proud that an Officer closely associated with Changki has now returned to Nagaland as a General. It is our prayer that you have a successful tenure at 3 Corps.

Our villagers are eagerly awaiting your visit to Changki and will be obliged if you could kindly spare sometime from your busy schedule of engagements and pay a visit to Changki preferably in the month of October'97.

With sincere regards,

Yours sincerely,

Chairman, Village Council, 2/10/97.
Changki village: Mokokchung

Col S S Tinaikar
CO

10 PARA(SF)
C/o 56 APO

41478/SST

09 May 03

My Dear General,

1. I write to express immense gratitude for being a fantastic role model for myself and I'm sure many others in our Army.

2. I have always held you in great admiration since our short association in 1988. Young, inexperienced and given to a cavalier apch to soldiery, your professionalism was electrifying. That first impression is undying, indelible and has remained as a perfect guide, a lodestar to follow. Lucky are those who served with you and grew with you in service.

3. I have tried to emulate you in many ways, with little success; minor habits which add up to a great personality. Sometimes I wonder how you could hold your own in an environment so different in morals, dignity and dedication.

4. I must confess that you have influenced me

2

in many ways. On the eve of your retirement, I can only thank you for being the great soldier that you are and for discharging your duties with unmatched commitment. I hope our Army puts forth more like you. It inspires us to soldier on for our Army and country.

With Every Good Wish and Best Regards,

I remain,

Yours Sincerely,

[signature]

Lt Gen R K Nanavatty, PVSM, UYSM, AVSM
GOC-in-C
HQ Northern Comd
C/o 56 APO

जनरल एन सी विज
पी वी एस एम, यू वाई एस एम, ए वी एस एम, ए डी सी
General N C Vij
PVSM, UYSM, AVSM, ADC

सेना मुख्यालय
नई दिल्ली - 110 011
ARMY HEADQUARTERS
NEW DELHI - 110 011

A/00043/1/COAS

01 Jun 03

My dear Rostum,

1. Now that you have "hung your Spurs" (boots for an Infantryman), Rostum, I would once again like to reiterate a few sentiments. And these are sans, the politeness and formalities of the "Dining Out".

2. You have been a **great friend and a colleague**. A **gentlemen** to the core from whom one could emulate many things; at least I tried to pick up some.

3. Your contribution to the Army has been monumental. I can well judge the pressures of "the Northern Command", especially with the benefit of my last three assignments of the DGMO, VCOAS and now that of the Chief. All that I can once again repeat is that, you have **done the Army well** and **proud !**

4. I am sure that you shall continue to retain interest in the "happenings in the Army". It shall be a **pleasure for me** to **have suggestions from you** . I shall certainly look forward to them.

5. May I also take this opportunity to wish you and Suniti the very best of luck and **God speed** in the years to come !

With lots of love from me & Rita to both you & Suniti.

Yours ever,
Nirmal

Lt Gen RK Nanavatty, PVSM, UYSM, AVSM (Retd)
C/o HQ Northern Command
C/o 56 APO

HEADQUARTERS NORTHERN COMMAND

SPECIAL ORDER OF THE DAY

BY

LT GEN RK NANAVATTY, PVSM, UYSM, AVSM
GOC-IN-C NORTHERN COMMAND

C/o 56 APO	SATURDAY	31 MAY 2003

1. On relinquishing the appointment of GOC-in-C Northern Command on my retirement, I wish to convey my deep and sincere gratitude and appreciation to all ranks.

2. In the year 2001, you neutralised a total of 2177 terrorists; the largest No ever in a single calendar year, since the start of the current phase of the conflict in 1989. This was despite approximately five months of 'non initiation of combat operations'. In 2002, despite strenuous preparations for conventional general war, you continued to prosecute relentless counter terrorist operations resulting in the successful conduct of 'free and fair' elections to the J&K State Assembly – a landmark event. During this period of intense and sustained activity, through a display of controlled aggression, you ensured effective domination of the Line of Control resulting in complete moral ascendancy over the enemy. Your civic behaviour and conduct, strict adherence to the laws of the land and, sustained efforts at winning the hearts and minds of the local population have resulted in discernible de-alienation. Your selfless efforts have provided the state a rare opportunity to march decisively towards conflict resolution.

3. You have demonstrated extraordinary endurance, courage, steadfastness, self-sacrifice and sense of duty in sustained and relentless low intensity combat operations in Operations RAKSHAK and PARAKRAM in the command theatre. As your Army Commander, I could not have asked for more. I salute you and the many gallant men who have laid down their lives on the field of battle for the safety and honour of their country, the Army and their regiments.

4. There is no doubt that this is a 'war' we must win, however long it takes and whatever the price. And, win it you will if you are able to elicit the willing support and cooperation of the people in your fight against terrorism. I pray for you to be clear-headed, strong, resolute and disciplined.

5. I take this opportunity to wish you and your families the very best, in the future.

(RK Nanavatty)
Lieutenant General

Lieutenant General R K Nanavatty [Retired]

17 Atlantis
West Avenue
Kalyani Nagar
Pune 411 006
☎ +91 - [0]20 - 2668 3010
+91 - [0] 98227 90248
✉ rknanavatty@gmail.com

06 May 2007

Your interview with Karan Thapar on the CNBC Show, *India Tonight* on Monday, 30 April 2007 left me bewildered and dismayed.

You have already narrated your story of the Indo-Pakistan War of 1971 in your book - *Surrender at Dacca – Birth of a Nation.* Therefore, it is difficult to understand the purpose of the interview. Whatever the reason, it was ill timed. Two of the principle players whom you mention by name - Generals JS Arora and IS Gill – have passed on; and the Field Marshal - even if he were well today - would deem it beneath his dignity to join issue with you. What you have succeeded in doing, unwittingly perhaps, is to rake up controversy. General, I believe the media has used you.

I have little doubt that you speak of events truthfully, as you perceive them. However, in the interview, you come across as the person in sole charge of operations in Eastern Command – as though Lieutenant General JS Arora simply did not exist; you disparage your superiors and you make out as if history has been unkind to you. You were the Chief of Staff, Eastern Command during the war and not the Army Commander. By giving the Chief of Army Staff your advice without fear or favour, you only did your duty – rare, as it might seem today. Despite his angry reaction – as you put it - he apparently acted on the advice to *delay operations until the Army was ready* and steadfastly stood his ground vis-à-vis the government. The country awarded you the Param Vishist Seva Medal for distinguished services rendered in the war. You were promoted Army Commander and later appointed Governor of Goa and then Punjab - apt recognition of your contribution to the nation.

Sir, Field Marshal SHFJ Manekshaw, MC was the Chief of Army Staff and Chairman Chiefs of Staff Committee during the war. There are many who would like to lay claim to India's famous victory in Bangladesh but if we had lost that war, the nation would have held only one man responsible. A fine military leader, loved by the troops to this day; Sam Manekshaw is a legend in his lifetime. Ever generous in his praise for his peers and juniors he has invariably attributed his own success to luck – *kismet* as he calls it. Are we going to grudge Sam Manekshaw his slice of luck? Are we going to rob the Indian Army of one of its few genuine heroes? Are we going to deny the nation the opportunity to honour this great military leader?

With best wishes,
Yours sincerely,

Lieutenant General JFR Jacob, PVSM (Retired)
J 203 Som Vihar Apartments
New Delhi 110 022

NOO

Major General SK Singh
Colonel 8 Gorkha Rifles

भारतीय डाक
INDIA POST

YERWADA P O (411006)
SP EE142686707IN
Counter No:1,OP-Code:VVB
To:LT GEN JFR JACOB,PVSM
New Delhi, PIN:110022
From:NANAVATTY , KALYANINAGAR PUNE 6
Wt:20grams,Taxes:Rs.3.00
Amt:25.00 , 09/05/2007 , 08:23
<()>

LIST OF INTERVIEWEES

This is a list of serving and retired officers formally interviewed, informally spoken to, or corresponded with during research for this book.

Mr N.N. Vohra

General V.P. Malik

Air Chief Marshal S. Krishnaswamy

General N.C. Vij

General Bipin Rawat

General Sir Hew Pike, British Army

Lieutenant General Anand Sarup

Lieutenant General Satish Nambiar

Lieutenant General S.S. Mehta

Lieutenant General J.R. Mukherjee

Lieutenant General T.S. Shergill

Lieutenant General Arjun Ray

Lieutenant General K.K. Khanna

Lieutenant General K. Nagaraj

Lieutenant General Arvind Sharma

Lieutenant General R.B. Singh

Lieutenant General Tej Pathak

Lieutenant General P.C. Bharadwaj

Lieutenant General Mohan Pande

Lieutenant General Zameeruddin Shah

Lieutenant General P.C. Katoch

Lieutenant General V.K. Ahluwalia

Lieutenant General S.K. Singh

Lieutenant General J.D.S. Rawat

Lieutenant General Ranbir Singh

Lieutenant General S.S. Tinaikar

Major General C.S. Nugyal

Major General S.D. Mahanti

Major General Dalvir Singh

Brigadier R.R. Palsokar

Brigadier Shamsher Singh

Brigadier B.C. Muthana

Brigadier Trigunesh Mukherjee

Brigadier B.M. Panthaki

Brigadier Basant Ponwar

Brigadier S.S. Negi

Brigadier Loave Verma

Brigadier Rajesh Raman

Colonel Arjun Singh

Colonel Chandrakant Tembe

Colonel K.S. Mandana

Colonel Dilip Parab

Colonel Dorcha Lee, Irish Army

Colonel R.S. Sanghera

Colonel K.S. Aithmian

Colonel Sunil Mathur

Colonel John D. Britto

Colonel David Devashayam

Colonel K.A. Mohan

Colonel Gurdeep Bains

Colonel P.K. Mehrishi

Colonel Awadesh Kumar

Colonel Manish Sarin

Colonel Abhijeet Tembe

Shri S.M. Sahai, IPS

Professor Gautam Sen

Mr Ayaaz Khan

Mrs Suniti Nanavatty

Ms Erna Nanavatty

Rushad Nanavatty

Veer Nanavatty

Subedar Major (Hony Captain) Barta Bahadur Gurung

9 Hony Captains, Subedar Majors and Subedars who served alongside Nanavatty over the years.

NOTES

Introduction

1. B.H. Liddell Hart, *Strategy: The Indirect Approach* (New Delhi: Pentagon Press, 2012), 335.
2. Rostum K. Nanavatty, *Internal Armed Conflict: Forging a Joint Civil–Military Approach* (New Delhi: Pentaon Press, 2013).
3. Subaltern history broadly refers to a 'bottom-up' approach to writing history that largely relies on a hierarchical colonial style that banks heavily on recollections.
4. Stanley Weintraub, *15 Stars* (New York: NAL Caliber, 2007), xi.
5. Prem Shankar Jha, 'The Forgotten Prime Minister', *Biblio: A Review of Books,* Vol. 27, April–June2022.
6. Robert S. McNamara, *In Retrospect: The Tragedy and Lessons of Vietnam* (New York: New York Times Books, 1995), xvii–xviii.

Chapter 1: Early Days

1. Lietenant General A.M. Sethna, 'Parsis in the Armed Forces', Presentation at the Bombay University in March 2000 to honour Sir Pherozeshah Mehta. From the Nanavatty Papers.
2. Afshin Marashi, *Exile and the Nation* (Austin: The University of Texas Press, 2020), 8–13. For equally authoritative works on the Parsi community in India, see Eckehard Kulke's *The Parsees* and

Jesse Palsetia's *The Parsis of India*. For breezy narratives from the Nanavatty collection of books and papers, see Adil J. Govadia's *Beyond Borders and Boundaries: History of Parsi Migration, Enterprise and Philanthropy* and Prochy N. Mehta's *Who Is a Parsi?*

3. Nanavatty interview, 16 May 2022.
4. 'The London Gazette', 23 June 1922, p. 4716 at https://www.thegazette.co.uk/London/issue/32722/page/4716/data.pdf.
5. Nanavatty interview, 16 May 2022.
6. Nagaland Government Note on Shri K.J. Nanavatty, Nanavatty Papers. The note offers a crisp overview of Kaikhushru's career.
7. Nanavatty interview, 16 May 2022.
8. Ibid.
9. Ibid.
10. Nanavatty's Report Card from St Peter's, accessed from his records at Rajkumar College, kind courtesy, Sujan Chinoy, an alumnus of the College, a distinguished diplomat and currently the Director General of Institute for Defence Studies and Analyses, New Delhi.
11. Report Card from Rajkumar College, kind courtesy, Sujan Chinoy.
12. Max Hastings, 'The Prince and the Sweeper's Son—Old Boys of India's Finest', *The Standard,* London, 10 April 1984, 22–23. Nanavatty Papers.
13. Mr Peter Rogerson, OBE, email correspondence with Nanavatty, 1 September 2022.
14. Nanavatty interview, 16 May 2022.
15. Report Card from Rajkumar College. Kind courtesy Sujan Chinoy.
16. Email correspondence between the author and Mr Ayyaz Khan, 3 July 2022.
17. For an insightful biography of Lieutenant General P.S. Bhagat by his daughter, see Ashali Varma, *The Victoria Cross: A Love Story: The Life of Lt Gen. P.S. Bhagat, PVSM, V.C.* (Self-published in India, January 2014.
18. Telephone conversation, 1 May 2023 and email correspondence with a detailed write-up on Nanavatty from Brig. Shamsher Singh (retd.), 10 May 2023.
19. Interview with Prof. Gautam Sen, 4 June 2023.
20. Nanavatty interview, 16 May 2022.

21. Lieutenant General A.M. Sethna, 'Parsis in the Armed Forces', Presentation at Bombay University in March 2000 to honour Sir Pherozeshah Mehta. From the Nanavatty Papers.

Chapter 2: Into the Deep End with the Gorkhas

1. Arjun Subramaniam, *India's Wars I: A Military History 1947–1971*, (New Delhi: HarperCollins, 2016), 215, 233. For a detailed overview of the entire conflict, see Chapters 14–17.
2. From the War Diary of 2/8 GR, accessed at Dehradun on 15 November 2022.
3. Syed Ata Hasnain, 'Epic Battles: Revisiting Jaswantgarh and Rezangla of 1962 on their Anniversaries', *Swarajya Magazine*, 17 November 2019, https://swarajyamag.com/defence/epic-battles-revisiting-jaswantgarh-and-rezangla-of-1962-on-their-anniversaries. Also see, Arjun Subramaniam, *India's Wars I: A Military History*, 242–243.
4. R.D. Palsokar, 'Red Pompons: History of the 8th Gorkha Rifles, 1947–1992', (Dehradun: Gorkha Training Centre, 1993).
5. Detailed battle notes from Colonel Janak Sesodia (Retd) and several phone conversations in January 2022.
6. Palsokar, Red Pompons. Also see War Diary, 2/8 GR.
7. A battalion of the Indian Army normally comprises four Rifle companies with each company having three platoons. The strength of a battalion averages between 800–1000 troops.
8. This is from the War Diary of 2/8 GR, accessed at Dehradun on 15 November 2022. Also, refer to the detailed interview with Nanavatty on 16 May 2022.
9. Colonel Janak Sesodia (Retd), one of the officers taken prisoner by the Chinese, forwarded extracts from the War Diary of 2/8 GR to the author.
10. Nanavatty interview, 16 May 2022.
11. Nanavatty interview, 16 May 2022. Also see Nanavatty Papers, 'Analysis of the 1962 Conflict', June 1963.
12. Ibid.

13. For a detailed overview of the United Nations Neutral Repatriation Committee (UNNRC), see Arjun Subramaniam, *India's Wars I,* 313–315.
14. Nanavatty Papers, 'Analysis of the 1962 Conflict', June 1963.
15. For a detailed general review of Thimayya's resignation episode, see C.B. Khanduri, *Thimayya: An Amazing Life* (New Delhi, KW Publishers, 2006), 282–295.

    The episode reveals the deep and debilitating schisms that existed within the politico-military interface of the time because of the dominating and condescending approach of the Defence Minister V.K. Krishna Menon towards senior military leadership.
16. 'Analysis of the 1962 Conflict', Nanavatty Papers.
17. Arjun Subramaniam, *India's Wars II: A Military History 1972–2020* (New Delhi: HarperCollins, 2020), 37–73. Chapters 4 and 5 offer a detailed overview of the Naga insurgency.
18. Richard Miers, *Shoot to Kill* (London: Faber and Faber, 1959). The author was a successful Battalion Commander during the 'Malayan Emergency' in the late 1950s.
19. Nanavatty interview, 16 May 2022.
20. Nanavatty Papers, 'Hostile: A Naga Encounter', Infantry Journal, Autumn 1963.
21. Ibid.
22. Ibid.
23. Arjun Subramaniam, *India's Wars II,* 49–51.
24. Nanavatty Papers, 'Hostile: Naga Encounter'. Also, refer to the telephone conversation with Colonel Arjun Singh on 27 June 2022.
25. Nanavatty interview, 16 May 2022.
26. Nanavatty interview, 07 August 2018.
27. Nanavatty interview, 23 May 2022
28. End of Course Report, Nanavatty Papers.

Chapter 3: Peacetime Soldiering

1. Nanavatty Papers.
2. The Colonel of the Regiment is a tradition and a position the Indian Army inherited from the British. All serving officers of the

regiment above the rank of Colonel vote to select the Colonel of the Regiment, who is generally chosen from one of the senior-most serving generals from that Regiment. Towards the closing stages of his career, Nanavatty was the Colonel of 8 GR.

3. Arjun Subramaniam, *India's Wars I,* 359.
4. 'Fort William: The Rise and Fall of an Imperial Empire,' at https://indianculture.gov.in/node/2790482, accessed 28 May 2023.
5. Nanavatty interview, 23 May 2022.
6. Course Report, Nanavatty Papers.
7. Nanavatty interview, 23 May 2022.
8. Newsletter of the 2nd Battalion of the 8th Gorkha Rifles, sometime in 1968, soon after the battalion moved out of Fort William, from the Nanavatty Papers.
9. Nanavatty interview, 23 May 2022.
10. Lieutenant General Anand Sarup, MVC (Retd) interview, 25 June 2022.
11. For an account of the Battle for the Buthidong Tunnels in WWII during the Burma Campaign, see Anne Baird, 'The Tunnels Battle', *BBC WW2 People's War Homepage,* https://www.bbc.co.uk/history/ww2peopleswar/stories/66/a5373966.shtml.
12. Arjun Subramaniam, *India's Wars I,* 107–108.
13. Colonel Dileep Parab's written notes on his recollections of Nanavatty as a mentor and soldier, correspondence with the author, 12 July 2022.
14. Notes from Dileep Parab.
15. Nanavatty and Lieutenant General Anand Sarup, MVC (Retd) interview, 25 June 2022.
16. Interview with Lieutenant General Anand Sarup, MVC (Retd), 25 June 2022. Also, refer to Nanavatty's interview on the same day.
17. Course Report, Nanavatty Papers.
18. Nanavatty interview, 25 June 2022.
19. Major R.K. Nanavatty, 'Training the Infantry Company Commander', paper written at the Infantry School, Mhow, 1969–1971, Nanavatty Papers.
20. Nanavatty papers, from a page-numbered and neatly indexed Blue Cloth-bound Diary, 'Rommel Papers', 60–63.

21. Ibid., 'Israel's Army and the Making of a Commander', 73–74.
22. Nanavatty interview, 26 June 2022.
23. From the Nanavatty Papers. Sam Manekshaw replied similarly to Nanavatty in the US, but the letter is missing from Nanavatty's repository of correspondence.
24. Nanavatty interview, 26 June 2022.
25. Nanavatty interview, 26 June 2022.
26. Major R.K. Nanavatty, 'The Last 200 Yards and Fighting on the Objective', 1972–74, a paper written as a Company Commander when 2/8 GR operated in J&K.
27. Securing a 'Competitive Vacancy' to attend the Staff College meant that an officer would be eligible to compete for a slot to attend the Staff Course at one of the many Staff Colleges abroad from friendly foreign countries.
28. In the Indian Army, a division and corps are commanded by a General Officer Commanding (GOC) of the rank of Major General and Lieutenant General respectively. They are also called division commander or corps commander. The seven Army Commands are commanded by Lieutenant Generals who are called General Officer Commanding-in-Chief or GOC-in-C. They are also called army commanders.
29. Quotations from the 'Blue Diary', Nanavatty Papers.
30. Nanavatty interview, 26 June 2022.
31. Major R.K. Nanavatty, 'Training of Armoured and Mech Forces', 1976–77, a paper written during his tenure as the Brigade Major of 1 Armoured Brigade, from the Nanavatty Papers.
32. Nanavatty interview, 26 June 2022.
33. 'Class of 1966 Yearbook', published by Lawrence School, Sanawar, 2017. The Yearbook is edited by Mrs Suniti Nanavatty.
34. From the author's first conversation with Suniti Nanavatty on 26 June 2022.
35. Ibid.

Chapter 4: First Command

1. Yigal Allon, *The Making of Israel's Army* (New York: Universe Books, 1970), 251.

2. Nanavatty interview, 26 June 2022.
3. From the Nanavatty Papers. Nanavatty never went unprepared for an address to the officers and men, and his papers include cue cards of several speeches and talks he delivered throughout his career. The speech cards reminded the author of Winston Churchill's statement when asked about his oratory skills; he said, 'There is nothing such as an extempore speech or talk.'
4. Blue diary of notes, quotations and excerpts from good books on military history, Nanavatty Papers.
5. Nanavatty interview, 26 June 2022.
6. Major R.K. Nanavatty, 'Leadership Training in the Army', 1975, Nanavatty Papers. A formal service paper cum presentation that Nanavatty made at DSSC Wellington while undergoing the Staff Course in 1975, it has comments by the Senior Instructor at the end of the paper that read, 'You have an excellent comprehension of the subject, and your paper is well-reasoned, covering the essential details. A good effort.'
7. PTI, 'Man gets killed while collecting empty shells near firing range', *India Today,* 18 May 2016, https://www.indiatoday.in/pti-feed/story/man-gets-killed-while-collecting-empty-shells-nr-firing-range-610736-2016-05-18. Also see, Express News Service, 'Scrap Dealer arrested with ammunition explosives of the Indian Army in Ahmednagar, *The Indian Express,* 23 July 2023, https://indianexpress.com/article/cities/pune/scrap-dealer-arrested-with-ammunition-explosives-of-the-indian-army-in-ahmednagar-8855007/.
8. Nanavatty interview, 26 June 2022.
9. For a good description of the strategic importance of this area, see Ankit Pada, 'Geographical Curse: India's Vulnerable Chicken's Neck', *The Diplomat,* 8 November 2013, https://thediplomat.com/2013/11/geographys-curse-indias-vulnerable-chickens-neck/.
10. Nanavatty interview, 26 June 2022.
11. Nanavatty interview, 26 June 2022.
12. Suniti Nanavatty interview, 26 June 2022.
13. See Arjun Subramaniam, *India's Wars I,* 412–413.
14. Nanavatty interview, 26 June 2022.
15. All these papers form part of the rich repository in the Nanavatty Papers. Also, refer to Nanavatty's interview on 26 June 2022.

16. Notes on Weapon Training in the Indian Army (79–81), Nanavatty Papers.
17. Ibid.
18. Lieutenant Colonel R.K. Nanavatty, Notes on 'Improving Performance Levels in the Army' (79–81), Nanavatty Papers. The notes contributed to a paper by the same name that Nanavatty wrote before relinquishing command of 2/8 GR.
19. Notes from Dilip Parab.
20. Email correspondence with Lieutenant General Aiyengar, 31 July 2022.
21. From the farewell speech by Nanavatty at DSSC Wellington, Nanavatty Papers.

Chapter 5: Learning from the Americans and the British

1. Lieutenant Colonel R.K. Nanavatty, Organisation and Conduct of Instruction—United States Army Infantry School (USAIS), presentation delivered to the Senior Command Course, November 1977, Nanavatty Papers. The presentation has a detailed overview of the functioning of USAIS.
2. Nanavatty presentation and interview on 22 August 2022.
3. Nanavatty interview, 22 August 2022.
4. Nanavatty presentation.
5. Nanavatty interview.
6. Nanavatty interview, 22 August 2022.
7. Note from Colonel Dorcha Lee (retd.), Irish Army, who did the Course with Nanavatty, email correspondence with the author, 29 July 2022.
8. Ibid.
9. Ibid.
10. Ibid.
11. Nanavatty interview, 28 August 2022.
12. Nanavatty interview, 28 August 2022.
13. Ibid.
14. Nanavatty interview, 28 August 2022.

15. Henry Jones, 'The Falklands will always be special to me, says Lt Col H Jones' grandson', *Independent*, Asia Edition, 28 May 2022, https://www.independent.co.uk/news/uk/british-argentine-falklands-victoria-cross-port-stanley-b2089305.html.
16. Ibid.
17. Draft notes on Colonel Nanavatty's visit to HQ Director Special Air Service (SAS) & SAS Gp, 22 February 1985, Nanavatty Papers.
18. Telephonic conversation with Lieutenant General Nambiar.
19. A copy of the letter can be accessed at https://defenceforumindia.com/threads/that-famous-letter-from-general-k-sundarji.2927/.
20. Demi Official letter to Colonel R.K. Nanavatty from J.F. Ribeiro, IPS. DGP, Punjab, 05 October 1986, from the Nanavatty Papers.
21. Nanavatty interviews and interview with Suniti Nanavatty.
22. Notes on 'Restructuring Special Forces', Nanavatty Papers.
23. Arjun Subramaniam, *India's Wars II,* 173–178.
24. Arjun Subramaniam, *India's Wars II,* 173–178.
25. Nanavatty interview, 28 August 2022.

Chapter 6: Into Sri Lanka with the Para Commandos

1. Nanavatty Papers.
2. Ravi Nair, 'The Birth of the Para Commandos', *India–Pakistan War of 1965, https://www.bharat-rakshak.com/ARMY/history/1965war/441-the-birth-of-the-para-commandos.html.* Also see Arjun Subramaniam, *India's Wars I: A Military History 1947–1971* (New Delhi: HarperCollins, 2016), 281–282.
3. Arjun Subramaniam, *India's Wars II: A Military History 1972–2020* (New Delhi: HarperCollins, 2020), 79–82.
4. Arjun Subramaniam, *India's Wars II: A Military History 1972–2020* (New Delhi: HarperCollins, 2020), 79–82.
5. For a detailed overview of the Jaffna University operation see, Arjun Subramaniam, *India's Wars II*, 189–193.
6. Nanavatty's comments on the first draft of the chapter in an email on 2 September 2022.
7. Nanavatty's comments on a draft chapter, 2 September 2022.

8. The detailed telephone conversation on 14 August 2022 with Colonel Awadhesh Kumar (retd) settled in Agra.
9. Handwritten notes from Sri Lanka on the recommended tasking for the para commando battalions. Nanavatty Papers.
10. Major General Dalvir Singh, 'Reflections on Gen Nanavatty', email note of 6 August 2022.
11. Final reflections, Email Note from Lieutenant General Tej Pathak, 2 September 2022.
12. Diary jottings from Nanavatty Papers. Also, see the author's email exchanges with Lieutenant General Tej Pathak on 2 September 2022.
13. Telephonic interview with Colonel John Britto, 7 March 2023.
14. 'Snatch Operations' were practised by the British Army in Northern Ireland in urban and built-up areas. They were precise intelligence-driven operations meant to capture leaders and cadres of the Irish Republican Army. Nanavatty observed and studied this during his week-long stint with a British Army battalion preparing for deployment in Northern Ireland.
15. Nanavatty interview, 22 August 2022.
16. Note on Nanavatty from Lieutenant General Tej Pathak.
17. Draft letter from Nanavatty to Lieutenant General Rodrigues, 2 March 1989, Nanavatty Papers.
18. Major A.N. Nayyar, 'Operation Merry Lane', '*Pratividrohi*', March 1994, the Journal of the CIJWS. From Nanavatty Papers.
19. Colonel Awadhesh Kumar interview.
20. For a detailed account of Colonel Chapman's exploits in Malaya, see Freddie Spencer Chapman, *The Jungle Is Neutral: A Soldier's Three-Year Jungle Escape from the Japanese Army* (London: Marshall Cavendish, 2015).
21. Dalvir Singh, Email Note.
22. DO letter from Major General S.C. Sardeshpande to Brigadier R.K. Nanavatty, 14 February 1989, Nanavatty Papers.
23. Email to the author from Lieutenant General S.S. Tinaikar, 25 January 2023.
24. Brigadier R.R. Palsokar, *Ours Not to Reason Why: With the IPKF in Sri Lanka* (Pune: Sunidhi Publishers, 2017) 125–126.

25. Lawrence E. Cline, 'Pseudo Operations in Counterinsurgency: Lessons from Other Countries', *SSI Monograph*, US Army War College,https://www.globalsecurity.org/military/library/report/2005/ssi_cline.pdf. The paper does not cover operations conducted by the Indian Army as these were never openly publicized.
26. Draft Report, 'Op Pawan-Para CDO Operations: Observations and Comments', 1 March 1988, Nanavatty Papers.
27. Draft letter to Lieutenant General V.K. Nayyar, 1 March 1988. Nanavatty Papers
28. Draft letter to Deputy OFC, IPKF, Sri Lanka diary, Nanavatty Papers.
29. Draft DO letter to Lieutenant General B.C. Joshi, 8 June 1988, Nanavatty Papers.
30. Notes on 'Restructuring Special Forces', Nanavatty Papers.
31. DO letter from Colonel S.S. Tinaikar to Nanavatty, Nanavatty Papers.

Chapter 7: On the Saltoro Range

1. Colonel Dilip Parab, who served with Nanavatty as one of his Company Commanders, was in the personnel branch of the Army (MS Branch) and recollected the glee with which the civilian officer looking after the posting of brigadiers received Nanavatty's letter volunteering to command the Siachen Brigade. Refer to the note and email correspondence with Colonel Parab.
2. Harish Kapadia, *The Siachen Glacier: A Historical Review* (102 Infantry Brigade: Partapur, 2011), 1–3. Harish Kapadia wrote the booklet for officers and men who serve on the Siachen Glacier.
3. Nanavatty interview, 29 February 2024.
4. Ibid.
5. Amit Paul, 'Myths and Facts about Siachen', *The Statesman,* 13 April 2022, https://www.thestatesman.com/opinion/myths-facts-siachen-1503059919.html.
6. Arjun Subramaniam, *India's Wars II,* 97–103.
7. Telephonic Interview with Major General Chandan Nugyal, 10 September 2022.

8. Pervez Musharraf, *In the Line of Fire: A Memoir* (London: Simon & Schuster, 2006). Except for a small paragraph in Chapter 7, no mention is made in the book of Musharraf's tenure as Brigade Commander of 323 Brigade, the Pakistan Army Brigade he commanded in 1987–88.
9. DO letter written by Brig. Chandan Nugyal on the last day of his Command of the 102nd Infantry Brigade, 30 September 1988, Nanavatty Papers.
10. Nanavatty interview on Siachen, 18 September 2022.
11. Nanavatty interview, 29 February 2024.
12. Draft Standard Operating Procedures for the Siachen Battle School, January 1989, Nanavatty Papers.
13. Nanavatty interview, 19 September 2022.
14. Nanavatty's first briefing to his Commanding Officers, 15 November 1988, Nanavatty Papers.
15. Ibid.
16. Telephonic interview with Brigadier Raghbir Sanghera, 15 September 2022. Sanghera is now settled in the US in Virginia on the outskirts of Washington, DC.
17. Conversations with Lieutenant General M.K. Mago in 2022. The author was the President's Chair of Excellence at the National Defence College, where the general was commandant.
18. The gist of the operation has been extracted from Nanavatty's draft notes, from which an official 'OP IBEX: 11 April–6 June 89 After Action Report' was rendered to Divisional HQ in early June 1989. Nanavatty Papers.
19. Lieutenant Colonel Syed Ishfaq Ali, *Fangs of Ice* (Rawalpindi: Pan America Commercial, 1991), 87–117. Also see, Lieutenant Colonel S.M.H.Y. Naqvi, 'The Battle of Chumik', *Pakistan Army Journal,* Vol. XXX. No. 4, December 1989.
20. Kevin Fedarenko, 'Experiencing Siachen War (Part 3)', 8 September 2011, https://hassaanrabbani.wordpress.com/2011/09/08/experiencing-siachen-war-part-3-by-kevin-fedarko/. This is the best western account that is available on the Siachen Conflict.
21. Arjun Subramaniam, *India's Wars II,*114–118.
22. Draft notes on Op IBEX 'After Action Report', Nanavatty Papers.

23. Ibid.
24. Nanavatty interview, 29 February 2024.
25. DO letter from Nanavatty to Lieutenant Colonel P.S.R. Hallikeri, 8 June 1989.
26. Nanavatty interview, 19 September 2022.
27. From Nanavatty interview, 18 November 2019. Also see Arjun Subramaniam, *India's Wars II: A Military History 1972–2020,* 120.
28. Nanavatty interview, 29 February 2024.
29. For the draft questionnaire and Nanavatty's cryptic encapsulation of the survey findings, see 'Folder on Leadership', Nanavatty Papers.
30. Ibid.
31. Nanavatty interview, 18–19 September 2022.
32. DO letter from Major General Raghavan to Brigadier Nanavatty, 16 November 1990, Nanavatty Papers.
33. DO reply to the above letter from Nanavatty, 21 November 1990, Nanavatty Papers.
34. DO letter from Colonel Braganza to Brigadier Nanavatty after completing his tenure, 16 October 1990.
35. Nanavatty's email to Nitin Gokhale on the most memorable recollections of his Siachen tenure, 6 February 2014.
36. Nanavatty email to Nitin Gokhale.
37. Dinakar Peri, 'India Protests Chinese road construction at Shaksgam Valley in Pakistan-occupied Kashmir', *The Hindu,* 2 May 2024, https://www.thehindu.com/news/national/india-lodges-protest-against-beijings-construction-in-shaksgam-valley-rejects-china-pakistan-boundary-agreement/article68131742.ece.
38. The quote is attributed to Stephen Cohen, a US specialist in South Asia. See 'Siachen dispute: India and Pakistan's glacial fight', *BBC News,* 12 April 2014, https://www.bbc.com/news/world-asia-india-26967340.
39. Adapted from an article by Suniti Nanavatty in the Army Wives Welfare Association Magazine, 2002, titled 'The Commander and His Ibex'.
40. Suniti Nanavatty, 'The Commander and His Ibex'.

Chapter 8: Interlude between Operations

1. DO letter from Lieutenant General B.C. Joshi to Brigadier R.K. Nanavatty, 7 November 1990, Nanavatty Papers.
2. Informal conversation with Commander Akhshay Joshi (retd.), October 2022.

Chapter 9: Covert War in Baramulla

1. Arjun Subramaniam, *India's Wars II: A Military History 1972–2020* (New Delhi: Harper Collins, 2020), 244–249.
2. Ibid.
3. Arjun Subramaniam, *India's Wars II,* 250–251.
4. Nanavatty interview, 6 Oct 2022
5. For an appropriate definition of Fidayeen attacks, see Syed Firdaus Ashraf, '10 Fidayeen attacks that shocked the nation', 6 January 2016, https://www.rediff.com/news/report/10-fidayeen-attacks-that-shocked-the-nation/20160106.htm. For an academic description of suicide attacks, see Ariel Marari, 'Suicide Terrorism'. In R.I. Yufit & D. Lester (Eds.), *Assessment, Treatment, and Prevention of Suicidal Behavior* (New York, John Wiley & Sons, 2005), 431–435. Taken from abstract at https://psycnet.apa.org/record/2004-21460-017.
6. Interview with Colonel P.K. 'Royal' Mehrishi (retd.), 2 December 2022. PKR was a Major and the GSO-2 (Ops) in HQ 19 Infantry Division. He accompanied Nanavatty on several visits to forward units and was responsible for organizing much of Nanavatty's Staff work.
7. From an email note from Colonel Kuldip Singh Aithmian, 9 December 2022. Aithmian was the CO of 15 PUNJAB for the entire duration of Nanavatty's tenure as the divisional commander.
8. Nanavatty interview, 6 October 2022. Also see notes made for a presentation to the GOC-in-C Northern Command, 8 October 1993, Nanavatty Papers.
9. Interview, Colonel Mehrishi.
10. Interview, Colonel P.K.R. Mehrishi, Recollections of the night patrol.
11. Notes on 'Counter ANE Operations' concept, 12 February 1994, Nanavatty Papers.

12. Nanavatty interview, 6 October 2022.
13. Notes on Familiarisation briefing for Army Commander, Nanavatty Papers.
14. Nanavatty interview, 6 October 2022.
15. Informal telephone conversation with Mrs Padmanabhan, 15 March 2022.
16. Note of 26 November 2022 in response to the author's query on the nature of 'Punitive Operations' in 19 Infantry Division.
17. Ibid.
18. Notes on 'Counter ANE Operations' concept, 12 February 1994, Nanavatty Papers.
19. Notes on 'Instructions for Road Opening and other Defensive Tasks', Nanavatty Papers.
20. Detailed note on the operation from Raman, 27 November 2022 and DO letters from Nanavatty on the operation.
21. Ibid.
22. Emails from Brigadier Trigunesh Mukherjee, 29 October–5 December 2022. Mukherjee was the commander of 323 Brigade, which operated in the 19 Division Area of Responsibility (AOR) for almost six months and did a fine job.
23. Ipsita Chakravarty, 'They sprang from the earth: It's been 70 years since tribal forces poured into Kashmir', Scroll.in, 26 October 2017, https://scroll.in/article/854235/they-sprang-from-the-earth-its-been-70-years-since-tribal-forces-poured-into-kashmir. Also see Andrew Whitehead, *A Mission in Kashmir* (New Delhi: Penguin, 2008). Excerpts from that book are available at https://www.andrewwhitehead.net/for-the-conversion-of-kashmir.html.
24. Nanavatty interview, 6 October 2022.
25. Notes on the 'Outline Plan to stabilize Baramulla', Nanavatty Papers. Refer Nanavatty interview, 6 October 2022.
26. Telephonic interview with Colonel Aithmian, 5 September 2022. Also, refer to the email exchange of 12 September 2022.
27. Demi-Official Letter from Major General Nanavatty to Sh. Hakim Mansoor, District Magistrate, Baramulla, 20 November 1993, Nanavatty Papers.
28. Ibid.

29. Interview Lieutenant General J.D.S. Rawat, 1 November 2022.
30. DO letter from Nanavatty to Major General Ashok Mehta, 10 September 1994. Also see Major General Ashok Mehta, 'On the Road to Peace', *The Tribune*, 25 August 1994.
31. Dinesh Kumar, 'Army Plan Pays off in Valley', *The Times of India*, 4 January 1994, Cutting from Nanavatty Papers.
32. Luis White, *Fighting and Writing: The Rhodesian Army at War and Postwar* (New York: Duke University Press, 2021), Chapter 3 at https://doi.org/10.1515/9781478021285.
33. Nanavatty interview, 6 October 2017. The author also discussed the issue with Nanavatty during a series of interviews in 2017. The incident is in the author's book, *India's Wars II*.
34. Ibid.
35. Notes on 'SOPs for Military-Civic Action', Nanavatty Papers.
36. Interview with Lieutenant General J.D.S. Rawat , 1 November 2022.
37. The LeT was proscribed as a terrorist outfit by the US only in December 2001.
38. 'Lashkar Tactics and Fighting Prowess', Nanavatty Papers.
39. Interview with Sh. Shiv Sahai, IPS, additional secretary, Government of India, 2 November 2022. Sahai was the Superintendent of Police in Baramulla and worked well with Nanavatty to create synergies between the army and the J&K Police.
40. Ibid.
41. DO letter from Nanavatty to Sahai, 6 September, Nanavatty Papers.
42. Rawat interview.
43. Nanavatty interviews.
44. Written note from Brigadier Sushil Negi, 4 January 2023.
45. Recollections of a letter he wrote to all his brigade commanders in September 1994. Nanavatty interviews.
46. Obituary in the Afternoon Despatch Courier, Bombay, 13 February 1995, Nanavatty Papers.
47. Nanavatty's address to officers, faculty members, and special invitees at Pune University on the 'Sit in J&K' on 30 January 1995.
48. Interview with General V.P. Malik, former army chief, 3 October 2022.
49. Nanavatty interview, 12 November 2022.

Chapter 10: Return to the Northeastern Cauldron

1. Nanavatty Papers.
2. DO letter from Grewal to Nanavatty, 31 August 1997, from the Nanavatty Papers.
3. Gurinder Singh, 'A Decade of Ceasefire in Nagaland', *Strategic Analysis,* Vol. 31, No. 5, September 2007, 815–832, https://doi.org/10.1080/09700160701662302.
4. Nanavatty interviews, 12 and 13 November 2022.
5. For a detailed overview of the origin of the Naga people and their migration into the hilly tracts of northeast India, See Y.D. Gundevia, *War and Peace in Nagaland* (Dehradun: Palit & Palit, 1975). For an excellent overview of the insurgency in Tripura see, Biswajit Ghosh, 'Ethnicity and Insurgency in Tripura', *Sociological Bulletin,* Vol.52, No.2 (September 2003), 221–243. For a detailed analysis of the conflict and ethnic strife in Assam, see Bhaskar Gogoi 'An Overview of Conflict and Insurgency with Special Reference to Assam', *International Journal of Trend in Scientific Research and Development*, Vol. 3, Issue 2, February 2019, 356–359, https://www.ijtsrd.com/papers/ijtsrd20320.pdf.
6. 'Military Strategy for NE 1998-99: Nagaland', 12 October 1997, Nanavatty Papers.
7. Ibid.
8. A Press Release was sent to Army HQ, New Delhi, from 3 Corps HQ, Dimapur, on 10 January 1998. From Nanavatty Papers. Also see Udayan Namboodri, 'Militants force candidates to back out from contest in Nagaland', *India Today,* 16 February 1998, https://www.indiatoday.in/magazine/nation/story/19980216-militants-force-candidates-to-back-out-from-contest-in-nagaland-825709-1998-02-15.
9. 'Nagaland: Assessment of Post Election Scenario', 18 March 1998. From Nanavatty Papers.
10. National Consortium for the Study of Terrorism, University of Maryland, An Emeritus Center of Excellence of the US Department of Homeland Security, https://www.start.umd.edu/gtd/search/IncidentSummary.aspx?gtdid=199911290005.
11. Nanavatty interview, 6 April 2023.

12. Staff Reporter, 'George Fernandes strikes a warm note with political parties, underground in a visit to Nagaland', *India Today,* 20 April 1998, https://www.indiatoday.in/magazine/indiascope/story/19980420-george-fernandes-strikes-a-warm-note-with-political-parties-the-underground-in-nagaland-826183-1998-04-19.
13. Nanavatty interview, 6 April 2023. In this interview, Nanavatty recalled his impressions of George Fernandes, Governer Ved Marwah, other politicians he interacted with and some commanders who served with him.
14. Nanavatty interview, 13 November 2022.
15. DO letter from Nanavatty to Shri Rishang Keishing, Chief Minister of Manipur, 27 November 1997.
16. Draft notes on 'Outline Concept of Operations: Manipur', 2 November 1997, diary notes from Nanavatty Papers.
17. Lieutenant General.Rostum Nanavatty (Retd.), 'Manipur: Restoration of Normalcy', Short Paper, 10 December 2004. Nanavatty Papers.
18. Nanavatty interview, 6 April 2023.
19. https://www.satp.org/satporgtp/countries/india/states/manipur/data_sheets/majorincidents.htm. Table of casualties as per diary jottings, Nanavatty Papers (Manipur folder).
20. A Staff Reporter, 'RPF Calls for end to all interaction with Army', *Imphal Free Press,* 17 April 1998, Nanavatty Papers.
21. Undated Press Release, 'Human Rights and the Security Forces', Nanavatty Papers.
22. Nanavatty interview, 13 November 2022.
23. 'Profile of Lieutenant General Nanavatty,' email note from Lieutenant General Arvind Sharma (Retd.), 28 January 2024. Sharma served as a divisional and corps commander under Nanavatty.
24. Interview with Major General A.K. Channan, 5 January 2023.
25. Ibid.
26. Ibid.
27. Biswajit Ghosh, 'Ethnicity and Insurgency in Tripura', *Sociological Bulletin,* 52(2), September 2003, at https://journals.sagepub.com/doi/10.1177/0038022920030204.

28. Draft notes on 'Military Strategy for Tripura', 19 October 1997, Nanavatty Papers.
29. Nanavatty interviews, 12 and 13 November 2022.
30. DO letter from Nanavatty to Lieutenant General Ravi Eipe, 20 December 1997, Nanavatty Papers.
31. DO letter from the chief secretary, Govt. of Tripura to Nanavatty appreciating the contribution of 3 Corps towards the successful conduct of elections, 21 February 1998, Nanavatty Papers.
32. Nanavatty interview, 13 November 2022.
33. For an excellent academic analysis of Tripura's politics, see Harihar Bhattacharya, *Radical Politics and Governance in India's North East: The Case of Tripura* (London: Routledge, 2018). The book traces the evolution of a hybrid political strategy that allowed the Left to accommodate non-class tribal communities.
34. Nanavatty interview, 12 and 13 November 2022.
35. Ibid.
36. Nanavatty interview, 13 November 2022.
37. 'Yearbook Class of 1966', Lawrence School Sanawar, 2017, Nanavatty Papers.
38. This is an adaptation of an article by Suniti Nanavatty for the Army Wives Welfare Association (AWWA) Magazine titled 'A Profile in Courage: Nitu's Story'.
39. Telephonic interview with Major General S.D. Mahanti (retd), 16 December 2023.
40. DO letter from Nanavatty to Lieutenant General Kalkat, 7 August 1999.

Chapter 11: A Minefield Called Northern Command

1. Nanavatty Papers. Chibber wrote several letters to Nanavatty when the latter was the Army Commander in Northern Command.
2. DO letter from Nanavatty to Lieutenant General M.L. Chibber (retd.), 19 February 2001, Nanavatty Papers.
3. Arjun Subramaniam, *India's Wars II: A Military History 1972–2020* (New Delhi: HarperCollins, 2020), 285–289.

4. Express News Service, Explained Snippets: 'When Vajpayee Announced J&K Ceasefire, and what happened next', 14 May 2018, at https://indianexpress.com/article/explained/explained-snippets-when-vajpayee-announced-jk-ceasefire-and-what-happened-next-5175523/.
5. Rajesh Ahuja, 'Looking Back: The Ceasefire in Kashmir in 2000 saw more violence but lasted longer', *The Hindustan Times*, 17 June 2018, https://www.hindustantimes.com/india-news/looking-back-the-ceasefire-in-2000-saw-more-violence-but-was-longer/story-eD1BIfi109TFgopGgz12BJ.html, accessed 4 March 2023.
6. Nanavatty's Comments in the Draft of Chapter 11, 14 March 2024.
7. Lieutenant General John Ranjan Mukherjee, *A Soldier for Life: My Story* (New Delhi: Vij Books, 2021), 239–247.
8. Nanavatty Papers.
9. J.N. Dixit, 'India and Pakistan: Beyond the Agra Summit', *India International Centre Quarterly*, Vol. 28, No3, Monsoon 2001, 133–148. The article, written just before the author assumed his post as Foreign Secretary, is a nuanced attempt to justify NICO despite its failure.
10. Data Sheet J&K, https://www.satp.org/datasheet-terrorist-attack/fatalities/india-jammukashmir.
11. Nanavatty comments, 14 March 2024.
12. Nanavatty interviews, 7 August 2018.
13. Ibid. Also see Happymon Jacob, *Line on Fire* (New Delhi: Oxford University Press, 2019), 1–6.
14. Ibid.
15. Nanavatty Papers
16. Series of Telephonic Conversations with Lieutenant General Panag in February 2023.
17. Ibid. Also discussed in Nanavatty interviews, 7 August 2018.
18. 'Jammu and Kashmir: The Way Ahead', Keynote Address by the General Officer Commanding-in-Chief Northern Command, Lieutenant General R.K. Nanavatty, National Seminar at Jammu University organized by 16 Corps on 31 October 2001. From the Seminar Collation Folder, Nanavatty Papers.
19. Jammu Seminar, 31 October 2001.

20. Pradeep Dutta, 'We have right to strike but end alienation too: J&K's top Army Officer', *The Indian Express,* Jammu, 31 October, from Seminar Collation folder, Nanavatty Papers.
21. Jammu Seminar Collation Folder.
22. Nanavatty interviews, 13 November 2022.
23. Telephonic interview with Lieutenant General V.K. Ahluwalia, 21 February 2023. Ahluwalia, then a brigadier, served an extended tenure as the brigade commander of 161 Brigade.
24. Ahluwalia Interview
25. Lieutenant General R.K. Nanavatty (Retd.), 'Low-Intensity Conflict in the State of Jammu and Kashmir', Address to the 44th NDC Course, 20 October 2004, Nanavatty Papers.
26. Nanavatty Keynote Address, Jammu Seminar, 31 October 2001.
27. Ibid.
28. DO letter from Captain A.J.L. Gomes to Nanavatty, 5 March 2001, Nanavatty Papers.
29. Amrita Nayak Dutta, 'China Study Group the elite Indian govt body that guides policy on ties with Beijing', *The Print,* 18 July 2020, theprint.in/theprint-essential/china-study-group-the-elite-indian-govt-body-that-guides-policy-on-ties-with-beijing/463078/.

Chapter 12: Almost War and Adios

1. Nanavatty interview, 23 February 2023.
2. Conversation with Air Chief Marshal Krishnaswamy at a reception at Air House, New Delhi, in October 2019.
3. Rajat Pandit, 'Govt. Revises Union War Book to meet current situation', *The Times of India,* 15 September 2010, https://timesofindia.indiatimes.com/india/govt-revises-union-war-book-to-meet-current-situation/articleshow/6554663.cms.
4. Nanavatty interviews, 07 August 2018.
5. Telephonic conversation with Lieutenant General Rajan, former military advisor to General Padmanabhan, June 2022.
6. Conversations with Lieutenant General Nagaraj and Lieutenant General Nanavatty, August 2018.
7. Nanavatty interviews, 23 February 2023.

8. Telephone conversation with Lieutenant General Mohan Pande, former divisional commander of the 26th Infantry Division, 22 February 2023.
9. DO Letter from Nanavatty to Lieutenant Colonel Sunder Singh, CO 19 JAT, 24 September 2002, Nanavatty Papers.
10. General Ashok K. Mehta (retd), 'Point 5353 Still in Pakistan's Possession: India's Kargil Agenda Is Incomplete', *The Tribune,* Chandigarh, 13 July 2004, https://www.tribuneindia.com/2004/20040713/edit.htm#4, accessed 20 February 2023. Also refer to the short telephonic interview with Lieutenant General Ranbir Singh (retd), 20 February 2023.
11. Arjun Subramaniam, 'From Kargil to Parakram: A Lesson in Forceful Persuasion', *The Hindu,* 27 July 2012, https://www.thehindu.com/opinion/op-ed/from-kargil-to-parakram-a-lesson-in-forceful-persuasion/article3687855.ece.
12. 'Ultras Kill 12 in Kathua', The Tribune News Service, Hiranagar, 1 October 2001, https://www.tribuneindia.com/2002/20021002/main2.htm.
13. For a detailed explanation of the historical and statistical analysis of the run-up to the 2003 CF and its aftermath, see Happymon Jacob, *Line of Fire* (New Delhi: Oxford University Press, 2019), 124–167.
14. Nanavatty interviews, 7 August 2018.
15. Strobe Talbott offers an excellent US perspective on the 2001–2002 Crisis in his book. See Strobe Talbott, *Engaging India: Diplomacy Deterrence and the Bomb* (Washington DC: Brookings Institution Press, 2006). Also, See P.R. Chari, Pervaiz Iqbal Cheema and Stephen. P. Cohen, *Four Crisis and a Peace Process: American Engagement in South Asia* (Washington DC: Brookings Institution Press, 2007). Both books offer excellent Western perspectives on Exercise Brasstacks, India's 1998 nuclear tests and Operation PARAKRAM.
16. Conversation with Nanavatty, 25 April 2020.
17. Nanavatty Papers.
18. Rekha Chowdhary and Nagendra Rao, 'Elections 2002: Implications for politics of Separatism', *Economic and Political Weekly,* Vol. 38, No.1 (Jan 4–10, 2003), 15-21, https://www.jstor.org/stable/4413038. Praveen Swami offers an excellent overview of the 2003 CF and the subsequent dialogue process between India and Pakistan in a Special

Report published in March 2005 by the United States Institute for Peace (USIP) titled 'Quickstep or Kadam Tal? The Elusive Search for Peace', https://www.usip.org/publications/2005/03/quickstep-or-kadam-taal-elusive-search-peace-jammu-and-kashmir.

19. DO letter from Nanavatty to CM Mufti Mohammad Sayeed, 14 February 2003, Nanavatty Papers.
20. Draft letter to Army HQ, 13 April 2002, Nanavatty Papers.
21. 'Strategy for the Resolution of Conflict in J&K', Nanavatty Papers. Several drafts of the paper are available in the Nanavatty Papers. Over the years, Nanavatty has dissected and deconstructed the strategy in several presentations.
22. Recollections from the closing address by the Chief of Army Staff at the Army Commander's Conference in October 2002, Nanavatty interview, 6 April 2023 and Nanavatty Papers.
23. Excerpts from a presentation made to the group at Udhampur a month before Nanavatty retired from service, Nanavatty Papers.
24. Arjun Subramaniam, 'Lieutenant General Nanavatty's Kashmir Road Map was Prophetic', The Print, 12 August 2019, https://theprint.in/opinion/lt-gen-nanavattys-kashmir-roadmap-was-prophetic-he-now-calls-modi-govt-move-a-bold-step/275671/, accessed 4 March 2023.
25. Nanavatty interview February 2023.
26. Short note on his recollections of Op SARP VINASH from Lieutenant General H.S. Lidder (retd.). Refer to the email from Nanavatty, 24 March 2024.
27. Ibid
28. 'Operation SARP VINASH', Parliament question by Chandra Nath Singh and V. Saroja, 24 July 2003, https://eparlib.nic.in/bitstream/123456789/451273/1/64216.pdf. Chandra Nath Singh and V. Saroja were members of the 13th Lok Sabha.
29. I interviewed Colonel Mohan (retd.) by telephone on 2 March 2023. Colonel Mohan has been associated with Nanavatty since he was a young para commando in Sri Lanka and won a Vir Chakra for gallantry.
30. Telephonic interview with Colonel Mohan (retd.), 2 March 2023. Colonel Mohan has been associated with Nanavatty since he was a young para commando in Sri Lanka and won a Vir Chakra for gallantry.

31. For a detailed explanation of Nanavatty's reservations on the fence, see Rostum K. Nanavatty, *Internal Armed Conflict in India* (New Delhi: Pentagon Press, 2013), 104.
32. Ibid, Note 49, 126–7.
33. Telephonic interview with General N.C. Vij, 26 September 2023.
34. DO letter from Lieutenant General (Retd) S.K. Sinha, Governor of Jammu & Kashmir, 13 February 2004.
35. DO letter to Brajesh Mishra, National Security Advisor, 23 October 2003, from the Nanavatty Papers.
36. Amazon reviews at https://www.amazon.in/Internal-Armed-Conflict-Rostum-Nanavatty/dp/8182746752.
37. Gautam Sen, 'Reviewing Internal Armed Conflict in India: Forging a Joint Civil-Military Approach', *CLAWS Journal,* Summer 2013, 241–252, https://archive.claws.in/images/journals_doc/1394685847Gautam%20Sen%20CJ%20Summer%202013.pdf
38. Conversation with Veer Nanavatty, 11 February 2023.
39. Veer Nanavatty interview—corroborated by Nanavatty during a subsequent conversation on 22 February 2023.

Chapter 13: Soldiering, Leadership and Strategy

1. General Carl Von Clausewitz, *On War*, New and Revised Edition with an Introduction and Notes by Colonel F.N. Maude (Late RE), Book 1, Chapter 3 (The Genius for War), First published after Clausewitz's death in 1831, from the Clausewitz Reference Archive at https://www.marxists.org/reference/archive/clausewitz/works/on-war/book1/ch03.htm.
2. 'Thoughts on leadership', email from Nanavatty to the author on 30 March 2024.
3. The Nanavatty Papers contain speeches by Field Marshal Slim on 'Leadership, Morale and Courage' given while he was Governor-General of Australia in the 1950s.
4. Blue diary of jottings, reflections on myriad issues of soldiering, Nanavatty Papers.
5. Blue Diary, Nanavatty Papers.

6. Probal Dasgupta, *Watershed 1967: India's Forgotten War over China* (New Delhi: Juggernaut, 2020)
7. Telephonic conversation with Probal Dasgupta, 27 February 2023.
8. Ibid.
9. Interview with veterans from 2/8 GR at the unit location in Dehradun, 12 November 2022.
10. Ibid.
11. Folder and notes on 'Leadership Directives', 1993, Nanavatty Papers. Also, see James G. Hunt and John D. Blair's *Leadership on the Future Battlefield* (University of Texas: Pergamon Brassey's, 1985).
12. Recollection of 'Talking points at the Army Commanders Conference', 24 October 2002, Nanavatty interviews.
13. Email exchange and interview with Lieutenant General Arjun Ray, 29 October and 6 November 2022.
14. Note on General Nanavatty from Lieutenant General Mohan Pande, who served under him as a division commander in Northern Command, 26 March 2023.
15. Ibid.
16. Pande notes.
17. Pande note on Nanavatty.
18. Nanavatty interview, 23 February 2023. Also, see the handwritten jottings on 'Review of warfighting aims vis-à-vis Pakistan' and Nanavatty Papers.
19. Telephonic interview with General V.P. Malik.
20. Telephonic conversation with Brigadier Loave Verma (retd.) and his subsequent note on his impressions of Nanavatty, 6 January 2023.
21. Extracts from an email from Muthana to Nanavatty, 13 April 2024.
22. Interview with Lieutenant General Arjun Ray, 6 November 2022.
23. Nanavatty interview, 12 and 13 November 2022.
24. Telephonic interview with General V.P. Malik, 3 October 2022.
25. Nanavatty's approach and frustration at being unable to get through to New Delhi on the evolving crisis in Manipur is reflected in his letter to General Malik after the latter's visit to 3 Corps. DO letters folder, Nanavatty papers.
26. Telephonic conversation with Gen. Panag, 15 September 2022.

27. The essence of Nanavatty's assessment of the situation in Manipur in the late 1990s remains valid even in contemporary times, see Arjun Subramaniam, 'Little has changed in Manipur over 25 years: A heady cocktail of ethnic and tribal strife', Firstpost, 23 June 2023, https://www.firstpost.com/opinion/little-has-changed-in-manipur-over-25-years-a-heady-cocktail-of-ethnic-and-tribal-strife-12777832.html.
28. Notes made after a talk at the Defence Services Staff College, Wellington, 4 March 2017, Post-retirement DO folder, Nanavatty Papers.
29. Leadership presentation by Nanavatty at the Indian Military Academy, 17 October 2007, Nanavatty Papers.
30. Nanavatty interview, 22 February 2023.
31. This incident has been reproduced with the explicit permission of Lieutenant General Zameer Uddin Shah. Shah has also written about it in his book *The Sarkari Mussalman.* See Lt Gen. Zameer Uddin Shah, *The Sarkari Mussalman: Life and Travails of a Soldier Educationist* (New Delhi: Konark Publishers, 2018), 87.
32. Demi-Official letter from Nanavatty to Jacob with a Speed Post receipt, 6 May 2007.
33. Ibid.
34. Note on Nanavatty from Major General Dalvir Singh.
35. Telephone conversation with Srinath Raghavan, 1 November 2023.
36. Raghavan recalls this quote by Sir Michael Howard, which the latter often used in his writings and conversations.

INDEX

Abdullah, Farooq, 259–261, 273
Abdullah, Omar, 257–258, 273
Constitution of India, abrogating Articles 370, 278
accidents, 179, 234; in Calcutta, 180; in Nagaland, 179; near Mhow, 179; at Warminster, 180
Actual Ground Position Line (AGPL), 139, 145, 147–150, 152–154, 156, 158, 275
Additional Director General of Perspective Planning (ADG PP), 112
Advani, L.K., 276–277
'After Action Report,' 108, 132, 135, 160, 212
'After the clearance of Jaffna Town by the IPKF,' 128
Agra Summit, 253–255
Ahluwalia, Harpal 'Harry' Singh, Group Captain, 161, 165, 262
Ahluwalia, Lt. Gen. V.K., 261–262
Ahmedabad, 12–14, 16–17, 245
Aide-de-Camp (ADC), 52, 65, 191, 308
airborne forces, 97, 99
Air Force, 83, 144, 160, 164–165, 297
Air Officer Commanding J&K (AOC J&K), 297
Airy, V.P. (Ved), Brig., 89–90
Aithmian, K.S. Col., 188, 201
Aiyengar, S.R.R., Lt. Gen., 95
AK-47 rifles, 159, 203, 306
Alexander, John, 101
Ali, Syed Ashfaq, Lt. Col., 159
Allon, Yigal, 64, 76
All Party Hurriyat Conference (APHC), 186
All Tripura Tiger Force (ATTF), 238–239
Along, 28, 36
Alpha Company, 26–28, 47, 86; PLA attack on, 27
Amardhoj, 42–43
ambush, 41, 44, 47–48, 207, 211, 227, 233, 236, 240–241, 244, 279–280
Amiot, Bob, 101
animal transport (AT), 152
Annual Confidential Report (ACR), 168, 237, 301
anti-LTTE insurgents, 124
Anti-National Elements (ANE), 184, 202–203
Anti-Tank Guided Missiles (ATGMs), 149

Arctic Warfare Cadre, Lympstone, 108
Area of Operations, 44, 151, 165, 208
Area of Responsibility (AOR), 40, 44, 145, 151, 188–189, 191, 194, 199–201, 206–207, 210, 212; Mendhar Sector of 16 Corps, 263
Arjun Vihar, 132, 172
Armed Forces, 2, 5, 9, 21, 23, 59, 64–65, 182, 187, 261, 266–268, 271–272
Armored Fighting Vehicles (AFV), 72
Armor Officers' Advance Course, Fort Knox, 98
Armoured Brigade, 68, 71, 74, 76–77, 101, 297; Patiala, 69
Armoured Corps Centre and School, Ahmednagar, 68
Armoured Personnel Carrier (APC), 70
Armoured Regiment Combat Group, 70
Army and Air Force, joint operation, 270
Army Aviation, 157, 160–161, 164
Army Aviation Cheetah (SA 315-B Lama) helicopters, 145, 165
Army Battle Physical Efficiency Test (BPET), 37
Army Commander, 70, 82, 153, 205, 209, 261, 298–299, 301, 307
Army Medical Corps (AMC), 22
Army Ordnance Corps (AOC), 22, 164
Army Rifle Association (ARA), 62
Army Service Corps (ASC), 22
Army Training Command (ARTRAC), 112
Army War College (AWC), 64
Army Welfare Education Society (AWES), 282–283
Arunachal Pradesh, 19, 25, 217, 222, 232
ASHA, 214
Assam, 26, 85, 232, 238, 283
Assam Rifles, 26–27, 32, 37, 44, 217, 219–220, 222, 227, 236–237, 239, 241
Assistant Quarter Master General (AQMG), 26–27, 32, 37, 44, 77, 219–220, 227, 236–237, 239
Ati Vishisht Seva Medal (AVSM), 283
'Attitudes,' 133–134
Attri, H.C., 22–23
Aurora, J.S., 307
Aurora, Lt. Gen., 307
AWWA Journal, 'Nitu's Story' for, 244
'Azadi,' 185–186, 215

Bahadur, Indra, 42
Bahini, Mukti, 63
Bahri, N. (Nico), Brig., 114
Bahuguna, A.N., Major, 142
Bakshi, Z.C.(Zoru), Lt. Gen., 69, 71
Balakot, JeM training camp at, 270
Balaram, K., Lt. Gen., 96; as Gen., 87
Balasingham, Anton, 124, 126
Bana Post, 155
Bangladesh, 1, 36, 38, 55, 63, 230, 238, 241, 307; campaign, 1971, 24; war, 55
Bangladesh Rifles (BDR) Battalions, 56
Baramulla, 184, 186–188, 192, 196, 198–199, 203–204, 208–212, 246, 283, 292, 296; Dinesh Kumar on, 204
Barooah, B.K. (Manju), 29–30
Base Camp, 144–149, 153, 156–158, 161, 166, 168

'Base Realignment and Closure' (BRAC), 97
Basic Free Fall course, 110
Battalion Release Point, 82
Battalion Sikh Light Infantry, 13th (13 SIKH LI), 118
'Battlefield Milieu 2015,' 113
Battle Honour Sanjoi, 52
Battle Physical Efficiency Test (BPET), 37, 53
"Battle Report", 169
Belgaum, 178–179, 181
Bengal, 85, 238
Benning, Fort, 48, 65–66, 69, 77, 96–97, 102
Bhagat, P.S., Brig., 19, 21
Bhagavad Gita, 295, 308
Bhardwaj, P.C. Brig., 224
Bhatia, 'Jimmy,' Air Mshl, 297
Bhindranwale, Sant Jarnail Singh, 118
Bhutan, 83, 87–89, 92
Bilafond La Pass, 139, 141–143
biographies, 4–6, 124; Fromm on, 6
Birdwood, William Riddell, FM, 10
'Bleeding India with a Thousand Cuts,' Zia-ul-Haq, 251
'blue diary,' 290–291
Bofors, 153, 262
Boomer, 172, 179, 214, 216, 242
Border Action Teams (BAT), 254
Border Security Force (BSF), 56, 188, 191, 202, 239, 251
Braganza, Nevis, Col., 153
Bragg, Fort, 48
Brar, T.P.S. (Tippy), Lt. Gen., 248
Bravo Company, 27–29, 43, 47, 56–57, 59–60
Brigade Major (BM), 68, 76, 244
Brigade 'Sparrow' or Signals officer, 172
Brigadier General Staff (Operations), 178
British Army, 72, 92, 105–106, 109–110, 295; Military Attaché's, 107
British Army School of Infantry, Warminster, 65, 95, 104
British Army Training Unit Suffield (BATUS), Canada, 72, 110
British Indian Army, 10, 105
Bukhari, Asif Riaz, Brig., 161–162
Bumla-Tawang Axis, 57–59, 93
Burma Campaign, 33, 290
Bush, George, 256
Buthidaung–Maungdaw region, battles of, 57
Butt, Maqbool, execution of, 185

Calcutta, 12, 49–51, 53–54, 57, 180, 217, 236
Camp Hebron, 223
'Capabilities,' 133
Carl Gustav, 84mm 160
Ceasefire (CF), 218–220, 222–227, 230–231, 236, 245–246, 270, 284; Ground Rules (CFGR), 222–224, 241; with NSCN (IM), 224
Central Armed Police Forces (CAPF), 118, 187, 223–224, 230, 236, 251
Central Paramilitary Forces (CPF), 238
Centre for Environmental Planning and Technology (CEPT), 244
Chair Professor of Chhatrapati Shivaji Chair for Excellence, fellowship, 285
Chand, Bidhi, 86
Changki, 47, 49, 242
Channa, Vijay, Brig., 141–142

Channan, Ashwini, Maj., 237
Channan, Nitu, 244
Chapman, Freddie Spencer, Col., 130
Charlie Company, 27–28, 30, 37, 43–44, 46–47, 49, 52, 77
CHASE, 129
Chaudhuri, J.N., Gen., 53
Chauhan, O.P.S., Col., 199
Chauhan, Prakash, Lt. Col., 77
Chavan, Y.B., 12, 50, 306
Cheshire, Leonard, Lord, 214
Chhabua, 26, 36
Chhamb, 117, 274
'Chhuppa Rostum,' 182
Chibber, M.L., Lt. Gen., 141, 247
Chief of General Staff (CGS), 33
China, modus operandi of, 32; occupation of Tibet, 25; operations, 93; patrols, 27, 29, 171; PLA columns, 27; war, 1962, 4, 19
China Study Group, 264
Chorbatla-Shungroti sub-sector, 256
Chowdhary, Shankar Roy, Gen., 218, 245
Chumik Camp, 156–157, 163
Chumik Glacier, 156, 162
Churachandpur killings, 230, 304
Chushul, 25, 264
COAS, 115, 135, 168, 254, 274, 276
COIN warfare, 285
College of Combat, 63–65, 74, 179
Colonel GS (Ops), 186
Commander Artillery (C Arty), 152–153
Commander HQ PARA Cdo Task Force (Adhoc), 116
Communist Party of India (Marxist) (CPI (M)), 239–240
Cooch Behar, 88, 91, 95
'cordon and search' (C&S), 187, 207–208
Corps Battle School in Khrew, 209
corps commander, 81, 85, 87, 141–142, 218, 225, 229, 236, 242, 245, 248, 252
Corps of Signals, 20, 95
Counter Anti National (CANE), 184, 206, 213
'Counter Groups,' 211; ' Enterprising COs, 204
counterinsurgency, 1, 26, 55, 63, 136, 191, 203, 235–237, 239–240, 252, 296; operations, 2, 35–36, 43–44, 46, 49, 69, 203, 217; semi-urban, 204
Counterinsurgency and Jungle Warfare School (CIJWS), 55, 63, 241–242
Counterinsurgency Force (CIF), 114, 248, 275, 279, 308; Doda-based Delta, 308
counterterrorism (CT), 113, 118, 187–188, 190–192, 194, 196–199, 204, 206–207, 211, 248, 251–253, 255, 262, 267, 273
covert war, 2, 185, 207–208, 252–253, 255, 275, 284
Cromwell, Oliver, 266
CRPF battalion, 56
Cursetji, Jal, Adm., 23

Dadi (uncle), 10; as soldier, 11
Dagger, Akhnoor, 84
Dakota aircraft, 26
Dalton, Peter, 101
Dar, Abdul Majid, 196
Dar, Moti, Lt. Gen., 215
Dar, S.N. Lt. Col., 66
Daruwalla, Maja, 52
Dasgupta, Probal, 292–293
data-driven predictive analysis, 207

De Britto, John, as Colonel., 124–127, 209; as Major, 123; intelligence gathering team in CAPRICORN, 124, 126
Declaratory Punitive Policy (DPP), 254–255, 284–285
Defence Attaçhé, 103
Defence Services Staff College (DSSC), 67–68, 80, 95–96, 103, 178, 298, 304; Wellington, 91
Dehradun, 1–2, 18, 37, 56, 112, 173, 214, 287–288; 'Saltoro' in, 2
Delta Company, 27, 29, 47
Dewan, Ashok (Tally), 84
Dhan (mother), 9, 11, 14, 16–18, 24
Dima Halam Daogha (DHD), 220
Dimapur, 36–37, 216–217, 223, 226, 228
Dinjan, 24, 26, 36
Directing Staff (DS), 22, 63, 74, 91, 95
Directorate of Perspective Planning (PP), 112
Director Cdo Cell, 132
Director General of Military Operations (DGMO), 116, 118, 123, 133, 135, 161, 201, 226, 229, 253–254, 264
The Disruptor, Jha, 6
division commander, 81, 161, 168, 177, 182, 185, 213, 235, 263, 298–299
Dogar, Yasub Ali, Brig., 162
Dogra Regiment, 48, 157–160, 162–163, 170, 263, 269–270
Doig, Desmond, 53
D'Sena, Owen, 15
Dual-Task Formation (DTF), 263
Duleepsinhji, 15

Eastern Ladakh, 2, 7, 264
East Pakistan. *See* Bangladesh
Eelam People's Revolutionary Liberation Front (EPRLF), 123
Eisenhower, 5
Election Commission of India, 273
Electrical and Mechanical Engineers (EME), 22
Emergency Commissioned Officer, 31, 51
Erna (sister), 7, 9, 14, 24, 72; joining Paville Fashions, 18
Europe, 126; holidaying in, 111
Evans, Humphrey, 5
exfiltration, 38, 193

Falklands, 108
familiarization, 68, 144, 193
Fangs of Ice, Ashfaq Ali, 159
Fedarenko, Kevin, 159
Fernandes, George, 166, 227–228, 260, 280
Ferozepur, 75, 77, 79, 82–83, 85, 88–89
Fidayeen attacks, 187, 207
Field Firing Ranges, 67, 87, 92, 180; Raimatang, 85
Fighting and Writing, White, 204
Force Oriented Doctrine (FOD), 103
foreign terrorists (FT), 208, 211, 252–253
formation commanders, 3, 63, 91, 189, 208, 256–257, 261
Fort William Battalion, 51
Forward Logistics Base (FLB), 142
Forward Policy, 33
Fromm, Erich, 6
Full Spectrum, Subramanian, 3–4, 43
Future Battlefield Milieu, 303

Gaidinliu, Rani,' 228
Gandhi, Indira, 141

Gandhi, Rajiv, 115
Garhwalis, 61, 167
General Officer Commanding (GOC), 57, 59–60, 69, 84–85, 87, 130, 132–133, 150–151, 156–157, 183–186, 189, 191, 218, 220, 267–268
Ghandhi, Adi R., Air Mshl, 23, 297
Gharaya, J.S., Maj. Gen., 79
Ghuman, G.S., Col., 142
Gill, Gurbux Singh, Brig., 31–32, 34
Gill, I.S. (Inder), Lt. Gen., 69–70, 81, 304, 307
Global War on Terror (GWOT), 256–257
Goel, J.N., Maj. Gen., 130
Gokhale, Achyut Madhav, 170, 228
Gokhale, Nitin, 170
Golden Temple, Amitsar, 109, 118
Gomes, A.J.L., Capt., 263
Gore, Anand: as Captain, 37, 47; as Lt. Colonel., 29, 37, 47
Gorkha Battalion, 31, 91, 235
Gorkha, Johnny, 54, 59, 72, 79–80, 85, 88
Gorkhalis, 25, 30, 33, 36, 73, 88, 293–294
Gorkha Rifles, 7, 22, 25, 47, 63, 76, 102, 291–293, 309
Gorkha Training Centre, Dehradun, 56; Shillong, 84
Grad-P Rocket Launchers, 149
grenade attacks, 187, 207
GRENADIERS, 89–90
Grewal, Sarabjit Singh, Lt. Gen., 217–218
'Grey Zone' conflict, 7
GUARDS, 114, 118, 141, 144, 148, 154, 164, 170
guides, 29, 190, 195, 278–279, 295, 306
Gulmarg, 148, 166, 194, 210, 248
Gunners, 68, 149, 153, 261
Gupta, Indrajit, 229
Gurung, Bajar Bahadur Sub Maj., 56–58, 294
Gurung, Chitra Bahadur, 58
Gurung, Kaman Singh, Sub., 46
Gurung, Kumraj, Lan. Nk., 41–42, 49
Gurung, Mandal, 42
Gurung, Mukesh, 191
Gurungr '31 Dil Bahadur,' HavildaDil Bahadur, 31, 40
Gyong Glacier, 157–158, 163
Gyong La Pass, 139, 156

Haider, Salman, 259
Hakim, Mansoor, 201–202
Hallikeri, P.S.R., Lt. Col., 162
Handwara, 187, 195–196, 199
Harkat-ul-Ansar (HuA), 184, 208
Harkat-ul-Mujahideen (HuM), 208
Hashimara/ Hasimara, 82–85, 88–90, 95, 242
Havelock-Allan, Henry, Lt. Gen., 105
HAWS team, 167
Heavy Machine Guns (HMGs), 149
Hector (uncle), 11
Hegde, Niranjan, Brig., 199, 204
Helicopter Task Force, 142
'help the people to help themselves' principle, 206
Herzog, Chaim, 71
high-altitude warfare, 92, 108
High-Altitude Warfare School, Gulmarg, 166
Higher Command Courses (HC), 63–64, 147
Hilkaka/Hill Kaka, 262, 274, 278–281
Hindu-Muslim riots, Ahmedabad, 12
Hizbul Mujahideen (HM), 186, 204, 206, 209–212, 253

Hobkirk, Basil, Maj., 148–149
Hooda, Lt. Gen., 272
Hoon, P.N., Lt. Gen., 141–142
Howard, Michael, Sir 309

ibex, 174–176; with gobex kids, 176
Imphal Free Press, 233
'Improving Performance Levels in the Army,' 94
Improvised Explosive Devices (IED), 136, 187, 207
Independent Infantry Brigade, 188, 199, 251
India and Pakistan hostility 1965, 48
India and Pakistan war 1971, 102
India-China War of 1962, 25, 31, 35, 37, 171
Indian Advanced Landing Ground (ALG), 171
Indian Air Force, 5, 15, 23, 43, 142, 160, 164, 170, 228, 265, 271; Vampire jets, 43
Indian Army (IA), 195; Early Warning (EW) Company, 58–59; frontline in Ladakh, 19; Intelligence Corps and School, 203; Mechanized Infantry Battalion, 126; officer, 101, 305
Indian Army Liaison Officer (IALO), 65, 95, 103–107, 109, 111–112, 114
Indian Cancer Society in Bombay, 13
Indian diplomat in Birmingham, execution of, 185
Indian Marine Special Forces (IMSF/later as MARCOS), 122, 126
Indian Military Academy (IMA), Dehradun, 7, 18–22, 25, 48, 54, 59, 298, 305
Indian Military Training Team (IMTRAT), 86
Indian National Congress (INC), 23, 273
Indian Peacekeeping Force (IPKF), 115, 118–120, 122–123, 126, 128–129, 131, 133, 135; capture of 'Ranjit,' 123; 'snatch Operation,' 123, 126
India-Pakistan War: 1965, 4, 20, 23, 55, 117, 138, 307; 1971, 4, 55, 90, 100, 111, 307
India-Sri Lanka Accord (ISLA), 115
India's Wars, Subramanian, 1
India–US relations, 65
Indigenous Nationalist Party of Tripura (INPT), 238–239, 241
Indo-Tibetan Border Police (ITBP), 251, 265
Indra Col, 138–139
Infantry Brigade, 26–28, 31, 36, 62, 146, 152–154, 161, 168, 170, 173, 188, 196, 198; at Partapur, 138
Infantry Day, 205
Infantry Officers Advance Course (IOAC), 65, 97–98, 102
Infantry School, 48, 53, 55, 62–63, 65, 98–99, 103, 105, 108, 178, 181, 291, 293; Commando Course at, 47; Platoon Weapons (Officers) Course, 52–53; 'Training the Infantry Company Commander,' 64
infiltration, 38, 52, 90, 93, 193–194, 196, 254, 256, 258, 263, 281
Institute of Defence Studies and Analyses (IDSA), 56, 112
intelligence, 11, 44, 120–124, 128–129, 183, 190, 200, 202, 206–207, 223, 253, 258, 279
Internal Armed Conflict In India, Nanavatty, 285
International Border (IB), 232, 251, 270, 275; in J&K., 258

interrogation, 194, 203; techniques, 200
Inter-Services Intelligence (ISI), 186, 208, 212; under CIA, 185
Irish Republican Army (IRA), 109
Islamic Jihadi, 277

Jacob, J.F.R., Lt. Gen., 307
Jaffna Peninsula, 115–116, 119, 122, 124, 128–129, 131, 135
Jaish-e-Mohamed/ Mohammed (JeM), 186, 208, 212, 253
Jamir, S.C., 219, 225, 246, 286: assassination-attempts on, 226
Jammu and Kashmir (J&K), 2, 67, 182, 184–186, 208–209, 213, 215–217, 247–248, 252–258, 260, 266–267, 274–278, 280–281, 283–285, 303; Assembly election, 185, 269, 273; state police, 187, 251; Tangdhar region in, 52
Jammu and Kashmir Liberation Front (JKLF), 185–186
Jaswantgarh, 26, 61
JAT, 167, 217, 262, 269
Jatar, S., Maj. Gen., 272
Jayewardene, 115
Al-Jehad, 206
Jetley, V.K. as Colonel., 114, 268; as Lt. Gen., 267
Jha, Prem Shankar, 6
Al-Jihad Group, 212
joint operations, 170, 210, 297, *see also* Army and Air Force, joint operation
Jones, H., Lt. Col., 108
Joshi, Akshay, 178
Joshi, B.C. (Bipin), as Lt. Gen., 123, 180; Maj. Gen., 113–114, 116, 135, 182, 191
Joshi, H.C. (Joe), Lt. Col., 67, 178
Jungalwala, Pilloo, 172
Jungle Warfare School, 55, 241
Junior Commander's (JC) Course, 62
Junior Commissioned Officers (JCOs), 31, 45, 48, 62, 78, 80, 87, 162, 167, 170, 294–295

Kalkat, Onkar Singh, as General, 50, 57, 60, 62–63, 135, 245; as Lt. General., 133; as Major General, 50, 63, 65
Kaluchak incident, 268–269, 272, 299
Kanglei Yawol Kanalup (KYKL), 231
Kankesenturai, (KKS), 125–126
Kanwar, Brig. S.P.S., 192
Kapadia, Harish, 139
Karakoram (KK) Pass, 151, 171
Karakoram Ranges/ Great Karakoram Range, 138–139, 145, 151; Eastern, 137–139, 171
Karakoram Wing of Ladakh Scouts, 141, 157, 163
Kargil Conflict, 4, 162, 236, 251–252, 270, 302
Kartoos (Black Bear), 242
'Kashmir Banega Pakistan,' 185
Kashmir Light Infantry (JAK LI), 198
Kashmir Valley, 2, 67, 185, 198, 204, 248, 278, 280; and 'Azadi,' 185; conflict, 252; separatists, 257–258; terrorist groups, 253
Katharine (Kate) Bernsohn, 244, 287, 291
Kaul, B.M., Lt. Gen., 27, 33
Kaushik, O.P., Col., 105, 112
Kazinag Dhar range, 189, 194, 198
Keishing, Rishang, 230, 235, 246, 304
khaki beret, 187–188
Khan, Amanullah, 185–186
Khan, Ayaaz, 17
Khan, Akbar, Col. 57

Khanna, H. M., Lt. Gen, 215, 252
Khanna, K.K., as Lt. Colonel., 73; Maj. Gen., 274
Khanna, Suniti. *See* Nanavatty, Suniti
Khaplang, S.S., 222
Khrew, 67, 77, 209
Khud race, 36, 81
Kiddie, Abdul Razak, 15
Killinochi-Vavuniya axis, 129
Kilo and Victor (commonly called Kilo Force and Victor Force), 55–56, 248
kinetic operations, 206, 210, 218
Kirti Chakra, 79
Kler, Gurdev Singh, Brig., 69
Kohima, 43, 220, 226, 243
Korean War, 33
Kothavala, Dhanjishah, 9
Kothavala, Hector Ratanji Kothavala, joining Bombay Police, 11
Krishna Rao, K.V. Gen., 104
Krishnaswamy, S. 'Kichcha,' A.C.M., 182, 266
Kuki (Kuki National Army), 220, 229–230, 232
Kuki-Mizo-Chin vigilante groups, KNA and ZRA, 230
Kulkarni, Ramesh, Lt. Gen., 156
Kulkarni, Sanjay, Capt., 142
KUMAON, 141
Kumar, Awadhesh, Col., 120–121, 129
Kumar, Narinder 'Bull,' Col., 141
Kumar, Sushil, Adm., 267
Kumar, Vijayant, Capt., 160
Kumaramangalam, P.P. Gen., 51
Kupwara, 208–209

Lachhampur patrol incident, 205
Ladakh Range, 19, 25, 33, 72, 138, 145, 174, 176, 183, 248, 264
Ladakh Scouts, 141–142, 148, 157, 163, 264
Lal, P.C., A.C.M., 5
Lama, Dalai 14th, escape to India, 25
Langer, Sanjeev, Col., 275
Lashkare-Taiba/Lashkar-e-Taiba/ Lashkar-e-Toiba (LeT), 184, 186, 208, 212, 253; attack on Parliament, 266
leadership style, 7, 211, 245–246, 295–296, 302
'Leadership Training in Army,' 80
'leader tracking maps,' 207
Lee, Dorcha, Col., 101–102
Lee, Eileen, 102
left out of battle (LOB), 30, 65
Leonard, Baroness, 214
Lidder, Hardev Singh 'Hardy,' Col., 1, 64, 115, 130, 132, 279–280
light machine gun (LMG), 40, 42, 52, 62, 70, 87, 149
Limaye, A.V.M., 297
'Limited Offensive Operations in Defence,' 93, 297
Line of Actual Control (LAC), 2, 32, 59, 93, 171, 248, 264–265
Line of Control (LoC), 187–188, 190, 193–195, 251–252, 254–256, 263, 267, 270–271, 275, 278, 281–282, 284; in Mendhar Sector, 262; with Pakistan, 2, 139, 255, 258, 285; PA post on, 269; of Zoji la, 248
Line of Fire, 143
Locally Trained Militant (LTM), 206
Liberation Tigers of Tamil Eelam (LTTE), 115, 118, 122–126, 128–129, 135–136; Jyothi, 126–127; Mahattya, 126; Susai, 126

MacArthur, 5

Mackay, Ian, Brig., 105
Madan, Vijay, Brig., 104–105, 107
Madon, Manek, Air Mshl, 23
Maginot Line complex, 93
Mago, Manoj Kumar, Lt. Gen., 154–155
'Mago Trolley,' 155
Mahajan Field Firing Ranges, Rajasthan, 72
Mahanti, S.D. Maj. Gen., 240, 245
Mahar Regiment, 69
Maha Vir Chakra, 79, 90
Maira, Som, 72–73
Major, Fali A.C.M., 23
Major General General Staff (MGGS), 182–183, 215, 218, 268, 274, 277, 285
Majumdar, R.K., Major, 30, 43
'The Making of the Israeli Army' by Yigal Allon, 64
Malhi, I.S., 261
Malik, V.P., as Lt. Gen, 215
Malik, V.P. as General, 215, 218, 241, 300, 302, 306
Mandanna, K.M. (Ben), Captain, 56
Mandhoj, Havildar, 40
Manekshaw, Sam, as FM, 18, 23–24, 47, 50–54, 65–67, 188, 304, 307
Manekshaw, S.H.F.J. (Sam) as Lt. Gen., 47, 50
Manipur, 23, 86, 217, 219–220, 228–230, 232–238, 244, 246, 303–304, 306; Churachandpur (Lamka), 229; insurgency, 23, 237; militants, 236; police, 230, 237–238; violence in, 244
Mann, Jaswant, Major, 68
Mann, S.S. (Sukhi), Col., 110, 115, 119, 130, 132
Manoeuvre Captain's Career Course' (MCCC), 98
Manoeuvre Centre of Excellence, Fort Moore, Georgia, 98
'no man's land,' 193
Maratha Light Infantry Regimental Centre, 22, 180
Marathas, 167
Marshall, 5
Marwah, Ved, 235
Masih, Ajay, Brig., 169
Master, Jal, Brig., 143
Master, T.J., Air Mshl, 23
Mazumdar, S., Maj. Gen., 89
McNamara, Robert S., 6–7, 124–126
Mechanized Infantry Regiment, 76
Mechuka, 24–25, 27–30, 33, 37, 294
Megh Force, 117
Mehrishi, P.K. 'Royal,' Maj., 187
Mehta, Ashok, Maj. Gen., 203, 260
Mehta, Pherozeshah, Sir, 23
Mehta, Shamsher, Lt. Gen., 1–2, 62, 267
Meitei/ Meiti, 86, 220, 230–232, 235, 246
Meiti insurgent groups, 231
Meiti Pangal, 230
Menon, Prakash, Lt. Gen., 154
Menon, V.P., 304
Mhow, 47, 50, 52, 62–63, 67, 74–75, 97, 107, 179, 291
Miers, Richard, Col., 36
Military Assistant (MA), 235
Military Attaché in London, 66, 95, 106, 112
military historians, 6, 34, 64, 213, 292, 309
Military Secretary (MS), 22, 84, 91, 103–104, 138, 169, 178, 182, 261, 300–301
Military Training Directorate, 104
Mishra, Brajesh, 284
Mizo Church–sponsored agreement, 229

Mizoram, 43, 63, 217, 219–220, 242
Mohan, K.A., Capt., 127, 280–281
Mokochung-Wokha area, 47, 222, 224
Montgomery, British FM, 268
Moolgaonkar, S., A.C.M., 171
Mountain Brigade, 47, 57, 61, 82–84, 86, 89, 91, 145, 256, 306
Mufti, Mehbooba, 274
Muivah, Thiungaleng, 222
Mukherjee, Trigunesh, Brig., 196–198
Mukherjee, John Ranjan, Lt. Gen., 248, 252–253
Mukti Bahini, 63, 65
Murlidhar, 86
Musharraf/ Musharaff, Pervez, as Brigadier, 143; as Gen., 143, 251–253, 255–256, 270
Muslim Mujahedin, 196, 207
Muslim United Front, 185

Nadimarg incident, 276
Nadkarni, Adm., 149
Nagas, 38, 41–42, 46, 222, 225–226, 230, 232, 245–246; rRebellion, 35
Naga Army, 43
Naga groups, 36, 226
Naga guerrillas, 7
Naga Hills & Tuensang Area (NHTA), 35–36, 43, 47
Naga Hostiles, 35, 38, 46; counterinsurgency, 2
Naga insurgency, 35, 50, 218, 222
Naga–Kuki clash, 233
Nagaland, 35–36, 38, 43, 46, 49–50, 217–220, 222, 225–228, 232, 235–236, 242, 245–246, 286, 303–304; Assembly election 1998, 230; ceasefire in, 47; formation of, 12; Gaon Bura, 38, 45–46, 242; police, 223
Nagalim/Greater Nagaland, 230, 232, 246
Naga National Council (NNC), 35, 222
Nagaraj, Lt. Gen., 268, 271
Nagrota, 248
Nambiar, Satish, Lt. Gen. 111
Nanavatty, K. Rostum/'Nana'/ Rostum/Rusty, 8, 13–21, 72–75, 88, 90–91, 95, 102–104, 119, 131–132, 138, 172–175, 181, 214, 242–243, 281–282, 287–288; as Acting Major, 52; Arjun Ray on, 298; Arvind Sharma on, 235; Ayaaz Khan on, 17; birth of, 9; calligraphic writing, 112; Chanan on, 237; College life of, 14–15; as Intelligence Officer and Assistant Adjutant, 52; Jojo' Sengupta on, 20; Lee on, 102–103; letters of, 284; as Lieutenant General., 1, 78, 97, 217, 247, 267, 283, 285, 290; Loave Verma on, 301; as Maj. Gen., 184, 204, 213; Malik on, 215; Mehrishi on, 187; on mother, 13; Muthana on, 302; Negi on, 212; Pande on, 300; promotion, 216; Raghavan on, 308; Sahai on, 210; schooling, 14, 16–17; as Second Lieutenant, 25; Sen on, 21; Shamsher Singh on, 20; sports of, 15; writings, 64, 94
'Nanavatty Factor,' 169, 300
'The Nanavatty Papers,' 3, 6
Nanavatty, Jal (elder brother), 10; joining Education Corps, 11
Nanavatty, Kaikhushru (Keki) Jehangir (father), 10–14, 16–17, 24, 66, 213, 228, 305; dealing with dacoity menace, 13; death of, 213; in police, 12
Nanavatty, Rushad, 75, 88–90, 95, 104, 111, 172–175, 179, 214, 242,

244, 285–287, 291; birth of, 75; to Doon School, 173; education of, 244; Navjote ceremony of, 172; at St Stephen's College, 244
Nanavatty, Suniti., 73–75, 88–91, 95, 104, 106, 109, 111, 119, 131–132, 172–174, 181–182, 214–216, 242–244, 282–283, 287–288; and adult literacy classes, 89; to Mhow, 74; and Next-of-Kin (NOK), 243, 282; on Rangapahar, 242; at Rushad's school, 111
Nanavatty, Veer, 104, 111, 119, 132, 172–175, 181, 214, 242, 244–245, 286–288, 291; birth of, 91; at CEPT, Ahmedabad, 244–245; Doon School entrance exam, 181; joining military school, 181
Nanda, B.C., 150
Nanda, S.M., Adm., 5
9/11 terror attacks, 256PUNJAB, 186, 188–189, 199–201, 203, 211
National Conference (NC), 185, 247–248, 252–253, 255–256, 259–262, 267–271, 273, 276, 278, 280–281, 299, 304, 308
National Defence Academy (NDA), Khadakvasla, 18–20, 177
National Defence College (NDC), 147, 154, 177–178, 181–182, 199, 262; Course, 177–178, 181, 262
National Liberation Front of Tripura (NLFT), 238–239
National Security Advisory Board (NSAB), 284
National Security Council Secretariat (NSCS), 178, 209
National Security Guard (NSG), 118, 122, 235
National Socialist Council of Nagaland (Isaac & Muivah) (NSCN (IM)), 218–220, 222–227, 231, 236, 241, 245
National Socialist Council of Nagaland NSCN (Khaplang) (NSCN (K)), 219, 222–226, 246
Navjote ceremony, 172
Nav Kalpana, 68
Nayyar, Anil: as Captain., 124, 127; as Major, 128; Strike Troop of, 126
Nayyar, V.K. 'Tubby,' Lt. Gen., 134
NC-Congress alliance, 185
Negi, Sushil, Col., 212
Nepal Domiciled Gorkhas, 293
Newman, David, 101
Nissangong–Mechuka–Tato–Along, 26–28
Non-Commissioned Officer (NCOs), 24, 31, 48–49, 62, 78, 87, 97, 107–108, 167, 295
Non-Initiation of Combat Operations (NICO), 114, 252–255, 263
North-east (NE), 19, 24, 50, 216–217, 219, 234, 239, 243, 284, 286, 303; inter-factional clashes, 224; operations in, 7; states as 'Chickens' Neck,' 83
North-East Frontier Agency (NEFA), 19, 25, 33, 57, 86, 92
Northern Army Commander, 2, 7, 84, 191, 206, 243, 253, 261, 264, 267, 282, 272, 276, 281–282, 294, 298, 302, 304, 308
North Kashmir, 184, 208, 215; Machhil Sector, 270; operations in, 7
'nothing to report' (NTR), 40, 236
Nubra River, 139, 144–145, 149, 171
Nugyal, Chandan, Brig., 143–144, 148, 161

Oberoi, Tirath Singh, Lt. Col., 48

observation post (OP), 59, 144, 149, 165, 170
Offensive Air Support (OAS), 297
Operation BLUE STAR, 109, 118, 136, 143, 168
Operation CAPRICORN, 124–125, 127
Operation CHUMIK, 159
Operation CORPORATE, 108
Operation GULMARG, 57, 185
Operation IBEX, 157, 161–164, 166
Operation KABADDI, 255–257, 260–261, 271, 278, 300
Operation KOH-E-PAIMA, 269
Operation MEGHDOOT, 2, 108, 136, 138, 141, 144–145, 147–148, 154–156, 163–166, 169, 208
Operation NYLON, 129–130
operation PARAKRAM, 2, 139, 251, 269–273, 278–279, 300
Operation PAWAN in Sri Lanka, 115–116, 119, 130–131, 133, 136, 279–280
Operation RAKSHAK, 182, 191, 213
Operation SANGRAM, 267, 278
Operation SARP VINASH, 279–280
Operation VIJAY in Kargil, 236
order of battle (ORBAT), 145, 148, 189, 248
Ours Not to Reason Why, Palsokar, 131
Over Ground Workers (OGWs), 190, 195, 201–203, 207, 232

Padha, K.C., Col., 132
Padmanabhan, Roopa, 193, 282–293
Padmanabhan, S. (Paddy), as Lt. General., 192–193, 204, 209; as General, 204, 253–256, 266–268, 275–276, 281, 283, 304
Pakistan, 2, 4, 35–36, 101–102, 138–139, 141–143, 171, 215, 251–252, 254–258, 260–261, 269–270, 272–273, 275, 284–285; ceasefire offer, 284; covert war in J&K, 184, 247; 1971 War in East, 1, 4, 138; trained militants (PTMs), 184, 206, 208, 270
Pakistan Army (PA), 142, 161–163, 165, 168, 190, 193–194, 251, 253–256, 258, 263, 269–270, 282, 284
Pakistanis, 102, 155, 159–160, 253
Pakistan Occupied Kashmir (PoK), 171, 185–186, 258, 266, 272
Palaly Airfield, 119–120, 124–126, 130
Palestine Liberation Organization (PLO), 185
Palsokar, R.R., Brig., 131, 179
Palsokar, Villol, 179
Panag, H.S., as Brigadier., 256; as Lt. General., 304
Pande, Mohan, Lt. Gen., 269, 298–300
Pangal community, 231
Pangong Tso, 22, 264
Panipat Company, 19, 21–22
Panthaki, Behram, Lt., 52, 65, 86, 91
Panthaki, Zenobia, 5
Parab, Dileep/Dilip Second Lieutenant, 58–60, 91, 94
Parab, H.S. Col., 59
Parachute (Commando) (PARA Cdo), 2, 7, 109, 114, 117–118, 120, 122, 131, 279–281; operations in Sri Lanka, 134; Task Force, 116, 120, 129; as Tiger Troop, 124
Parachute Regiment, 133–136
Param Vir Chakra, 22–23

Param Vishisht Seva Medal (PVSM), 283, 307
Parliament attack, by LeT, 262, 266, 271–272
Parsis, 9–10, 23–24, 74; Sanjan settlement of, 10
Partapur, 138, 141, 147–148, 155–157, 167, 172, 174
Pashtun terrorists, 208. *see also* foreign terrorists (FT); Pakistan terrorists
Passing Out Parade (POP), 21
Patankar, Vinayak, Lt. Gen., 248, 276
Pathak, Tej, Col., 122–124, 127, 130, 132
Pathania, R.S. Lt. Col., 49, 53, 62
Patney, Vinod, Air Mshl, 2
peaceful resolution, 252, 275–276
'peace station,' 26, 50
People's Conference, 261
Peoples Democratic Party (PDP), 273
People's Liberation Army (PLA) of China, 25, 27, 29, 60, 93, 231, 264; offensive operations, 93
People's Liberation Organization of Tamil Eelam (PLOTE), 123
People's Revolutionary Party of Kangleipak (PREPAK), 231
Permanent Vehicle Check Points (PVCPs), 199, 202
Phizo, A.Z., 35
Pillai, G.K. (Gopal), 229
Pillai, S.K., Lt. Gen., 181
Pir Panjal Range, 183, 188, 195, 248, 254, 262, 268, 278, 280
Pithawala, Cyrus, Maj. Gen., 23
Platoon Commander's (PC), 62; Wing at Infantry School, Belgaum, 178
Ponwar, Vinayak, Brig., 241
Population Services International (PSI), 287
Porter, Wayne, 101
Prabhakaran, 123–124, 128
Prakash, Arun, Adm., 2
Prasad, Sri, 60
prisoner of war, 29, 87
professionalism, 107, 136, 224, 290
Pseudo Gang Operations, 121, 133–134, 204–206
Pulwama, 278
Pune, 1, 171–172, 178–181, 213–215, 281, 283, 285–287
punitive operations, 26, 262, 284, 297
Pun, Major G.D., 26–27
Purdy, Lee, 101

Al-Qaeda, 208, 256

Radhakrishnan, Sarvepalli, 21
Rafiabad Area, 188–189, 196, 198
Raghavan, as Major General, 161, 174; General, 132, 150, 154, 157, 162–163, 168, 174, 177, 201, 308–309
Raghavan, Srinath, 308
Raghavan, V.R., Brig., 150, 168, 201, 268
Rai, Mangla, Sub., 144
Rajkumar College (RKC), Rajkot, 14–17
Rajouri-Mendhar-Poonch Sector, 279
Rajput Regiment, 63, 65, 195–196
Rajputs, 167
Raman, Rajesh, Second Lt., 195–196
Ramanna, Raja, 166
Rampur Brigade, 261
Rangapahar, 217, 242–243; Spear Top at, 242
Ranjitsinghji, 14
Raphael, Robin, 214, 260, 288

RAPHAEL'S mission, 214
Rashtriya Indian Military College (RIMC), 2, 20, 59, 73; Old Boys Reunion at, 2
Rashtriya Rifles (RR), 114, 191, 229, 248, 279
Rawat, Bipin, Maj., 192
Rawat, J.D.S., Lt. Col., 202–203, 206–207, 211
Rawley, N.C., 27
Ray, Arjun, Lt. Gen., 248, 264, 298, 302
'Receiving Areas,' 190, 195
regimental medical officer (RMO), 29, 263
Remount Veterinary Corps (RVC), 22, 207
rendezvous (RV), 40, 42, 195
'Reorganization of the Infantry Battalion,' 180–181
Research and Analysis Wing (R&AW), 123–124
Rest and Recuperation ("R&R"), 54
'return to their units' (RTU), 66
Revolutionary People's Front (RPF), 231, 233
Ribeiro, Julio, 113, 213
Rocket Launcher (RL) 84mm, 186
Rodrigues, S.F., as General, 180; as Lt. Gen., 113, 123, 127
Rogerson, Peter, 8, 16; Order of the British Empire (OBE) for, 15
Rommel, FM, 21, 64, 78, 94, 189
'The Rommel Papers,' 64
Rostum, *see* Nanavatty, K. Rostum
Royal Bhutan Army, 86
Royal Marine Commando Mountain, Lympstone, 108
Roychowdhury, Shankar, Gen., 216
Rules of Engagement (ROE), 186, 193, 296
Sahai/Sahay, Shiv, 209–211
Sahni, D.S.R. Lt. Gen., 150, 156–157, 182
Saini, S.K., Lt. Gen., 262–263
Salahuddin, Syed, 186
Saltoro Kangri, 139, 144
Saltoro Range, 2, 108, 137–139, 141, 145, 152, 156–159, 163, 171, 288
SAM-7 Surface-to-Air Man-portable air defence system (MANPADS), 168
Sandhu, C.S., Wng. Com., 142
Sanghera, Raghbir, Lt. Col., 155
Sanghera, Raghbir Brig., 154
Sardeshpande, S.C., Maj. Gen., 119, 130
Sarkar, Manik, 240–241
Sarma, B.C. (Roni), 30, 51
Sarup, Anand, Maj., 49, 51, 55–58, 61–62, 76, 92, 112
Satakha–Zunehboto–Atoizu area, 43–44, 46, 52
Saxena, Girish Chander, 261, 277
Sayeed, Mufti Mohammad, 273–274
School of Infantry, Warminster, 65, 104, 106
Schools Liaison Officers, 110
Second Burma Campaign, 22
Security Forces, 233–234, 237, 239, 252
Sehgal, Harjot Singh, Maj., 146, 153
Sehgal, Vinod Maj. Gen., 104
Sema Naga, 43–44, 222, 225
Sen, Gautam, 21, 285
Sengupta (Jojo), Rita, 20
Sengupta, J.K. 'Jojo,' 20–21
Senior Command Courses, 63, 74–75, 77, 162
Seth, Nadirshah, 11
Sethi, Maj. Gen., 183
Sethna, A.M., Lt. Gen., 23
Sethna, A.M., Lt. Gen., 9

Shah, Zameeruddin, Brig., 306
Shaksgam Valley, 138, 151, 171
Shamshabari Ranges, 262
Sharif, Nawaz, 251
Sharma, J.K. Col., 156
Sharma, Arvind, Maj. Gen., 235
Sharma, Om Prakash, 228
Sharma, V.N. Gen., 135
Shaurya Chakra, 196
Shekhar, Chandra, Lt. Gen., 229
Shergill, T.S. (Maun), Lt. Gen., 68, 94, 225
Shimla Agreement, 258
Shirin (aunt), 11
Shrivastava, O.N., 235
Shyok River Valley, 139, 145, 171, 264
Siachen, 2, 136–139, 141, 144–145, 154, 156, 165, 167, 169, 171–172, 182, 184, 246, 248, 251; conflict, 143, 170; operations in, 7
Siachen Battle School (SBS), 144, 146, 148–149, 158, 168
Siachen Brigade, 130, 143–144, 268, 283
Sia Kangri, 139, 141
Sia La Pass, 139, 141–142, 150, 155
Sihota, Gurbaksh, 267
Sikh Regiment, 15, 22, 143
Sikh Regimental Centre, Ramgarh, 143
SIKH UTT, 158
Siliguri, 20, 83
S.L. Rifle, 7.62 mm, 52, 149, 294
Singh (Dhante Pun), Onkar, Maj. Gen., 57
Singh, R.B., as Lt. General., 248; as Major General, 224, 236
Singh, Ajai Lt. Col., 71
Singh, Arjan, Marshal of Indian Air Force, 5
Singh, Arjun Major, 43
Singh, Bakshi Jogender Lt. Gen., 217
Singh, Balwant, 13
Singh, Dalvir: as Colonel, 115, 122, 130, 308; as Major General, 308
Singh, Depinder Lt. Gen., 5, 123
Singh, Dushyant, Air Vice Marshal, 164
Singh, Gurpreet, Col., 84
Singh, Hanut, Brig., 71
Singh, Harbaksh Lt. Gen., 5, 51, 117
Singh, Jaswant, 276, 304
Singh, L.T., 86
Singh, Ranbir, Col., 269
Singh, Randhir, Maj. Gen., 5
Singh, Sagat, as Lt. General., 304; as Major General, 60
Singh, Shamsher: as Brigadier., 20; as Lt. Colonrl., 37; as Colonrl, 37, 46–47, 49, 53
Singh, S.K., Maj. Gen., 84
Singh, Surender Lt. Gen., 191–192
Singh, V.K., Lt. Gen., 63
Singh, V.P., 6
Singh, W. Nipamacha, 235, 237
Sinha, Arvind, Maj., 146
Sesodia, Janak, 26–27, 77
Situation Report (Sitrep), 144, 306
Slim, W.J. (Bill), Lt. Gen., FM, 21, 105
'Snatch Operations,' 123, 126, 134
Snow and Avalanche Studies Establishment, Manali, 146, 166
A Soldier for Life, Mukherjee, 253
Sood, S.D. (Shubhi), 5
Sood, V.K., Maj, 32
Sopore, 186–187, 199, 203–204, 208–209
South Asia Terrorism Portal (SATP), 233, 255
South Assam, 219–220; Masimpur in, 236
Southern Glacier Battalion, 169

'Speaking Truth to Power,' 305–306
Special Action Group (SAG), 118, 122
Special Air Service (SAS), 109–110, 114
'Special and Stay Behind Missions,' 93
Special Forces (Airborne), 136
Special Forces (SF), 109–110, 114–117, 130, 132–133, 135–137, 186–187, 203, 206–207, 209, 219, 222–225, 234, 280–282, 302; PARA Cdo units into, 115
special operations, 116–117, 131, 137
Special Protection Group, 118
Special Service Group (SSG), 157–158
Spl Ops, 133, 136
sports, 15, 17, 54, 68, 77–78, 83, 101, 105, 244
Sri Lanka, 7, 19, 115–117, 119–120, 122–123, 126–128, 130–131, 134, 136, 190, 279–280; 54 Inf Div to, 115; PARA Commandos in, 2
Sri Lanka Army (SLA), 115, 135
Srinagar, 67, 141–142, 187–188, 192, 199, 248, 276, 283
Staff College, 55, 67–68, 104; Camberley, 106
'stalling of the J&K Peace Initiative,' 254
Standard Operating Procedures (SOPs), 79, 236, 306
Standing Orders for War and Peace, 79
Station Swimming Pool incident, 79–80
Sten Machine Carbine, 9 mm, 27, 46
St Joseph's Franciscan Convent, Pakistani tribesman ravaged, 198
'Strategy for Resolution of Conflict in J&K,' 260, 277
St Xavier's College, Bombay, 18
subalterns, 23–24, 30, 36, 228
Subrahmanyam, K., 56, 112
suicide attacks, 187, 207
Sumi, Khetovi, 225
Sundarji, K. as General, 56, 69, 71–72, 85, 91, 104–105, 112–115, 136, 297, 304; as Lt. General., 69, 76, 85, 104; as Major General, 69
Surankote, 278, 280–281
surveillance, 122, 129, 160, 195, 297
Swu, Isaac Chishi, 222
Syndicate Directing Staff (DS), 63

Taare Zameen Par, 287
Tactical Exercises without Troops (TEWT), 99
tactics, techniques and procedures (TTP), 121
Taliban, 208
Taliha, 30
Tamenglong, 37, 228
Tangkhul, Hansi, 222, 226–227, 246
Tangkhul Nagas, 230, 235, 246
Tanzeems, 195, 208, 211
Tarapore, Adi, Lt. Col., 23
Task Force (TF), 120–121, 123, 142
'Tasking,' 133–134
Tato, 26, 29–30
Tawang–Sela–Darang–Bomdila Axis, 25–26, 37, 57, 60, 92
Taylor, Derek, as Colonel, 29; Lt. Colonel., 26
Teachers' Training Workshops in Army Schools, 243
Tembe, Chandrakant (Chandre), 84
Teram Shehr Plateau, 139, 151
terrorism, 185, 188, 190, 201–202, 234, 247, 254, 257, 275, 298

terrorist groups, 195, 205, 211, 275; killing of policemen, 209
Thapa, Dhan Singh, Major, 22
Thapar, Karan, 307
Thimayya, K.S., Gen., 33, 59
'thinking soldier,' 64
Thoise airbase, 147
Thomas, Mathew, Lt. Col., 62–63
Thorat, Raghunath, 58, 86, 88
Thorat, S.P.P., Lt. Gen., 5
Thulasidas, 239
"Tigers", 128–129, 131
Tike Pun, 45
Tinaikar, S.S., as Colonel, 136; as General, 131
Topaz Armoured Personnel Carrier (APC), 70
'Training of Armoured and Mechanised Forces,' 67, 71
Tripura, 217, 219–220, 222, 228, 238, 241–242, 303; elections in, 240; insurgency in, 238; State Level Coordination Committee (SLCC), 240
Tripura National Volunteers (TNV), 238
Tripura Rifles, 239–241
Tukhovi, SS Brig., 45–46
Turkestan La, 139
Tuting, 27–28

Udhampur, 144, 182, 214, 268, 297; Tara Mount, 282
Udhampur Nursery School, 283
Union War Book, 267
United Bengal Liberation Front (UBLF), 239
United National Liberation Front (UNLF), 231, 233
Unit Training Team (UTT), 148
urban counterinsurgency grid, 203
urban counterterrorism grid, 202
Urban Counterterrorist (CT), 109
Uri, 199, 292
USAIS (US Army Infantry School), 65, 77, 97, 102
US Army Physical Tests, 101
US defensive doctrine, 103
'Use of the Armed Forces in Aid to Civil Authority", dissertation, 182
Uttam Yudh Seva Medal (UYSM), 283

Vaidya, General A.S., 141, 168
Vajpayee, Atal Bihari, 252–253, 256, 266
'Valley based Insurgent Groups' (VBIG), 220; under the RPF banner, 220, 231–233, 237
Vas, Eric, Maj. Gen., 64, 85
Verma, Ashok, Maj. Gen., 65
Verma, Inder: as Lt. Gen., 229, 241; as Major General, 183, 186, 209, 215
Verma, Loave, Lt. Col., 302
Victoria Cross (VC), 108
Vij, N.C. as General, 266, 281–282, 297; as Lt. General, 266
Village Public Telephone (VPT), 263
Vir Chakra, 111, 160, 274
Vishisht Seva Medal, 149
Vohra, N.N., 276, 304

Walong sectors, 24–27, 294
Wani, Ishfaq Majeed, 186
Wardak, Abdul Rahim, Lieutenant, 101–102
Warminster, 65, 95–96, 104–107, 132, 180
'no war-no-peace,' 236
War of Atonement, Herzog, 71

Watermanship Training, 90; Camp on River Sankosh, 85
Weapon Training (WT), 19, 92
weekend, 72, 111, 114, 226, 244; travel, 111
Weintraub, Stanley, 5
Wellington, Nilgiris, 68, 80, 91, 95, 304
Western Army Commander, 1, 81
Westmoreland, W., Gen., 101
White, Luise, 204
World War, I, 11, 58, 154
World War II, 10, 15–16, 19, 21, 24, 33, 35, 38, 92, 94, 193
Wynter-Blythe, Mark Alexander, 17

Yadav, Col., 65
Yadava, J.B.S., Lt. Gen., 248
Young Officers (YO), 62–63, 78, 97, 291–293
Yudh Seva Medal (YSM), 127

Zakhama, 36, 220
Zeliangrong Naga tribes, 228
Zia-ul-Haq, Muhammad, 185
Zingrulma Glacier, 166
Zoroastrianism, 172
Zoroastrians, 9, 75
Zoumi (Zoumi Revolutionary Army), 220, 229–230, 232

ABOUT THE AUTHOR

Air Vice Marshal **ARJUN SUBRAMANIAM** is an accomplished military historian and the author of the two-volume *India's Wars: A Military History*. Subramaniam was the President's Chair of Excellence in National Security Affairs at the National Defence College, New Delhi, from February 2021 to March 2023; a Visiting Fellow at the Harvard University Asia Center and the Changing Character of War Programme, Oxford University; and Visiting Professor, Fletcher School of Law and Diplomacy. He is currently a Visiting Faculty at Kautilya School of Public Policy, Hyderabad, and several war colleges across the three services.

ALSO BY THE AUTHOR

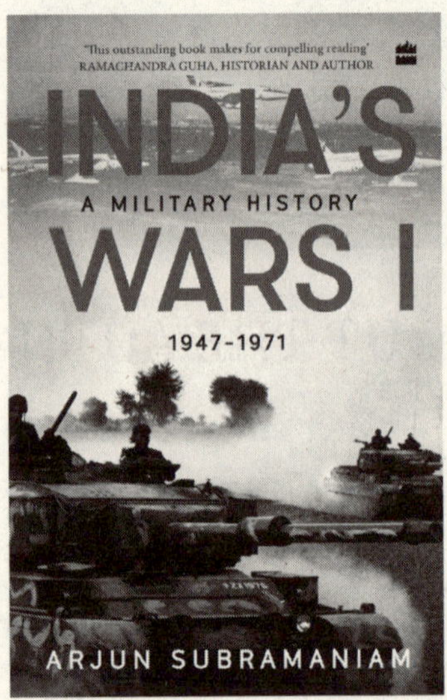

The armed forces play a key role in protecting India and occupy a special place in people's hearts. Yet, standard accounts of contemporary Indian history rarely have a military dimension.

In *India's Wars I: A Military History 1947–1971*, serving Air Vice Marshal Arjun Subramaniam, who has a PhD in Defence and Strategic Studies, seeks to give India's military exploits their rightful place in history. Beginning with a snapshot of the growth of the armed forces, he provides detailed accounts of the conflicts from Independence to 1971: the first India–Pakistan war of 1947–48, the liberation of Hyderabad and Junagadh, the campaign to evict the Portuguese from Goa in 1961, and the full-blown wars against China and Pakistan.

At the same time, *India's Wars I* is much more than a record of events. It is a tribute to the valour of the men and women in olive green, white and blue in the hope that it reaches out to a large audience, specially the youth. It highlights ways to improve the synergy between the three services, and emphasizes the need for wider discussions on matters related to national security.

Laced with veterans' exhilarating experiences in combat operations, India's Wars fuses the strategic, operational, tactical and human dimensions of war with great finesse. Deeply researched and passionately written, it unfolds with ease and offers a fresh perspective on independent India's history.

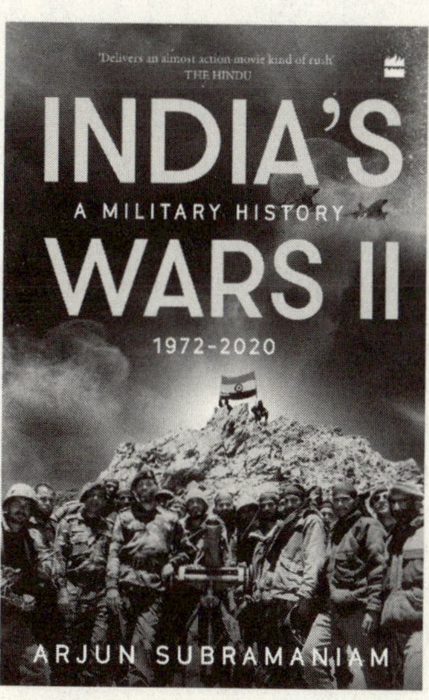

The armed forces have played a key role in protecting India's sovereignty and raising its stature as a stable democracy and responsible regional power. Though the nation's soldiers, sailors and airmen occupy a special place in people's hearts, standard narratives of contemporary Indian history rarely cover the military dimension. In his first book, *India's Wars I: A Military History 1947–1971*, Arjun Subramaniam attempted to set this right by taking readers on a journey until the liberation of Bangladesh in 1971.

India's Wars II: A Military History 1972–2020 takes the story forward. It is a sweeping account of war and conflict in contemporary India over the past five decades. Covering every major operation that the armed forces have participated in—including the Kargil conflict of 1999, insurgencies in the North-east, terrorism and proxy wars in Jammu and Kashmir, separatist violence in Punjab, the IPKF intervention in Sri Lanka, and the continued stress along the LoC and LAC—it fuses the strategic, operational, tactical and human dimensions of war and conflict into a racy narrative that reflects their changing character in modern time.

As deeply researched and passionately written as the previous volume, this is a befitting sequel that brings up to date a unique endeavour to offer a fresh take on independent India's history.

HarperCollins *Publishers* India

At HarperCollins India, we believe in telling the best stories and finding the widest readership for our books in every format possible. We started publishing in 1992; a great deal has changed since then, but what has remained constant is the passion with which our authors write their books, the love with which readers receive them, and the sheer joy and excitement that we as publishers feel in being a part of the publishing process.

Over the years, we've had the pleasure of publishing some of the finest writing from the subcontinent and around the world, including several award-winning titles and some of the biggest bestsellers in India's publishing history. But nothing has meant more to us than the fact that millions of people have read the books we published, and that somewhere, a book of ours might have made a difference.

As we look to the future, we go back to that one word—a word which has been a driving force for us all these years.

Read.

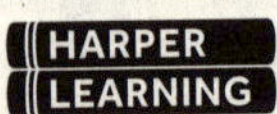